COMMUNITY WELFARE

ORGANIZATION:

Principles and Practice

ARTHUR DUNHAM
Professor of Community Organization
School of Social Work,
University of Michigan

Thomas Y. Crowell Company · NEW YORK

1957

Library of Congress Catalog Card Number: 58-6099

Manufactured in the United States of America
By Vail-Ballou Press, Inc., Binghamton, N.Y.

To My Wife,
Esther S. Dunham

FOREWORD

THIS BOOK IS INTENDED as a basic analysis and discussion of the principles and practice of community welfare organization. It is hoped that it may be useful in at least four different ways: (1) As a textbook for courses in community welfare organization. The book covers materials that might go into a semester's introductory course in the subject, plus a semester of a more technical generic course in community organization practice. (2) As a basis for discussion groups or for systematic self-study by professional workers who wish to improve their own equipment in community organization. (3) As a working tool and reference book for the community organization practitioner, the social welfare executive, and others concerned with community organization. (4) As a source of information and suggestions on particular aspects of the subject, for social workers in other specializations, for representatives of other professions and disciplines, for citizens concerned with social welfare, and for representatives of other nations and cultures.

The book is divided into three parts. Part I, An Introduction to Community Organization, includes background chapters on social work and social welfare and on the community; a discussion of the basic nature and relationships of community organization, and of social action. Part II, on Agencies and Programs, begins with a chapter on history, followed by a general view of local community organization agencies and some extended case illustrations of community organization in action. The following chapters contain fairly detailed discussions of councils, chests, united funds, social service exchanges, and of community organization on the statewide, national, and international levels. A special chapter deals with the exciting contemporary subject of community development in newly developing countries. Part III, on Community Organization at Work, begins with three somewhat technical chapters on the foundations of community organization practice, personnel, and the generally neglected subject of records. The next five chapters, on methods, committees, and guiding principles, are of special concern to the practitioner of community organization, but they may have considerable application to anyone who participates in such activities. The final chapter, on frontiers of community organization, is an attempt to look at community welfare organization today and to consider some of the possible directions which it may take in the years ahead.

Much use has been made of illustrative case materials; and charts and other figures have been used where it seemed appropriate. Each chapter is followed by a carefully selected list of suggestions for further reading, and by a number of questions and problems. These latter are not academic exercises; they are regarded as an integral part of the total presentation, and it is hoped that they will be as useful to the practitioner as to the student. These lists, together with material in the appendices, include not only specific questions but also references to definitions, checklists and analysis blanks for use in actual every-day social work practice, and a variety of case problems.

Some of the emphases which have been sought in this book are these: The attempt has been made to define terms and state concepts clearly; to emphasize primarily the generic process of community organization as an aspect of social work and social welfare; to keep the subject in balance, from united funds to the United Nations; to present issues, controversies, and problems fairly; to write simply and directly, with a minimum of professional jargon; and always to keep the focus on the practical use of the process of community organization.

I have sought to attain accuracy of statement, but with the hundreds of facts and details involved in a manuscript of this sort, errors and omissions are not unlikely; and of any such I shall be glad to be informed. I have tried to bring the discussion of facts and developments, so far as possible, up to the fall of 1957; but for any subject that changes as rapidly as community organization, complete up-to-dateness could be obtained only by a looseleaf publication, with weekly revision sheets!

This volume has grown out of about forty years of experience in social work — twenty years of practice, chiefly in community organization, on the local, state, and national levels, and some twenty years of teaching, study, and research. At this point it is impossible to disentangle what has emerged from reading and study, from conferences, classes, discussions with colleagues and students, and from actual experience.

My debt to Wayne McMillen and to those who have followed in his footsteps as writers of basic books on contemporary community organization will be apparent. I am deeply appreciative of their contributions to the literature of community organization. A number of friends and colleagues have at various times critically reviewed drafts of portions of this manuscript, and have generously given me the benefit of their criticisms and their thinking. Among these are: Lyman S. Ford and Merrill K. Krughoff, of United Community Funds and Councils of America; Gordon Berg, formerly with UCFC, now with United Community Services of Charlotte, N.C.; Charles H. Alspach and Glen Leet, of the United Nations Secretariat, and Mohamed M. Shalaby, formerly connected with the Secretariat; George W. Rabinoff of the National Social Welfare Assembly; representatives of the statewide citizens welfare associations of New York, Pennsylvania, and Ohio; Cecilia Craig of the United Community Services of Detroit; Faye Portner Soffen, formerly a member of the faculty of the School of Social Work of the University of Michigan; and Rilma O. Buckman of the Toledo Council of Social Agenices.

Among others who have in many ways stimulated and influenced my thinking about community organization, through their writings and through personal contacts are: Walter W. Pettit, Russell H. Kurtz, the late Robert P. Lane, Leonard W. Mayo, Arlien Johnson, Hertha Kraus, Clarence King, Wilber I. Newstetter, Ralph H. Blanchard, Violet M. Sieder, Bradley Buell, and Ernest B. Harper; my colleagues and many individual students at the University of Michigan School of Social Work, the New York School of Social Work of Columbia University, and elsewhere, both in the United States and in other countries; and a number of members of the former Detroit and Ann Arbor Community Organization Discussion Groups.

To all these and to many other friends, colleagues, and students, I am deeply indebted. The final responsibility for this manuscript is of course mine alone.

The greatest debt of all — for encouragement, sustained interest, wise counsel, and companionship through the years during which I have been concerned with this undertaking — can be expressed only in the dedication.

ARTHUR DUNHAM

Ann Arbor, Michigan
December, 1957

CONTENTS

FIGURES

I.

An Introduction

to

Community Organization

_____

I.

SOCIAL WORK AND SOCIAL WELFARE

THE SOURCES OF SOCIAL WORK

MODERN SOCIAL WORK IS A RESPONSE to problems as old as humanity. Sickness, old age, widowhood, orphanhood, domestic discord, physical handicaps, maladjusted personalities, and crime are problems which have been with man since the dawn of history. Some ancient methods of dealing with these problems are still being used. No one knows how long orphaned children have been receiving foster family care. Families and friends have provided dependents with the necessities of life for untold generations. Among English-speaking peoples, this has been a recognized service of government for more than three centuries.

Nevertheless, modern social work differs, in many essentials, from earlier efforts to minister to human needs.

The contrast between social work today in the modern city and the methods of helping people in a rural village as recently as sixty years ago may be seen in this illustration.

In 1889 a young bride went with her husband to live in a village on the Dakota prairies. Elsa Schrader had come to this country from Europe as a grown woman. She had no particular cultural or material advantages over her new neighbors. Yet, as the years passed, her neighbors found themselves constantly turning to Elsa for advice and help when beset by troubles. It was she who went to the aid of a half-starved, friendless dressmaker and started her on the road to self-support and friendship. Elsa went farther than anyone else in seeking to help the Miller clan, who lived in poverty and squalor, across the tracks. When the minister's wife lay near death, Elsa organized the women neighbors to give constant nursing care. She prepared a special diet for the sick woman, and took the woman's two-year-old daughter into her own home. Elsa did these things quite naturally and simply, as the expression of neighborliness and friendship.

In later years, Elsa and her family moved to a large city. About the time of World War I, one of her daughters, upon completion of college, chose social work as a vocation. When her training started, she began to see a relationship between the things her mother had done in the little Dakota village and what social workers were doing in the city. The same spirit of the good neighbor which had actuated her mother now actuated the various city agencies.

Back in the village Elsa had given "relief" to those who were in need, found employment for the dressmaker, placed the child of a sick mother, provided bedside nursing, and mobilized resources to save a woman's life. The same problems recurred in the city — but how vastly magnified! Hundreds of sick people needed care; poverty stalked through whole districts of the city; unemployment threatened thousands of homes; and every year scores of orphaned children had to be placed in foster family homes and institutions.

The activities of the good neighbor and the informal helping of those in distress by relatives and friends are important sources of modern social work. Other sources are the activities of churches and religious orders, medieval guilds, fraternal organizations, various governmental activities, and individual and group philanthropies.

The motivations for providing social welfare services are as varied as the sources from which the aid originated. Among them are religious concern or belief; philanthropy; a moralistic desire to "make over" human beings; fear and repression; economic gain; self-expression or self-glorification on the part of donors and founders of charities; scientific investigation; humanitarianism; and the democratic motive of joint responsibility.

WHAT ARE SOCIAL WORK AND SOCIAL WELFARE?

TO THE ORDINARY CITIZEN as well as the board member who suddenly finds himself in the midst of the social welfare activities of a community, social work must initially appear hopelessly chaotic. Modern social work is a relatively new profession, and its domain is necessarily less precisely defined than that of a long established profession such as medicine or law.

FIELD AND PROFESSION

This confusion is heightened by loose and conflicting terminology — for example, consider the terms "social work" and "social welfare." Social work and social welfare mean two different things. Social welfare is a broad *field* of human effort, in which there are many types of agencies and services. Social work is one *profession* within that field.

Social welfare may be defined as *organized activities for the promotion of social well-being through helping people to meet needs in such areas as family and child life, health, social adjustment, leisure time, standards of living, and social relationships.* Social welfare services are concerned with individuals, groups, communities, and larger population units; these services include care, treatment, and prevention.[1]

Social work in the United States has been thus defined:

> Whether the emphasis is on individual or group activities, modern social work may be described as a professional service to people for the purpose of assisting them, as individuals or in groups, to attain satisfying relationships and standards of life in accordance with their particular wishes and capacities and in harmony with those of the community.[2]

It has been said that social work in all countries has three common characteristics: (1) it is a helping activity; (2) it is a "social" or nonprofit activity; (3) it is a liaison activity, through which individuals and groups may tap all the available resources in the community to meet their needs.[3]

The origins of professional social work in the United States may be traced back to the rise of the charity organization movement in the 1870's and the establishment of what is now the National Conference on Social Welfare. Evidence of the growth of social work as a profession after World War I include the development of the spe-

[1] Compare Walter A. Friedlander, *Introduction to Social Welfare* (New York, Prentice-Hall, 1955), p. 4.
[2] Arlien Johnson, "Social Work as a Profession," SWYB, 1943, p. 511.
[3] United Nations. *Training for Social Work* (Lake Success, N.Y., 1950), p. 13. See also pp. 8–17.

cialized processes of casework, group work, and community organization; the expansion of facilities for professional education; the rise of the professional associations; the growth of a professional literature; and the movement toward legal regulation of social work practice. Social work has only recently passed the period of the early pioneers, but with every decade its professional foundations are becoming more securely grounded.

The effective operation of social welfare agencies requires the cooperation of at least five and sometimes six groups: social workers; other professional social workers (doctors, psychiatrists, accountants, etc.); non-professional workers; volunteers (not used by all agencies); "consumers" or recipients of the services; and supporters of the agencies through taxes or contributions. At present, only a minority of social work positions are occupied by persons who are fully qualified through graduate professional education.

CHARACTERISTICS OF MODERN SOCIAL WELFARE

SOCIAL WELFARE SERVICES are *a response to human needs.* A particular service may focus on individuals, a particular group, a community, or a larger population group.

Social welfare services today are *organized.* This is a response to the complexities of modern urban society. Even in a small city, needs are so extensive, so complex, and usually so massed in certain geographical areas that they can no longer be cared for by the direct, personal ministrations of neighbors, but must be delegated to specialized agencies. Such an agency may be a separate organization, such as a family service society or Y.W.C.A., or it may be a subordinate unit of a larger organization, such as the school social work or visiting teacher service in a public school system, or a social service department of a hospital. The private fee-charging practitioner is extremely rare in social welfare. Often an agency conducts several services: a county welfare department, for example, may administer several types of public assistance and also special services to children. Conversely, in a large community the same type of service may be administered by several different agencies; thus, child placement may be provided at the same time by a governmental department and by denominational and nonsectarian voluntary agencies.

Social welfare agencies are *specialized.* In a community of any considerable size no one agency can cover the multiplicity of needs. The extent and variety of the work demands both a division of labor and the development of specialized services and skills. In spite of the existence of multi-functional agencies, a fairly high degree of specialization is the general rule.

Social welfare services are *extensive*. It is estimated that the total costs of governmental and voluntary social welfare services and social insurance were about $19,600,000,000 in the United States for the year ending June 30, 1954. Of this amount, about $10,700,000,000 was accounted for by social insurance and related programs. Nearly $1,500,000,000 is spent annually on social welfare programs benefiting the 8,000,000 people of New York City.[4]

SOCIAL WORK PROCESSES

THREE BASIC PROCESSES ARE USED by social workers in giving professional services: social casework, social group work, and community organization. In addition, administration and research are sometimes described as "enabling processes."[5] The term "process" suggests that each of these aspects of social work is "concerned with on-going, dynamic, changing manifestations of interaction."[6]

Besides the social work processes, many other methods are employed by social welfare agencies. Among these methods are: (1) medical diagnosis and treatment; (2) specialized consultation, such as legal aid, consultation by psychologists, home economists, etc.; (3) institutional care and treatment; (4) mass recreation; (5) mass education in such areas as health, child care, safety, and inter-cultural relations; and (6) enforcement of public regulations, such as those relating to public health, child labor, and commercial recreation.

CLASSIFICATION OF SOCIAL WELFARE AGENCIES

SOCIAL WELFARE AGENCIES may be classified by auspices, by functional fields (or types of problems dealt with), and by geographical area.

In terms of *auspices*, agencies may be governmental (public) or voluntary (private). Governmental agencies are established by law,

[4] Wayne McMillen, "Financing Social Welfare Services," SWYB, 1957, pp. 264–265. Community Council of Greater New York, news release, June 14, 1957.
[5] Werner W. Boehm, "Progress Report on the Study of the Curriculum in Social Work Education," *Social Work Education*, Vol. V, February 1957, p. 2.
[6] Arlien Johnson, "Community Organization in Social Work," SWYB, 1945, p. 93. Social action is sometimes regarded as an additional social work process; in this volume it is considered an aspect of community organization. See ch. 6.

directly or indirectly, and are supported by taxation. Voluntary agencies are usually organized through the association of interested persons or the action of other organizations. A voluntary agency may be sponsored by a particular group such as a religious denomination, a fraternal order, a labor organization, a cultural group, a social or a civic organization; or it may be completely non-sectarian and independent.

According to *functional fields*, agencies may be classified as follows:

1. Family welfare — including agencies dealing with income maintenance, financial need, and family casework.

2. Child welfare — primarily casework and institutional services to children, including children who are dependent or neglected, children born out of wedlock, and children with serious behavior problems.

3. Health — including public health departments, health promotion agencies, clinics, and hospitals.

4. Physically handicapped — including services relating to identification, diagnosis, treatment, vocational rehabilitation, and care, of the physically handicapped, and prevention of physical handicaps.

5. Mental health — diagnosis, treatment, and care of the mentally ill, mentally retarded, and epileptic; as well as preventive mental health programs. These agencies are usually separate from general health agencies.

6. Adult offenders — agencies dealing with crime, crime prevention, adult offenders, and discharged prisoners. This field does *not* include agencies dealing with behavior problems of children, such as juvenile courts and juvenile training schools, which are properly classified under child welfare.

7. Recreation and informal education — including many group work and so-called character building activities.

8. Planning, coordination, and program development — specialized community organization agencies, such as community welfare councils, community chests, social service exchanges, and most national and many statewide agencies.

9. Other — including state welfare departments and some other public welfare agencies.[7]

---

[7] For other functional classifications of social welfare agencies, see: Friedlander, *Introduction to Social Welfare;* Philip Klein *et al., Social Study of Pittsburgh* (New York, Columbia University Press, 1938), pp. 359, 916–921; Bradley Buell and associates, *Community Planning for Human Services* (New York, Columbia University Press, 1952), p. 10.

By *geographic levels,* agencies may be classified as local, state, national, and international. Variations of these general groupings are: metropolitan, "twin-city" or "tri-city" agencies, inter-county or district welfare agencies, and interstate or regional agencies.

Two other classifications should be suggested. (1) *Consumer-service agencies* serve clients or consumers directly. The vast majority of social welfare agencies are within this classification. They give public assistance, child guidance service, or institutional care; or they provide group work, mass recreational, or health services. These consumer-service agencies are subdivided into institutional or non-institutional agencies, on the basis of whether the clients live at the agency or not. (2) The *non-consumer-service agencies* do not serve clients directly: they serve other agencies, or the community as a whole. Most agencies concerned primarily with community organization are non-consumer-service agencies: community chests, community welfare councils, social service exchanges, and statewide and national agencies. The same is true of certain public welfare agencies: for instance, the Children's Bureau or the Bureau of Public Assistance in the Department of Health, Education and Welfare, and certain divisions of state welfare departments.

To understand how a social welfare agency fits into the community welfare picture, the answers to these questions should be determined:

1. Is the agency governmental or voluntary?
2. In what functional field does it operate?
3. Is it a consumer-service or a non-consumer-service agency; institutional or non-institutional?
4. What are its specific functions?
5. What territory does it serve?
6. How is it organized?
7. How is it supported?

THE ORIGINS OF SOCIAL WELFARE AGENCIES

SOCIAL WELFARE AGENCIES ORIGINATE in many ways. Governmental agencies have their origin in *law,* directly or indirectly. Most are created by explicit statutory provisions. Sometimes an agency is created by *administrative action* by a governmental official or another agency. The Federal Department of Health, Education and Welfare, created by a presidential Reorganization Plan in 1953, is an example of this method of establishment. An international, intergovernmental agency, such as the United Nations (which is concerned with social welfare at many points) may be created by agreements among a number of nations.

A typical method of establishing non-governmental social welfare agencies is by the *voluntary association* of an interested group. About a hundred years ago Alexis de Tocqueville observed that "Americans of all ages, all conditions, and all dispositions, constantly form associations."[8] Again, he remarked: "In no country in the world has the principle of association been more successfully used, or more unsparingly applied to a multitude of different objects, than in America. Beside the permanent associations which are established by law under the names of townships, cities, and counties, a vast number of others are formed and maintained by the agency of private individuals."[9]

The voluntary agency is likely to pass through the stages of a consciousness of need on the part of one or more persons, spreading the concern to a larger group, effecting a temporary organization, obtaining financial support, building a permanent organization, and beginning active operations.

Occasionally, an agency may be established by the *direct action* of a few individuals. Missions with social service as well as religious functions, and also some children's agencies, have sometimes been started by individuals working almost single-handed. It is often difficult for such agencies to continue as recognized agencies unless they develop a form of organization that attracts community interest and support.

Sometimes an agency is established by *bequest,* as was Girard College in Philadelphia, a well-known institution for dependent boys; or by *gift,* as was the Children's Fund of Michigan. Flexibility in such gifts or bequests is of great importance, so that agencies and programs may adapt themselves to new needs and changing conditions.

A voluntary agency may also be established by *some other organization or group* — a church, a religious order, an association of college alumni, a men's service club, or a community welfare council. An agency may be organized as a *local branch of a national or state agency:* for example, a chapter of the American Red Cross or a local Boy Scout council.

[8] *Democracy in America* (London, Saunders & Otley, 1840), p. 220.
[9] de Tocqueville, *American Institutions and Their Influence* (New York, A. S. Barnes & Co., 1855), p. 189. The tendency which de Tocqueville observed has of course been enormously increased by urbanization and improved communication.

Sometimes, a department or committee of an agency *separates itself* from the parent organization to form an individual agency. Charity organization societies frequently organized committees or departments which eventually became separate housing or tuberculosis associations.

Occasionally, a new agency may even arise from a definite *schism* in the parent agency: for example, the Volunteers of America were formed as a result of a split-off from the Salvation Army.

Agencies may be formed by *merger* as well as by division. An Association for Jewish Children in one large city was formed as the result of a consolidation of a foster family placing agency and two children's institutions. Some agencies are formed by *federation or joint action of other agencies.* Community welfare councils, federations of settlements, and national agencies such as the Family Service Association of America or United Community Funds and Councils of America, are examples.

SOCIAL WORK AND MODERN LIFE

PREVENTIVE EFFORT OR MORE INTELLIGENT and equitable social organization could undoubtedly reduce or eliminate some social welfare services. The development of social insurances, for example, might eliminate the need for all but a relatively small amount of public assistance. This does not mean, however, that social welfare services in general are therefore merely dependent upon social or economic inequities.

Modern social work has become a recognized adjunct to community life. We are not likely, in the foreseeable future, to develop a social order where there will be no need for skilled help with problems of individual adjustment. The future prospect of increased leisure time will itself necessitate additional leisure-time services. Wherever several social welfare agencies exist, and wherever people seriously seek to work out better relationships and better ways of living, community organization will be an important part of the task.

QUESTIONS AND PROBLEMS

1. Does the distinction between social work and social welfare, as suggested in this chapter, seem valid? Why or why not?

2. Examine critically some of the definitions of social work and social welfare referred to in Appendix B. Compare them with those given in the text. If you do not find satisfactory definitions for both terms, try to construct your own definitions.

3. Look through a social service directory for your own or some other community. Find agencies that illustrate various functional fields, geographic levels, auspices, service processes, and other categories suggested in the chapter.

4. Write a descriptive report on a social welfare agency, following the Outline for such a report in Appendix C.

5. How important are volunteers in modern social welfare services?

SUGGESTIONS FOR READING [10]

Fink, Arthur E.; Wilson, Everett E.; and Conover, Merrill B., *The Field of Social Work* (New York, Holt, 3rd ed., 1955, 630 pp.). A recent edition of one of the best texts on social work.

Friedlander, Walter A., *Introduction to Social Welfare* (New York, Prentice-Hall, 1955, 683 pp.). An excellent textbook, focused on the field of social welfare.

Hollis, Ernest V. and Taylor, Alice L., *Social Work Education in the United States* (New York, Columbia University Press, 1951, 422 pp.). Report of an important study of social work education. Chapters I–III contain valuable descriptive material regarding social work. (A 48-pp. Abridgement of this volume was published by the American Association of Social Workers in 1952.)

Howard, Donald S., "The Common Core of Social Work in Different Countries," NCSW, *Social Welfare Forum*, 1951, pp. 19–36. Suggests a definition and principles believed to be internationally applicable to social work.

Howard, Donald S., "Fifty Years of Social Work in the World," *Fifth International Conference of Social Work* (Paris, 1950), pp. 26–81.

Kasius, Cora (ed.) *New Directions in Social Work* (New York, Harper, 1954, 258 pp.). Stimulating articles on the present status of and the outlook for social work.

Lee, Porter R., *Social Work as Cause and Function and Other Papers* (New York, Columbia University Press, 1937, 270 pp.). The title paper, on the changed role of social work, from a series of crusades to a function of an orderly society, is especially suggestive.

Pray, Kenneth L. M., *Social Work in a Revolutionary Age and Other Papers* (Philadelphia, University of Pennsylvania Press, 1949, 308 pp.) The title paper, pp. 225–243, is particularly interesting as an interpretation of social work.

Social Work as a Profession (New York, published for Council on Social Work Education, by National Committee on Social Work in Defense Mobili-

[10] See list of Basic References on Community Organization and explanatory note, and list of Periodicals.

zation, 1953, 36 pp.). Probably the best available brief description of social work as a profession in the United States.

Social Work Year Book, 1957. Russell H. Kurtz, ed. (New York, National Association of Social Workers, 1957, 752 pp.). See especially: Nathan E. Cohen, "Social Work as a Profession," pp. 553–562, and the historical article by H. L. Lurie on "The Development of Social Welfare Programs in the United States," pp. 19–45.

Wilensky, Harold L. and Lebeaux, Charles N., *Industrial Society and Social Welfare* (New York, Russell Sage Foundation, 1958). The impact of industrialization on the demand for and supply and organization of social welfare services in the United States.

Note: Under Basic References, see especially Buell and associates, *Community Planning for Human Service; National Conference of Social Work, Proceedings; Social Work Year Book,* 1929–1954; also, under Periodicals, see *Social Work* and its predecessor, *Social Work Journal.*

2.

THE COMMUNITY AND SOCIAL WELFARE

COMMUNITY SETTINGS AND SOCIAL WELFARE

EVERY LOCAL SOCIAL WELFARE AGENCY operates in one or more communities. A social welfare agency is therefore vitally affected by the community in which it exists. It must adapt to the needs and conditions of the community, and must work with the available resources and leadership. The city slum, the mining town, the suburb, and the rural village all differ in needs and resources. Community standards and attitudes are other determinants of social welfare programs: standards of living, attitudes toward racial or nationality groups, toward relief and social welfare clients, toward cooperation with state and national programs, and so on. Above all, the community's understanding of social work and social needs are of vital importance. *The general level of social welfare organization and practice in a community cannot rise much higher than the level of the community's understanding of social welfare.*

The social worker, then, needs to know something about communities in general and especially the particular community in which he works.

WHAT IS A COMMUNITY?

A community involves an aggregation of *people* and a *place* or geographical entity. But what is the element that makes a particular population group a community? Is it common living conditions, common interests, shared facilities, political or social organization, or something else? [1]

The following definition will serve our purposes: *A community is a group of human beings, settled in a fairly compact and contiguous geographical area, and having significant elements of common life, as shown by manners, customs, traditions, and modes of speech.* According to this view, the community is not a mechanism but a growth; it need not be coterminous with a political unit; there may be communities within communities, as, for example, a Mexican community in an American city. The size of a community may range from a half-dozen houses to the Greater New York metropolitan area or a large county, provided it is a fairly compact and contiguous area.

TYPES OF COMMUNITIES

Communities are frequently classified in four ways: (1) by the size of the population (large city, small village); (2) by their economic bases (a mining town, a fishing village); (3) by their relationship to governmental units (the city of New Orleans; a Connecticut town) and (4) by a special character of the population (Harlem; Chinatown; the Greek section; Hobohemia).

For the purposes of social welfare, the following classification of communities is based on the economic, social, or cultural focus of interest of the community. Communities as described below are more or less nearly coterminous with governmental units. Some communities may fall into more than one of the following categories.[2]

1. *Metropolitan centers* of 500,000 population or more. The large city is usually an industrial, commercial, and cultural center.

2. *Industrial* cities, towns, and villages. Some have diversified industries, and some are centered about one industry — mining, lumbering, fishing, steel, automobiles, shoes, furniture.

3. *Commercial* cities, towns or villages. These are primarily trading centers.

[1] See Jessie Bernard, *American Community Behavior* (New York, Dryden Press, 1949), pp. 34–35; Amos H. Hawley, *Human Ecology* (New York, Ronald Press, 1950), pp. 180, 257–258; Herbert H. Stroup, *Community Welfare Organization* (New York, Harper, 1952), pp. 6–9; and especially, R. M. MacIver, *Community* (London, Macmillan & Co., 3rd ed., 1936), pp. 22–23.
[2] This classification is adapted from Eduard C. Lindeman, *The Community* (New York, Association Press, 1921), pp. 40–57. For other classifications, see Ray Johns and David F. DeMarche, *Community Organization and Agency Responsibility* (New York, Association Press, 1951), pp. 12–15, and Stroup, *Community Welfare Organization*, ch. 3.

4. *Governmental* cities and towns; the national and state capitals, and county seats, concerned primarily with the business of government.

5. *Educational* towns or villages. Such communities are centered about universities, colleges, teacher training schools, and so forth.

6. *Institutional* towns or villages. Such a community is one whose life centers primarily about an institution — a hospital, medical center, a sanitarium, or the like. In many cases the institution itself forms a smaller community within the town.

7. *Suburban* communities. The suburb is the residential community near a larger city, usually with a considerable number of persons who regularly commute to the city.

8. *Resort* communities. Typical of these are seaside and mountain resorts; centers for hunting, fishing, winter sports; villages adjoining national parks or natural attractions.

9. *Agricultural* villages. Such villages are trading and social centers for the surrounding agricultural districts.

10. *Open country* communities. Such a community may center about a school, church, general store, gasoline station, or some combination of these.

11. *Ideological* communities. These are the so-called "intentional communities" based primarily upon common religion, ideology, or artistic interests: religious communities of Mennonites, Hutterites, Shakers, Mormons, etc.; cooperative farms or villages; and so on.[3]

THE SOCIAL WORKER AND THE COMMUNITY

No social worker is prepared to practice social work intelligently in a community until he knows certain basic facts about that community. Those facts fall under the following headings: geography; history; population; government; housing and planning; economic basis of community life; educational, health, recreational, social welfare, and religious resources; and community attitudes and relationships.

A social worker who seeks basic information about the community may use the outline on pages 19–20, expanding it in accordance with his needs. Ordinarily, the worker can acquire most of this information

---

[3] There is a fascinating literature both on the literary utopias — from Plato's *Republic* to Aldous Huxley's parody, *Brave New World* — and on actual experiments with ideological, "utopian," or cooperative communities. See Stroup, *Community Welfare Organization*, ch. 4; Henrik F. Infield, *Utopia and Experiment* (New York, Praeger, 1955).

within the first two months on a job. A good deal of the information will be picked up without much special effort, and the rest can be obtained by a limited amount of research and interviews.[4] The larger a community is, the more likely it will be that much of this information will be available in digest summary form. In larger cities the worker's agency should be able to help him in his orientation to the city.

The social worker must see the community as a dynamic organism. It embraces individuals, groups, and institutions with complex and ever-changing patterns of relationships. The social worker knows that individuals change, and he is aware that groups also change, since they are made up of changing individuals and changing relationships between these individuals. The social worker, knowing that the community also changes, must realize his responsibility and that of his agency in helping make that change for the better.

To this end, the social worker must acquire knowledge of his community and must form the habit of objective appraisal.

COMMUNITY YARDSTICKS

The following list may be helpful in the evaluation of the strengths and weaknesses of a community.[5]

1. **Community planning.** What are the community's natural resources? Is the community consciously planning for its future? Is it making the most of its resources? What is the status of the community in respect to highways, transportation, utilities, and convenience of living?

2. **Housing.** Is the housing adequate in quantity and quality for all the residents of the community?

3. **Government.** Is there effective democratic local government? Are there sound relationships between the local government and state

[4] For an organization or group that wishes to undertake a community self-study, several guides are available. See especially Roland L. Warren, *Studying Your Community* (New York, Russell Sage Foundation, 1955); and Richard W. Poston, *Democracy is You* (New York, Harper, 1953). Also consider Wayne McMillen's suggestion of a "community abstract," in his *Community Organization for Social Welfare* (Chicago, University of Chicago Press, 1945), pp. 239–241.
[5] Adapted from a pamphlet by the author, *Friends and Community Service, in War and Peace* (Philadelphia, American Friends Service Committee, 1942), pp. 21–22. For other suggestions as to criteria for community life, see Lindeman's list of the values which an ideal community should furnish to its people, *The Community*, pp. 14–15; Earle Lippincott, *Our Home Town* (New York, Association Press, 1949), pp. 8–11; Stroup, *Community Welfare Organization*, ch. 4; and United Nations, *Declaration of Human Rights*.

and federal governments? Are there special political problems, such as indications of corruption, governmental incompetence, poor quality of leadership, or long-continued dominance by one political party?

4. **Economic life.** What is the degree of economic security in the community? How satisfactory are industrial development, employment, and distribution?

5. **Education.** Is there a system of free public education? Are there adequate facilities for the entire community? Is education adapted to the needs of various types of individuals?

6. **Health.** Is there a healthy community environment, and are there adequate public health and medical services?

7. **Recreation.** Are there sufficient opportunities for the constructive and creative use of leisure time?

8. **Welfare Services.** Are there adequate resources in the area of social welfare, including services for the treatment and care of those who have physical, mental, or social handicaps?

9. **Religion.** Is there freedom of religion? Are there adequate opportunities for religious expression? Is there freedom for those who do not wish to participate in organized religious activities? To what extent do organized religious groups render community services or participate vitally in the life of the community?

10. **Community attitudes.** To what degree is the community characterized by: freedom of opportunity; freedom of expression; freedom for voluntary associations; freedom from discrimination against minorities; freedom from the disruptive effects of war or deeply divisive conflicts? To what extent may all participate in community-wide activities? Is there a democratic spirit and an underlying sense of unity in community life?

Obviously, this list cannot take the place of research or technical appraisals. In spite of its limitations, however, such a checklist may be of considerable value in locating some of the major needs or problems in a community.

In these first two chapters we have considered the nature of social work and social welfare today, and the importance of the community in respect to social welfare. We are now ready to raise the question, What *is* community organization?

QUESTIONS AND PROBLEMS

1. Examine critically some of the definitions of community referred to in the chapter. Which of these definitions seems to you most valid? If none of

the definitions seems satisfactory, try to construct a definition of your own.

2. How large do you think a community should be?

3. Give some illustrations of the effects of the community setting on social welfare services, in a particular community.

4. *Report on a Community.* Select some community that you know well. Make a brief written report on this community, using the following outline. This report is an attempt to identify quickly the major characteristics of a community. This is the sort of information that a social worker might want about a community if he were considering taking a position there or undertaking some service such as a study, field trip, consultation, etc. This report is not intended to involve any elaborate research; approximate dates and figures will serve the purpose, in the case of most of the items.

IDENTIFICATION

(1) Name of community

(2) In what county and state is the community located?

(3) What is the population?   Source of information?

(4) Does the community correspond identically or approximately with a governmental unit: city, county, village, etc.? If so, give name and type of unit.

(5) Classification: type of community?

(6) What are the major geographical characteristics of the community?

(7) When was the community first established?

(8) Note any major foreign-born or racial groups in the community.

(9) What is the main economic basis of the community? How do most of the people make their living?

(10) What is the form of local government?

RESOURCES

(11) Note any special features of interest in regard to the following types of community resources: (a) educational, (b) health and medical, (c) recreational and leisure time, (d) welfare and civic, (e) religious, (f) housing and community facilities — transportation, utilities, etc.

PROBLEMS

(12) Are there slums or problem areas within the community? If so, describe.

(13) Are there special problems connected with any minority groups. Describe.

(14) Are there significant conflicts or tension situations in the community? Describe.

EVALUATION

(15) What would you say are the dominant psychological characteristics of the community — interests, traditions, attitudes, etc.?

(16) In respect to social welfare: (a) What would you say are the major strengths of this community? (b) Major weaknesses?

(17) Is there, in your judgment, an outstanding need for some particular "next step" in social welfare in this community? If so, what?

SUGGESTIONS FOR READING

The texts by Hillman, Johns and DeMarche, Murphy, and Stroup all have chapters on the community. (See Basic References.)

Bernard, Jessie, *American Community Behavior* (New York, Dryden Press, 1949, 688 pp.). Sociological analysis of problems confronting American communities.

Biddle, William W., *The Cultivation of Community Leaders: Up From the Grass Roots* (New York, Harper, 1953, 203 pp.). Development of leaders for volunteer community activities. Based primarily upon the experience of the Earlham College program in working with small communities.

Hunter, Floyd, *Community Power Structure: A Study of Decision Makers* (Chapel Hill, University of North Carolina Press, 1953, 352 pp.). A basic sociological study of community power structure and relationships.

Hunter, Floyd; Schaffer, Ruth Connor; and Sheps, Cecil G., *Community Organization: Action and Inaction* (Chapel Hill, University of North Carolina Press, 1956, 268 pp.). A sociological study of a self-study of health problems in Salem, Massachusetts.

Lindeman, Eduard C., *The Community* (New York, Association Press, 1921, 222 pp. OP). An unusually valuable and stimulating analysis of the subject of the community and the organization of community forces.

Lippincott, Earle, *Our Home Town* (New York, Association Press, 1949, 70 pp.). An aid to citizen groups in appraising their communities.

MacIver, R. M., *Community: A Sociological Study.* (Published, 1917. London, Macmillan & Co., third edition, 1936, 446 pp.) Especially ch. II. MacIver's philosophical approach is of unique value for social workers.

Morgan, Arthur E. *The Community of the Future and the Future of the Community* (Yellow Springs, Ohio, Community Service, 1957, 166 pp.). Considers the possibility of future communities that may combine the desirable features of the village and the city, and how such communities may be brought into being.

―――― *The Small Community* (New York, Harper, 1942, 312 pp.). The importance and values of the small community; contains a chapter on the community council.

Poston, Richard W., *Democracy Is You* (New York, Harper, 1953, 312 pp.). An outline and suggested methodology for community self-study.

Sanderson, Dwight and Polson, Robert A. *Rural Community Organization* (New York, Wiley, 1939, 448 pp.). A valuable sociological textbook on rural community organization.

Steiner, Jesse Frederick, *Community Organization* (New York, Century, rev. ed., 1930, 453 pp., OP). The first six chapters deal largely with the nature of the community.

Warren, Roland L., *Studying Your Community* (New York, Russell Sage Foundation, 1955, 385 pp.). An outline for community study. A successor to Joanna C. Colcord's *Your Community* (1939, 1947).

3.

WHAT IS COMMUNITY ORGANIZATION?

___

WHY COMMUNITY ORGANIZATION?

COMMUNITY ORGANIZATION IS NEEDED for social welfare because situations exist in which no direct and immediate service to an individual or group will meet the need. Frequently there must be a community-wide mass attack upon a problem. Let us look at an illustration of such a problem.

A caseworker in a public assistance agency finds that a family receiving assistance is living in a house unfit for human habitation. The roof leaks; the place cannot be heated; a hard rain transforms the cellar into a lake; and the whole structure is on the verge of collapse. The caseworker, after a good deal of effort, helps the family to move out of this hovel and to establish itself in a decent neighborhood.

A month later a new family is assigned to her. To her horror she discovers that they are living in the same house from which she has just helped the first family escape. Here is the whole job to be done again! The caseworker sees herself spending her professional life helping families move out of that house so that other families can move in. Distraught at such a prospect, she brings it up at the weekly district staff meeting.

The caseworker's story provokes a torrent of discussion. Every one of her colleagues has had the same sort of experience. One worker questions: "What's the use of talking about decent family life unless people can live in decent homes?" Another observes that this is a problem which cannot be solved by giving assistance to individual families; there must be some over-all approach to the problem of housing in the district.

The district superintendent and the staff are so concerned that they bring the matter to the attention of the administrator of the municipal public welfare department. The administrator discusses it with the public welfare board of the city. The members of the board are impressed with the case illustrations presented by the workers. The department arranges for and assists in a housing survey in the district. The workers get addresses, locations and all the necessary details. It becomes clear that there are equally urgent housing problems in other parts of the city. A group of citizens organizes a Citizens Housing Association to work for better housing, town planning, and zoning. The Community Welfare Council takes a hand. Citizen groups begin to call upon the Mayor and members of the city council. The city government becomes actively concerned. Negotiations are begun with the federal government regarding a slum-clearance project. Within two years both governmental and voluntary agencies are working vigorously on a housing program for the city.

In this instance, the casework approach was recognized as inadequate and was succeeded by a community organization approach.

Again, a settlement, with an excellent, though small, program may spark a community-wide study resulting in the development of a sound city-wide recreation program. A rural child-welfare worker, in addition to her casework duties, may find herself speaking to various groups, interpreting the child welfare needs of the county; serving on a committee concerned with juvenile delinquency; conferring with officials regarding questions of interagency relationships; and helping to organize a county community welfare council.

The term "community organization" came into use about the time of World War I, and has been variously defined.[1]

In this book the term will be used with the following meaning: *Community organization for social welfare (or community welfare organization) is the process of bringing about and maintaining adjustment between social welfare needs and social welfare resources in a geographical area or a special field of service.* Community welfare organization is a process comparable to casework or group work.

[1] The term is not entirely satisfactory, and various substitutes for it, such as social welfare planning and social welfare organization have been proposed. However, "community organization" seems pretty firmly fixed in history, literature, and practice.

SOCIAL WELFARE NEEDS

Community organization is called into being by *needs* relating to the field of social welfare as we have previously defined it. Some of these needs may be community-wide, such as the need for fuller knowledge of community problems, for better coordination of agencies, for better understanding and support of social welfare efforts. Some needs may relate to certain aspects of community life, such as family welfare, child welfare, health, or recreation. Or needs may be more specific: the need for more adequate public assistance grants, better standards in the public health department, a child guidance clinic, a playground in a particular section, or better housing for a minority group.

These needs are not always obvious. The question may arise: Who is to define what is a social welfare need at a particular time and place?

For example, in a city public welfare department, the average load may be 175 cases per visitor — a figure which precludes any extensive casework service aside from the actual administration of assistance. The director of the department may believe that such supplementary casework service is vitally necessary, and that the average case load per visitor should be reduced to about 75 to make this possible. From his standpoint, there is a social welfare need for more funds for administration and for more staff members. On the other hand, the mayor may believe the agency should do no more than determine economic need and give assistance; he may even think there is no good reason why the average case load per visitor could not be increased to 200 or 250.

Again, a particular group of physicians and laymen may believe that there is an overwhelming need for the establishment of maternal health clinics that will give contraceptive information and advice to married persons, at the discretion of the physicians in charge. Another group, who reject birth control on moral and religious grounds, will see no need whatever for these clinics; in fact, they may feel that there is a need for educational activity, pressure methods, or even the enactment of legislation to prevent these clinics from coming into existence.

There is no authoritative method for determining the valid social welfare needs in all situations. Finding the facts and obtaining the judgment of experts may be of great help; but these procedures will not solve the inevitable disagreements that stem from different value-judgments.

The needs in any situation are defined by those concerned. They may be defined through trial and error, disagreement, conflict, domination, compromise, or integration of thinking. Frequently the definition of needs, or at least the determination of what shall be done about them, is bound up with decisions of voters, taxpayers, contributors, members of a constituency group, or other persons in positions of power in a community.

SOCIAL WELFARE RESOURCES

Social welfare needs are met by the use of certain *resources*. Sometimes existing resources can be mobilized, expanded, or better utilized; sometimes new resources must be created. The term *resources* includes not only social and health agencies but also other organizations, groups, and individuals; staff personnel; physical equipment; laws; funds; leadership; volunteer participation; factual materials; public understanding; good will; and capacity for united planning and action.

All the following are resources for meeting social welfare needs.

A family service agency is organized in a city where one has never existed before.

A men's service club promotes better services for crippled children.

A child welfare worker in a rural county enlists the interest of a dynamic superintendent of schools; this leads to closer cooperation between the schools and the social welfare agencies, particularly in the area of child behavior problems.

A combination gymnasium and auditorium is added to a community center building, greatly increasing its program possibilities.

A new, well-qualified executive comes to an ineffective public health agency. By giving dynamic leadership, employing trained personnel, and improving procedures and records, he raises the standards of the agency substantially.

Over a five-year period, a community chest increases the annual amount raised from $800,000 to $1,100,000.

ADJUSTMENT BETWEEN NEEDS AND RESOURCES

The *aim* of community organization is to bring about *a progressively more effective adjustment* between needs and resources. However, there are times — during a depression or war, for example —

when the community organization worker must battle desperately just
to maintain what has already been achieved.

When we speak of welfare needs and welfare resources, we are
not talking about static elements, but about variables. Community
organization operates in a world where, to use Walter Lippman's
phrase, "whirl is king"; it must be viewed as something in motion; it
will never stand still to be looked at properly. Community organization is a dynamic process.

This adjustment may be not only in a community but in any other
geographical area. It may be concerned with the whole field of social
welfare, or it may focus on one special field of service. This may be a
functional field (child welfare, health, etc.) or a special racial, religious, or cultural group. Even in such instances, however, at least a
secondary relationship to a geographical area is implied. For example:

> The community organization process is applied to recreation and
> informal education in a particular community by the community wel-
> fare council, while the National Recreation Association is concerned
> with recreation throughout the United States.
>
> The state mental health society is interested primarily in com-
> munity organization for mental health on a statewide basis.
>
> The National Conference of Catholic Charities is concerned with
> Catholic social welfare services throughout the United States.
>
> The World Health Organization is concerned with international
> health problems.

The adjustment of social welfare needs and resources may be accomplished in a variety of ways. It may be done democratically or
autocratically. A local welfare agency may be established through
democratic thinking, planning, and participation, or it may be set up
by a highly centralized totalitarian national government, in accordance
with a rigid uniform plan, and without consideration of the wishes of
the community. In both cases those concerned would be attempting
to adjust resources to needs. Most of us who live in a democratic
society would think that the democratic, cooperative way is the
right way, and that the autocratic way is socially undesirable.

However, the process would be community organization in either
case, since it would be concerned with the adjustment of needs and
resources. Community organization must be defined objectively, in
terms of *the nature of the phenomena and objectives* involved. It cannot be defined in terms of value-judgments or subjective criteria of
social desirability. Thus one cannot say, "A community chest forced

a merger on these two agencies against their wishes; that is undemocratic procedure, *therefore* it is not community organization." If it is not community organization, what is it? Is a merger of two agencies community organization in one town and something else in another? Community organization, if done undemocratically, does not cease to be community organization; but *it ceases to measure up to what we, in a democratic society, regard as sound standards of community organization.*

SOME OTHER CONCEPTIONS OF COMMUNITY ORGANIZATION

Three contemporary contributions to the subject of community organization should be especially noted, since they are important in current thinking and practice.

Wilber I. Newstetter and his associates at the University of Pittsburgh School of Social Work have stressed "social intergroup work" as being the aspect of community organization which is "probably unique in social work practice." Social intergroup work is conceived of as a process of promoting mutually satisfactory relations between groups and using these relations to further social work goals.[2]

Intergroup relations are certainly one of the most important aspects of community organization, but there seems to be no convincing evidence that "intergroup work" is any more uniquely social work practice than a number of other community organization activities.

Murray G. Ross defines community organization as a process by which a community identifies its needs or objectives, establishes priorities among them, finds the resources for dealing with them, takes action in respect to them, "and in so doing extends and develops cooperative and collaborative attitudes and practices in the community."[3]

This emphasis upon the involvement of the total community points out an important social ideal. However, it seems doubtful whether, in practice, the process which Ross describes can ordinarily be carried out by any except smaller communities. In any case, there appears to be no warrant, in practice or in accepted usage, for restricting the

[2] Wilber I. Newstetter, "The Social Intergroup Work Process," NCSW, 1947, pp. 205–217; "Teaching Community Organization in Schools of Social Work," in Wayne McMillen, *Community Organization for Social Welfare*, p. 61. See also Helen D. Green, *Social Work Practice in Community Organization* (New York, Whiteside and Morrow, 1954), ch. 3.

[3] Murray G. Ross, *Community Organization, Theory and Principles* (New York, Harper, 1955), p. 39.

term community organization to instances where the total community rather than certain portions of it are involved.

Violet M. Sieder has identified five stages in the development of community organization objectives:

(1) Efforts, through the social service exchange or otherwise, to prevent "client abuse" of services offered by independent agencies.

(2) Emphasis upon the integration of services, particularly through community chests and community welfare councils.

(3) Attempts to "relate the resources of agencies, both public and voluntary, to the needs of people."

(4) Emphasis upon process, upon analyzing "causative factors," and upon prevention.

(5) A focus on community organization as a "direct service to communities," with the goal of achieving an integrated community.[4]

These are all valid approaches to community organization. As Miss Sieder points out, they are not mutually exclusive: rather "they are all still necessary and in effect in most community planning organizations."

The emphasis in this book on the adjustment of needs and resources is based upon the conviction that, if the inner as well as the more material community resources are taken into account, the adjustment transcends environmental manipulation and becomes a sound and basic approach to community welfare organization.

QUESTIONS AND PROBLEMS

1. Formulate your own definition of community welfare organization.

2. What seem to be the main points of agreement and disagreement in the definitions on community welfare organization which you have read?

3. What is the relationship between community welfare organization and "social intergroup work"?

4. Should the ideas of cooperation and democracy be introduced into the definition of community welfare organization? If so, how?

SUGGESTIONS FOR READING

(For Chapters 3, 4, and 5)

The most thorough discussions of the nature of community welfare organization are to be found in the Basic References — particularly Robert P.

[4] Violet M. Sieder, "What is Community Organization Practice?", NCSW, Social Welfare Forum, 1956, pp. 161–163.

Lane, "The Field of Community Organization" and the *Social Work Year Book* articles on community organization.[5]

Barry, Mildred C., "Current Concepts in Community Organization." NCSW, *Group Work and Community Organization, 1956* (New York, Columbia University Press, 1956), pp. 3–20. Suggests a system of concepts for community organization and illustrates them from practice.

Carter, Genevieve W., "Practice Theory in Community Organization." (Paper presented at National Conference on Social Welfare, 1957, mimeographed, 28 pp.) Discusses the nature of "practice theory" and suggests five levels of knowledge in theory-building.

Cockerill, Eleanor E. (ed.), *Social Work Practice in the Field of Tuberculosis.* (Pittsburgh, University of Pittsburgh, School of Social Work, 1954, 223 pp.) Wilber I. Newstetter: ch. 4, "The Concept of the Community and Other Related Concepts," pp. 65–100. Also ch. 5, discussion: "A Closer Inspection of the Processes Utilized in Community Organization," pp. 101–108.

Kurtz, Russell H., "The Range of Community Organization." (NCSW, 1940, pp. 400–412.) A valuable discussion of eight "bench-marks" that describe major variations in community organization.

Lane, Robert P., "Report of Groups Studying the Community Organization Process." (NCSW, 1940, pp. 456–473.) Committee report: the "second Lane Report" — a sequel to the report of 1939 (see Basic References).

Mayo, Leonard W., "Community Organization in 1946." (NCSW, 1946, pp. 129–138.) The outlook on community organization shortly after the end of World War II.

Newstetter, Wilber I., "The Social Intergroup Work Process." (NCSW, 1947, pp. 205–217.) Analyses of the nature of the social intergroup work process and the functions and role of the social worker as a "disciplined enabler." (See also the reference under Cockerill, editor, above.)

Pray, Kenneth L. M., "When is Community Organization Social Work Practice?" (NCSW, 1947, pp. 194–204.) Included also in Pray, *Social Work in a Revolutionary Age and Other Papers* (see bibliography, ch. 1).

Sieder, Violet M., "What Is Community Organization Practice in Social Work?" (NCSW, *Social Welfare Forum,* 1956, pp. 160–174.)

[5] The first *Year Book*, in 1929, contained merely a brief "coordinating article" on "Community Organization." In the four issues during 1933–1939, the terms "social planning," "social planning and program promotion," or "social welfare planning" were employed. In 1941, the *Year Book* adopted the term, "Community Organization for Social Work"; since 1949, the article has appeared as "Community Organization for Social Welfare."

4.

MAJOR CHARACTERISTICS

———

KIPLING'S "SIX HONEST SERVING MEN" who taught him all he knew (what, why, when, how, where, and who) have served all kinds of persons from learned philosophers to cub reporters. These questions provide a natural framework for many types of analysis, and they may be used to advantage in the present attempt to analyze the nature and characteristics of community welfare organization. If we apply these questions to community organization, we shall ask:

What is community organization?
Why is it practiced?
Where is it practiced?
Who practices it?
When is it practiced?
How is it practiced?

The first question — What is community organization? — has been answered in Chapter 3. Community welfare organization is a *process* of social work, comparable with casework or group work. The essence of this process is the attempted adjustment of social welfare needs and resources in a geographical area or special field of service. Community organization includes factfinding insofar as factfinding is intimately related to the adjustment of resources to needs; and it includes social action insofar as social action relates to social welfare.

Leonard W. Mayo has pointed out that "community organization projects tend to focus primarily on agencies, on a social or health problem, or on a given geographical area."[1] Community organization also often involves one or more of the following factors: (1) mass attacks upon problems; (2) intergroup and interorganization relationships;

[1] Mayo, "Community Organization in 1946," NCSW, 1946, p. 131.

30

(3) the development of comprehensive social welfare programs; and (4) education and interpretation.

Community organization is concerned with the discovery and definition of needs, with elimination and prevention as well as treatment, and with the constant readjustment of resources to meet changing needs.

WHY IS COMMUNITY ORGANIZATION PRACTICED?

The *aim* of community organization is to bring about a progressively more effective adjustment between social welfare needs and resources. But this cannot be done wholesale. One cannot just start out on Monday morning and simply begin bringing about an adjustment between needs and resources. The broad aim must be narrowed to more specific objectives.

These secondary objectives are the channels through which community organization expresses itself. They are the *functions* — the jobs to be done by community organization agencies and workers.

These functions are: [2]

1. *To secure and maintain an adequate factual basis for sound planning and action.* (Factfinding.)

2. *To initiate, develop, modify, and terminate social welfare programs and services.* (Program development.)

3. *To establish, maintain, and improve social welfare standards, and to increase the effectiveness, efficiency, and economy of operation of social welfare agencies.* (Standards.)

4. *To improve and facilitate inter-relationships, and to promote coordination between organizations, groups, and individuals concerned with social welfare programs and services.* (Coordination.)

5. *To develop better public understanding of social welfare needs, resources, objectives, services, methods, and standards.* (Education.)

6. *To develop adequate public support of, and public participation in, social welfare activities.* Financial support includes income from tax funds, voluntary contributions, and other sources. (Support and Participation.)

These will be discussed in more detail in the next chapter.

[2] Compare Robert P. Lane, "The Field of Community Organization," NCSW, 1939, pp. 500–501.

WHERE IS COMMUNITY ORGANIZATION PRACTICED?

Community organization takes place outside as well as inside the field of social welfare. Chambers of commerce, councils of churches, municipal research bureaus, citizens' organizations to promote better government, county and city political organizations, and adult education councils are concerned with community organization, whether or not they use the phrase. So also are general community councils, village improvement associations, and community development agencies.

Community organization, in spite of the local connotation of the term "community," may be carried on in any geographical area; it may operate on any geographical level or between any geographical levels.

The State Charities Aid Association of New York has done distinguished work in statewide community organization. The federal Children's Bureau and the National Social Welfare Assembly are concerned with community organization on the national level.

Where community organization operates between geographical levels, it is usually a two-way process; that is, it may operate from the lower to the higher level as well as from the higher to the lower. Figure 1 illustrates this point.

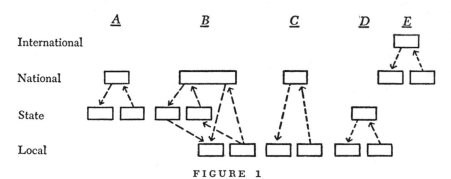

FIGURE 1

INTER-LEVEL OPERATION OF COMMUNITY ORGANIZATION.

A. NATIONAL-STATE.   B. NATIONAL-STATE-LOCAL.
C. NATIONAL-LOCAL.   D. STATE-LOCAL.
E. INTERNATIONAL-NATIONAL.

The Bureau of Public Assistance of the federal Department of Health, Education, and Welfare may help a state welfare department work out a state plan for aid to the blind under the Social Security Act. (Example A.)

In the case of a national organization for the physically handicapped, which has both state and local branches, the process may operate between the national-state, national-local, and state-local levels. The national agency carries on research, publishes a monthly bulletin, holds national and regional conferences, and gives field service. It uses the community organization process in aiding the state and local branches in program development, raising standards, and fund raising. The state and local units, in turn, help mold the national program through their studies, practice, and experimentation, and through participation in the agency's national conference and on its board and committees. (Example B.)

In still other cases, relationships may be national-local, as between the Family Service Association of America and its local members (Example C.); or state-local, as between a state welfare department and county public welfare agencies (Example D.); or international-national, as between the World Health Organization and a national department of health (Example E.).

WHO PRACTICES COMMUNITY ORGANIZATION?

Community organization is practiced by: (1) workers in agencies such as chests, councils, and so on; (2) executives of these community organization agencies, who divide their time between administration and community organization; (3) executives of consumer-service agencies, whose jobs involve some community organization as well as administration; (4) social workers, such as those in settlements, rural child welfare services, and health agencies, who combine casework or group work with community organization; (5) consumer-service workers (caseworkers or group workers) who use the community organization process occasionally and incidentally — for example, in interpreting their jobs and their agencies; and (6) laymen, who, as volunteers, solicit for the community chest, serve on boards and committees, and render service in many other ways. In some cases where, for example, a group of laymen undertake to organize a family service society or a tuberculosis association, the community organization process may be carried on for a time by laymen alone.

Within the field of social welfare, *community organization is a primary function of some agencies and a secondary or incidental function of practically all others.* Community organization is obviously the primary function of the community welfare council or community chest. These agencies do not ordinarily give direct service to consumers. Their service is to other agencies or to the public or a portion of the public. But *any* consumer-service agency is concerned with program development, interpretation, financial support, and community and inter-agency relationships. Community organization, then, is used to a greater or lesser degree by all social welfare agencies.

WHEN IS COMMUNITY ORGANIZATION PRACTICED?

Community organization is, of course, practiced constantly. But there is an aspect of time that is of practical importance in the analysis of community organization activities, record-keeping, and program direction.

Community organization activities may be *continuous,* as in the case of the operation of the social service exchange or information and referral service; they may be *temporary* projects, as in the case of a study, a series of eight weekly training sessions for volunteers, or a legislative campaign; or they may be *occasional,* such as meetings of a community welfare council or field visits from a national agency. This classification of activities is discussed in Chapter 16.

HOW IS COMMUNITY ORGANIZATION PRACTICED?

Community organization always begins as a response to a *problem,* expressive of a need. For example:

How can a community develop more cooperation and eliminate duplication of service among health agencies? How can agencies and social workers interpret social welfare more effectively to organized labor, to the churches, and to the general public? How can the number of separate appeals to contributors in a community be reduced? The attempt to solve any one of these problems would lead to the use of the process of community organization.

The practitioner of community organization uses certain *methods.* A method is, of course, the way in which the job is done. It is a direct answer to the question, How?

Take, for example, the question: How can a community find out the nature and extent of its health problems? The answer may be, make a *study* through the community welfare council: that is, use the method of factfinding. The first steps toward factfinding may involve *analyzing* what will be involved in the study, drawing up a tentative *plan, organizing* a committee, calling a *conference* of representatives of interested organizations, and *interpreting* the need for the study to groups from whom support is wanted.

METHODS OF COMMUNITY ORGANIZATION

To date, there has not been sufficient careful recording of community organization activities to serve as a sound basis for an adequate scientific analysis of the methods of community organization.

However, the study of a considerable volume of community organization material, in various forms and settings, suggests that there are at least fourteen fairly distinct major methods. It is clear that they are used in all sorts of combinations and relationships to one another.

These fourteen methods are listed below, grouped under four general headings. Italics denote the six methods most commonly used in the various types of community organization.

PROGRAMMING.   *Factfinding, analysis,* evaluation, *planning.*
COORDINATION AND INTEGRATION.   *Conference,* consultation, negotiation, *organization.*
EDUCATION AND PROMOTION.   *Education,* legislative promotion, non-legislative social action.
FINANCING.   Fund-raising, federated financial campaigning, joint budgeting.

KINDS OF PERSONAL RELATIONSHIPS

Casework involves primarily interpersonal ("one-to-one") relationships. Group work involves both group and interpersonal relationships. Community organization involves interpersonal, group, and intergroup relationships. Some relationships which appear to be interpersonal may also be intergroup in the sense that the individuals involved represent two different groups. Illustrations of these three types of relationships in the practice of community organization are: (1) The executive of the community chest interviews a "leading citizen" about taking a key position in the campaign. Here the relationship, or at least the actual interview contact, is interpersonal. (2) A committee of the staff of the city welfare department plans a year's program of interpretation of the services of the department. In the planning by this committee, group relationships are paramount. (3) The health division of the community welfare council holds a meeting to consider certain problems of preventive effort and health promotion. Here intergroup or interagency relationships are involved.

Administration, like community organization, clearly involves all three types of relationships; and this is true of research also, where the personal interview, the committee or group meeting, and the intergroup committee may all be found.

PRINCIPLES OF COMMUNITY ORGANIZATION

HOW SHOULD COMMUNITY ORGANIZATION be done? Are there any general *principles* that may guide us in deciding what is sound or good or socially desirable community organization? The formulation of principles involves judgments as to values. It is assumed that principles of community organization in a democratic society would be in harmony with the basic concepts of democracy. For example, such principles as the following would probably elicit rather general agreement among American community organization workers:

Social welfare programs should be based upon and responsive to needs.

So far as possible, all groups affected by a program should have a part in shaping and directing the program.

Voluntary cooperation is the key to effective community organization.

Social welfare programs should stress prevention.

QUESTIONS AND PROBLEMS

1. Give examples of the community organization process illustrating:
a. The focusing of the process on (1) agencies, (2) a social welfare problem, (3) a geographical area.
b. A mass attack on a problem
c. Intergroup relationships
d. The development of a social welfare program
e. The use of each of the six community organization functions
f. Community organization on or between statewide, national, and international levels
g. The use of the community organization process, (1) by a consumer-service agency, (2) as part of the job of an executive of a

consumer-service agency, (3) by a caseworker or group worker, (4) in a situation in which laymen participate in the process

h. The use of various methods of community organization

i. A situation involving a principle of community organization

2. Consider some major social welfare problem in your own or another community — for example, the prevention and treatment of juvenile delinquency, developing a program for the aging or for retarded children, or an adequate public health program; bringing about the establishment of a needed new agency; or bringing order out of chaos in the field of child care and foster family placement. How might the problem be approached from the standpoint of community organization?

SUGGESTIONS FOR READING

See Suggestions for Reading for chapter 3.

Note also the chapters on community organization in the texts by Fink and others, *The Field of Social Work;* and Friedlander, *Introduction to Social Welfare* — listed in Suggestions for Reading at end of ch. 1.

5.

RELATIONSHIPS AND CHANNELS

COMMUNITY ORGANIZATION AS AN INTEGRAL ASPECT OF SOCIAL WORK

IN THE EARLY DAYS OF SOCIAL WORK, its various processes were not clearly identified or differentiated. However, from about World War I until approximately 1950, one of the major emphases and trends in social work was the emergence, identification, analysis, and development of the various processes — casework, group work, and community organization. Casework as a process was defined and analyzed, and the foundations of practice were laid between about 1917 and 1929. Group work followed a somewhat similar process about 1935–1936; community organization during 1939–1946. Since 1950, however, there has been a strong trend toward *integration in social work* as contrasted with the previous emphasis upon the separate processes.

All the processes of social work deal with human beings, social situations, and social relationships. All of them deal, in one way or another, with the problems of adjustment and growth. They all require a basic understanding of the dynamics of individual behavior, group behavior, and of community and social life and social institutions. They all require practitioners who possess certain knowledge, skills, attitudes, and professional self-discipline.[1]

In a discussion of "Basic Values in Social Work," Elmer J. Tropman

[1] Ernest V. Hollis and Alice L. Taylor, *Social Work Education in the United States* (New York, Columbia University Press, 1951), pp. 222–224; see also Campbell G. Murphy, *Community Organization Practice* (Boston, Houghton Mifflin, 1954), pp. 77–139.

has stressed principles which are clearly applicable to all forms of social work. For example:

Self-determination.   The individual, the group, and the community have the right to choose their own goals.

Individualization.   People, groups, and countries differ from each other, and therefore require differential treatment.

Participation.   There must be participation of persons, groups, or communities for which service is offered or planning is done. We plan *with* — not for.

"The ultimate good of all must take precedence over the interests of the individual worker or agency."

"People and communities can change and be helped to change." [2]

In this book we shall be concerned mainly with those aspects of community organization which are distinctive from other processes of social work; but beneath all of these is the solid foundation of common social work objectives, knowledge, concepts, skills, attitudes, philosophy, and values. Community welfare organization is *an integral aspect of social work.*

CASEWORK AND COMMUNITY ORGANIZATION

We may discern a broad parallelism between the usual steps of the casework process and the community organization process. In casework the successive steps would usually include: (1) defining the general nature of the problem presented, (2) psychosocial study, (3) diagnosis and formulation of treatment plans, (4) treatment, (5) evaluation.[3] In community organization the process is likely to include: (1) the recognition of the community organization problem, (2) analysis of the problem, which may involve factfinding, (3) planning what to do about the problem, (4) action to meet the problem, and (5) evaluation of the action and its results.

Each process begins with a problem. Each involves analysis of the problem, though the term "diagnosis" is more likely to be used in casework. Formal factfinding (psychosocial study) appears to be more an integral part of the casework process than of the community organization process *at this point*. That is, social study is ordinarily a step in the handling of any case, whereas formal factfinding is not

[2] Elmer J. Tropman, *Basic Values in Social Work,* talk before Social Workers Club of Buffalo, April 12, 1955. Mimeographed.
[3] Compare Florence Hollis, "Social Casework," SWYB, 1954, p. 475.

necessarily a step in the planning of every community organization project. Community organization problems are larger than individual case problems, and the major facts about a community situation may be generally known at the time a particular problem arises. However, formal factfinding is often undertaken as part of the action on a community organization problem; indeed, it may be the essence of a particular community organization project, such as a study or survey.

Both processes involve planning, action or treatment, and evaluation. Moreover, the process, in each instance, fans out into a variety of methods and procedures at the point of action.

In some other respects, casework and community organization differ. The focus of casework is work with individuals and families. The focus of community organization is meeting broad social welfare needs in communities or other territorial units. In meeting these needs it deals largely with agencies, programs, services, committees, groups, and intergroups.

In casework the relationships are primarily interpersonal, and the client-worker relationship is unique in its nature and quality. In community organization, all kinds of relationships are found — personal, group, and intergroup. The community organization worker has a helping relationship with his consumer group, but this relationship differs from that between the caseworker and the client.

The caseworker uses fewer methods, but he uses a number of them more intensively; the community organization worker uses many different methods, but in the main he makes less intensive use of any one method than the caseworker does. Even conference as a method of community organization has scarcely the commanding place in community organization that the interview has in casework.

Casework and community organization differ materially regarding records. In casework there is one basic, and practically universally used type of record — the case record. In spite of the differences of opinion about just what should go into the case record and how it should be kept, there is agreement among all respectable caseworking agencies that there must be a case record, and that the record should contain at least some identifying data, some analysis of the problem, and some narrative of the efforts of the agency to help the client work out his problem. In community organization there is no one type of record that holds a position comparable to the case record. Indeed, there is no one variety of record (other than administrative records such as minutes) that is universally used in community organization.

Casework, as a form of professional practice, is substantially in advance of community organization. Its methods and techniques are much better understood; its philosophy, in spite of differences in schools of thought, is more clearly formulated; its literature is more adequate; casework practice, supervision, and teaching are all generally in advance of comparable phases of community organization.

GROUP WORK AND COMMUNITY ORGANIZATION

The group and group process are the essence of group work; they are also among the most important aspects of community organization. The element of group leadership is important in both processes, although the community organization worker is likely to have a somewhat different relationship with the group than the group worker has because the groups with which the two are involved usually differ in composition, objectives, and procedures.

Organization is likely to be a part of both processes, although its manifestations may be comparatively simple in group work and often highly complex in community organization.

Both group work and community organization depend primarily upon voluntary cooperative actions; both are educative rather than manipulative. Both processes commonly involve cooperation of professional social workers and laymen and both have a relation to social action. Community organization includes social action for social welfare purposes; in group work, however, it is often a part of group interests and expression.

Community organization is more diverse than group work and probably has more diverse specialties. The group worker, like the caseworker, probably uses fewer methods and these more intensively, while the community organization worker uses more methods, less intensively.

Of course, group work and casework both deal directly with consumers, whereas community organization deals with agencies, the community, or the general public. In many ways community organization is more comparable to administration than either casework or group work. There is, however, an area where group work shades into community organization. This is particularly true where there are groups of residents who participate not only in certain recreational or informal educational activities but also in community program building or social action.

The development of group work records lies somewhere between casework and community organization records: group work records have developed further than community organization records but not as far as casework records.

ADMINISTRATION AND COMMUNITY ORGANIZATION

The term "administration" is used here in the sense of the supporting or facilitating activities which are necessary and incidental to the giving of direct service by a social agency. Administrative activities range from the determination of function and policies, and executive leadership to routine operations such as keeping records and accounts and carrying on maintenance services.[4]

Every social welfare agency exists for the purpose of giving some form of service to either consumers, all or part of the general public, or to other agencies. But every agency has a secondary function — administration, the facilitation of the actual giving of service.

Community organization and administration are separate processes, but they have much in common. In general, neither community organization nor administration deals directly with consumers. The two processes employ many of the same methods: conference, factfinding, analysis, evaluation, planning, organization, and education. Both involve a wide variety of activities and extensive use of a large number of different methods.

In some cases not only are common methods used, but the nature of the activities is such that these activities must be classified as both administration and community organization. For example:

> The board of an agency adopts a plan for an expanded service program involving the addition of a new department. This involves increasing the budget to be presented to the community chest. The board's action is certainly administration: its decision facilitates the agency's giving of direct service. But it also relates to a change in the agency's program, and therefore to the community's social welfare patterns and the general adjustment of social welfare needs and resources.

> Other illustrations of activities which appear to be at the same time administration and community organization include: (1) an executive's relationship with his board of directors; also the relationship of a public welfare executive to an advisory board; (2) the public relations and fund-raising activities of agencies; and (3) a

[4] See article on "Administration of Social Agencies," SWYB, 1957, and in other recent issues of the *Year Book*.

public assistance department's raising of standards by adopting higher personnel requirements.

However, community organization and administration have differences as well as similarities.

First, their objectives are different. Community organization is concerned with the adjustment of needs and resources in a geographical area or field of service; administration is concerned with facilitating the services of a particular agency.

Second, their territorial foci are different. Administration focuses primarily inward, upon the operation of a particular agency. To the extent that administration is concerned with extra-agency relationships, it deals incidentally with the relationships of *this* agency to other agencies. That is, administration as such is agency-centered. Community organization, on the contrary, is typically community-centered; its interest focuses primarily upon directing social resources effectively to meet the social welfare needs of the area. Community organization is concerned with the community as a whole and not with any single agency. Even where a community welfare council is interested in starting a new child guidance clinic, thus helping a specific community center to reorganize its program, the focus of interest is still the provision of more adequate social services for the community rather than the internal operation of one agency.

Third, the total content, or subject matter, of community organization and of administration differs materially. Community organization is typically concerned with a variety of agencies and types of services, with programs and community patterns, with coordination, broad interpretation, and enlistment of public support. Administration usually relates to one agency, giving one type of service, or to a limited number of specialized services. In facilitating the giving of these services, administration is concerned with job analysis, employment, and personnel records; with interdepartmental organization structure and methods of transmitting policies and instructions; with records, filing, bookkeeping, and telephone service; with the maintenance of good physical working conditions and the purchasing of current supplies.

Fourth, many of the methods used in the two processes are separate and distinct. For example, drafting a set of job specifications, collecting and passing on estimates for a new mimeographing machine, employing a staff worker, and keeping financial accounts are definitely identified with administration. On the other hand, giving consultation to a representative of another agency regarding the problems of that agency, planning and conducting a joint financial campaign, and drafting a brief in support of a bill in the legislature are methods of community organization.

COMMUNITY ORGANIZATION FUNCTIONS

We have seen that community organization is an integral part of social work, and we have compared it with other social work processes. Now we must examine in more detail the six distinctive functions of community organization or the channels through which the process operates.[5]

To secure and maintain an adequate factual basis for sound planning and action. This is the foundation for all community organization. Standards and practices, agency programs, coordination, education, and support should all rest upon a basis of ascertained fact. Facts are needed regarding the area in which the community organization agency is at work; the nature, volume, and cost of social welfare services, and the nature and extent of social needs.

We have suggested that research is one of the enabling processes of social work, but that factfinding is one of the functions of community organization. There is no necessary contradiction between these two positions. Factfinding, which is closely related to the problem of bringing about a better adjustment between needs and resources, is an aspect of community organization; more formalized and generalized factfinding which is not intimately related to "programming" or the development or operation of social welfare services is research rather than community organization.

PROGRAM DEVELOPMENT

To initiate, develop, modify, and terminate social welfare programs and services. Activities relating to social welfare programs are at the center of community organization. Here, community organization most directly affects the social welfare patterns of the community, state, or nation.

---

[5] Five of these six functions were first identified by W. Frank Persons, as "objectives of a welfare council," in his report of a plan for *The Welfare Council of New York City* (N.Y., The Coordination Committee, 1925). With some variations these objectives were used by the present writer in articles in the SWYB, 1933–1937, and in the Lane report, "The Field of Community Organization," NCSW, 1939.

The phrase "program development" should be broadly construed. It may include any or all of the following types of activity: (1) The organization or reorganization of an agency. (2) The modification of an existing program. Any change that substantially adds to, subtracts from, or modifies an agency's total service is program development. (3) The merger of two or more existing agencies, or similar cooperative organizational arrangements. (4) The termination of social welfare agencies or programs. (5) Opposition and resistance to proposed program developments, when these seem unsound. "Program development" may be preventive as well as promotional. (6) The planning and execution of synthesized programs in particular functional fields — child welfare, health, recreation, etc. (7) The planning of an adequate welfare program for a community or other area. This is one of the broadest undertakings to be found in community organization. The community welfare council and the statewide citizens' welfare association are examples of agencies concerned with such enterprises.

IMPROVING STANDARDS

To establish, maintain, and improve social welfare standards, and to increase the effectiveness, efficiency, and economy of operation of social welfare agencies. The two main aspects of this function are: first, the setting up of criteria for determining sound performance; and second, helping agencies and workers to measure up to these criteria in practice.

A standard is a yardstick or norm — a criterion for measuring adequacy or effectiveness.[6] Standards are an attempt to determine in advance what is to be considered an acceptable achievement in reference to a particular type of agency, service, or situation. They may relate to any type of consumer service, to community organization, or to administration. Standards may be quantitative, as in respect to adequacy of assistance budgets, or qualitative, as in an attempt to define the qualities needed by executives of agencies.

Standards may be written or unwritten. In general, they are more significant when they are written. Many standards referring to various aspects of social welfare are available in published form. Some are confined to broad statements of principles, like the famous report of the first White House Conference on Child Welfare, in 1909, or the

---

[6] Compare: Gertrude M. Hengerer, *Social Welfare Standards: A Compilation of Health, Welfare and Recreation Standards of National Voluntary Agencies.* (Los Angeles, Welfare Council of Metropolitan Los Angeles, 1950), p. 23.

"Basic Standards in Philanthropy" included in the annual *Giver's Guide* of the National Information Bureau. Some formulations are specific and detailed, like the standard budgets for public assistance agencies. Some standards may take the form of a checklist or schedule, perhaps with numerical rating scales. Some standards are embodied in membership requirements.

The first step is the initial setting up of the standards — the formulation of sound criteria. A second step is to maintain these standards so far as possible — assuming that they are sound — when they are attacked, perhaps by economic or political groups who find them a threat, or when the standards are brought under pressure by economic difficulties, war, or disaster. A third step is to recognize the necessity of periodical review of even the best standards, to revise them as may be required in the light of changing circumstances.

Even more difficult than the formulation of standards is the attempt to help agencies and workers measure up to these standards. This means helping an agency to increase its efficiency, effectiveness, or economy of operation. "Efficiency" is primarily a quantitative concept: it is the ratio between the investment of time, money, and energy and the resulting production. "Effectiveness" suggests primarily a qualitative judgment: an agency's effectiveness is increased if it does a better quality of casework or group work — if it accomplishes its aim more fully.

The term "economy" applies primarily to financial operations. Governmental and voluntary social welfare agencies are financed by funds from the public. Obviously these agencies ought to operate without spending more money than is necessary to perform their tasks effectively and efficiently. However, it is vital to recognize that a current reduction of expenditures for social services is not necessarily true economy in terms of long-range expenditures. A valid concept of economy in social welfare must be coupled with the concepts of effectiveness and efficiency.

Community organization agencies may use various methods to promote greater effectiveness, efficiency, and economy of operation in the agencies which they serve. In general, there may be either a group approach or an individual approach to the raising of standards. Illustrations of the group approach are: joint surveys; the publication, study, distribution, and joint discussion of standards; and the sharing of experience through conferences and council division meetings. The individual approach includes field service and technical advice, consultation, and assistance to a particular agency.

COORDINATION

To improve and facilitate inter-relationships, and to promote coordination between organizations, groups, and individuals concerned with social welfare programs and services. Coordination is so fundamental a part of social welfare organization that it has sometimes been thought to be the whole of it. One of the early council of social agencies executives said that his council was "nothing whatever except a plan for making team work easy and natural." [7]

Teamwork is basically a matter of spirit and attitudes rather than of machinery. "In cooperation, the most logical arrangements are less important than good will." [8] Real teamwork grows out of the will to work together, a spirit of unity and solidarity. It is a state of mind rather than a machine-made product.

The very organization of a federative agency such as a community welfare council or community chest is an expression of a desire for better teamwork and a step in the direction of achieving it. One of the most important aspects of the council is that it establishes a central point for social welfare services in the community — an organization representing all or most of the welfare agencies, and which is available, when needed, for sponsoring or administering a project of common interest such as the making of a survey, the publication of a social service directory, or the calling of a public meeting to discuss a relief crisis.

The method of conference, while used in connection with all the objectives of community organization, is particularly applicable to obtaining better teamwork because group discussion is by its nature an integrative process.

Community welfare councils may conduct certain common services for their member-organizations or the general public. Social service exchanges, community information and referral services, volunteer bureaus, and research bureaus are among the more common types of such joint services.

North, in his description of the desirable attributes of a community welfare program, suggests that some of the factors underlying coordination may be: specialization in function, reciprocal use of each other's services, specialization in types of cases, division of territory,

[7] Fred C. Croxton of the Columbus, Ohio, Council, quoted by Edward T. Devine in "Central Councils of Social Agencies," *The Survey,* Vol. 47, January 21, 1922, p. 624.
[8] Quoted on the title page of Persons, *The Welfare Council of New York City.*

common use of equipment, pooling of information, and joining of forces to accomplish a common task.[9]

EDUCATION

To develop better public understanding of social welfare needs, resources, objectives, services, methods, and standards. Adequate interpretation of social welfare programs and services is fundamental to their support and therefore to their existence. This is true whether the agencies in question are governmental or voluntary.

Any profession needs to interpret itself to the public if it wishes public understanding of its aims, services, and professional status. This is particularly important for social work — a newcomer among the professions — which depends upon the general public's support for services rendered largely to groups unable to pay for these services. Widespread understanding of social work is necessary if social services are to be effectively used by those who need them. There is at present a vast amount of ignorance and misunderstanding of social work.

Education is perhaps the most pervasive and widely practiced function of community organization agencies. The function of education is one that every social worker needs to know something about; most community organization workers need some technical skill in this area, and some must qualify as experts in interpretation and public relations.

As in the case of factfinding, a specialized set of methods is used for interpretation.

SUPPORT AND PARTICIPATION

To develop adequate public support of, and public participation in, social welfare activities. Governmental agencies are of course financed primarily from tax funds. Public welfare appropriations have in recent years been among the largest expenditures of government; and the obtaining of adequate appropriations for these purposes may be much more than a matter of administrative routine, and may even involve widespread and highly organized activities on the part of voluntary agencies.

Voluntary agencies obtain financial support chiefly from voluntary contributions, through a community chest or otherwise; other sources

[9] Cecil Clare North, *The Community and Social Welfare* (New York, McGraw-Hill, 1931), pp. 21–23.

of income may include membership fees, earnings (fees for service, etc.), income from endowments, payments from tax funds (for board of children in foster homes, for example), grants from foundations, and so on. Raising money through voluntary contributions is generally accepted as the basic test and index of community support for chests and voluntary agencies.

Along with the securing of funds goes the enlistment of volunteer participation in social welfare. This includes not only those who contribute hours of volunteer service, supplementing the services of the paid staff, but also the services of those who serve on boards and committees of both governmental and voluntary agencies.

INTER-RELATIONSHIPS OF FUNCTIONS

If these six functions are the channels through which the community organization process expresses itself, *every community organization activity relates to one or more of these functions.* They afford also a means of analyzing the objectives and relative emphases of programs and projects of community organization agencies.

These six functions of community organization are closely interrelated. A single activity may involve several objectives. A survey of the welfare agencies within a community is concerned, first of all, with factfinding; but beyond this purpose may be the goals of raising the standards and practices of agencies, improving coordination, affecting agency programs, educating the public regarding problems and services, and enlisting public support for a sounder and more adequate social welfare program.

All these six functions contribute, whether individually or in combination, to the general aim of attaining a better balance between social welfare needs and social welfare resources.

QUESTIONS AND PROBLEMS

1. Analyze the report of a community welfare council, or a statewide or national community organization agency, or the recommendations of a community welfare survey or study. Classify the projects or activities (or recommendations) according to the six functions of community organization outlined in this chapter. Do you find any activities that do not fit into any of these categories? Are there any indications that the statement of functions should be modified?

2. Try to make a comparative analysis of community organization and either casework or group work, as social work processes. Consider such

matters as: essential nature of the process, purpose, philosophy, settings, major methods, skills required by the practitioner, participation of laymen in the process, types of records, training for use of this process, major current problems.

3. What social welfare agencies that have a definite function of coordination exist in your community? Through what methods do they seek to promote coordination?

4. Analyze a set of published standards relating to some area of social welfare. Consider such points as: title; by whom issued; for what audience; year of issue; scope; form of presentation (general or specific statements, checklist, rating scale, etc.); purpose of the standards; how and by whom formulated; provisions for enforcement, if any (how and by whom); any evidence as to use or application of these standards, or results of their use; any indication of procedure for revising these standards.

5. Give examples of activities of a consumer-service agency which you would classify as: (a) direct service, (b) administration, (c) community organization.

SUGGESTIONS FOR READING

In addition to the references below, see Suggestions for Reading for chapter 3.

In the Basic References, see especially Green, *Social Work Practice in Community Organization,* ch. VI, and Murphy, *Community Organization Practice,* Pt. II.

References regarding factfinding, program development, education, and financing, are suggested at the end of chapters 20 and 21, respectively.

COMMUNITY ORGANIZATION AND SOCIAL WORK

Hollis, Ernest V. and Taylor, Alice L., *Social Work Education in the United States.* (See bibliography ch. 1.) Competencies expected of all social workers are discussed on pp. 220–225.

Johnson, Arlien, "Community Organization in Social Work" SWYB, 1945, pp. 92–98. An unusually stimulating article on community organization, the meaning of methods and skills, etc.

Murray, Clyde E.; Bowens, Marx G.; and Hogrefe, Russell, *Group Work in Community Life* (New York, Association Press, 1954, 245 pp.). These records illustrate the borderline between group work and community organization.

COORDINATION

Gunn, Selskar M. and Platt, Philip S., *Voluntary Health Agencies: An Interpretive Study* (New York, Ronald Press, 1945, 364 pp.).

Johns, Ray, *The Cooperative Process Among National Social Agencies* (New York, Association Press, 1946, 290 pp.).

U. S. Federal Security Agency, *Teamwork in Community Services, 1941–1946: A Demonstration in Federal, State, and Local Cooperation* (Report of the Office of Community War Services, Federal Security Agency. Washington, 1946, 80 pp.).

STANDARDS

Dimock, Marshall Edward, *The Executive in Action* (New York, Harper, 1945, 276 pp.), ch. XII, "The Measurement of Performance."

Hengerer, Gertrude M., *Social Welfare Standards: A Compilation of Health, Welfare, and Recreation Standards of National Voluntary Agencies* (Los Angeles, Welfare Council of Metropolitan Los Angeles, 1950, processed, 112 pp.). An invaluable pioneer study; lays a foundation for further research.

Johns, Ray, *Executive Responsibility* (New York, Association Press, 1954, 258 pp.), chs. 9 and 17.

Norton, William J., *The Cooperative Movement in Social Work* (New York, Macmillan, 1927, 373 pp.), ch. XIV, "Improving Standards of Social Work."

6.

SOCIAL ACTION

WHAT IS SOCIAL ACTION and what is its relationship to social work and to community organization? Some discussion of this question is essential to an understanding of community organization. The term social action is used in a specialized sense in relation to social welfare and the advancement of social causes.

In this sense, it may be defined as *efforts to bring about change or prevent change in current social practices or situations, through education, propaganda, persuasion or pressure, in behalf of objectives believed by the social actionists to be socially desirable.* Ordinarily, social action involves organized efforts to influence public opinion or official policy or executive action through enlistment of the support of groups or individuals.

This definition involves the following corollaries and implications.

1. Social action is always concerned with a proposal for change in current social practices and the advocacy of or resistance to such a proposal. A campaign might be waged to establish a national system of health insurance, to extend an existing civil service merit system, or to abolish the poll tax in a state. But there may also be "defensive" social action, carried on to preserve something that already exists. Freedom of the press may be defended against the threats involved in a censorship bill; an existing and effective civil service system may be defended against crippling amendments; confidentiality of public assistance records may be defended against proposals for making public the names of relief recipients.

2. Social action involves a goal accepted as desirable by the

social actionists. The social actionist has a defined objective; he knows what he wants. He is not trying to promote open-minded exploration or objective deliberation of a question. He already has what he believes is a sound answer, and his intent is to see that this answer is adopted and translated into action.

Back of the social action may be any amount of research, exploration, and discussion; but "social action" itself begins at the point where there is a definite promotional goal and where the social actionists set out to achieve that goal.[1]

3. Social action always involves an attempt to bring about action by some person or persons other than the social actionists.

These persons who are the "subjects" of the social action (that is, those toward whom the social action is directed) may be voters; legislators; public officials such as a mayor, superintendent of schools, or social welfare commissioner; or other groups or persons having power to take desired action.

In every case, social action involves an attempt to convert, to persuade, or to "pressure" some person or group to accept a particular point of view or follow a particular course of action. The "subject" of the social action is always a person or group that has (or is believed by the social actionists to have) the necessary power to accomplish what the social actionists desire.

It has been suggested that the organization of a labor union or consumers' cooperative is social action. This seems a mistake. The organization of a membership group is simply voluntary organization, whether the association is a religious group, a political party, a cooperative, a labor union, or a garden club. Any of these groups may engage in social action after it is organized, but its initial organization does not in itself ordinarily involve social action.

Neither is the attempt to enlist membership, adherence to a pledge, or financial support from the general public social action. The evangelistic revival, the attempt to gain signatures to a safe driving pledge, the community chest campaign, are all promotional efforts outside the area of social action.

4. Social action may embrace such methods as education, propa-

---

[1] For a different point of view, see John G. Hill, "Social Action," SWYB, 1951, pp. 456–458. Mr. Hill lists five "elements . . . in the various methods employed in social action:" (1) Research. (2) Planning a solution. (3) Enlisting public support. (4) Presentation of the proposal to those with authority to implement it. (5) Enforcement. All these are certainly part of the total community organization process which may be used, but it seems logical to restrict the term social action to the third and fourth, and in some cases, the fifth, of these items.

ganda, persuasion, or pressure, but it obviously does not include physical coercion or compulsion.

Social action involves commitment to a cause. It is by nature propagandistic, and frequently militant in spirit, and may involve various forms of psychological or social pressure.

The reason for eliminating physical coercion as an element of social action is that "social action" becomes an essentially meaningless phrase if it is stretched to include everything from legislative promotion to police raids, street fighting between strikers and strike breakers, mob violence, civil insurrection, and foreign war. All these activities lie in the realm of direct physical action. In every case the effort is to *force* the opponent to take some action (such as forcing a sheriff to hand a prisoner over to a mob) or to force him to accept or submit to some actions directed against him. It is intended that he shall have no choice; the will of the actors is forcibly imposed upon him.

In social action, on the contrary, the subject of the action is usually not thought of as an opponent; he may be in a neutral public position or he may even be a trusted leader, urged by his followers to take a particular course of action in a specific instance. Furthermore, social action does not prevent the subject from making his own decision. Paradoxically, social action leaves the final decision to the subject, but it tries by various means other than physical coercion to make all except one course of action so uncomfortable or undesirable as to induce him to decide in accordance with the wishes of the social actionists!

5. The objectives and methods of social action may be legal or illegal. If we define social action in terms of the phenomena involved, we cannot take the varying test of "legality" as an element in the definition.

A particular action may be legal in one country and illegal in another, or legal in one state or city of the United States and illegal in another; or legal at one time and illegal at another, in the same country or state. A public meeting on "The Rights of Freemen" would probably be legal in a democratic nation but illegal in a totalitarian state. Is the meeting, then, "social action" in the democracy but not in the totalitarian state? Advocacy of disarmament will probably be legal in a democracy in peacetime but illegal in the same country if it is at war. Yet the action is the same in both cases.

If "social action" is to have any real meaning, it must be defined *in terms of the essential nature of the phenomena*. If this is true, then social action may be either legal or illegal.

This is not an argument in defense of social action activities which are in violation of law. Whether violation of law in behalf of one's convictions is ever justifiable is an entirely different question, totally irrelevant to this issue. One may accept the conclusion that social action may be legal or illegal. One may or may not add to this conclusion the belief that, "All violation of law is unjustifiable. Some social action is violation of law, therefore such social action is unjustifiable."

This question of legality is not likely to have much application to social action in behalf of social welfare objectives. Much social action in respect to social welfare is concerned with changing existing legislation, but the procedure of promoting legislation to change existing statutes is, of course, perfectly legal; and the question of the legality of objectives or methods does not commonly arise in respect to social action for social welfare.

6. The only test of the social desirability of the objective that can be applied is that the social actionists regard it as socially desirable.[2]

Any attempt to limit social action to action in behalf of "socially desirable ends" immediately runs into difficulty. Who is to decide what is "socially desirable"? Are there any absolute or objective standards that would authoritatively decide, for example, such questions as the following:

Shall a system of universal military training or peacetime conscription be adopted?

Shall clinics operated with tax funds furnish contraceptive information to married persons, on request?

Or even:

Shall the state have one over-all department of social welfare or separate departments of welfare, mental health, and corrections?

Shall the director of the state welfare department be appointed by the Governor or by the State Welfare Commission?

Shall the administration of general assistance be highly centralized, under the control of the state, or largely decentralized, with local control and little state supervision?

In each of these cases, and in thousands of other controversial situations, there is no "one right answer" which will commend itself to all intelligent people. Judgment as to "social desirability" involves

[2] John A. Fitch in his paper on "The Nature of Social Action," NCSW, 1940, p. 488, presents a different point of view; he would restrict social action to furthering "objectives that are both legal and socially desirable."

judgment as to values; it is a subjective, individual judgment, and therefore not a sound criterion for determining what is or is not "social action." The only practicable test is whether the social actionists themselves regard their objectives as socially desirable. The Fascist, the Communist, and the advocate of a capitalist democracy are all social actionists, if each believes that his objectives are socially desirable.

7. Social action is to be identified with certain methods and procedures rather than certain social values. Social action in itself is neither good nor bad. It may be used for good, bad, or indifferent purposes.

8. Specific methods of social action may be socially desirable or socially undesirable, expedient or inexpedient, in various types of situations.

Public speaking and discussion, newspaper publicity, use of radio and television are methods of social action taken for granted in this country. The bribery of a legislator or public official, on the other hand, is not only socially unacceptable and unethical, but it is also criminal.

Threats of political reprisals and certain types of over-aggressive high-pressure methods are usually inexpedient, as they are liable to awaken psychological resistance and stir up hostility for the future as well as in the present.

9. Social action may or may not be within or closely related to the area of social welfare, depending upon the objectives and the subject matter in any specific instance.

An attempt to secure the enactment of a new adoption law or of a bill to reorganize the state corrections system is obviously within the area of social welfare. Bills to establish a state civil service system, to eliminate racial discrimination in employment, or to set up a public works program to relieve unemployment are at least closely related to social welfare, and social welfare organizations might be interested in any or all of them.

On the other hand, the question of the rorganization of the Federal or a state judiciary, whether or not a state shall impose an income tax, or whether a treaty with a foreign power shall be approved—all these matters transcend the limits of the field of social welfare in the technical sense.

Social action for purposes of promoting social welfare should certainly be broadly rather than narrowly construed, and it should be understood to include the promotion of preventive legislative and similar measures as well as modifications of existing patterns.

IS SOCIAL ACTION COMMUNITY ORGANIZATION?

Insofar as social action is a part of social work, it is an aspect — and an important one — of the process of community organization.

The reasons for this conclusion are these: (1) If community organization is the effort to bring about adjustment between social welfare needs and resources, part of the job is done through voluntary group or intergroup activities — developing agency programs, organizing federative bodies, etc. — and part by seeking authoritative sanctions, such as legislation, regulations, and official administrative decisions. Any line between these two parts of the job is artificial rather than logical. (2) Social action, as an aspect of social work, appears to be always concerned with some aspect of the adjustment of social welfare needs and resources. Social action, like community organization in general, is concerned with elimination and prevention as well as treatment of difficulties in community and social life. Social action, through legislation, is frequently concerned with two of the specific functions of community organization — the development of social welfare programs and the improvement of standards. (3) Community organization and social action draw on common methods, particularly in the area of interpretation, organization and promotion.[3]

SOCIAL WELFARE AGENCIES AND SOCIAL ACTION

Kenneth L. M. Pray has stated three principles as applying to the participation of social welfare agencies in social action: (1) The agency should act only in areas appropriate to its function. (2) It should act only within the limits of the actual agreement of its lay

[3] The writers on social action in the SWYB have usually regarded it as a separate process. See SWYB: John A. Fitch, 1941, pp. 507–508; Sydney Maslen, 1949, p. 473; John G. Hill, 1951, pp. 455–456; Sanford Solender, 1957, pp. 517–518. The main arguments in favor of this position appear to be: (1) that social action has "a connotation quite distinct from that generally attributed to community organization"; (2) that its significance is such that it cannot properly be regarded as a subdivision or special aspect of community organization; and (3) that community organization is limited to voluntary action and does not extend to the invocation of authority by the community or state, through legislation or otherwise.

In any case, the question is not crucial. Regardless of any academic classifications, the phenomena and problems of social action and community organization are and will remain inescapably intertwined. The community organization worker will have to continue to engage in social action, and if it is a separate process he will have to develop skill in two processes of social work instead of one.

and professional elements. (3) It should not engage in partisan politics.[4] These principles seem eminently sound.

A voluntary child-placing agency might well take a position on any legislation relating to the welfare of children. It is doubtful that it should engage in social action regarding state supervision of homes for the aged or a constitutional amendment providing for the election of the Governor for a four-year instead of a two-year term.

In the case of a proposed child labor law where most of the board members of the children's agency are opposed to the bill and a substantial majority of the staff are in favor of it, it would certainly be unwise for the board to adopt a resolution putting "the children's aid society" on record against the bill. Under present practices, the board usually represents primarily the contributors to the agency. But the agency includes a professional staff. The board members are under no obligation to accept the conclusions of the staff members about the child labor bill; but it is doubtful that they have any moral right to ignore the conclusions of the staff and to adopt a resolution against this bill in the name of *the agency*.

The question may be raised as to *how much unity* the agency should have before it engages in social action. If a bare majority of board and staff approved the child labor bill and the issue were a violently controversial one, the board would probably be ill-advised to endorse the bill. Usually action on a particular issue of this sort is not justified if it means a serious risk of splitting the agency or leaving a substantial minority feeling that they have been overridden and perhaps misrepresented to the public. One could not insist upon unanimity as a preliminary to social action, but it would seem reasonable that there should be a clear and substantial majority — perhaps as much as two-thirds.

Partisan politics raises another sort of question. In a particular political campaign, a Governor with a fine record of social accomplishment may be running for reelection. Although a large majority of both the board and staff of an agency favor this candidate, the organization still has no moral right as a social welfare agency to endorse this candidate. As Mr. Pray has suggested, there are always a variety of issues involved in a partisan contest, and it is difficult to decide the relative importance of particular social issues in the over-all decision as to which party should assume the reins of government.

[4] Kenneth L. M. Pray, "Social Workers and Partisan Politics," *Compass*, Vol. XXVI, June 1945, pp. 3–6; and "Social Work and Social Action," NCSW, 1945, pp. 348–359.

In addition, it is reasonably certain that the agency derives its support from adherents of both major political parties; and certainly they have not contributed to the agency with the idea that it shall become a mouthpiece for one party and against another, even in a single election.

However, this principle would seem to apply rather strictly to partisan politics but not to non-partisan social welfare issues.

The Michigan Legislature passed what many social workers regarded as a superior social welfare reorganization act in 1937. The act came before the voters on a referendum in 1938. Here the issue was non-partisan (the Act had been sponsored by both Republicans and Democrats) and there was no reason, as far as partisan politics was concerned, why a voluntary social agency should not support or oppose the act, in this election, on its merits.

Another qualification should be added here in respect to governmental welfare agencies. *It is not a proper function of a governmental administrative agency to campaign to influence the thinking or voting of voters or legislators on political or governmental issues.*

This does not mean that a public welfare agency may not vigorously defend or press its budget, through all proper official channels. It may also quite properly interpret its program, standards, objectives, and the needs in its field to the Governor, budget director, legislators, and to the public. However, it should not get into legislative campaigning. Even in a case like that of the Michigan welfare referendum, where the issue was non-partisan, where vital social welfare issues were involved and much was at stake, it would appear inappropriate for a governmental administrative agency to become involved in a campaign to influence the action of the voters.

A community welfare council is comparable to an individual agency, as far as these principles are concerned. The council's function — the bringing about of a better adjustment between welfare needs and resources — is broader than that of any one consumer-service agency. The council may find it more difficult than the individual agency to gain agreement on matters of social action, since the council is, to a large extent at least, a federation of agencies.[5] The council should, of course, avoid participation in partisan politics. Even in a case where a council decides not to take an official position on a controversial issue, it may with complete propriety do everything pos-

[5] See, however, Violet M. Sieder's thoughtful article, "The Community Welfare Council and Social Action," NCSW, *Social Work in the Current Scene*, 1950, pp. 22–41.

sible to help its constituency to understand the issues involved and the arguments advanced, pro and con, on the question.

SOCIAL WORKERS AND SOCIAL ACTION

It may be taken for granted that *every social worker should be concerned with social action.*

If social work as a profession is concerned about a wholesome, rich, and abundant life for everyone, then it is logical for social workers to try to probe beyond end-results, to uncover causes; to seek for prevention rather than merely care or treatment; to refuse to continue, as Grace Coyle has said, merely "to pick up the pieces without even attempting to stop the breakage."

At least four types of channels are open to the social worker in respect to social action. He may act as an employee of a social welfare agency, as a member of the profession of social work, as a worker, or as a citizen.

If a social agency engages in social action, the social worker, as a member of the staff may have a part in these social action activities.

As a member of the profession of social work, the social worker may express himself through the professional association and certain other channels. The professional association is concerned with professional standards and relationships, as well as with broad social welfare programs. It may elect to participate in social action within its "area of competence" and of interest as a professional organization. The principles suggested by Mr. Pray apply to the professional association as well as to the social agency. The association should limit itself to social action appropriate to its function; there ought to be a substantial majority if the group is to take official action; and it would be completely inappropriate, even if practicable from the standpoint of agreement, for it to engage in partisan politics. Social workers are freer in their participation in social action, collectively, as members of professional associations, than as employees of individual agencies. In practice, however, professional associations may tend to be fairly cautious and conservative in social action, especially since much of their leadership usually comes largely from older members of the profession and those with more of a stake in the status quo.

The social worker may participate also, primarily in his capacity as a professional person, in a state conference on social welfare, of the "action" type, or a "social workers club." Both of these organizations are usually composed of laymen as well as social workers. Their functions may be stated quite broadly, so the matter of action may rest chiefly on the question of internal agreement and on the need for avoiding partisan political commitments.

The social worker may join with other employees, both professional and non-professional, and may become a member of a labor union. The union is concerned primarily with the economic interests of its members and other workers. However, a particular local or national union may have a concern for certain broad social welfare objectives and standards of effectiveness, adequacy, etc. The union is not a professional organization, but the two may find themselves working hand in hand on certain issues. The union is likely to be more militant than the professional association: it will have fewer inhibitions as to function, its membership and leadership are likely to be more representative of younger persons, and its traditional role takes struggle and conflict much more for granted.

There would seem to be no reason why the union, like any other interest group of citizens, should not engage in social action in any area where it can command sufficient internal agreement. The union might, on occasion, even ally itself with a political party, if it were convinced that its aims could best be achieved through the success of that party.

The social worker who has a deep concern about social action, particularly in respect to basic social and economic issues, will probably have to find a good deal of his self-expression through "citizens organizations" of various sorts outside the field of social welfare. Among the channels which are open to him as a citizen are organizations to promote or oppose specific social, economic, and political changes; social, civic, patriotic, religious and other organizations, parts of whose programs are concerned with social action; and political parties and organizations.

FREEDOM AND SOCIAL ACTION

How free is the social worker to engage in social action? Among the factors which may tend to limit the social worker's complete freedom in respect to social action are the following: (1) civil service limitations; (2) the worker's relationships to his agency; (3) community pressures; and (4) the individual's conception of what is appropriate for him as a professional social worker.

If the worker is employed in a governmental agency which operates under civil service, he will be able to vote as he pleases and discuss his political opinions in private, but he will not be able to take a position of public leadership in politics. This is a necessary price to be paid for having a technical career service in government which will operate continuously and competently under any political party that comes into power. If an individual social worker finds that active participation in politics is necessary and important to him, he had better find a job outside the civil service.

In the area of worker-agency relationships, it seems possible to state several principles of action.

First, *the social worker, while on the job, is the representative of the agency. He is therefore not free to engage in social action, on the job, except as the representative of the agency.*

Second, as Mr. Pray has pointed out, *the worker-client relationship must not be used to promote social action.* The worker-client relationship is a helping or service relationship; to exploit it for purposes of social action is a betrayal of the social worker's professional role.

In a group work agency this means that the worker should carefully avoid any manipulation of the group or exploitation of the worker-group relationship to advance social action causes in which the worker is interested. At the same time, he may perform a real service for the group by helping the members to gain information, to weigh arguments pro and con, and to learn to think for themselves about current issues.

In the third place, *the worker should avoid doing anything that will seem to commit his agency to a position to which it is not in fact committed.*

Allied to this is a fourth principle: *that the worker should avoid utilizing agency facilities or prestige to further social action in which he is personally interested, but with which the agency as such is not involved.*

Agency letterheads are for the transaction of agency business; the agency office, with its equipment and supplies, is designed for agency purposes. The worker has no right to use his official position on campaign literature, in newspaper publicity, or otherwise, for the purpose of forwarding causes to which the agency as an agency is not committed.

All this may seem mainly negative and limiting. But there is another side to the picture. *The social worker should be free, off the job, to engage in such social action as may seem to him appropriate.*

In practice, this personal freedom of the social worker is likely to differ substantially at different times and places. Both community and agency pressures may be applied. A small community, where "everybody knows everybody else" and where political and economic orthodoxy is the rule, may attempt to control or censor the social worker's activities. In the larger city, he may be more anonymous, and differences of opinion may be more taken for granted. A conservative agency board may be shocked at some manifestation of social action on the part of a worker, whereas a more liberal board may regard the same action as a matter of personal decision for the worker. Moreover, there is a tendency toward the abridgement of personal freedom and civil liberties in time of war or popular hysteria.

There is also the practical difficulty of deciding, especially in the case of an executive, when the social worker is "off the job." Can the executive of the family service society act with complete freedom, on any matter of social action, as long as it is after the closing of the office at five o'clock? Or will he always be so much a symbol of the family service society that any social action in which he becomes involved will inevitably, in the public mind, be connected with the society? A workable answer will probably lie somewhere in between the two extremes; the line will be drawn slowly and with difficulty; it will, for a long time, vary irregularly from community to community, and from one phase to another of the public mind and temper.

Certainly, *if social workers are to enjoy a large measure of personal freedom, they will have to pay the price for it;* and part of that price will be some risking of security or even the loss of jobs; some experiencing of social disapproval, isolation, and ostracism. If social workers want a large measure of personal freedom, they, like others, will have to win it and hold it.

The question of the social worker's contribution *as a professional person* raises other considerations than are involved in his actions as a citizen only. *The social worker may properly be an adherent of any cause on the basis of his convictions; but his acceptance of a role of leadership or public advocacy, on matters involving essentially technical issues, should normally be within his area of professional or avocational competence.*

Porter R. Lee has stressed the importance of professional competence as a qualification for leadership or advocacy.[6] However, there are a good many questions of public policy which do not involve *primarily* abstruse technical issues. For example: Shall we have the long or short ballot? Shall public personnel operate under a civil serv-

[6] Lee, *Social Work as Cause and Function*, pp. 260–261.

ice merit system? Shall we have a state fair employment practice act? Granted that there are technical aspects to all these subjects; still, the main issues seem clearly enough drawn so that the social worker, if he is competent to give leadership, may claim the same right to give it that is exercised without question by the business man, the clubwoman, or the politician. To be sure, the social worker will give leadership here as a citizen rather than as a professional person; but he must not be eliminated from leadership merely *because* he is a professional person.

There is also such a thing as "avocational competence." A social worker may have been a member of consumers' cooperatives and credit unions for ten or fifteen years; he may have read the literature of the subject, worked on committees and boards; served for three years as president of his local cooperative; worked on the board of the credit union; he may have read, thought, and talked cooperation for a decade or two. Such a person has never had any formal training in this area and would not consider his knowledge in this field as part of his professional equipment as a social worker; but he has probably attained a degree of practical "avocational competence" which qualifies him highly for leadership in the cooperative movement.

In this whole area of social action we must recognize the importance of the *acceptance of difference,* between laymen and social workers and among social workers themselves. *Personal freedom, group freedom, and a large degree of mutual acceptance and tolerance are basic to effective democracy.* The integration attained in the working of the democratic process is not a regimented uniformity but a unity born of diversity.

QUESTIONS AND PROBLEMS

1. *Definitions of Social Action.* Try to formulate your own conclusion as to what social action is. Read at least two of the definitions in Appendix B. Analyze them and compare them with the one suggested in the chapter. If none of these definitions seems satisfactory, try to formulate your own.

2. Which of the following would you classify as social action? Why? (a) Efforts to promote passage of a bill to publish names of recipients of public assistance; (b) a community recreation survey; (c) the establishment of a family service society in a community; (d) propaganda activities carried on by a political party; (e) the annual tuberculosis Christmas seal campaign; (f) protests to the school board against segregation or desegregation in the public schools; (g) a mob breaks up a meeting on civil

rights; (h) a group of consumers organize a consumers cooperative; (i) a group of public assistance clients "demonstrate" before the public assistance office, carrying signs expressing their grievances; (j) strikers engage in picketing; (k) a non-violent boycott of a bus system is carried on by a minority racial group as a protest against discriminatory practices.

3. In a hard-fought presidential campaign, the executive of a youth service agency is asked to become a member of a campaign committee for one party. Should he accept? Under any conditions? Under certain conditions? If so, what conditions?

4. A community chest executive says, in a talk to a professional group, that he believes it is his duty not to ally himself with any "partisan or divisive group" or any "controversial cause," where his affiliation might be a detriment to the chest's appeal to the community. What do you think?

5. What do you think of the principle suggested in the chapter regarding support and leadership in social action causes?

6. A social work executive is asked to write his representative, on his agency letterhead, endorsing (a) a housing bill, (b) a fair employment practice bill. What should he do?

SUGGESTIONS FOR READING

Articles on social action and its relation to social work appear in all issues of the *Social Work Year Book* since 1939, except 1954.

Case materials will be found in King, *Organizing for Community Action* (see Basic References), as well as in the items by Lane and Earl below.

References on methods of social action are appended to ch. 21.

Burns, Eveline M., "Social Action and the Professional Worker," *Compass*, Vol. XXVIII, May 1947, pp. 37–40. See also discussion of this article in *Compass*, January 1948, pp. 29–31.

Coyle, Grace L., *Group Experience and Democratic Values* (New York, Woman's Press, 1947, 185 pp.) Part III, "Social Work and Social Action."

Deutsch, Albert, "There Were Giants," *Channels*, Vol. XIX, Oct.–Nov. 1941, pp. 1–4, 18. The social action tradition in social work. See also "Town Meeting on Giants," *Channels*, Vol. XIX, Dec. 1941, pp. 23–26, 36.

Earl, Lawrence, *The Battle of Baltinglass* (New York, Knopf, 1953, 241 pp.). An historical narrative of social action that arose from an incident in an Irish village.

Fitch, John A., "The Nature of Social Action" (NCSW, 1940, pp. 485–497). A valuable and historically important paper. The author did much to make social workers social-action conscious.

Hathway, Marion, "Social Action and Professional Education" (NCSW, 1944, pp. 363–373).

Kasius, Cora (ed.), *New Directions in Social Work* (see bibliography, ch. 1). Harry L. Lurie, "The Responsibilities of a Socially Oriented Profession," pp. 31–53. Donald S. Howard, "Social Work and Social Reform," pp. 159–175.

Lane, Robert P., "An Agency Initiates Social Action" (NCSW, 1946, pp. 172–177). Social action by a community welfare council.

Lee, Porter R., *Social Work as Cause and Function, and Other Papers* (see bibliography, ch. 1). "The Social Worker and Social Action," pp. 257–270.

Lurie, Harry L., "Social Action: A Motive Force in Democracy" (NCSW, 1941, pp. 631–641).

Pray, Kenneth L. M., "Social Work and Social Action" (NCSW, 1945, pp. 348–359). Included also in Pray, *Social Work in a Revolutionary Age and Other Papers.* (See bibliography, ch. 1.)

—— "Social Workers and Partisan Politics," *Compass,* Vol. XXVI, June 1945, pp. 3–6.

Sieder, Violet M., "The Community Welfare Council and Social Action" (NCSW, *Social Work in the Current Scene,* 1950, pp. 22–41).

Youngdahl, Benjamin, "Social Workers: Stand Up and Be Counted," *Compass,* Vol. XXVIII, March 1947, pp. 21–24.

II.

Agencies

and

Programs

———————————————————————

7.

HISTORICAL DEVELOPMENT

———

THOUGH THE TERM "COMMUNITY ORGANIZATION" was not common before about 1912–1916, the *fact* of community organization, in the sense of the development of social welfare services and programs to meet needs, must go back as far or almost as far as organized social service efforts.

A fascinating glimpse of an early chapter in community organization is given by Jane Addams:

> "The Society for Superseding the Work of Climbing Boys" [chimney sweeps] was founded in 1803 by some kind hearted people whose names have not been preserved. They first offered a prize of two hundred pounds for the best sweeping machine which should obviate the necessity for boys. Secondly, they promoted a bill to protect the boys, but although it passed the House of Commons, it was rejected by the Lords, possibly not because the Lords were more hard hearted, but because the chimneys in the old mansions and manor houses were hopelessly crooked and could not be swept by machinery. Thirdly, they appointed their own private inspectors to watch the conduct of the master sweepers, and maintained these inspectors for seventy years. They also purchased sweeping machines and rented them to small masters for one shilling, six-pence a week. They continually badgered the insurance companies to demand the use of these machines; finally in 1875 they succeeded in passing a law of regulation and safeguard for their grimy little proteges.

We have here an epitome of the most advanced philanthropy, stimulation of inventions which shall relieve the poor from degrading drudgery, cooperation with commercial enterprises, and finally protective legislation. But these obscure people whose hearts were wrung over the conditions of chimney sweeps did even better than that. They were pioneers in the establishment of the modern principle of inspection, which when taken over by the government as an extension of the function of the state, is ably defended by the economist, but which was after all inaugurated by the Philanthropist. May we not credit to their initiative this most valuable instrument of the modern state? [1]

There is a fascinating and almost untouched field for research in the use of community organization for social welfare prior to the beginnings of modern social work. However, for our present purpose, it will suffice if we begin with the charity organization movement in the United States, which marked the first substantial recognition of some of the most important aspects of what we have since come to call community organization.

As a supplement to this chapter, there is included in Appendix A a chart of some Major Chronological Developments in Community Welfare Organization in the United States, 1870–1957.

There have been three major periods in the development of community welfare organization in the United States since 1870. The first may be called the *charity organization period,* because community organization was most clearly and broadly expressed through the charity organization societies during these years. This period extended from about 1870 — a few years before the establishment of the first American charity organization society (COS) — to 1917, when the war chests associated with World War I were being organized extensively in American communities.

The second period may be designated by its most striking characteristic — *the rise of federation,* through chests and councils. It lasted from the rise of the war chests, in 1917, to about 1935, when the Social Security Act set the stage for the development of the public welfare programs of today.

The third period, from 1935 to the present time, is harder to designate because we are still in the midst of it. It may be tentatively characterized as a period of *expansion and professional development,* since it has been marked by a recognition of the broader implications of community organization and by an increased concern with the

[1] Jane Addams, "President's Address: Charity and Social Justice," NCSW, 1910, pp. 3–4.

analysis of the process and the development of professional skill in its use.

THE CHARITY ORGANIZATION PERIOD

THE CHARITY ORGANIZATION PERIOD was an era of beginnings in social welfare. The first striking developments were in the area of state organization. The first state board of charities had been established in Massachusetts in 1863, and by 1870, similar authorities had been created in six other states. In 1872, came the establishment of the State Charities Aid Association (SCAA) of New York, the first of the statewide citizens welfare associations.

One of the landmarks in the history of social welfare in America was the organization of the National Conference of Charities and Correction. The Conference held its first annual meeting and began the publication of its annual *Proceedings* in 1874. In 1917, it assumed the name, the National Conference of Social Work, which was changed in 1956 to the National Conference on Social Welfare. The National Conference has served as the forum for all American social welfare, and its *Proceedings* give the best stream-picture available of American thinking and experience in respect to social welfare over a period of more than eighty years. Later, the National Conference of Jewish Charities (1899) and the National Conference of Catholic Charities (1910) were established, as organs of expression for the Jewish and Catholic groups in social welfare.

The first city-wide charity organization society in the United States was established in Buffalo in 1877. It traced its lineage to the London charity organization society, established in 1869. Leadership in the organization of the Buffalo society was given by Rev. S. H. Gurteen, an English clergyman, who had formerly been associated with the London society and who had moved to Buffalo about 1873. The new movement spread rapidly to other cities, and by 1883, charity organization societies had come into being in some 25 American cities.

The charity organization movement was concerned with two things — the giving of more effective and more adequate personal service to families and individuals who needed it, and a cooperative approach to the "charitable" or social welfare problems of the community. That is, in the language of modern social work, these societies were concerned with social casework and with community organization.

In addition to their services to individuals, the charity organization societies sought to promote cooperation among social welfare agencies; to "expose impostors," and "prevent wilful idleness"; to "establish relations of personal interest and sympathy between the poor and well-to-do"; to "prevent pauperism"; and to "collect and diffuse knowledge" regarding social welfare.[2] Regardless of the forms of expression, all this was related to the fact of community organization.

In following out these aims, many charity organization societies were led into the establishment of new community services, such as anti-tuberculosis committees, housing committees, child labor committees, remedial loan committees, etc. The New York Charity Organization Society, among other services, established a periodical, *Charities*, which was a forerunner of *The Survey*; established the New York School of Social Work, the first school of social work in the United States; was instrumental in planning and carrying through the Pittsburgh Survey of 1907–1908; and initiated a field service which was the predecessor of a national agency in this field.[3]

From the soil of the charity organization movement grew the social service exchange and the community welfare council, or council of social agencies.

The first forerunner of the social service exchange was the Boston Registration Bureau, organized in 1876 by a group of volunteers, primarily as a central record of relief received by families, from various sources, and of other facts regarding the families. About 1906–1909 the original conception of a central record gave way to the modern idea of a *central index*, with *identifying information only*; and this has been the continuing form of the social service exchange in American communities.

Most of the early exchanges were established and operated by charity organization societies. As councils of social agencies and community chests were established in large numbers during the 1920's, more and more social service exchanges were established by or transferred to councils and chests.

The first council of social agencies was organized in Pittsburgh in 1908. Most of the early councils stemmed from the charity organization movement; much of the local leadership came from COS execu-

[2] Amos G. Warner; Stuart A. Queen; and Ernest B. Harper, *American Charities and Social Work* (New York, Crowell, 1930), p. 207.
[3] Frank D. Watson, *The Charity Organization Movement in the United States* (New York, Macmillan, 1922), pp. 530–531, 337. See also Edward T. Devine, *When Social Work Was Young* (New York, Macmillan, 1939).

tives; and the earliest national field service to councils came from the staff of what is today known as the Family Service Association of America.

At the same time as primary leadership in community organization was coming to be exercised more and more by chests and councils, the charity organization societies were tending to give more intensive concern to social casework and less to community organization. Growing experience indicated (1) that casework and community organization represented separate specializations; (2) that a consumer-service agency could not expect to give effective leadership in joint planning and particularly in the coordination of its sister agencies; and (3) that planning and coordination ought to be closely linked up with joint financing. After World War I the family rather than the community became the primary focus of interest of the charity organization societies; they concentrated more and more on family social work, and they tended to change their names to family welfare or family service agencies.

The social settlement, another pioneer organization, was concerned with group and recreational activities and with the welfare of the neighborhood or local community within the larger city.

A passage from the journal of Edward Denison, the first actual settlement pioneer, shows the community organization process at work even before the organized settlement had come into existence. Denison was a young English gentleman who, becoming dissatisfied with volunteer service for a relief society, took up his lodgings in Stepney, in 1867. On August 7, 1867 he wrote in his journal:

> My opinion of the great sphere of usefulness to which I should find myself admitted by coming to live here . . . is completely justified. All is yet in embryo — but it will grow. Just now I only teach in a night school, and do what in me lies in looking after the sick, keeping an eye upon nuisances and the like, seeing that the local authorities keep up to their work. I go tomorrow before the Board at the workhouse, to compel the removal to the infirmary of a man who ought to have been there already. I shall drive the sanitary inspector to put the Act against overcrowding in force with regard to some houses in which there have been as many as eight and ten bodies occupying one room. It is not surprising that the street in which this occurs has for months been full of small-pox, scarlet fever, and typhus . . . These are the sort of evils which, when there are no resident gentry, grow to a height almost in-

credible, and on which the remedial influence of the mere presence
of a gentleman known to be on the alert is inestimable.[4]

In this one paragraph there are suggestions of beginnings of casework, adult education (closely related to group work), and community organization, including social action!

Community organization, though not always identified in those
terms, has, from the beginning, been one of the major characteristics
of settlement programs. The settlement movement has a major concern with the well-being and development of the neighborhood or
local community, in addition to the settlement's clubs and classes,
group work, educational, and recreational activities. Some of the
distinctive aspects of the settlement's use of the community organization process are: (1) The emphasis upon the urban neighborhood.
In this interest it has been followed by various other agencies, including district or neighborhood councils, the Cincinnati Social Unit
Experiment of 1917–1919, Urban Leagues, and perhaps the wartime
"block" organizations. (2) Its emphasis upon experimentation, demonstration, and a changing and evolutionary program. (3) Its emphasis
upon the self-organization of the residents of a community to bring
about the needed changes through direct efforts, mobilization of local
resources, and democratic social action.

Many of the national welfare agencies which have come to play
so important a part in American social work were organized during
the charity organization period. Of 256 national voluntary welfare
agencies listed in the *Social Work Year Book, 1947*, only 9 had been
established prior to 1870, whereas 97 were organized during the
period 1870–1919.[5]

American "social surveys" find some of their forerunners in certain
English studies such as Charles Booth's work on *Life and Labour of
the People of London* (1892); in more or less journalistic volumes on
social conditions; in studies by settlements, such as Hull House in
Chicago and South End House in Boston; and in certain sociological
studies of communities.

In 1905, the editorial staff of the *Charities and Commons* under-

---

[4] Sir Baldwyn Leighton (ed.), *Letters and Other Writings of the Late Edward
Denison, M.P. for Newark,* p. 37. Quoted by Robert A. Woods and Albert J.
Kennedy in *The Settlement Horizon: A National Estimate* (New York, Russell
Sage Foundation, 1922), p. 19.
[5] Marvin L. Diller, *National Social Welfare Agencies: A Classification and Analysis
Based upon the Directories of the Social Work Year Book 1947* (Master's thesis,
University of Michigan, Institute of Social Work, Detroit, 1948; typed), p. 27.

took a study of the city of Washington. In 1907–1908, the Pittsburgh Survey was carried out under the same auspices, and the results were later published in four large volumes. In 1909, *Charities and Com-mons* was renamed *The Survey*, a name which it bore, with minor variations, to its discontinuation in 1952. In 1912, a Department of Surveys and Exhibits was established in the Russell Sage Foundation. This became a center for information, advice, and assistance with surveys; and in 1914, the Department conducted a comprehensive survey of Springfield, Illinois, the reports of which were published in a series of pamphlet volumes.

The survey method gradually came into use by many national and other welfare agencies. Many studies were made of special functional fields or of specific agencies, and for some years probably more emphasis was placed on such studies than on broader community or community welfare surveys. In recent years there seems to have been another swing toward comprehensive community welfare surveys, as indicated by studies in Boston, Milwaukee, Cincinnati, and other cities.

The state conference of social work became firmly established during this first period of community organization. The earliest conference was organized in 1881 in Wisconsin; by the end of World War I there were conferences in 32 states.

THE RISE OF FEDERATION

THE CENTRAL PHENOMENON in the second period of community organization (1917–1935) was the rise and the rapid growth of community chests and councils of social agencies. Financial federation among voluntary social welfare agencies seems to have originated in Liverpool, England, about 1873. In Denver, a combination charity organization society and joint fund-raising agency was organized as early as 1887. The first federations of Jewish agencies were established in Boston and Cincinnati in 1895 and 1896. A small financial federation was formed in Elmira, N.Y., in 1909.[6]

However, the Cleveland Federation for Charity and Philanthropy is usually thought of as the first modern community chest. In 1900, the Cleveland Chamber of Commerce organized a Committee on Benevolent Associations, the first of the municipal charities endorse-

---

[6] Two sources for the early history of the chest movement are: William J. Norton, *The Cooperative Movement in Social Work* (New York, Macmillan, 1927), and *Yesterday and Today with Community Chests* (New York, Community Chests and Councils, 1937).

ment committees. In 1907, this committee made a study of the financial support of 61 Cleveland social agencies. They found that the number of contributors was small; half of the money collected came from 74 persons; generous individuals were burdened by innumerable appeals; the average cost of money-raising was about 20 per cent; some sound agencies were having hard financial sledding while other less important ones were laying up a surplus. The Committee urged a new plan of financial federation. The Cleveland Federation was organized in 1913; the new venture was successful from the start, and it prompted similar efforts in a number of cities.

The entry of the United States into World War I, in 1917, led to a mushroom growth of "war chests," or financial federations concerned wholly or partially with war appeals, in 300 to 400 communities. In the period following the War, and particularly during the 1920's, many war chests were made over into peacetime community chests; other new chests were organized. By 1930, the community chest plan had become the established pattern for the financing of most of the important voluntary welfare agencies in large cities. When the community chest was organized in community after community, during the 1920's, a council was often set up in connection with the chest, or an existing council was brought into close relationship with the chest. Chests and councils began to be thought of as parts of one movement and as allied agencies for joint financing, community planning, and coordination.

During the early years of the depression the chests intensified their money-raising efforts; but by 1933 it was evident that the needs of the depression must be met primarily from governmental funds. Developments since the depression have included the war chests and the state chests of World War II, the problems of "multiple appeals" since the War, and the rise of the united funds.

The American Association for Community Organization (AACO), was organized in 1918 as the national agency for chests and councils; this later became known as Community Chests and Councils of America (CCC) and, in 1956, it was renamed United Community Funds and Councils of America. In 1923, the Association cooperated with Ohio State University in offering an eight-weeks' course for training of community chests executives. This ultimately grew into a school of social work, which has maintained an emphasis on the training of chest and council personnel.

The AACO and the Cleveland Welfare Federation also initiated a study of the Volume and Cost of Social Work, in Cleveland, in 1924; this led, in 1928, to a joint project for the registration of social statistics, under the auspices of the AACO and the University of Chicago. In the further development of statistical reporting important contributions were made by several national agencies, both governmental and voluntary.

At least three other types of councils originated about the time of World War I. The Cincinnati Public Health Federation, established in 1917, was probably the first independent "health council" in an American city. Some of the first rural "community councils" were organized in Massachusetts between 1912 and 1918. The first "co-ordinating council" traces its origin to 1919, in Berkeley, California. By the early 1930's, the plan began to spread through California and later beyond the borders of that State.

Between 1863 and 1917 state public welfare agencies were, in the main, either supervisory "state boards of charities" or administrative "boards of control." In 1917, the first modern state department of public welfare was created in Illinois. The state welfare agencies are today the keystones in our state systems of public welfare, and in the aggregate they use community organization in a vast number of services and relationships.

The establishment of new national agencies continued during this period of 1917–1935. The American Association of Social Workers, organized in 1921, was the first general professional organization for social workers, including, of course, those who specialized in community organization. The founding, in 1930, of the American Association of Public Welfare Officials, now the American Public Welfare Association, heralded the increasing importance of public welfare.

The Department of Surveys and Exhibits of Russell Sage Foundation gradually shifted its emphasis from surveys to interpretation and in 1934, it became the Department of Social Work Interpretation. As early as 1921, representatives of the Department assisted in the organization of the Social Work Publicity Council (now the National Publicity Council for Health and Welfare Services), as a national agency concerned with problems and methods of interpretation and public relations — one of the basic aspects of community organization.

The beginnings of closer cooperation among national agencies were evidenced by the organization of the National Health Council in 1921, and the National Social Work Council in 1922. These organizations applied the council of social agencies idea on the national level.

COMMUNITY ORGANIZATION AND PUBLIC WELFARE

⟨THE THIRD PERIOD IN COMMUNITY organization history, from 1935 to the present, has been characterized by expansion and professional development. The first important aspect of this period is the greater use of the community organization process in the field of public welfare.⟩

The stock market crash of 1929 heralded the beginning of the depression of the 1930's. By 1930, unemployment was already widespread; and unemployment and the need for relief increased in severity, each year, for the next several years.

Councils of social agencies were well established in most large cities and many smaller cities by 1929; their machinery and their experience in community organization were drawn upon in a large degree in the organization of "mayors' committees" and other early efforts to organize "emergency relief" in local communities. On the national level, several voluntary agencies — among them the American Public Welfare Association, the Family Welfare Association of America, and Community Chests and Councils — developed special emergency programs, which included, in one or more instances, fact-finding studies, production of handbooks and other material for unemployment relief agencies, consultation, and special field service. During 1931, a "welfare and relief mobilization" was carried on in the form of a special field service given by Community Chests and Councils, in cooperation with the President's Organization on Unemployment Relief. This project involved special field service to chest and non-chest cities; it was an effort to meet the emergency relief needs largely with private funds. In 1932, a United Educational Program was organized by the National Social Work Council to enlist public understanding and support of essential social services during a time when desperate economic need was concentrating attention more and more upon relief needs and services. In 1932, 397 community chests raised $101,000,000 as compared with $84,000,000 raised by 386 chests during the preceding year. In 1933, however, the amount raised by 401 chests fell to $77,000,000.[7] Each year, from 1930 on, it became increasingly evident that only government and governmental funds could cope with the major problems of the depression.

Even more important than these activities of the voluntary agen-

[7] *Yesterday and Today with Community Chests* (New York, Community Chests and Councils, 1937), p. 16.

cies were the immense growth of public welfare agencies and the enormous enlargement of their services and budgets; the emergence of a much greater degree of leadership from governmental agencies and the shift from local to state and federal leadership in the field of public welfare.

Along with these changes went a corresponding increase in the use of the community organization process by these public agencies. Vast new responsibilities were assumed by the federal and state governments for the development of social welfare programs, for the setting of standards, for the marshaling of support, and for all that these implied in factfinding, public education, and coordination of effort with other governmental agencies and with voluntary organizations. As Federal Emergency Relief Administrator, Harry L. Hopkins made decisions regarding program and standards that were incomparably more far-reaching than the operations of the half-dozen largest community chests and councils of social agencies in the country.

The Social Security Act of 1935 moved even further in the direction of federal and state governmental leadership. Several features of the Act were significant from the standpoint of community organization:

1. It created a new federal agency, the Social Security Board (later the Social Security Administration), with vastly important functions in respect to programs and standards; and it conferred comparable functions upon the Children's Bureau and certain other federal agencies in respect to particular services.

2. It established the "state plan" as the basic administrative device by which a state could secure approval of its program and the granting of federal aid.

3. It established the principle of state leadership in planning and in carrying on public welfare programs.

4. It established certain standards, particularly in reference to public assistance — statewide coverage, standards of eligibility, "fair hearing" or right of appeal, etc.

5. It extended child welfare services to children in rural areas, emphasized the preventive as well as the rehabilitative aspects of casework, and envisaged "developing state services for the encouragement and assistance of adequate methods of community child welfare organization." This is probably the first instance of the term "community organization" in a federal statute.

The creation of the Federal Security Agency by a presidential reorganization plan in 1939, and the transfer of the Social Security

Board to this agency, was another step of major importance. In 1946, the Agency was strengthened and partially reorganized. In 1953, several years of effort culminated in the establishment as a successor to the Federal Security Agency of a Department of Health, Education, and Welfare. Thus, in a hundred years, the federal government has moved from President Pierce's veto of Dorothea Dix's resolution (1854), with its implications of federal non-participation in social welfare, to the establishment of a cabinet department with broad responsibilities for leadership, program operation, and support in the areas of health, education, social welfare, and social insurance.

PROFESSIONAL DEVELOPMENT

⟨THE TREND OF CONTEMPORARY THINKING about community welfare organization dates chiefly from 1939⟩ An exploratory study-group project was developed under a Section of the National Conference of Social Work in 1938–39, and the activities of six local committees culminated in a committee report which was the first cooperative and widely circulated statement regarding the nature of "generic" community welfare organization.[8]

The study project continued a second year and resulted in a second report at the 1940 National Conference. In accordance with a recommendation in this Report, a Continuing Committee on the Study of Community Organization was organized. Before an active program could be initiated, America's entry into World War II brought wartime responsibilities to many of the committee members, and the committee became inactive for the duration of the war. In 1944, some informal conversations were held, looking toward the organization of some sort of broader group for the study of community organization; but the continuance of the war delayed action until 1946.

⟨In May 1946, at a meeting held at the National Conference of Social Work, in Buffalo, the Association for the Study of Community Organization (ASCO) was organized. Its purpose was "to increase understanding and improve professional practice of community organization for social welfare."⟩Membership was open to anyone with a "serious interest" in community organization — in other words, to anyone willing to pay the dues. In practice, however, the leadership of ASCO and most of the participation in it came primarily from professionally qualified community organization executives, practitioners,

[8] Robert P. Lane, "The Field of Community Organization," NCSW, 1939, pp. 495–511.

and teachers. Increasingly, ASCO moved in the direction of becoming a professional organization.

ASCO's membership varied from about 500 to 1,000 individuals. Its budget was usually in the neighborhood of $2,000. It never had an executive secretary; the President gave volunteer executive as well as official leadership, and everything that was done, except office administration and clerical work, was accomplished through the volunteer efforts of members of the Association. During the first years, the official "headquarters" of ASCO followed the presidency from Detroit to Philadelphia to Columbus, Ohio. During 1951–1955, the headquarters of ASCO were located in the offices of the American Association of Social Workers, and AASW furnished office services on a contractual basis.

In spite of these handicaps, ASCO developed an active program which included: (1) publication of a *Newsletter* and a quarterly bibliographical checklist of *Current Publications on Community Organization;* (2) encouragement of local Community Organization Discussion Groups, which existed at various times in 15 or 20 different communities; (3) promotion of publication of materials on community organization, including a *Community Organization Monographs* series in which three case records and a bibliography were published; (4) meetings, in connection with the National Conference, on topics of interest to community organization practitioners; (5) some study, discussion, and experimentation respecting community organization records; (6) liaison service with other national organizations, and representation of community organization practitioners.

In 1955, ASCO merged with six other professional organizations to form the National Association of Social Workers. A Committee on Community Organization has been created as an integral part of the organization of NASW; it has planned a program including exploration of basic issues and problems in community organization, chapter activity in this area of social work, production and promotion of published material, and other activities.

Paralleling these developments in the National Conference of Social Work were the activities of a group of teachers of community organization within the American Association of Schools of Social Work. A Committee on Community Organization, appointed as a subcommittee of the Curriculum Committee of the Association, was active from 1939 to 1945. The committee made a questionnaire study of courses in community organization in the schools; developed some degree of integration of thinking about the subject; explored the subject of community organization case records; prepared bibliographies; and made some suggestions regarding course content.

Community organization has been recognized as an integral and important aspect of social work education in the Hollis study (1948–1951) and in the activities of the American Association of Schools of Social Work and its successor, the Council on Social Work Education, looking toward the development of improved and more highly integrated curricula in schools of social work. Several workshops on community organization have been held in connection with various annual meetings of the AASSW and CSWE.

At present, there is an active committee of the Council on Social Work Education concerned with the production of Teaching Materials in Community Organization.

More important, perhaps, than any specific organizational developments has been the stimulation of professional thinking as evidenced and enhanced by public discussions and additions to the literature of the subject.

Wayne McMillen's *Community Organization for Social Welfare*, published in 1945, was the first contemporary textbook on community organization and was undoubtedly the most important single contribution to the literature of the subject up to the time of its publication. It was the first of a series of textbooks and collections of case materials that have done much to present factual material in systematic form, to clarify concepts, and to stimulate thinking.

WORLD WAR II AND COMMUNITY ORGANIZATION

SOCIAL WELFARE PROBLEMS in World War II had three main causes: (1) the transfer of several million men and a substantial number of women from civilian to military status; (2) the development of large-scale war industries, often in small communities or rural areas; and (3) preparing for the possibility of enemy attack.

Wartime community problems involved at least four different types of communities: the military camp or post, the community near the military camp, the war-industry community, and the home community. In many instances the most vital needs related to the provision of adequate facilities for housing, health, education, recreation, and other services. In a society that knew more about engineering than human relations, technological planning forged far ahead of planning for human beings. A *Survey* article in 1942 described a war plant located "in a semi-rural area without apparent thought for housing, transportation, water supply, sewage disposal, schools, recreation or medical care for its several thousand workers." There were a "noisome trailer camp," overcrowded schools, tarpaper sheds, inadequate water lines, and sewage in open ditches.

(Community organization found itself grappling with the problem of providing minimum necessities of decent living for the thousands of war workers who were earning good wages but were often unable to purchase the physical necessities of a good or even normal life.) Other problems ranged from providing "day care" for children of working mothers, to aiding Japanese and Japanese-Americans, evacuated from the West Coast to inland war relocation centers, and frequently later resettled in other communities.

There was a notable increase in federal leadership and participation in community organization, though no single federal agency had sole responsibility for it. The Office of Civilian Defense served as a center for the coordination of federal civilian defense activities. Local defense councils, in addition to their protective functions (air raid warden services, etc.) performed a great variety of community organization services in the fields of health and welfare. Various patterns of cooperation and relationships were worked out by defense councils and community welfare councils. Some of the most important demonstrations in our history of local governmental bodies concerned with community welfare organization were given by the defense councils. From their experience came some important questions as to the place of government in future health and welfare planning.[9]

The Office of Community War Services (OCWS) in the Federal Security Agency was given direct responsibility for recreation and social protection (social hygiene) programs, but it served also to some extent as a federal planning and coordinating agency for health and welfare.

Developments in the area of national voluntary wartime services included modifications of function and program and the organization of special war projects and services; the immense expansion of the program of the American Red Cross; an increased emphasis on coordinative effort, with the growth of several new national councils or federated bodies; the organization of some new agencies, especially those concerned with wartime appeals for foreign relief; and developments in the field of federated financing. Among the national agencies created to meet wartime needs were the United Service Organizations (USO),

[9] See Thomas Devine, "Community Organization under Public Auspices. 1. From the Federal Viewpoint." NCSW, 1944, pp. 408–409.

a union of forces on the part of six national agencies, to serve the needs of military personnel and defense communities; the American War-Community Services; the President's War-Relief Control Board; the National War Fund; and the National Budget Committee.[10]

{Another wartime development of significance for community organization was the growth of closer relationships between organized labor and social work.}In 1942, the American Federation of Labor and the Congress of Industrial Organizations entered into an agreement with Community Chests and Councils that labor would "throw its weight behind the newly developing war chests of the country" and that "community chests and war chests would attempt to obtain recognition for organized labor by placing labor leaders in active positions in the campaign and on governing bodies and by asking employers, in soliciting contributions, to work, insofar as possible, through joint labor management committees." [11]

One of the striking characteristics of community organization during the War was the immense increase in volunteer service. Civilian defense councils, the American Red Cross, the USO, and other agencies were active in the recruitment and use of volunteers. As early as 1942, the Office of Civilian Defense reported 7,250,000 active volunteers in all types of work, with 1,500,000 in health, welfare, and related fields.[12] OCD later estimated that as of December 31, 1943, there were 4,306 civilian defense volunteer offices. Under the leadership of Community Chests and Councils and other national agencies, continuing attention has been given to the problem of how a maximum amount of citizen participation and volunteer service may be enlisted in the operation of social welfare programs and activities.

RECENT DEVELOPMENTS

ALTHOUGH MORE THAN TEN YEARS have passed since the end of World War II, it is still too early for us to have much perspective on the community organization developments of this postwar period in which we are living. It is even somewhat doubtful whether these years can be accurately designated as a postwar period in view

[10] See Chapters 11 and 13. See also: Wayne McMillen, "Wartime Developments in Federated Financing of Social Work," in: Helen R. Wright (ed.), *Social Service in Wartime* (Chicago, University of Chicago Press, 1944), pp. 144–168.
[11] McMillen, *loc. cit.*, pp. 157–158.
[12] Katharine R. Van Slyck, "The Awakened Volunteer Interest," NCSW, 1942, p. 247.

of the war in Korea during 1950–1953, the "cold war," and the recent disturbances in Hungary and the Near East. Obviously, the workings of the community organization process reflect these uncertain, tense, and confused years.

Some recent developments which seem of major importance from the standpoint of community welfare organization may be summarized as follows:

(There have been *new areas of emphasis* in social welfare and therefore in community organization.) Services to veterans was one field of central importance immediately following World War II. The rehabilitation of the physically and mentally handicapped, mental health planning, problems of the aging, and the prevention and treatment of juvenile delinquency are among other areas of special concern. In respect to older persons, a fairly extensive literature has developed; surveys, broad planning, and action programs are common; and service to the aging is today one of the important functional divisions of the field of social welfare.

In regard to juvenile delinquency, there have been four important national developments. A Special Juvenile Delinquency Project, initiated in 1952, culminated in a National Conference on Juvenile Delinquency in 1954. A Division of Juvenile Delinquency Service has been established in the Children's Bureau; a five-year Citizens Action Program has been launched with foundation support; and a Senate subcommittee has studied the subject and has proposed federal legislation, embodying grants-in-aid to the states in connection with programs for combatting juvenile delinquency.[13]

The New York City Youth Board is one local agency that has developed an extensive preventive program, including the use of casework, group work, and mass recreation facilities. An "aggressive casework" unit has been established in the City Department of Public Welfare. The workers "view the community as the client. They seek out families in need of assistance and visit them with perseverance and persistence, eventually establishing the necessary relationship."[14]

(There have been important developments in the area of *financing and central planning* for social welfare.)

There has been a growth in the number and size of independent fund-raising campaigns, particularly on the part of some of the large national health agencies. Community chests have been deeply con-

[13] Norman V. Lourie, "Juvenile Deliquency," SWYB, 1957, pp. 330–341.
[14] Bertram M. Beck, "Juvenile Delinquency," SWYB, 1954, p. 298.

cerned over the problem of multiple appeals. An increasingly strong
movement has developed for the extension of joint financing through
united funds or *extended federation campaigns.* There has been sharp
opposition and widespread controversy. During recent years there
have been numerous reorganizations among chests and councils, many
of these in connection with the establishment of united funds.

The publication of *Community Planning for Human Services* by
Bradley Buell and associates, in 1952, is an important event from the
standpoint of community welfare planning. While its analysis of social
welfare problems under the headings of dependency, ill-health, maladjustment, and recreational need is not all-inclusive, it presents the
clearest picture of American social welfare problems, service functions, and service systems that has yet been seen. Drawing on an
intensive study made by Community Research Associates in St. Paul,
Minnesota, this volume suggests that the four types of problems described are inextricably intertwined, that a disproportionate amount
of time and money is being spent on a relatively small proportion of
families in the community, and that drastic changes are needed in
community planning if health and welfare services are to be really
effective in treatment and prevention. The book is an analysis of needs
and problems rather than a blueprint for reconstruction, but it contains some suggestions as to desirable paths of exploration and experimentation. Community Research Associates is itself carrying on a program of local experimentation in partnership with selected communities. Allowing for all the questions and criticisms that have been or
may be advanced in reference to various aspects of its analysis and
conclusions, this volume still appears to be one of the most creative,
provocative, and valuable contributions to community organization
thinking and literature within the last thirty years.

There are encouraging signs of broader and more effective cooperation on the part of *national agencies.* The reorganization of the
National Social Work Council into the National Social Welfare Assembly, in 1945, is a landmark in the history of national welfare agencies.
Several former specialized councils of national agencies are now parts
of or affiliated with the Assembly. Other evidences of new or enlarged
cooperation have been seen in the National Budget and National
Quota Committees, and the programs of the United Defense Fund
and the United Community Defense Services, referred to below.

The end of World War II has obviously not brought about international peace. The "cold war," a vast national defense program, and
uneasiness and disturbances in various parts of the world are among

the new and difficult conditions of chronic crisis under which social welfare and community organization must currently operate.

Some of the special social welfare needs created by the present situation relate to: the armed services, civilian mobility, atomic energy installations, and civil defense.

Two of the most important developments in response to these needs have been the program of the United Community Defense Services (UCDS), a federation of national agencies to help defense communities meet their problems during 1950–1956, and the operation of the United Defense Fund (UDF), during 1950–1955, as a national agency for the financing of national health and welfare services related to the defense effort.

Foundations play an important part in the financing of many special programs and projects in social welfare. There have been two recent congressional investigations of foundations, directed particularly to the question of whether foundations were engaging in un-American or subversive activities. The Cox Committee concluded, in 1952, after examining a considerable number of witnesses, that "on balance the record of the foundations is good." The Reece Committee, in 1954, brought in a report attacking the foundations, but the Committee was widely criticized for its methods of gathering evidence and conducting the hearings. Two members of the committee in a minority report observed that, "We are presented with an inquiry in which facts have played no part." Several of the major foundations issued spirited public statements not only denying the charges of the committee, but also strongly asserting their commitment to freedom of thought and inquiry as a foundation for a democracy.[15]

Another aspect of social welfare financing which has attracted considerable public attention is the subject of *charitable frauds*. An authority on social welfare financing has estimated that "of the $5,-400,000,000 contributed to philanthropy in 1954, 3 per cent or approximately $162,000,000 may have been wasted on dishonest, incompetent, or borderline charities." [16]

A New York legislative committee in 1953 uncovered five areas of fraudulent or undesirable practices: (1) misrepresentations of the true programs of the soliciting organization; (2) unauthorized use of

[15] F. Emerson Andrews, "Foundations and Social Welfare," SWYB, 1957, pp. 274–280. "The Foundations Defend Freedom of Inquiry," *Social Service Review,* Vol. XXIX, March 1955, pp. 76–77; copyright, 1955, University of Chicago. By permission of University of Chicago Press. See also: Bernard DeVoto, "Guilt by Distinction," *Harper's Magazine,* Vol. 210, April 1955, pp. 14–15, 18–21.
[16] Wayne McMillen," "Financing Social Welfare Services," SWYB, 1957, p. 266.

names as sponsors; (3) inadequate financial and other records and reports; (4) operation of so-called charities as "fronts" for commercial or personal enterprises; and (5) excessive administrative and fund-raising costs, with the result that only a small percentage of the contributor's dollar goes for social welfare purposes. Remedial legislation was enacted in New York State, although the legislative committee emphasized that the basic answer to the problem is public education rather than legal control. A National Conference on Solicitations has been established and is seeking to educate contributors to wise giving and avoidance of charity frauds.[17]

International social welfare has gained commanding importance in the world today, and community organization is an integral part of this picture. The United Nations, with its various organs and specialized agencies, the Organization of American States, technical assistance under the auspices of the United States Government, the UN expanded program of technical assistance, the International Conference of Social Work, individual voluntary agencies for carrying on international service, and the American Council of Voluntary Agencies for Foreign Service are all important elements in the area of international social welfare.

The enormous growth of programs of *community development,* particularly in relation to newly developing or technically less developed areas, is one of the most important trends, within recent years, in international social welfare.

Some of the emphases in community development also manifest themselves in community welfare organization in the United States: recognition of the goal of working with the whole community, and a greater emphasis on self-help.

There are some indications of a trend toward more consumer-controlled, consumer-related, *self-help social welfare movements.* Alcoholics Anonymous (established 1935) is probably the best-known example; there are organizations of former mental patients and of physically handicapped persons; and the current movement on behalf of retarded children began, in some places, as a movement by the *parents* of retarded children. There were some advisory committees of the unemployed during the depression; there have been "patients councils" in some mental hospitals; and in one instance, a social action

[17] McMillen, *loc. cit.* State of New York. *Report of the Joint Legislative Committee on Charitable and Philanthropic Agencies and Organizations* (Legislative Document, 1954, No. 26. Albany, 1954), pp. 15, 17–18. "National Conference on Solicitations," *Social Service Review,* Vol. XXIX, June 1955, p. 200.

project was undertaken by patients at a Veterans Readjustment Center, to save the Center from liquidation through legislative action.[18]

QUESTIONS AND PROBLEMS

1. Compare the general status and development of community organization in 1908; 1919; 1929; 1935; 1941; 1945; today. Do you see any sound reasons for picking any of these particular dates?

2. Compare the historical development of community organization services in your community with the general outline given in the chapter. In particular, find out, for your community, the dates and something of the circumstances of the beginnings of the major community organization agencies, and any other outstanding events and dates in the history of these agencies.

3. Summarize the history of some one aspect of community organization referred to in the chapter—chests, councils, the survey movement, national agencies, etc.

4. Make a study of one or more "self-help movements" in relation to social welfare in the United States.

5. Prepare a brief history of a specific community organization agency. Try to get beyond a mere listing of dates and events: try to find out not only *what* happened, but *how* and *why* it happened. What sort of problems were encountered, and what were the responses to these problems in terms of agency organization, program, policies, etc.? Who were some of the key persons in this development? What do you find are the most valuable sources of information for this study?

6. Identify five national leaders, present or past, in the area of community welfare organization. What has been the nature of the contribution of each of them?

7. Prepare a biographical sketch of some community organization leader, together with as complete a bibliography as you can collect of his professional writings.

8. List five books that are of major importance in community welfare organization today. Prepare a bibliographical citation on each of them, including a few sentences of objective description. Add critical or evaluative comments, if you wish.

SUGGESTIONS FOR READING

There is no comprehensive contemporary volume on the history of social work and social welfare in the United States. Texts such as those by Fink

---

[18] Dorothy Robinson, *A Campaign of Patients to Save the Veterans Readjustment Center of Ann Arbor* (Ann Arbor, University of Michigan, School of Social Work, Master's Thesis, 1950). For other examples of community projects reflecting self-help see: *Promoting Social Welfare Through Self-Help and Cooperative Action in the United States* (New York, American Association of Social Workers, 1954).

and Friedlander (see bibliography, ch. 1), contain some historical material. The texts by Murphy, Johns and DeMarche, and Green contain chapters on the history of community organization, and McMillen has valuable material under specific topics. The *Social Work Year Book* articles include a limited amount of historical material. (See Basic References.)

Bruno, Frank J., *Trends in Social Work, 1874–1956* (New York, Columbia University Press, 2nd edition, with supplement by Louis Towley, 1957, 462 pp.) Includes chapters on chests, councils, and some other aspects of community organization.

Colcord, Joanna C., "The Impact of the War upon Community Welfare Organization" (NCSW, 1943, pp. 241–251).

Devine, Edward T., *Social Work* (New York, Macmillan, 1922, 352 pp.). Social work in the early 1920's.

———— *When Social Work Was Young* (New York, Macmillan, 1939, 163 pp.). The author's adventures in social work, particularly in New York, in the early 1900's. A good deal of the content relates to various aspects of community organization.

Dillick, Sidney, *Community Organization for Neighborhood Development — Past and Present* (New York, Woman's Press and Morrow, 1953, 198 pp.). The history and present status of "neighborhood community organization."

Dunham, Arthur, "The Literature of Community Organization" (NCSW, 1940, pp. 413–424). Literature, existing and needed, in 1940.

Ford, Lyman S., "The Effect of World War II on Community Organization for Health and Welfare" (NCSW, 1944, pp. 392–401).

Glenn, John M.; Brandt, Lilian; and Andrews, F. Emerson, *Russell Sage Foundation, 1907–1946* (New York, Russell Sage Foundation, 1947, 2 vol.). The history of a foundation which has played an important part in social work.

Kasius, Cora (ed.), *New Directions in Social Work*. (See bibliography, ch. 1.) Bears upon contemporary history, developments, and outlook for social work.

Mayo, Leonard W., "Community Planning for Health and Welfare" (NCSW, *Social Welfare Forum*, 1952, pp. 220–231). A balanced and thoughtful view of community organization in 1952.

Norton, William J., *The Cooperative Movement in Social Work* (New York, Macmillan, 1927, 373 pp. OP). An authoritative volume on the community chest and the chest movement to 1927.

Phillips, Wilbur C., *Adventuring for Democracy* (New York, Social Unit Press, 1940, 380 pp.). Contains a detailed account of the Cincinnati Social Unit experiment of 1917–1919.

Social Work Journal, Vol. XXXVI, July 1955. The final issue of this Journal, before the AASW became a part of NASW, contains several articles reviewing social welfare progress during the past few decades.

Steiner, Jesse Frederick, *Community Organization* (New York, Century, rev. ed., 1930, 453 pp. OP). The pioneer textbook on the "community movement" and community organization. Extremely valuable as a historical reference.

Warner, Amos Griswold; Queen, Stuart Alfred; and Harper, Ernest Bouldin, *American Charities and Social Work* (New York, Crowell, 1930, 616 pp.). "American charities" in the 1890's and social work at the beginning of the 1930's.

Watson, Frank Dekker, *The Charity Organization Movement in the United States* (New York, Macmillan, 1922, 560 pp.). An authoritative history of the charity organization movement.

8.

COMMUNITY ORGANIZATION IN ACTION

THE PREVIOUS CHAPTER HAS GIVEN some idea of how community organization developed historically. This chapter has a double purpose: (1) to outline the main types of social welfare agencies which practice community organization — particularly the local agencies whose primary function is community organization; and (2) to give some examples of community organization in action, in order to convey something of the feel, the atmosphere, and the color of community organization.

In his paper on "The Range of Community Organization," Russell H. Kurtz traces the development of community organization in "a pioneer community in which, at the outset, no social services exist." The community grows; social work — and with it community organization — makes its appearance and becomes more and more important. Mr. Kurtz identifies eight "bench-marks" in the evolution of community organization:

1. Community organization is effectively practiced in certain circumstances by laymen without the help of professionals.

2. Community organization is necessarily practiced by every social agency in its struggle for survival and development.

3. The community organization process is used between agencies in all communities, even where formal councils do not exist.

4. The community organization process is used intensively by some specialized agencies, such as councils (and, of course, chests) organized for this purpose.

5. Community organization is practiced vertically, between a local agency and its state and national affiliates, as well as horizontally in the local community.

6. Community organization is generally a joint process in which professionals and non-professionals participate, with the non-professionals always having the last word.

7. The community organization process is used on the state level by both public and private agencies, both horizontally and vertically.

8. Community organization is practiced in the "community" of the nation by public and private agencies individually and collectively, as on the lesser levels. Laymen participate in the process here as elsewhere.

Summarizing, Mr. Kurtz says, "We find the community organization process being used for social welfare purposes on all jurisdictional levels, by single agencies and among groups of agencies; and we also find it employed between levels in a variety of relationships." [1]

COMMUNITY ORGANIZATION AGENCIES

THERE ARE MORE COMMUNITY ORGANIZATION agencies in operation than are generally recognized, even by social workers. We shall identify some major types of local agencies which make primary use of this process. Where a type of agency is discussed in a special chapter in this book, the chapter number will be indicated in parenthesis.

The *community welfare council* (Chapter 10) is the central local agency for health and welfare planning. The council may be related in various ways to the *community chest* (Chapter 11). Sometimes the chest and council are united in a single agency. The *united fund* is an extension of the plan of joint financing of agencies.

Frequently, a community welfare council has divisions concerned with specialized functional fields, such as family welfare, child welfare, health, recreation, and also with certain processes such as casework and group work. Sometimes, however, there are *specialized councils*, such as a child welfare council or recreation council, instead of a central council with divisions. One type of specialized council, the *health council*, has developed as a distinctive type of agency which may exist separately from a community welfare council. There is a national Conference for Health Council Work, established in 1926,

[1] The preceding paragraphs are quoted and paraphrased from Russell H. Kurtz, "The Range of Community Organization," NCSW, 1940, pp. 400–412.

and having 70 individual members.[2] *The federation of settlements* is another distinctive type of coordinating organization in a special field. There may be also hospital councils, boys and girls work councils, camping associations, etc., which may be outside the structure of the community welfare council.

District, community, or neighborhood councils in cities are local bodies which sometimes spring from local initiative and sometimes are developed through the efforts of a citywide community welfare council, or occasionally through governmental agencies. They are usually connected with a community welfare council (Chapter 10). *Coordinating councils* were initiated in California about forty years ago, with a primary focus on juvenile delinquency. Such councils have now usually broadened their interests to include other social welfare and neighborhood problems.

The *community council* has usually been associated with smaller communities and often with rural community organization. Such a council seeks community improvement through community study and action. It is likely to be composed of representatives from the major civic, educational, governmental, and welfare interests in the community. The council is an instrument of over-all community integration and action, and is often closely bound up with programs of adult education or "citizenship education." Such a council is not interested *primarily* in community welfare organization but rather in the total community life. However, the council's program should *include* community welfare organization, and in any case it is an important instrument for community organization in small communities and rural areas. In some cases there are statewide organizations of local councils — for example, the New York State Citizens Council and California Community Councils. In other cases local councils may be promoted or assisted by a state university or a statewide organization.

Jewish welfare federations are central financing and coordinating organizations for local Jewish social welfare agencies. Jewish federations have various relationships to community chests. In some cases Jewish *welfare funds* serve as instruments for central fund raising and budgeting for national and overseas agencies appealing to Jewish communities. In some cities *Jewish community councils* exist. These are concerned with all phases of Jewish community life, including the promotion of coordination among Jewish groups, development of Jewish

[2] SWYB, 1957, p. 665. See also: Yolande Lyon, *Stepping Stones to a Health Council* (New York, National Health Council, 2nd ed. 1952).

cultural activities, and promotion of better relationships among Jewish and non-Jewish groups.

The *Catholic Charities* is the official agency of the Catholic diocese for planning, coordinating, financing, and sometimes directly administering social service programs under Catholic auspices. Catholic agencies and fund-raising activities have various patterns of relationships to community chests.

Endorsement bureaus or committees may be maintained by chambers of commerce or other agencies for the purpose of endorsing voluntary social welfare agencies which seek public support and which measure up to certain stated standards. Membership in a properly operated community chest constitutes a *de facto* endorsement; so the endorsement function is concerned chiefly with non-chest agencies. In some cities agencies appealing for public support must obtain a license from a municipal authority.

A *community trust* is a foundation — usually local — which receives and invests capital gifts and bequests and distributes the income, and in certain cases portions of the principal, to social welfare agencies. Grants are made by a committee of representative citizens in accordance with the instructions of the donors, but the committee is vested with discretionary power to change the beneficiary of a gift if the original purpose becomes obsolete or inadvisable with the passage of time.

The *social service exchange,* or central index of families and individuals known to social welfare agencies as clients or applicants, is most likely to be a department of the community welfare council, but it may be a bureau of a governmental or voluntary agency or an independent agency. (Chapter 9.)

The *National Association of Social Workers* (NASW) is the national professional organization for social workers. The Association and its local *chapters* are concerned primarily with the development and improvement of professional practice and standards. Aside from this primary interest in standards, chapters may engage in factfinding and educational projects, and in activities bearing on the development of social welfare programs. These are aspects of community organization. Some of these activities may involve social action, at least within what is considered to be the professional area of competence of the members.

The *social workers club,* which exists in some communities, is a group less sharply defined than a professional association. It is usually open both to persons employed on social work jobs and to others interested; there are no requirements as to education and experience. This type of organization, in most cases, probably has two main functions. It may hold program meetings of an educational nature, whose content may either be restricted to social welfare or may take in a wider range of social, political, economic and other topics, and it may serve a social and recreational function. In some cases, such a club may engage in social action, passing resolutions, or seeking to advance particular pieces of social legislation, or it may otherwise use the process of community organization; this latter is in most cases a secondary function.

Labor unions of employees of social agencies are usually industrial unions, including in their membership professional, clerical, and maintenance workers. The unions are part of the American labor movement. They are concerned primarily with the economic protection and well-being of workers and their families. The unions may seek recognition by management, the establishment of collective bargaining, the negotiation of satisfactory labor contracts, and participation by the workers in the determination of program and policy. Unions are concerned with many matters relating to standards and programs; they may carry on factfinding and educational activities, and they have frequently engaged in social action in behalf of specific legislative measures and welfare programs. In these respects they are concerned with community organization as a secondary function.

There are many types of *local planning, promotional, and educational agencies in specialized fields.* In a single area, for example, there may be found an Urban League, an agency, either governmental or voluntary, for the improvement of intercultural relations, a consumers league, a housing association, associations concerned with mental health, tuberculosis, social hygiene, cancer, heart, crippled children and adults, muscular dystrophy, multiple sclerosis, etc. For the most part, these agencies are concerned with community organization rather than direct service.

The various types of statewide, national, and international agencies for community welfare organization are discussed in detail in Chapters 12, 13, and 14, respectively.

Some illustrations of community organization problems and activities will give insight into how the process of community organization is actually used.

"PROJECT NUMBER 1" IN KOREA

The first example is a story of rural community organization or "community development" in a Korean village.[3]

It was a March day in 1953, when two United Nations officials drove up in a jeep to Kam Chun Li, a Korean village of 800 people. The officials began to talk with some of the villagers. On every side they heard the same story. The villagers were hungry. The rice fields were not producing up to standard. An irrigation ditch had silted up, reducing the water flowing to the paddy fields. Their food supply was cut down — and there didn't seem to be much they could do about it.

The United Nations men had to go on to another appointment, but they agreed to come back. They returned and sat down to discuss the problem with the village president and the villagers. Out of the discussion a new idea began to take shape. To clear the silted ditch was an overwhelming job. No one or two or three men could do it. But suppose *all* the villagers worked together to clear the ditch? One of the UN men got out pencil and paper. How much of the ditch could one man clear in one day? How long was the canal? The official figured for a few minutes, then he looked up with an amazed expression on his face. With an investment of only 300 man days — ten men working for thirty days each — they could clear the ditch enough to increase their harvest by forty pounds of rice per head.

The villagers became excited over the prospect. But then a silence fell. Some were doubtful. It was too simple. There must be a catch somewhere.

That's right; there *is* a catch, the UN men agreed. Two catches, in fact. Nobody can pay you for this work. It will have to be volunteer work, done for the good of the village. Moreover, it is easy to arouse enthusiasm when everybody is together at a meeting, but it is harder to keep up the same spirit when there is sweat and hard work, day after day. It will depend on the spirit and pride of the villagers whether or not this job can be done.

The villagers were indignant. Their spirit was as good as that of any other community. They would clear the ditch and they asked no payment.

[3] Adapted from *Korea: The Task Ahead* (United Nations, Department of Public Information, 1955), pp. 17–26.

Finally it was decided, however, that while there would be no wages as such, each man should receive a token bonus of 25 hwan (12 cents) per man-day, in recognition of the fine spirit of the village and as a reminder of their commitment to finish the job.

In a simple ceremony the village president and one of the UN officials signed the first contractual agreement the villagers had ever seen. As a token of good faith, the village president received an advance of 1000 hwan — about five dollars.

The UN men drove off wondering whether they had started a program or whether they had been playing an elaborate game and wasting their time.

They came back in two days. The villagers had dug not the ten metres of the ditch which they had thought they could do in this time but *200 metres*. Before a week had passed the canal was free of silt and the water flowed through it at full strength. For a total cost of $40 cash and a collective contribution of hours of spare time, the value of the rice crop had been increased by about $3000, and the shadow of hunger was lifted from the village. Even more important, the villagers had learned what could be accomplished through co-operative effort. They had developed a new confidence in themselves, in what they could accomplish, and in the ability of their country to rehabilitate itself.

The results of Project Number 1 did not stop with Kam Chun Li. The neighboring villages heard about the cleared canal and requested meetings with the UN officials. It was generous of the UN to give Kam Chun Li a good irrigation canal, they said, but what about the other villages? They had their own problems and they needed help also. It was explained that neither the UN nor the government had given anybody a new canal. It was the spirit of the villagers of Kam Chun Li and the way in which they had worked that had cleared the canal.

What, said the spokesmen for the other villages, did the officials think that *their* villages did not have just as patriotic a spirit as the men of Kam Chun Li? They would prove what they could do. They determined that they would not only clear their canals of silt but they would pool the labor of nine villages to construct a reservoir which was needed to serve this whole local region.

And it was done. Within a few weeks the irrigation ditches were cleared and work was well under way on the reservoir. The Korean program of community development had begun.

Especially interesting in this illustration are the relation between the community organization specialist and the lay group, the enlistment of participation by the members of the community, and the workings of the community organization process in a village setting.

THE FLINT WORK PARTY

The second example of community organization is based on an event that occurred in Beecher Township, north of Flint, Michigan.[4]

Early on Saturday morning, August 29, 1953, hundreds of cars and people were streaming toward a great tent in an open space. Some of the men carried kits of tools; almost everyone had a hammer and saw. Suddenly quiet came over the crowd. An American flag was raised. A prayer was offered by a Roman Catholic priest. The loudspeaker sounded: "Is there an electrician in the area? Two bricklayers are needed right away. Please report to the registration desk." Thus began what was probably the biggest community "work party" ever held in the United States.

What was this all about? On June 8, Flint was ravaged by a tornado which left in its wake 116 dead, more than 900 injured, 400 houses demolished, and an estimated property damage of $12,000,000.

A Catholic priest, Father Henry W. Berkemeier, pastor of the Church of St. Francis of Assisi, conceived the idea that the people of Flint — and of other nearby communities if they wished — should spend a week-end working to rebuild the houses of their neighbors who had suffered from the tornado. Soon the idea began to catch. A committee of fourteen was formed, and before it had finished, it had increased to 1400. The mayor proclaimed a week-end for "Operation Tornado." The Junior Chamber of Commerce took over registration. Churches of all denominations took up the project; construction firms and unions pledged their support; restaurants and hotels provided box lunches for the volunteers and arrangements were made to put up out-of-town volunteers overnight in school buildings.

On the Friday evening before the work party, 3,000 volunteers

[4] From a paper by the author, "Action for Social Welfare—Its Meaning and Nature," in *Proceedings, Institute on Methods of Social Action, New Orleans, November 1953*, National Conference of Social Work and Louisiana Conference of Social Welfare, 1954. This statement is based upon accounts in *The New York Times*, August 30–31, 1953, and *Life Magazine*, Vol. 35, September 14, 1953.

had registered. But the next morning 1,200 more appeared who hadn't registered! Some came from as far as Detroit, 59 miles away. One planeload of plumbers came from Cleveland. Experienced union carpenters guided the work of amateurs — salesmen, auto workers, teachers, garage mechanics, business men, clerks, executives of industrial corporations, women and even schoolboys participated.

At the end of the two broiling summer days, 5,500 volunteers had contributed about 80,000 man hours of free labor, estimated at a minimum value of $160,000 in wages. The deeper values of what had been contributed, no one could assess. Nearly half of the demolished houses — 193 — were substantially rebuilt, 100 of them from basement to roof.

Among the elements of interest in this instance are: the *ad hoc* nature of this disaster reconstruction project; the spontaneity and extent of voluntary cooperation; the essentially lay direction, organization, and execution of the undertaking (at least as far as these accounts indicate); and the magnitude of the results accomplished.

"THE NEIGHBORHOOD IS OUR CLIENT"

The following account of a settlement's experience with community organization appeared as an article by Francis Bosworth, Executive Director of Friends Neighborhood Guild, Philadelphia. The article, entitled "The Neighborhood Is Our Client," appeared in the *Mail-o-gram* for March, 1949, published by the Health and Welfare Council of Delaware, Montgomery, and Philadelphia Counties. The article stands in its original form except for the omission of a few names of individuals and a few other slight changes.

Toward the end of 1943, we, as a Settlement, began to question much of what we did and why we did it. The neighbors came to our old Quaker Meeting House for clubs, sports, dances, crafts, and to talk over their problems. But was that enough?

We were in the heart of an expanding slum. People were surging up from the South into houses long abandoned. Houses without water, light or heat — without even window frames or doors were rented "as is." "Take 'em or leave 'em." The people took them. The Poplar Area (Market St. to Girard Ave. and Broad St. to the Delaware River) is 1-3/8 miles at its broadest. This area had a population of 49,000 in 1940, and has 72,000 today. In these eight years 853 houses have collapsed or have been demolished. Some 1400 have been converted to commercial purposes. Except for the Richard Allen Project *not a single new house has been constructed.*

A few hundred of these people were coming to the Guild to spend a few hours away from their wretched homes. We were trying to teach people how to live in the slums and like it. We realized that part of our job was to fill our neighbors with a mortal discontent before they would begin to search for new goals for living. We continued with our plan. We had no mass meetings or crusades. We were afraid of the inertia that often follows an all-out special event. We discussed neighborhood problems in small groups and home visits, waiting for their discontent to turn to thoughts of action, always asking, "What are you going to do about it?"

Under the leadership of the American Friends Service Committee (AFSC) 50 miners on relief in Western Pennsylvania were building their own homes at Penn Craft. In January, 1944, we approached the Service Committee to see if a Self-Help or Work Camp program could be jointly sponsored in our neighborhood, but they were unable to consider it at that time.

We opened a Self-Help Workshop in the Guild and some of the members began painting and fixing up one another's homes, but this often led to bitterness and frustration. Paint and paper do not stay on damp walls and people are hostile about improving the property of a negligent landlord. Several families did a fine job. They bought lumber, plaster and paint and spent nights laboring. They paid to have faulty plumbing and wiring fixed. In each case the owner promptly sold the remodeled house and evicted the tenants who had tried to make a home. The same families did not try again.

Now we began to question our responsibility to the larger community, the thousands who never came near us. What of the little ethnic pockets — "Roumanian Boulevard" (Brown Street), the large Russian Catholic community, the Polish section, the Marshall Street Jewish group, and later, the Puerto Rican colony? Neither the Guild nor its members could act for them. It was then we realized that our primary responsibility was not to those who came to the settlement — *our client* was the neighborhood, and everything we did must have a direct relationship to the welfare of the total neighborhood.

We began to move out into the area and new leadership joined in planning a new neighborhood. This broader program grew and by 1948, the Poplar Area was designated a division of the Philadelphia District of the Health and Welfare Council.

In the latter part of 1946, the chairman of the Guild Committee, opened the way for staff members of the Guild and the Self-Help Counseling Division of the AFSC to begin meeting to see if they could work together in urban redevelopment. In April, 1947, a memorandum was sent to the AFSC suggesting a housing rehabilitation project and in June the first meeting of the joint boards was held and it was agreed to go ahead.

A seven-man project committee, including the president of the Guild Adult Council was formed. The membership was now in action.

There followed a winter of continuous meetings, conferences and discussions. The Adult Council, with the help of the Philadelphia Housing Association, sponsored a series of Sunday Forums at the Guild and various ideas and possibilities were tested and new ideas were developed in these meetings.

In February, 1948, Area No. 10 was certified for redevelopment and the Community Worker of the Guild was spending a day a week at the City Planning Commission working on problems of occupancy and acquisition and studying suggested blocks for redevelopment. Agreements were reached on what kinds of work could be done by self-help. Trade Union representatives offered their full support to the proposed self-help aspects of redevelopment. The Extension Division of the School District of Philadelphia agreed to aid substantially in the Self-Help Workshop. Our architect had completed the first drawings and specifications and the Project Committee sent them out for estimates. Meetings were held with the City Planning Commission on total area plans. Parents and young people met at the Commission to discuss playground sites, changes in the transit system, and which streets should be closed off for better living.

The AFSC allocated money for a revolving fund and the chairman of the Project Committee began the long series of tedious conferences with the Federal Housing Administration to try to reach a formula which would allow us to proceed with safety. The features of mutual ownership, self-help and non-profit presented problems to the FHA. The joint efforts of all cooperating agencies are now prepared to present a plan for redevelopment as soon as the FHA agreement is reached.

Through all this the staff of the AFSC and the Guild were neither leaders nor planners, but rather enablers. We enabled board members to get together with neighbors and we enabled public and private agencies to be resources of the people by bringing them together in a common purpose. Credits have piled up for many people and agencies but they, in turn, will credit the effectiveness of neighborhood action and neighborhood leaders who believed it might happen.

This article shows a clearcut acceptance by a settlement of community organization responsibility — "our client was the neighborhood, and everything we did must have a direct relationship to the welfare of the total neighborhood."

Of special interest are the experimental approach and the step-by-step developments in trying to deal with this problem of housing. The number of different things that needed to be done and the number of organizations drawn into action may seem surprising, but both are frequent characteristics of community organization undertakings.

The catalytic nature of the community organization agency is highlighted. The agency secs its role not in "planning for" or "leading" or even "organizing" the community, but rather in "enabling" those who were concerned with the problem to get together and cooperate in seeking to solve it.

No attempt has been made to extend this account into a full-scale case record, bringing the story up to date; however, the reader may be interested in this note of what happened afterwards, written by the Director of Friends Neighborhood Guild in the summer of 1955.

The results from this program to date are: Area 10 became the first area of the city to be redeveloped which included razing an industrial slum to make a city playground of one block; demolition of all houses along the railroad for a green belt and parking area; demolition of other substandard houses for a well-planned public housing unit of 207 units which includes a small community center; and 167 units of State housing for middle income.

Friends Neighborhood Guild and the American Friends Service Committee purchased a square block of property for redevelopment. A mutual housing association was formed by which the block was tenant-owned on a cooperative basis. This allowed for a common court in the center of the block. The first 52 units have been completed and are occupied, and there are 45 units yet to be done. A club house which stood on one corner of the block has now been purchased by Friends Neighborhood Guild and turned into a community center.

The Board of Education has purchased all of the rest of the block around an elementary school which will become a playground. There has been physical replanning of the area with streets closed off and rerouting of surface transportation. However, these two Friends organizations are less concerned with the accomplishments than with the many problems they have raised and not solved and the rehabilitation yet to be done.[5]

COMMUNITY ORGANIZATION AND THE AGENCY EXECUTIVE

DIRECT-SERVICE AGENCIES use the community organization process at points where they are concerned with program development, standards, factfinding, community education, enlistment of support, and inter-agency relationships.[6]

In particular many of these community organization activities tend to attach to the job of the agency executive. In other words, *community organization is a normal part of the job of the executive of any consumer-service agency.*[7] Relationships with the board of directors or other superior administrative authority; the planning and development of program and policy; budgeting and participating in the obtaining of funds for operation; interpretation and public relations; and the broad area of "cooperative relationships," from the union of staff members and relations with other agencies through the community chest and council to the national agency — all these involve the use of the community organization process.

Nearly thirty years ago Paul L. Benjamin pointed out that "the social service executive is expected to be a jack-of-all-trades, to be all things to all men. He must be able to turn the trick of a good newspaper story, speak crisply and entertainingly before the Rotary Club, discuss profoundly the American Family before the Faculty Club, present clearly, in terse business terms a budget before the Budget Committee of the Community Chest, teach a group of his

[5] Letter to the author from Francis Bosworth, Executive Director, Friends Neighborhood Guild, August 1, 1955.
[6] Ray Johns and David F. DeMarche, authors of *Community Organization and Agency Responsibility* (New York, Association Press, 1951), found that 503 staff members of agencies maintained 5,524 inter-organization relationships. One nonsupervisory worker listed 57 such relationships! Relationships were classified as being concerned primarily with acquaintance, information, consultation, planning, or operating responsibility.
[7] Pierce Atwater, *Problems of Administration in Social Work* (Minneapolis, University of Minnesota Press, 1940); Margaret Logan Clark and Briseis Teall, *The Executive Director on the Job* (New York, Woman's Press, 1947); Ray Johns, *Executive Responsibility* (New York, Association Press, 1954); Harold Silver, "The Executive's Role in Administration," *Jewish Social Service Quarterly*, Vol. XXIV, December 1947, p. 193.

staff in case work or community organization, participate intelligently in countless committee meetings (we believe, somehow, that salvation comes through luncheons), answer a phone call at midnight (as I did several days ago) from a woman who wants to know what to do with a bed-ridden man in an alms-house in a neighboring county, be up-to-date in the literature of the field, be an active member of several "key" organizations, keep a competent staff recruited in spite of competition of higher salaries elsewhere and juggle a half-dozen committees successfully." [8]

In the same article Mr. Benjamin presents "One Day's Log." It appears that at least half the items — those which we have marked with an asterisk — involve some community organization content.

ONE DAY'S LOG

Morning

Read mail and dictated.

Interviewed man for vacancy on staff.

Conference with case supervisor concerning some organization policies.

Conference with supervisor of southern district about several difficult situations.

Made final arrangements for a new district office.

Went over with head janitor repairs needed in social service building.

*Conference with executive of the Children's Bureau.

*Finished work on the organization's budget for the next year.

Phone calls:

Had eight phone calls, including:

* 1. Executive of the Community Chest.
* 2. One of the secretaries of the Board of Trade concerning day nursery study.
* 3. Secretary of Social Service Exchange concerning plans for Christmas.

Noon

*Had lunch with chairman of the Case Work Council and discussed the employment situation with him.

---

[8] Paul L. Benjamin, "Executive Jack-of-all-trades," *Survey*, Vol. LXIII, February 15, 1930, pp. 577–578.

Afternoon and Early Evening

*Prepared a memorandum for a meeting with executive committee of community chest.

*Conference with representative of woman's club concerning a school study.

*Talked with executive of the Jewish Bureau for Social Service.

*Met with the director of the U.S. Employment Service and a committee to discuss an employment bureau.

*Went with a committee of the board to wait on executive committee of the chest to discuss the serious relief situation.

*Talked with the chairman of the building committee.

Benjamin Glassberg, in his diary of a relief administrator, indicates some of the community organization functions of a public welfare executive:

> The daily routine work of the organization involves, among other things, . . . hearing appeals of clients dissatisfied with their relief grants; meetings with other agency executives; addressing luncheon groups; and service on various public bodies. . . .
>
> The relief administrator will find a good deal of his time spent with the Board of Aldermen, the Mayor, or Board of Supervisors . . . The labor unions . . . may be fiercely antagonistic but both at times agree in feeling that the unemployed workers are not getting a square deal from the relief department, and countless delegations besiege the administrator to advise him of this. Citizens at large regularly write in concerning those who are receiving relief unjustly or of others who have unjustly been denied relief. Relief agencies throughout the country, anxious to know about this or that policy, frequently write for information. Just to make certain that the life of a relief administrator will not be a happy one, the union of the department employees will from time to time seek the opportunity of presenting its grievances, although these may largely be beyond the power of the administrator to correct.[9]

Mr. Glassberg's executive diary for a single month gives many specific illustrations of these general statements. The month begins with the executive's appearance before the Committee on County Institutions of the Board of County Supervisors; and some of the last

[9] Benjamin Glassberg, *Across the Desk of a Relief Administrator* (Chicago, American Public Welfare Association, 1938), pp. 7-8.

entries relate to a graphic illustration of "the cost of bad housing," the working out of a question of relationship with the District Attorney's office on cases of unmarried mothers, and interviews with the retiring and incoming presidents of the employees' union.

THE CHALLENGE OF COMMUNITY ORGANIZATION

THERE IS INFINITE VARIETY in the kinds of situations in which community organization may be used. No two situations are ever exactly the same.

Yet there is a generic process of community welfare organization which may be applied to different situations in varied settings; there is an underlying "unity in diversity."

The same methods are used over and over — conference, fact-finding, analysis, planning, organization, education,etc. The committee is a major instrument in use of these methods. These methods are used not in isolation but in all sorts of combinations. Some of the major skills of community organization relate to the selection and combination of methods and to timing in relation to action.

There are underlying principles of community organization which apply to any agency and any setting: needs should always determine service; voluntary cooperation is always to be desired; prevention is better than cure.

There is a rich fund of experience in regard to community organization to which a specific agency or worker may turn for help. To be sure, his own situation will be different in some ways from any other situation, but it will bear similarities to other communities, other agencies, other problems, which will probably make it responsive to a sound community organization approach.

QUESTIONS AND PROBLEMS

1. What agencies in your community are primarily concerned with community organization for social welfare? What additional agencies have an important coordinate or secondary function of community organization?

2. Prepare a descriptive report on a community organization agency — local, state, national, or international — using the Outline for a Descriptive Report on a Social Welfare Agency, in Appendix C, as far as it seems applicable.

3. For any large community it will be valuable to prepare an analytical chart of local agencies concerned primarily with community organization. The chart may include only federative agencies, that is, agencies which have

member organizations or affiliates, or it may include all agencies concerned primarily with community organization. The vertical columns may include any or all of the following items: name of agency; location; governmental or voluntary; year established; how originated; general functions; current major services or projects; territory served; federative or non-federative; if federative, how many member-agencies (total, operating agencies, others); basis for membership; organization (organizational and individual membership, board, departments, districts, etc.); size of professional staff; operating expenditures, last completed fiscal year (year, amount); amount distributed to member agencies; sources of support (community chest, member agencies, contributions, other); member of community welfare council, community chest, other local coordinating agency, state or national agency.

4. Assume a situation in an urban neighborhood similar to that pictured in Sidney Kingsley's play, *Dead End* (New York, Dramatists Play Service, 1938). Suppose a foundation was willing to give $1,000,000 "for the correction or improvement of conditions in the Dead End neighborhood." How could this money best be used?

SUGGESTIONS FOR READING

The Basic References contain a wealth of material on various types of community organization agencies. The following list contains some references on community organization in special fields or areas, some outside of social welfare, and on some of the most important community organization case materials.

COMMUNITY ORGANIZATION IN SPECIAL AREAS

Health

American Public Health Association, *Community Organization for Health Education* (Cambridge, Massachusetts, Technology Press, 1941, 120 pp.).

Gunn, Selskar M. and Platt, Philip S., *Voluntary Health Agencies: An Interpretive Study* (New York, Ronald Press, 1945, 364 pp.).

Rural Service

Hubbell, Helen C., "Come Into the Country," *Children,* Vol. I, January–February 1954, pp. 28–31. Community organization in a rural setting.

Sanderson and Polson, *Rural Community Organization.* (See bibliography, ch. 2.)

Other

American Association for Adult Education, *Community Education in Action: Report on Community Organization and Adult Education* (New York, American Association for Adult Education, 1948, 58 pp.).

Breckinridge, Elizabeth; Laue, Helen Graves; Little, Mary Hollis; and Manning, Helen. *Community Services for Older People.* The Chicago Plan. Prepared by the Community Project for the Aged of the Welfare Council of Metropolitan Chicago. (Chicago: Wilcox and Follet, 1952, 240 pp.)

Kraus, Hertha. "Community Planning for the Aged. Outline of a Working Hypothesis," *Journal of Gerontology*, Vol. 3, April 1948, pp. 129–40.

Seifert, Harvey, *The Church in Community Action* (New York, Abingdon-Cokesbury Press, 1952, 240 pp.).

White House Conference on Child Care and Protection (1930). *Organization for the Care of Handicapped Children* (New York, Century, 1932, 365 pp.). The section on "Educational Publicity for Promoting Social Work Programs" (pp. 209–44) relates to community organization by state welfare departments. No later comparable summary appears to exist.

THE EXECUTIVE AND COMMUNITY ORGANIZATION

Atwater, Pierce, *Problems of Administration in Social Work* (Minneapolis, University of Minnesota Press, 1940, 319 pp. OP). Includes chapters on public relations, fund-raising, and the executive and politics.

Johns, Ray, *Executive Responsibility: An Analysis of Executive Responsibilities in the Work of Voluntary, Community Social Welfare Organizations* (New York, Association Press, 1954, 258 pp.). Several chapters relate to various aspects of community organization.

Street, Elwood, *A Handbook for Social Agency Administration* (New York, Harper, 1947, 434 pp.). Includes chapters on committees, public relations, finances, etc.

CASE MATERIALS ON COMMUNITY ORGANIZATION

Alinsky, Saul D., *Reveille for Radicals* (Chicago, University of Chicago Press, 1946, 228 pp.). An account of certain local "people's organizations," with primarily lay, resident direction and participation.

COMMUNITY ORGANIZATION MONOGRAPHS. Published for the Association for the Study of Community Organization by Association Press, New York; Nos. 1–3 published in 1949, are community organization case records.

Platt, Clarice C. and Dunham, Arthur, *Community Organization for Child Welfare in Carver County*. (#1; 54 pp. OP)

Gordon, Spencer R., *The Reorganization of the Winston County Unemployment Relief Board*. (#2; 48 pp.)

Dunham, Arthur, *Pennsylvania's Ten Year Program for Child Welfare*. (#3; 38 pp.)

Council on Social Work Education. Teaching materials (case records) in community organization. Several such records have been published; some of them are specifically restricted to use in graduate schools of social work. (New York, The Council.)

Goodall, Frances, *A Narrative of Process in Social Welfare Organization: Step by Step through a Project in Community Planning* (St. Louis, Washington University, George Warren Brown School of Social Work, 1948, 116 pp.). A community organization process record.

McKee, Elmore M., *The People Act* (New York, Harper, 1955, 269 pp.).

Popular case stories "of how Americans are coming together to deal with their community problems."

Murray, Clyde E. *et al., Group Work in Community Life.* (See bibliography, ch. 5.)

Ogden, Jean and Ogden, Jess, *Small Communities in Action* (New York, Harper, 1946, 244 pp.).

Pettit, Walter W., *Case Studies in Community Organization* (New York, Century, 1928, 345 pp., OP). A pioneer volume of community organization case records.

Phillips, Wilbur C., *Adventuring for Democracy.* (See bibliography, ch. 7.)

9.

SOCIAL SERVICE EXCHANGES

THE SOCIAL SERVICE EXCHANGE is a community clearing house through which social welfare agencies dealing with families and individuals are enabled to work together for the best interests of those whom they seek to help. The exchange maintains an alphabetical card index of the names of families and individuals known to the social welfare agencies of the community as clients or applicants.[1]

The exchange's method of operation is extremely simple. When a social agency receives a new application for some form of social service for a family or individual, the agency can at once "inquire" of the social service exchange regarding the family and learn what other organizations are interested or have been interested in the family. The new agency is then in a position to consult with these other organizations, according to the nature of the circumstances. It may gain helpful insights through these consultations; and if several agencies are actively seeking to serve the family, they are enabled to act cooperatively, with mutual understanding, rather than in isolation or even in conflict with each other's plans and objectives.

The exchange is a community organization agency, although it is concerned with the facilitation of casework or individualized practice. The primary justification of the exchange, as with any other community organization agency, is that it promotes better service to consumers or clients. From the standpoint of the agency, the exchange is a community resource that enables the agency to operate with greater

[1] For other definitions see Kenneth I. Williams, "Social Service Exchanges," SWYB, 1957, p. 547; *Handbook on Social Service Exchange, 1946* (New York, Community Chests and Councils, 1940), p. 1.

efficiency and effectiveness. From the standpoint of the community's total social welfare pattern, the exchange is a device for helping agencies achieve better teamwork.

HISTORICAL DEVELOPMENTS

The social service exchange was the first local agency primarily concerned with community organization to be established in a considerable number of communities in the United States. The first exchange, the Boston Registration Bureau, founded in 1876, sought to establish a central record of families receiving relief and the amount they received. The gradual extension of the service to other agencies and a growing sense of the confidentiality of record material transformed the organization by 1906 into a clearing house operating a card index and handling identifying information only. This is the pattern which has been followed in the development of other social service exchanges. Other large cities followed the lead of Boston, and exchanges were established, usually in connection with the charity organization societies. Later a trend toward cooperative management developed, and many exchanges were organized under or transferred to the auspices of community welfare councils or community chests. The terms "social service exchange" and "social service index" tended to replace "registration bureau" and "confidential exchange," with their connotations of formalism and secrecy.

An American Association of Social Service Exchanges existed from 1919 to 1925, when it was succeeded by a National Social Service Exchange Committee in Community Chests and Councils.

During the depression of the 1930's the exchange proved an important resource, and some exchanges were established under the auspices of public welfare agencies. In recent years many exchanges have extended their areas of service, and some statewide plans for exchange service have been put into effect.

Of the 220 exchanges in operation in April 1956, 150 or 68% operated under the auspices of councils, chests, or united funds; 44 were under public welfare agencies; 7 were connected with family service agencies; and 19 were independently organized.[2] While some exchanges are financed entirely by a chest or governmental agency, the preferred method of support is by payments from the member agencies, prorated on the basis of use.

[2] Williams, *loc. cit.,* p. 549.

BASIC PRINCIPLES

There are certain basic principles underlying the social service exchange; a grasp of these is necessary to the understanding of it or to the intelligent use of its service.

1. **The exchange handles only "identifying information."** The inquiring agency gives only such information as the names, addresses, and ages of the members of the family. This is just enough to identify that particular family in the card index which may be so large as to contain several hundred families with the same surname.

2. **Inquiring about a person, or including his name in the exchange index, does not imply the casting of any "stigma" on him.** The exchange is not a "charity list." Even if it were an index of recipients of financial assistance, this would imply no stigma. But it is not this. The exchange is used by the most varied types of social and health agencies. During the First and Second World Wars, many American Red Cross home service sections inquired of social service exchanges, as a matter of course, on families under their care. The Red Cross did this in order to give the most effective service to these families. No one would be likely to suggest that this process cast any stigma upon these families.

It has also been an accepted policy of many progressive child-placing agencies to inquire of the exchange about families who offer their homes as foster homes for wards of the agencies, or who apply as prospective adoptive parents. The purpose of the agency's inquiry is to enable two child-placing agencies to keep clear of each other's active foster homes, to take advantage of each other's studies on rejected homes, and to avoid placing a child in a home where the family may be known to the children's protective agency or juvenile court as unfit to have children in their care. Of course, the persons who act as foster parents are giving rather than receiving social service, and many of them may be among the leaders of the community. If their names are included in the exchange index it is an additional indication that inclusion in the index is no reflection upon anyone.

3. **The records of the exchange are confidential, and the use of it is restricted to agencies desirous of cooperating to promote the welfare of the client.** Membership in the exchange is usually restricted to social and health agencies which maintain records and have standards of performance that will safeguard the handling of confidential information. Use of the exchange is not ordinarily permitted

to credit bureaus, collection agencies, newspapers, lawyers, detectives, business firms (including, usually, their personnel or welfare departments), or individuals, or, in most cases, to law enforcement or public prosecuting agencies. Where one of these organizations or an individual appears to have a sincere interest in the welfare of the client, the exchange can refer the organization to one of the regular member agencies.

Access to the files of a well-conducted exchange is rigidly limited to the staff, and it is expected that they are properly trained to respect the confidential nature of the information which they handle. No one is at liberty to run through the index. Thus, when a card is filed in the index — especially if it is a large one — the name is, to all intents and purposes, buried and lost, until another inquiry is made regarding that particular family.

4. The value of the exchange depends upon adequate use of it by social welfare agencies, in view of their respective functions and services.

Each agency should determine its policy in respect to use of the exchange, and clearing should be complete within the terms of that policy. Formerly it was assumed that most case working agencies should follow the policy of 100 per cent registration on all accepted cases. Actually, there was probably some selection in most fields, and in recent years the trend has been toward increasingly selective clearing.

5. Inquiry of the exchange should be made at the beginning of the agency's contact with the client. That is, cases should be cleared either at the time of application or immediately following the intake interview.

6. The practical usefulness of the exchange's service depends upon the agency's following up the reports of the exchange by consulting, planning, and working with other agencies.

Inquiry of the exchange and receiving the report are merely the first steps. Following up these first steps is the only way to translate the circulation of slips of paper into sound service and active teamwork with other agencies in behalf of the client. However, the decision as to which agencies shall be followed up and what use shall be made of the information received depends upon the individual situation.

EXCHANGE EQUIPMENT

The daily operations of the social service exchange center about its basic piece of equipment, the Name Index. This is an alphabetical card index of families about whom inquiries have been received.

Two factors have conditioned the development and adoption of filing systems in the social service exchange. The first is the fact that the same name may be reported under many variant spellings: such as Parrone, Pironi, Pirroni, Perrone, Porrone, Peron; Stuart, Stewart, Steward; and so on. The second factor is that the whole effectiveness of the exchange's service depends upon its ability to identify a family with certainty, if the name is in the index — even if it is there under a variant spelling.

In view of these two factors, only the smallest exchanges are likely to find the straight alphabetical system of filing satisfactory. This system may be applicable to exchanges with perhaps 5000 cards or less, although even then a good deal of cross-referencing of variant spellings is likely to be involved.

To meet the difficulties of the straight alphabetic system, most exchanges have turned to one of two types of alphabetic-phonetic systems. The older one, known as the Zone or Group System, seeks to file together under the most common spelling, names which are similar. Thus, the names Smythe, Smyth, Schmidt, Schmitt, Schmitz might all be cross-referenced to and filed as Smith. This system was highly developed by the Boston Central Index. The other system, the Soundex, which is sold by a commercial company, uses an ingenious method, based upon phonetic laws, by which all names are "coded" and filed according to the basic consonant sounds. For example, such names as Belanski, Belansky, Bolensky, Billinski, and many other variations will all be filed in one group, B-lmc, or, to use the numerical equivalent, B-452.[3] Thus, Sarah Belanski and Sarah Bolensky will be brought together in one place in the index. The Soundex brings together automatically the great majority of variant spellings which are

[3] In filing under the Soundex system, one leaves the initial letter as is, then eliminates a, e, i, o, u, h, w, and y and codes the remaining consonants by six basic sounds made by the human voice:

b = b — f — p — v	1	l = l	4
c = c — q — j — k — g — s — x — z	2	m = m — n	5
d = d — t	3	r = r	6

Two consonants which code to the same consonant are consolidated: that is, sk = c. Thus Belanski becomes B-lmc or B-452.

likely to be encountered. This system is used in most larger exchanges. In some cases the basic phonetic system of the Soundex is supplemented by such additional "family groups" of names as may seem necessary in order to catch variations in spelling not brought together by the phonetic code.

Other problems of filing in the Name Index relate to the question of whether to file the family Name Card primarily by the man's or woman's first name, in cases where both names are given, and the problem of bringing together under one first name the major foreign variants and nicknames. Thus, Mary may be used as the name for filing, whether the name on the inquiry is reported in that form or as Mae, May, Mamie, Mame, Mayme, Maria, Marie, etc.

In addition to the Name Index, the exchange requires a secondary geographical index known as the Street or Address Index. The Street Index contains the same names as are in the Name Index, but arranges these names *geographically,* by street and number, instead of alphabetically. On one card, for a single street and number, will be listed all the families inquired about at that address. (Only the surname of the family and the man's and woman's first names are usually entered.)

Experience indicates that if all inquiries are searched in the Street Index as well as the Name Index, many variant spellings and related families will be identified which would never be discovered through the Name Index alone, even if equipped with a phonetic filing system. The Street Index is a necessary adjunct to the Name Index, and a basic part of the exchange's equipment.

THE OPERATION OF THE EXCHANGE

The two basic record forms of the exchange are the Name Card, the master card in the Name Index, and the Inquiry Blank used by the agency. Samples of these forms follow. These are reproduced from the *Handbook on Social Service Exchange,* 1946.

The basic unit of operation of the exchange is the *inquiry.* This is a "clearing" (search of the exchange indexes) in which an agency requests a report of all agencies which have made previous inquiries on the family. In the case of a "recorded inquiry" or registration, which is the usual type, the inquiry is entered in the exchange indexes.

<table>
<tr><td colspan="2">SURNAME</td><td>CASE NUMBER</td></tr>
<tr><td colspan="2">Johnson</td><td>1234</td></tr>
</table>

SURNAME		CASE NUMBER
Johnson		1234

MAN'S FIRST NAME	OCCUPATION	BORN MO. DAY YR.
Thomas		1-6-14

WOMAN'S FIRST NAME	MAIDEN NAME	MO. DAY YR.
Margaret	Jenkins	3-15-16

OTHER MARRIAGES	COLOR
	W

ALIAS

Johns, Ted

ADDRESS

PREVIOUS ADDRESSES

CHILDREN'S NAMES	BORN MO. DAY YR.	CHILDREN'S NAMES	BORN MO. DAY YR.
Thomas	6-18-34		
George	5-20-36		
Margaret	9-6-38		

RELATIVES	ADDRESSES	RELATIONSHIP
Jenkins, Geo.&Julia	1322 South St.	P-2

VARIATIONS SPELLING	NO RECORD

INQUIRING AGENCY	DATE
FS	3-20-40

SOCIAL SERVICE EXCHANGE

300 Main Street   Middletown, U.S.A.

FIGURE 2

INQUIRY BLANK—SOCIAL SERVICE EXCHANGE

This form is used by the agency in making an inquiry of the exchange. It is filled out in duplicate and mailed to the exchange. The exchange enters its report on the original blank—either the name of one or more previously inquiring agencies or a report of "no record" or "not identified"—and mails it back to the inquiring agency. The duplicate blank is retained by the exchange, and may be used as an "out" marker for the Name Card while the latter is out of file.

SURNAME	#1	MAN'S		W	MO. DAY YR.
1. Johnson		Thomas			1-6-14

MAIDEN NAME		WOMAN'S			
2. Jenkins		Margaret			3-15-16

ALIAS	DATE	ADDRESS
Johns, Ted	'36	221 Main

OTHER MARRIAGES		
	'38	116 Knox
Josephine (Shields)	'40	221 Main
AnoW		

OTHER CROSS REFERENCES		
Fulton, Geo. XR		

	CHILDREN	MO. DAY YR.
3	Thomas	6-18-34
4	George	5-20-36
5	Margaret	9-6-38
6		
7		
8		
9		
10		
11		
12		

RELATIVES, ETC.	ADDRESS	KIN	TO
Johnson, Ralph&Dorothy (Brown)		P	1
Jenkins, George&Julia		P	2
Jenkins, Catherine, Middleton, Pa.		Rel.	

VARIATIONS

DATE	AGENCIES	DATE	AGENCIES
8-16-36	PhDPA		
4-8-38	PhDPA C (2)		
3-20-40	FS		
5-1-42	PhDPA		

FIGURE 3

NAME CARD—SOCIAL SERVICE EXCHANGE

This is the permanent card retained by the exchange for each family listed in the Name Index. It contains practically the same items of information as the Inquiry Blank, with the addition of the names of agencies which have inquired about this family and the dates of inquiries.

THE ROUTING OF AN INQUIRY

When a registration is received by the exchange, it normally passes through a number of steps. The following is an example of typical routing.

1. *Receiving.* The exchange receives the inquiry by mail, telephone, or messenger.

2. *Searching.* The inquiry is searched in the Street Index (usually first) and Name Index. The name may be "identified" or there may be "no record." The duplicate of the Inquiry Blank is entered in the Name Index; if there is a Name Card in file for the family it is removed and sent forward with the original Inquiry Blank for

3. *Reporting.* The inquiry is reported back to the agency, by mail, telephone, or messenger.

4. *Notifications* are typed and sent to agencies which have previously inquired about the family, if this is the policy of the exchange and the agencies in question.

Formerly, it was standard practice in the case of each new registration for an exchange to send notifications to all agencies which had previously registered that family. Theoretically, this made it unnecessary for an agency to inquire more than once about the same family. However, as indexes grew larger, the notification system involved a constantly increasing volume of paper work, much of which seemed of doubtful value. Current practice is varied and more flexible. Policy in regard to notification is worked out by the exchange and the various member-agencies; notifications may be sent only to those agencies which request this service, or perhaps sent only for limited periods of time after the original registrations. If an agency does *not* receive notifications, or if the established notification period has expired, the agency must reinquire (reregister) if a closed case again becomes active, and if the agency wishes to be brought up to date concerning the registrations of other agencies.

5. *Recording.* Entries are typed on the Name Card and, if there is a new address, on the Street Card. If the name was not previously in the index, new cards are typed.

6. *Filing.* The Name and Street Cards are refiled in the Name and Street Indexes, respectively.

7. *Statistics* are recorded, through counting and posting the pertinent items of information.

In addition to its basic business of clearing registrations or recorded inquiries, the exchange may handle a number of other types of clearings. These may include: (1) a recorded reinquiry (reregistration), (2) an inquiry for "information only," which is not recorded in the exchange indexes (a type of inquiry occasionally justified by circumstances); (3) a "relative inquiry" on a relative of a specified family or individual; (4) additional information, supplying additional or corrected identifying data on a family or individual inquired about previously; and (5) a cancellation or deletion from the exchange's records of a previous registration.[4]

SOCIAL CASEWORK AND THE EXCHANGE

HAS THE SOCIAL SERVICE EXCHANGE outlived its usefulness? This is a question that has been raised in recent years.

The number of exchanges in the United States and Canada declined from 320 in 1946 to 220 in 1956. During the five years 1951–1955, sixty-two exchanges were discontinued.[5] These liquidations of exchanges were apparently based upon marked decline in their use by agencies, united with a lack of conviction on the part of many agencies as to the usefulness of the exchange. One social worker, Morton I. Teicher, has attacked the exchange as being "unethical and undemocratic" and has proposed that it be abolished. He has raised, particularly, two questions.

1. In the course of the helping relationship, how can the worker introduce and make sound use of information, his possession of which is not known to the client?

2. Can a worker sustain a helping relationship when his conceptions of the situation are constantly colored by data about the client which the client has not shared directly and which, so far as the client knows, has not obtruded into the situation?

This article, proposing the abolition of the exchange, elicited some support and a good deal of vigorous dissent.[6]

The exchange grew out of the charity organization movement. In the casework of that day, emphasis was on avoidance of duplication in relief-giving and on the collection of a large volume of information about the client, both from the client himself and from collateral

[4] *Handbook on Social Service Exchange*, p. 27.
[5] Williams, *loc. cit.*, p. 550.
[6] Morton I. Teicher, "Let's Abolish the Social Service Exchange," *Social Work Journal*, Vol. XXXIII, January 1952, pp. 28–31. See also letters of comment, *ibid.*, April 1952 (pp. 105–110) and July 1952 (pp. 161–162).

sources — public records, relatives, employers, and so on. Today in many communities all forms of public assistance are administered by one integrated public welfare agency. Moreover, in modern casework primary emphasis is laid upon psychological factors and emphasis upon the development of a client-worker relationship. Some caseworkers today question whether information about another agency's contact can be of value unless such information comes from the client himself.

Allied to this is the question as to whether the client's name should be cleared in the exchange without his knowledge and consent. There is, of course, no secrecy about the existence of the exchange. The practical problems of gaining the client's consent to the use of the exchange center about the questions of the actual procedure to be followed; whether or not a person applying for help will be helped at the point of intake by an interpretation of a clearing house procedure; and whether, if he does consent, he will have been able to weigh the question thoughtfully or whether his consent may be perfunctory or dictated by a fear of the loss of a needed service if he should refuse.

The two questions here raised are far from being finally settled, and they merit much more exploration and discussion. Several recent thoughtful discussions by caseworkers, as well as action in certain cities, tend to confirm the historic values of the exchange, although stressing the need for more selective action rather than formalistic routine; and these discussions at least raise questions as to the need for or desirability of routinely securing the client's consent before using the exchange.[7]

A defense of the exchange and a discussion of its relation to social work today is found in a recent article by Stephen L. Angell and Frank T. Greving.[8]

The authors believe that the exchange can and should fit into the social work practice of today. They raise the basic question as to whether or not it is important that social welfare agencies work together instead of as isolated entities. They see the exchange as a tool for facilitating the helping process by making possible effective inter-agency communication. They believe there is some danger of an over-identification of casework with the goals and methods of

[7] Helen H. Perlman, "The Caseworker's Use of Collateral Information," NCSW, *Social Welfare Forum*, 1951, pp. 190–205. Sylvia Glasner, *New Ideas in Inter-Agency Communication: A Study of Multiple Registrations* (Philadelphia, Philadelphia-Camden Social Service Exchange, 1953). See also Williams, *loc. cit.*, bibliography.

[8] Stephen L. Angell and Frank T. Greving, "A New Look at the Social Service Exchange," *Social Work Journal*, Vol. XXXVI, January 1955, pp. 13–17.

psychiatry; of a trend for casework to become "an isolated counseling service," with a removal from the community's concern for broad social problems. They suggest that, if this happens, casework agencies will cease to be community agencies in the meaning within which they seek and obtain community support.

These authors suggest that the exchange may become a more dynamic force if agencies accept the full implication of their roles in social service, and if the exchange becomes more effectively related to councils in community welfare planning. They believe also that the exchange has possibilities as a medium for research, and that it could play a vital part in helping agencies locate and serve the "hard core" group of families with difficult, multiple and inter-related problems.

The Advisory Committee on Social Service Exchange of United Community Funds and Councils of America adopted a statement in 1955 expressing their continued support of the exchange, unless and until it becomes clear that it is no longer necessary under present conditions of social work practice. The Committee advocated objective research to determine whether (1) the exchange is needed in the typical urban community, (2) whether it is needed in certain types of communities only, or (3) whether it is no longer necessary. A special research committee under UCFC is proceeding with research along the lines of these suggestions. It has developed a method for studying the value or lack of value of the exchange, and this is being tested in a number of communities.[9] The next few years may be decisive in determining whether or not the social service exchange shall continue as a means of inter-agency communication and an adjunct to casework practice and to community organization.

QUESTIONS AND PROBLEMS

1. Try to arrange to visit a social service exchange.

2. Make a report on an exchange, considering such points as the following: organization; staff; membership requirements; what use by non-members; current budget; how supported; basis for payments by agencies; Name Index, size of card, filing system, estimated cards in index; is there a Street Index; procedure for handling an inquiry; use of telephone inquiries; what agencies use exchange most and on what basis (all cases? selective?); exchange policy regarding notifications, reregistrations, cancellations; interval between agency's sending of mail inquiry and receipt of reply; volume of work on a typical day — total clearings, recorded inquiries (registrations), identifications, notifications.

[9] Williams, *loc. cit.*, pp. 551–552.

3. What do you think of the validity of the exchange's existence and operation, from the standpoint of (a) democracy in social work practice; (b) sound casework practice; (c) sound community organization? Is there any conflict among these three?

4. Find out the policies and practice of a particular agency regarding its use of the exchange.

5. Assume that a young business man, a new member of the board of your agency, is reviewing the agency's budget. He asks, "What is this social service exchange, and why do we pay $200 a year to it?" Try to give him a brief, clear, simple, and helpful answer.

SUGGESTIONS FOR READING

The article on the social service exchange in the 1957 *Social Work Year Book* is an excellent brief introduction to the subject.

Angell, Stephen L., *A Report and Commentary on Minimum Standards for Operation of a Social Service Exchange* (New York, Community Chests and Councils of America, Social Service Exchange Bulletin 58, 1954, 6 pp.).

Angell, Stephen L. and Greving, Frank T., "A New Look at the Social Service Exchange" (*Social Work Journal*, Vol. XXXVI, January 1955, pp. 13–17). A valuable recent discussion of the exchange and its values and possibilities.

Community Chests and Councils of America. *Handbook on Social Service Exchange,* 1946 (New York, 1946, 42 pp.). A technical guide to the organization and operation of an exchange.

———— *Minimum Standards for the Operation of a Social Service Exchange* (Social Service Exchange Bulletin 57, New York, 1954, 10 pp.).

King, Edith Shatto, *The Social Service Exchange.* (Washington, Federal Security Agency, Social Security Board, Bureau Circular 16; 1943, 102 pp.). Somewhat out of date, but the most substantial discussion of the exchange and its problems thus far published.

Perlman, Helen H., "The Caseworker's Use of Collateral Information" (NCSW, *Social Welfare Forum,* 1951, pp. 190–205). A discussion of the use of the social service exchange.

Simcox, Beatrice R., *The Social Service Exchange. I. Its Function and Operation. II. Its Use in Casework.* Reprinted from *Journal of Social Casework* (New York, Family Service Association of America, 1947, 17 pp.).

Teicher, Morton I., "Let's Abolish the Social Service Exchange" (*Social Work Journal,* Vol. XXXIII, January 1952, pp. 28–31. See also letters of comment, *ibid.,* April 1952, pp. 105–110, and July 1952, pp. 161–162). The writer sums up the arguments for abolishing the exchange, in the light of modern casework practice.

Towle, Charlotte, "The Client's Rights and the Use of the Social Service Exchange" (*Social Service Review,* Vol. XXIII, March 1949, pp. 15–20).

IO.

COMMUNITY WELFARE COUNCILS

_____

WHAT IS A COMMUNITY WELFARE COUNCIL?

MORE THAN ANY OTHER ONE AGENCY, the community welfare council, or council of social agencies, typifies the workings of the process of community organization. Its very form is federative; its existence symbolizes the desire for cooperation. The council is concerned with all of the functions of community organization. Its activities represent the range of problems and the variety of methods with which the process of community organization is concerned. Moreover, the council operates on the local or community level; it usually includes most governmental and voluntary consumer-service agencies; and it is closer to their problems and interests than is any other community organization agency.

A community welfare council may be defined as *a federation or association of health and welfare agencies, and often also of civic organizations and individuals, in a local community; it is concerned with coordination of effort and joint planning and action, to the end that the social welfare needs of the community may be met as adequately and effectively as possible.*[1]

The awkwardness of this definition is due to the fact that it attempts to define a type of organization that is in transition. Traditionally, the "council of social agencies" has been just that — a council of health and welfare agencies. In smaller communities the council has often

[1] For other descriptive statements regarding community welfare councils, see: *Teamwork in Our Town: Through a Community Welfare Council* (New York, Community Chests and Councils of America, cited hereafter as CCC, rev. ed., 1954); Robert H. MacRae, "Community Welfare Councils," SWYB, 1957, pp. 185–191.

included civic organizations (chamber of commerce, labor unions, council of churches, service clubs, women's clubs, veterans' organizations) as well as operating agencies giving day-by-day social welfare services. Most councils also have had a few delegates-at-large or individual members. More recent thinking has suggested the name "community welfare council" to indicate an organization of agencies *and* citizens.

These elements are basic in respect to the community welfare council:

1. It represents citizens and social welfare agencies, laymen and social workers and it includes both governmental and voluntary agencies.

2. As far as the agencies are concerned, the council is a federation in which the agencies are represented by officially appointed delegates.

3. The council normally operates in a local community, whether this is conceived of as a large or small city, a county, or a metropolitan area which may embrace several adjoining counties.

4. The council's job is "health and welfare planning," or "overall community welfare organization." It is concerned with bringing about an adjustment between social welfare needs and resources in the community, or, as one council has stated it, effecting improvement in the quantity, quality, and arrangement of public and private health and welfare services in the community.

HISTORICAL DEVELOPMENTS

The beginning of the council movement as we know it today dates from 1908 when an Associated Charities, to be financed by a number of social agencies, was organized in Pittsburgh together with a "central council." There was an interlocking relationship between the Associated Charities and the council which was later terminated.[2]

Councils were organized in several other cities within the next few years. In the years following World War I, as the war chests became "peacetime chests" and the community chest movement rapidly gathered momentum, it became more and more common for chests and councils to be organized as more or less coordinate departments of "welfare federations," or for them to have other organizational or close working relationships.

By 1929, councils were established in most large cities and many smaller communities. In community after community, the council, in

[2] Watson, *Charity Organization Movement in the United States,* pp. 425–426.

the early thirties, found itself in a position of leadership or struggling to devise means for coping with the avalanche of unemployment and need. This was true particularly of the early depression years before the outlines of a real federal program for unemployment relief had emerged. Again, during World War II, councils performed vital services in coordination and health and welfare planning in local communities which found themselves grappling with new and almost overwhelming wartime problems. Various plans of cooperation were worked out between councils and Offices of Civilian Defense, in different communities.

There are some 500 community welfare councils in the United States today; [3] this includes practically all cities of over 100,000 population. Within the last few years councils and their programs and accomplishments have been sharply challenged in several communities; in some cases there have been conflicts between chests and councils. In some communities "united funds" have developed as broadened joint financing bodies, and structural reorganizations of chests and councils have taken place.

The full significance of these developments is not yet clear. At present the community welfare council is unquestionably the most firmly established and widely accepted local agency for broad health and welfare planning. At the same time the council is perhaps more nearly on trial today than at any time in the last twenty years; and it is under the necessity of demonstrating beyond question the basic contributions which it has made and is capable of making to the life of American communities.

THE COUNCIL'S FUNCTIONS

An active council does so many different things that it is hard to pick out its main patterns of activity. The total effect of a council seems highly miscellaneous if not disorderly, in comparison with the well-marked activities of a casework or group work agency or even a community chest.

The best clues to the understanding of the council and its activities may be found in two things: its basic *functions* and the kind of *organization units* through which it works. Community welfare councils perform seven fairly definite and well-marked functions.[4]

[3] *Teamwork in Our Town* (1954), p. 7.
[4] For other analyses of council functions and activities, see *Teamwork in Our Town* (1954), pp. 10–13; MacRae, "Community Welfare Councils," SWYB, 1957, pp. 186–187.

1. The council engages in *factfinding*, including collection and compilation of data and special studies. (This will be discussed later, in connection with the council's research service.)

2. The council serves as a *community clearing house* for social welfare experience and thinking — a center for conference, *joint planning and action*, coordination, and program development. This clearing house function may seem intangible, but it is highly important. *The council serves as a focus and center for social welfare in the community.* The council provides continuous machinery for conferring, planning together, and acting in concert. If there were no council it would be necessary to set up *ad hoc* machinery for each instance in which cooperative planning or action was needed. This would be slow and cumbersome, especially in a large city.

Specific examples of this function would include the following: A group of agencies in a particular functional field (health or recreation, for instance) meet together regularly, discuss their common problems, and try to work out cooperative solutions. . . . The casework and group work agencies work out a plan for making referrals, so that all of them may make better use of all the services available. . . . Through the council, both agencies and lay groups express the need for a child guidance clinic in the community. Sentiment is mobilized and plans are made for the organization and financing of the clinic. . . . The council sponsors a new adoption bill, upon which practically all of the family and children's agencies are agreed.

3. Councils administer *common services*. The social service exchange, information and referral service, and volunteer bureau are examples of such services. These are not direct consumer-services, but services to agencies or to the general public. The council is not a consumer-service agency, but a common service of the type mentioned above may appropriately be administered by the council where there is general agreement that it is better to have it organized under cooperative auspices than under the auspices of a specific agency.

4. The council provides *consultation and assistance* to individual agencies and organizations. The agency or the community group with a problem that involves a need for social services, or a problem relating to program, territorial scope, standards, service policies, or community relationships may turn to the council for consultation. This is largely a service by the council staff, although at times there may be group consultation from a division or committee of the council.

Specific illustrations would include: A council committee and staff member help two children's institutions to work out a merger. . . . The council, at the request of a settlement, helps the settlement to make a self-survey and to use the results in making major changes in its program.

5. Councils may participate in *joint budgeting,* through the community chests, and they work in close *cooperation with* financial federations and local governmental *appropriating bodies.* Joint budgeting is a basic function of a community chest, but the council should have a part in this budgeting process, since it involves social welfare planning and the council is the best central depository of knowledge about local social welfare needs and possibilities. The council should also follow closely the budgeting and financing of local public welfare services, and should be available to serve in an advisory capacity to public welfare agencies and public appropriating bodies.

6. The council *promotes public understanding* of social welfare needs, objectives, services, and standards. This will be discussed later, in connection with the council's public relations service.

7. The council may *promote or develop local community organization* in urban districts and neighborhoods and in suburban units, and develop relationships between local geographical units and the community welfare council. Community organization through local units is based on the fact that health and welfare planning cannot effectively be done wholesale for a large city.

COUNCIL ORGANIZATION

The council's functions are carried out through certain special types of operating units. There are wide variations in the organization of individual councils, but the following major elements are commonly found in councils, especially in larger cities: (1) membership; (2) delegate body; (3) board of directors; (4) operating units: functional divisions; departments administering common services; geographical units; units carrying on special temporary direct-service demonstrations (sometimes found under council auspices); committees; (5) executive and staff.

The simplified organization chart (Figure 4) depicts the more or less typical organization of a large-city community welfare council. The chart makes no attempt to include every aspect of the council's structure. It does not show administrative departments (accounting, office management, and so on), staff organization, district or neighborhood councils, divisional committees, or organizational relationships of the council to the community chest.

A simpler organization structure is desirable in smaller commu-

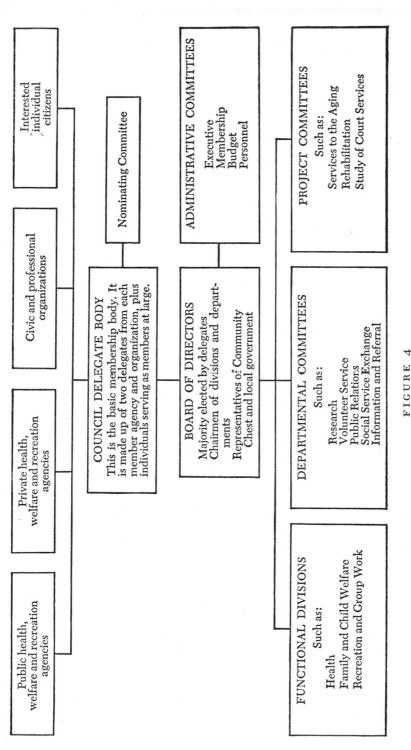

FIGURE 4

ORGANIZATION CHART FOR A TYPICAL COMMUNITY WELFARE COUNCIL.

From "Teamwork in Our Town" (1954), p. 14

The chart contains the following boxes and text:

Public health, welfare and recreation agencies

Private health, welfare and recreation agencies

Civic and professional organizations

Interested individual citizens

COUNCIL DELEGATE BODY
This is the basic membership body. It is made up of two delegates from each member agency and organization, plus individuals serving as members at large.

Nominating Committee

BOARD OF DIRECTORS
Majority elected by delegates
Chairmen of divisions and departments
Representatives of Community Chest and local government

ADMINISTRATIVE COMMITTEES
Executive
Membership
Budget
Personnel

FUNCTIONAL DIVISIONS
Such as:
Health
Family and Child Welfare
Recreation and Group Work

DEPARTMENTAL COMMITTEES
Such as:
Research
Volunteer Service
Public Relations
Social Service Exchange
Information and Referral

PROJECT COMMITTEES
Such as:
Services to the Aging
Rehabilitation
Study of Court Services

nities. For example, a small council may have short-term, *ad hoc* committees, instead of standing functional divisions; and some of the common services may be functions of the single council executive rather than departments.

MEMBERSHIP

Most councils are probably still primarily federations of agencies. Member-agencies which carry on operating programs of health and welfare services are of three kinds from the standpoint of their financial support: governmental agencies, voluntary agencies which are members of the community chest, and voluntary agencies which are not members of the chest. Each agency is usually represented by two delegates — one a member of the board of directors or other policy-determining body and the other the executive. In smaller communities particularly, the council may include not only operating agencies in the field of social welfare but also civic organizations which have an interest in social service. In addition it is common practice for the council to have some *ex officio* members (such as the mayor, superintendent of schools, etc.) and also a certain number of citizens-at-large as individual members.

More recent thinking about the council represents a different approach to the problem. The newer philosophy recognizes that *health and welfare planning concerns not only the existing social welfare agencies but also taxpayers and contributors, consumers, and the general public.* Not only should these various interests be represented as a matter of democratic procedure but there are also matters of social strategy involved. When major changes in existing welfare patterns are under consideration, it is desirable to have opinions of those who are detached from existing institutional programs as well as those who have the special knowledge that goes with the direction or operation of these programs. It is neither reasonable nor equitable to lay the full weight of health and welfare planning upon existing operating agencies. Moreover, the support and participation of those who provide funds and those who use services is needed, if there is to be community acceptance of plans and programs.

In the council's membership meetings each agency delegate and each individual member normally has one vote. The agency must invest its delegates with fairly broad discretionary powers, otherwise the necessity of referring every decision back for approval by the member agencies will render the council largely impotent.

There is no accepted formula as to the ratio between agency delegates and individual members. In a council where there are 50 agencies, there would be 100 agency delegates. The older type of council would probably not have more than 10 or 12 individual members. For the newer type of council, with the same number of agencies, the individual members should probably be not less than 30, and they might range from 50 to 100. It is not especially important that the voting strength of agency delegates and individual members should be equal; the important thing is that there should be substantial representation of the public in addition to the agencies. The individual members should give informal representation to various sections of the community, and to various interest groups. The number of such members may be determined by the number necessary to give adequate representation to various groups and the possibility of obtaining individuals who will be interested and reasonably active.

Individual members may be appointed by the board of the council or nominated by a committee and elected by the council membership. The individual members may be appointed for two or three year overlapping terms. The council will thus always have a group of members with some experience.

THE BOARD

The "membership" of a council of 50 to 150 agencies might range from 150 to 400 or more persons (depending on the number of individual members). A group of this size may participate in program meetings of various sorts, may serve as a group of ultimate control, and may register "yes" and "no" decisions on matters of broad policy; but such a group is too large to exercise detailed direction over program or policies.

The council therefore has a board of directors, commonly made up of the officers of the council, the chairmen of functional divisions and departmental committees, and other members elected by the council membership body, probably for overlapping terms. The board should include both laymen and professionals, but preferably at least two-thirds of the board members should be laymen. Ordinarily the president of the council and the chairmen of functional divisions should also be laymen.

OPERATING UNITS

The three major types of operating units within the larger councils represent three complementary approaches to the job of health and welfare planning: The *functional divisions* represent an approach by major fields of service or types of problems — health, recreation, etc. The *departments* represent certain common services; they cut across the lines of the functional fields. *Geographic units* — district councils, etc. — represent a unified geographical approach to the health and welfare problems of a particular section of the community.

Occasionally a council also carries on a temporary *demonstration project* which may involve direct service or a combination of direct service and community organization. An example would be a project for working with "street clubs" or gangs, in a given section of the city. In such a case the demonstration unit constitutes a fourth type of organization unit. A council should undertake direct service activities only in rare instances, if at all. Such projects may tend to distract the council's attention from the main job of coordination and planning, to remove the council from its position of detachment and objectivity in respect to operating programs, and perhaps to bring it into some competition with its member agencies. Where a demonstration project involves only community organization methods and not direct service, it can usually be carried on under one of the departments or functional divisions.

Committees represent a fifth type of organization unit. They are used in a variety of ways and are of major importance.

FUNCTIONAL DIVISIONS

A functional division is a *grouping of agencies* concerned with a specific field of service or type of problem. Thus, if a council has a children's division, all the agencies which work for children are automatically members of that division. The division is to be distinguished from a committee, which is usually a group of selected individuals rather than a formal grouping of all the agencies concerned with a problem.

The most common divisional groupings are: family and child welfare (these may be separate divisions), health, and recreation. There may be others, however, such as: aging, hospitals, physically handicapped, day care of children, etc. Multiple-service agencies may belong to two or more divisions.

If the general plan of the citizens-and-agencies type of council is followed, the division will have two delegates from each of the agencies in this functional field, plus a number of the individual members of the council. Unless it is very small the division will have officers and an executive committee, and probably other permanent or temporary committees. A large division may have subordinate sections such as settlements and community centers.

In a sense, a division is the council in miniature. Frequently much of the most effective work of the council is accomplished in the division, where agencies and individuals concerned with a particular field get together.

The degree of centralization or decentralization among the divisions differs from council to council. Ordinarily a recommendation or action by a division requires submission to the council board if it involves budgetary action or a commitment of the council as a whole, as in the case of a legislative proposal.

An active council division requires some staff service. In a large council there is usually a full-time professional staff member who serves as executive secretary or staff aide for the division, and in some cases there may even be one or more assistants. In somewhat smaller councils one staff member may serve two divisions, and in still smaller councils the executive may have to give staff service to all the divisions.

A DIVISION PROGRAM

The council division may carry on a great variety of projects and activities. For example, the program of the Family, Old Age, and Children's Division of the St. Louis Social Planning Council, for one year, included the activities which are briefly summarized below:

The Division planned a sectional meeting of the Annual Community Conference on Health and Welfare, on the subject "Where Are We in Child Welfare in St. Louis and St. Louis County?" . . . A Committee on Protective Services proposed a plan for a public protective service program. . . . Day care centers followed up the recommendations of a study of day care completed two years earlier. A consultant from the Child Welfare League of America aided in this work. A St. Louis club "adopted" the field of day care and planned to provide some of the special resources needed . . . A study of 18 children's institutions was begun *after almost a year's preparation* with board and staff members . . . The Conference of

Superintendents of Children's institutions continued active. An institute for cottage parents was planned. . . . A large committee, with five sub-committees, attacked the problem of mentally retarded children. . . . The Division participated in consideration of a proposed amalgamation of two family and children's agencies. . . . A largely attended luncheon meeting was held on "Older People in the Community." . . . The Division's annual meeting was a Board Member Institute. . . . Assistance was arranged for Selective Service Boards in investigating "hardship cases" of selectees. . . . Special studies related to: adoptive children and adoptive applicants; the experience of voluntary family agencies with financial assistance; an old folks home in a suburb; another old people's home, seeking membership in the Council and the Chest; and a voluntary veterans' agency.[5]

The examination of this summarized report of a functional division suggests a number of facets of council operation and of community organization in general. Among these are: the range of problems, interests, and services; the variety of methods used; the basic importance of factfinding as a foundation for almost everything that is done in planning and action; the importance of committee work; the skillful use of a variety of specialized consultants; the active participation and "involvement" of a wide range of organizations, groups, and individuals in the program of the Division; the use of conferences, institutes, and workshops for specialized groups; the occasional use of large meetings; the Division's consultation and assistance to individual agencies; the pervasive educational process that runs through the whole program; the recognition of limitations (statutory provisions, state jurisdictions, etc.); the inter-group relationships involving the Division and the Council Board, the Council and the Chest; and the careful and intelligent program accounting, including a carryover calendar of unfinished business at the end of the year.

DEPARTMENTS ADMINISTERING COMMON SERVICES

Most councils administer one or more common services which cut across functional lines and serve the agencies as a whole or the general public. In larger councils these services may be organized under separate departments; in smaller councils they must ordinarily

[5] St. Louis Social Planning Council, *Report to the Community . . . May 1, 1953*, pp. 5-9.

be carried on a part-time basis by the council executive or a staff member.

Five types of central services appear to be most common: social service exchanges, information and referral services, volunteer bureaus, research and statistical services, and public relations services. Other central services may include labor-welfare liaison, central purchasing, efficiency engineering, joint bookkeeping, central mimeographing, personnel advisory service, and other units. Any or all of these departments may have departmental committees which may be either directive (policy-determining) or advisory.

INFORMATION AND REFERRAL SERVICE

The information and referral service may carry on either or both of two related functions: (1) a public information bureau, to answer questions about the social welfare resources of the community — names and locations of agencies, descriptions of governmental and voluntary services available, and so on, and (2) a referral service, to interview specific individuals seeking services of various sorts and to refer them to appropriate agencies. In a large city the patterns of health and welfare services are so complex that there is vital need of some central bureau where there is expert knowledge and skilled counsel regarding available resources. The significance of the information and referral service, from the standpoint of community organization, includes these factors: (1) it helps to bring people and services together; (2) it interprets social services to key referral sources — industry, schools, police, churches, etc.; (3) it locates gaps in services and helps to meet needs through promoting flexibility in agency intake policies and bringing needs to the attention of planning groups.

VOLUNTEER BUREAU

A volunteer bureau combines some of the functions of a recruiting station, employment service, personnel department, and training center. The activities of a well-organized and active volunteer bureau may include any or all of the following:

1. Ascertaining the need for volunteer services.

2. Interpreting possibilities of volunteer service to agencies and stimulating the agencies to provide opportunities for important service by volunteers.

3. Recruiting volunteers.

4. Establishing and maintaining a central registry of volunteers.

5. Receiving "job requests" for volunteers, from agencies. This will probably involve working out adequate job specifications with the agencies. Job descriptions and job specifications are the only intelligent basis for making job placements, whether they are paid or volunteer positions.

6. Interviewing volunteers.

7. Referring volunteers to jobs in agencies.

8. Following up on referrals, with both agencies and volunteers.

9. Carrying on training activities for volunteers.

10. Giving appropriate recognition to volunteers who meet certain prescribed standards.

11. Keeping appropriate records.

12. Making reports.

RESEARCH AND STATISTICAL SERVICE

If the council's ideal is "an adequate factual basis for sound planning and action," every part of its program is intimately related to the department of research and statistical service.

Among the types of factual material likely to be needed by the council, its committees, and member-agencies, are facts relating to:

1. The community — its geography, history, government, population, economic and social make-up, and the various aspects of community life.

2. The nature, extent, and history of social welfare services and other resources for social welfare (civic organizations, for example), in the community.

3. The volume and cost of social welfare services.

4. Social welfare needs and problems, including indices of needs, unmet needs or gaps in service, and the flow of cases among agencies.

5. The effectiveness of social welfare services. Councils share with national agencies, local operating agencies, and other bodies the interest in developing adequate yardsticks for measuring results achieved by social welfare agencies.

6. Social welfare services in other communities — for purposes of reference, comparison, and suggestion.[6]

[6] Compare the statement in *Get the Facts* (New York, CCC, 1947, mimeographed, 4 pp.).

Many councils regularly collect data from the agencies and compile statistics regarding the health and welfare services given in the community.

A well-organized council becomes a depository for a vast amount of data regarding the community and its problems, the agencies and their services, and social welfare experience in other communities. While the council's facilities may be organized in various ways, there should be an intimate relationship between the research department and the council's library, subject file, and any unit that regularly clips local newspapers for items of social welfare interest.

A council department may publish a social service directory of local health and welfare agencies, as well as other handkooks or informational leaflets.

The council is almost always concerned with one or more surveys or studies. These may vary from a study of a specific agency applying for membership in the council or chest to a full-fledged community welfare survey. For some studies a research department may assume full responsibility; or it may serve as a technical consultant to a functional division or another department which may be conducting some inquiry in its own area. In still other cases a study may be made by an outside survey or study staff, and the research department may play a liaison and cooperative role.

The research department may serve as a consultant to the member agencies on matters of factfinding and research. It should also maintain liaison with any local school of social work, bureau of municipal research, or foundation, and with national and state agencies interested in social welfare research.

PUBLIC RELATIONS SERVICE

The council may have, or the chest and council may share, a department concerned with interpretation and public relations. Whether or not there is a special department, the council has a public relations function.

The council does not take over the public relations function of individual agencies; it supplements their efforts by attempts at broad-scale interpretation of the field of social welfare as a whole. It may use various media for this purpose — newspaper publicity, a news bulletin or house organ, special publications, radio and television broadcasts, a speakers bureau, and so on. The council may offer to the agencies a service of consultation and assistance in regard to public relations; it may also carry on activities directed specifically to special constituency groups — such as a board members' institute, a course for volunteers, a program of interpretation directed toward organized labor, employers, the churches, service clubs, and so on.

LOCAL GEOGRAPHIC UNITS

The "neighborhood" or local community approach to problems of social welfare in cities can be traced back to the settlement and the district committees of the charity organization societies.

Local geographic organization has become an increasingly important aspect of community welfare council programs during the past fifteen years. It is a natural and almost inevitable response to the facts of city life. The city needs to be broken down into more manageable units, and natural patterns for these units are usually at hand. Probably every city of 100,000 or over and many smaller cities have more or less well-marked natural local communities. The district councils, the most common form of local geographic organization under city-wide councils, are an attempt to bring community organization down to the local community, district, or neighborhood.

This local organization is an attempt at grass-roots community organization. The district council is a channel between city-wide social welfare programs and local communities. It seeks to improve conditions of local community life; to broaden education and enlist citizen participation; to bring social welfare programs and services closer to average citizens and consumers. The district council is based upon the eminently sensible idea of building up and strengthening the local units which make up the city.

The membership of a district council may be composed primarily of lay residents of the district or of local professional workers (social workers, teachers, nurses, etc.), or a combination of the two groups. A council composed of residents plus professional workers, but with a majority of residents, and with leadership coming primarily from the residents, would seem the soundest pattern in most cases.

Experience with district councils suggests that these factors make for the effectiveness of such local councils: [7]

The *district* ought to be a natural geographic community in the city rather than a mere artificial district, created by drawing lines on a map.

[7] This discussion is adapted in part from Violet M. Sieder, *Grass Roots Under City Streets* (New York, CCC, 1946, mimeographed).

The district should be small enough so that there is some sense of community solidarity and so that face-to-face contacts are relatively easy and frequent. Many district councils try to serve too large an area. In a city of a million, a district council may operate in an area with a population of 50,000 or 100,000; here the district itself is the size of a small city. Some experience points to the possibility of a "community council" or "district council" for approximately the area served by a high school, with a population of perhaps 50,000 to 100,000, and subsidiary "neighborhood councils," corresponding more or less to elementary school districts, with population averaging somewhere around 10,000. However, the implications of such a plan for a city of a million or more are rather staggering in terms of organization, staff service, and budget. The planning of district councils poses these questions: (1) Should a whole city be covered by district councils, or should they be developed exclusively or mainly in neighborhoods with a high incidence of social welfare problems? (2) What is the optimum size for a district or neighborhood council? (3) If the optimum size is a small population unit, how can the necessary organization, staff service, and budget be provided?

The *organization* of the district council should be simple and flexible. Major emphasis should be laid on "town meetings" of the whole council. Officers and an executive committee will be needed, as well as committees in charge of specific projects.

The *program* of the district council should be concerned with the whole field of social welfare and the whole area of neighborhood life; there should not be separate councils concerned with recreation, child welfare or juvenile delinquency, health, etc. A unified approach rather than segmentation is desirable for a small geographic unit of this sort.

The council's program should be concerned with community organization rather than operation of direct consumer-services. In this respect the district council is similar to the city-wide council.

The district councils should have close *relationships* with each other, with local health and welfare agencies, and with the central community welfare council. There is some difference of opinion as to whether district councils should be organizationally separate from or connected with the city-wide community welfare council. The two may gain mutual strength from their association; on the other hand, if district councils are separate, they may be more free in controversial matters of social action, and city-wide councils and chests may avoid occasional embarrassment caused by positions taken by specific district councils. In any case, the district council, in its practical operation, always represents a "two-way process": the mobilization and expression of local thinking and action in respect to city-wide agencies and the city-wide council, and the receiving of information, stimulation, and service from these city-wide resources.

There should be a major emphasis upon the development of *resident citizen leadership*. Along with this should go executive and professional service, preferably supplied by the community welfare council. In most cases a specific district council will have only part of the time of a staff worker. We need to know much more about how many councils of a given size and development may be effectively served by one worker, and what constitutes a reasonable work-load for such a worker.

In 1935 the Cleveland Welfare Federation completed a study of juvenile delinquency and its prevention in the Tremont Area, of about 20,000 population. In 1953, it was reported that, "Apparently as a result of the various activities which were conducted in the area as a result of the study, the delinquency rate among boys in the Tremont Area fell . . . about 70 per cent, and has continued at approximately this low rate." [8]

There have been proposals and some experimentation as to unification or closer coordination among the various types of services in a local district.[9] In addition, some community welfare councils have developed or are experimenting with various forms of organization for suburban units. Thus far, however, the district council is probably still the most promising single instrument for local geographic organization.

COMMITTEES

Committees are used at practically every point in the council's job. They may be attached to the board of directors, departments, functional divisions, district councils, other committees, or other organization units. Committees may be permanent or temporary; they may be composed of laymen, social workers, or both.

From the standpoint of function, council committees may include at least the following classifications:

[8] Unpublished document, Welfare Federation of Cleveland, 1953.
[9] See, for example, Roy Sorenson, "Case-work and Group-work Integration: Its Implications for Community Planning," NCSW, 1935, p. 321; and Ray Johns, *The Cooperative Process Among National Social Agencies* (New York, Association Press, 1946), pp. 246–247.

1. Administrative committees, concerned primarily with organization or administration. This would include executive committees of the council or functional divisions; directive or advisory departmental committees; committees on finance, personnel, nominations, etc.

2. Committees on functional fields or their sub-divisions or on special problems. Sometimes a council has committees (groups of individuals) rather than functional divisions (groupings of agencies) on family and child welfare, health, recreation, etc. Where there is a functional division, it may have continuing committees on special problems within its field. Thus a large child welfare division might have standing committees on such subjects as foster family care, institutional care for children, day care, behavior problems of children, and services to unmarried mothers. There may be also council committees on continuing program problems — such as aging, rehabilitation, vocational counseling — that may cut across traditional functional fields.

3. Permanent committees on special aspects of the council's program. Examples would include a committee to plan programs for meetings for the council or for a functional division; a study and planning committee for a division; a committee on joint budgeting (if the council serves as the agent of the chest for budgeting); a committee on long-time research plans; and so on.

4. Temporary committees in charge of specific projects or working on special problems, such as a committee to survey needs and facilities for convalescent care, to establish a child guidance clinic, to develop camping standards, to work out procedures for referrals between casework and group work agencies, or to work for the passage of the new Juvenile Court Bill, etc.

While it is often expedient to appoint a special *ad hoc* committee to direct a specific project, this need not be an invariable procedure. Certain projects may be in charge of standing committees of divisions or departments, such as those mentioned above; or some undertakings may be essentially staff projects, subject only to the supervision of the council executive and of executive committees of functional divisions.

5. Committees on technical practice, such as committees on social service exchange procedure, an advisory committee on the social service directory, a committee on research procedures, etc.

6. Committees on relationships between the council and other bodies, such as the community chest, other planning and coordinating agencies, governmental agencies, etc.

There are as yet no accepted norms as to the number and variety of committees that may be reasonably expected in a council of given size, or the relationships between members of committees and available staff service. General experience with committees does, however, suggest some general principles; these are discussed in Chapter 22.

Almost any council could improve the results it obtains from committees by observing the following:

1. Create a committee only when it is necessary; define the committee's assignment clearly; and set some deadlines for reports or action.

2. Keep an up-to-date index of the council's committees.

3. Once a year, conduct an administrative review of all committees, to check on each committee's activities. In particular, the following questions should be asked in regard to each temporary committee: Is the continued existence of this committee necessary? If so, why? What problems is it working on? How important are they? What did the committee accomplish last year? What does it plan to do next year?

ORGANIZATIONAL RELATIONSHIPS BETWEEN COUNCILS AND CHESTS

Where a council and a community chest exist in the same community there are almost always close organizational or other cooperative relationships between them.

The various patterns of chest-council relationships may be indicated broadly by the following greatly simplified diagrams.

FIGURE 5

FORMS OF COUNCIL-CHEST ORGANIZATION

Community	
Welfare	Federation
Chest	Council

1. Combined Chest and Council.

1. The council and chest may be more or less coordinate departments of a "community welfare federation," "united community services," or other single organization.[10] Sometimes the joint organization may be thought of as having three major functions: campaigning, budgeting, and social planning.

---

[10] The term "community welfare federation," however, does not always connote this type of organization. The term "federation" is sometimes used to denote a council and sometimes a chest!

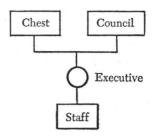

2. The council and chest may be separate agencies but may have a common executive and some common staff members or joint organization units, such as public relations, office management, etc.

2. Separate Chest and Council, with Common Executive.

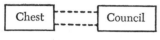

3. Separate Chest and Council, but with Organizational Inter-Relationships.

3. The council and chest may be separate agencies, with separate executives, but still have some organizational relationships, such as interlocking boards or joint committees.

4. The council and chest may be separate agencies with no organizational relationships, except that the council will probably be a member-agency of the chest. In this case the council and chest will probably depend for coordination upon informal working relationships between boards, committees, staff, etc. The council may also have advisory relationships to the chest regarding budgeting or other matters.

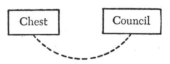

4. Separate Chest and Council, with Cooperative Working Relationships.

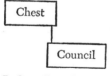

5. Council as Department of or Subordinate to Chest.

5. The council may be a department of the chest. This reflects the belief that the function of the council is less important than that of the chest, and that the council may therefore properly be subordinate to the chest.

6. The chest may be a department of the council. There are historical examples of this arrangement, whether or not there are any today. The traditional theory underlying this form of organization is that the council is the basic organization and that those member-agencies of the council which wish to engage in joint financing may form a community chest as a department of the council.

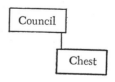

6. Chest as Department of or Subordinate to Council.

Opinions differ as to the best form of organizational relationships between council and chest, or whether there is actually any one "best" form for all communities. Number 4, with no organizational relationships between chest and council, is probably undesirable unless the informal cooperative relationships are so close that they transcend any need for formal organization. This type of organization is clearly undesirable if it implies antagonism, remoteness, or lack of cooperation.

Number 5, with the council as a department of the chest, seems thoroughly undesirable. It relegates health and welfare planning to a subordinate position; the council becomes a mere appendage to the chest. Number 6, with the chest as a department of the council, is likely to be equally unacceptable to the chest. As William J. Norton pointed out long ago, business leaders and contributors who volunteer for the chest job of joint financing are not likely to be willing to have their organization subordinate to a council which to a large extent represents health and welfare agencies.[11] The real argument then is between forms 1, 2, 3, and possibly 4. And the heart of the problem is, should the council and chest be essentially one organization or two?[12] Any sound solution should be based upon the following principles:

1. The relationship between the council and chest should be a cooperative one. Neither should be subordinate to the other.

2. There should be unity of purpose, practical cooperation, and close working relationships between the council and the chest. Whatever the form of organization, there should be a working partnership between them.

3. The council should be essentially autonomous and independent. Its policies and major decisions on matters of health and welfare planning should not be dictated primarily by financial considerations. The shadow of the campaign and the necessity of raising thousands or millions of dollars always hangs over the chest; it is inevitable that even the most far-visioned chest leadership should hesitate to take action that may antagonize important groups and make the difficult job of money-raising still more difficult.[13]

[11] William J. Norton, *The Cooperative Movement in Social Work* (New York, Macmillan, 1927), pp. 147–152.
[12] On this subject, see: *Teamwork in Our Town* (1954), pp. 25–27; Murphy, *Community Organization Practice*, pp. 257–259; Charles J. Birt, "Where Chest and Council Are One," *Community*, Vol. 24, May 1949, pp. 167–169; C. W. Pfeiffer, "A Vote for Separate Councils," (Los Angeles), *Community*, Vol. 29, February 1954, pp. 103–106.
[13] Compare: *Community Planning for Social Welfare: A Policy Statement* (N.Y., CCC, 1950).

This whole picture of council-chest organization has been further complicated by the development of "united funds" which include both the local chest agencies and certain national appeals. The national appeals are likely to be included on the basis of negotiation rather than on the basis of the traditional annual budgeting process which applies to local chest agencies.

Various organizational patterns have emerged. In some cases the chest has simply expanded its program, or the chest and the united fund have merged, so that the traditional pattern is retained: a chest or fund responsible for fund-raising and budgeting, and a council responsible for planning. In some communities there are now three central organizations: the united fund, which raises the money; the chest, which does the budgeting for the chest agencies; and the council, which is concerned with planning. In still other united fund communities, the chest, being left with only the budget function, has merged with the council to form an organization sometimes called "United Community Services," which does the planning and also the budgeting for local agencies. If this arrangement brings powerful citizen interests to the planning function, and if the integrity of the planning function and of agency participation are maintained, the net result may be a gain for the council and its cause. If, however, the united organization is dominated primarily by a fiscal point of view, and if the agencies are reduced to a powerless advisory status, the council will probably cease to be of any real importance, and untold damage may be done to the cause of health and welfare planning and to the community.

It is as yet too early to evaluate these developments. Aside from the complicating factor of the united fund, it would seem that in the large city the separate chest and council, with separate executives but with some organizational relationships, (form 3, above) would give the best prospects for success.

In the smaller city the problem is more difficult. Frequently the city can afford — or thinks it can afford — only one professional person for the whole job of joint financing and health and welfare planning. Even if a second person is employed, he is likely to be of limited experience, and not ready to assume the responsibility of serving as the executive of an independent council.

Where this situation obtains, the best solution may be the separate chest and council with a common executive (form 2, above) or possibly the combined chest and council in one organization (form 1), but with full recognition of the dual purpose of planning and joint financing. Such a situation makes extremely heavy demands upon the executive. It is a rare person who is at the same time equipped to be both a high powered campaign leader and a deliberate and creative planner. There is evidence that smaller cities are increasingly seeing the council function as sufficiently important to require well-qualified staff service. If such cities can find enough well-qualified staff members and if they are willing to pay for them, it is possible that even in some of the smaller cities there may be a trend toward separate chests and councils with separate executives, but with cooperative relationships.

It is highly desirable that the council should have a vital and formal relationship to the chest's budgeting of funds. Practice varies here. Sometimes, as indicated above, the chest and council are parts of one agency. Where they are separate, the chest may refer to the council for study and report problems of agency programs and relationships. Sometimes the council may appoint certain members of the chest budget committee, or the budgeting may be a joint activity of chest and council. Sometimes, the council actually does the budgeting for the chest. The process of budgeting represents the most important area of common ground between joint financing and "social planning."

FINANCIAL SUPPORT

Councils derive their chief support from community chests. Other sources of income include payments for use of the social service exchange, direct contributions, dues from voluntary and governmental agencies, endowments, appropriations from public funds, and grants from foundations.

In a few cities there are substantial appropriations to councils from governmental agencies. These appropriations are essentially different from the usual public subsidies to private agencies. The basic objection to subsidies is that public funds should not go where public control cannot follow: that tax funds should not be turned over to a voluntary agency to spend. The council, however, represents a partnership of governmental agencies, voluntary agencies, and citizens; the governmental agencies share in the control of the agency, and it would seem equitable that they should pay their share of the costs of health and welfare planning.

Where there is a community chest, agency membership dues and direct contributions from individuals are usually negligible. Grants from foundations are ordinarily for special studies, demonstrations, or other projects rather than for current operating expenses.

SOME COUNCIL ACCOMPLISHMENTS

Most of the accomplishments of community welfare councils cannot be satisfactorily measured by any methods yet devised. However, any estimate of the major accomplishments would include at least the following:

1. Councils have done much to establish *the spirit of teamwork* in social welfare, in local communities. They have also implemented the will-to-cooperate with machinery and devices ranging from divisional meetings to social service exchanges. Councils have done much to make teamwork easy and natural. Democracy itself is a vast cooperative enterprise, and community welfare councils, in encouraging cooperation and teamwork in an important segment of American life, have made a fundamental contribution to the life of a democratic nation.

2. In each community where an effective council exists, the council provides a *central point* for the social welfare efforts of the community. It provides certain *central machinery* which is always available and ready for use when needed, in the course of the day's work or in the face of a crisis.

3. Councils have performed an immense number of *concrete services* for their communities in the area of community organization. The annual report of any active council will carry its own proof.

4. Where the council has had strong leadership and vital participation it has usually become a kind of *"general staff"* for the social welfare forces of the community, analyzing facts and conditions, estimating resources, mapping out plans, and plotting the strategy of social welfare advances.

5. At its best, the council has helped to develop the idea of one *planned, integrated community welfare program* rather than a mere collection of separate agency programs. A few councils have caught this vision fully and are consciously working toward this goal. Many councils are as yet untouched by this idea; but more and more of them, we may be fairly certain, are gradually becoming aware of it.

COUNCIL PROBLEMS

In the light of a generation of experience, what are the major problems which councils face?

The *lack of inclusive and vital participation* is a common weakness.

This involves problems of adequate participation (1) by individuals as well as agencies, (2) by agencies in general, (3) by governmental agencies in particular, and (4) by laymen as well as social workers — especially laymen who have recognized leadership status among various interest groups.

One of the most frequent defects in councils is *the lack of a directed and focused program.* Often a council flounders in a welter of well-intentioned miscellaneous activities rather than carrying forward an ordered program. There may be too little selection of projects and establishment of priorities. There is frequently a lack of sound planning, conscious direction, adequate executive and professional supervision, and effective administrative controls. There is no more excuse for these deficiencies in a council than in a well-organized public welfare, family service, or group work agency.

Some councils *lack independence and autonomy;* they may be, in effect, appendages to the community chest. This weakness usually goes back to the form of organization, and to the quality of the council's leadership.

The community welfare council is frequently *lacking in strength and effectiveness.* The council has frequently been criticized for too much talk at too many meetings, and too little action. It often has difficulty in moving from study and discussion to action. Some persons see in this fact simply the council's lack of the "power of the purse" which the chest or the city government exercises, and believe that the council is inevitably and *per se* ineffective unless perhaps it serves as the budgeting agent for the chest. Even this is not a simple answer; for unless the council is democratically organized and has established widespread participation, the acceptance of the budgeting function may tend to make the agencies regard it as a separate authoritative body and to develop a "we and it" psychology.

To the extent that the council is a federation of agencies, it has some of the inherent weaknesses as well as strengths of a federation. There is always some danger that federative action will represent the least common denominator of convictions of the federated units. In matters of legislation and other controversial questions it is often questionable how far the council should go unless it has substantial agreement.[14]

The welfare of the community seems to require some degree of centering of power to act for the common good, greater than the tradi-

[14] In relation to this problem of the council and social action, see Violet M. Sieder, "The Community Welfare Council and Social Action," NCSW, 1950, pp. 22–41.

tional council of agencies has had. One answer probably lies in making over the council as a citizens-and-agencies body, where the federative nature of the organization will be somewhat minimized, and where representatives of the general public will play a more important part. Another answer lies in the recognition by individual agencies that unqualified individualism on the part of an agency will no longer work nor will it in the long run be tolerated by the supporting public; that every social welfare agency belongs fundamentally to the community, and that social agencies will have to surrender greater power to a central body to achieve more effective cooperative action. While the council has no administrative authority over the agencies, one can perceive the need for a greater degree of power to act by the council, based upon common consent and not upon any authority imposed from without. As one leader in the council field has observed, "By joining the council, the agency should say, 'We will be guided by the larger will, the broader study — the community need.'"

The publication of *Community Planning for Human Services* by Bradley Buell and associates (1951) [15] presents a challenge to councils, particularly in the area of *health and welfare patterns* in the community and *the evaluation of accomplishments and results of health and welfare services*. One community organization leader observes, "We need new patterns for organization of services, new clusterings of the specialties, more aggressive seeking out of problems, more continuity in treatment, and more concerted efforts at prevention and control of human maladjustment." All these needs go to the heart of the council's job.

Councils are sometimes *poorly organized and ineffectively administered*. Lack of adequate program control and direction, inadequate professional supervision, and inadequate records are three rather common weaknesses.

One problem which the council usually faces is *the difficulty of interpreting what it does and demonstrating what it accomplishes*. This is true not so much of the central services, which are fairly tangible and easily interpreted, but of the coordinating and planning function. The variety of the council's activities, the lack of quantitative measuring sticks, the frequent slowness in achieving certain results, the intangible elements involved — all are part of this difficulty. There is still another dilemma. If the council claims too much in its own name, the agency which has taken the action feels that it should have had the credit — with the result that it will have less enthusiasm for

[15] See Chapter 7, p. 86.

cooperative action in the future. If the council claims too little, however, and distributes all the credit to other agencies or groups, questions may arise as to why a council is needed.

Undoubtedly many councils *lack a sufficiently dynamic concept of their function*. Such councils may be more concerned with coordinating what already exists than planning and working to achieve what ought to be. A community has a right to expect understanding, imagination, vision, courage, and statesmanship from the leaders of its community welfare council.

"WHAT MAKES A GOOD COUNCIL"

The first Conference of Community Welfare Leaders, held under the auspices of CCC in 1953, laid down six principles and five "conditions for success" for councils:

SIX PRINCIPLES

1. Community planning is a democratic process, and therefore all major community groups should be included in its activities. The Council should include governmental and voluntary agencies, lay and professional interests, and citizen organizations having a concern in health, welfare and recreation. The Council should respect and build upon the autonomy of agencies and organizations.

2. Councils are concerned with the entire range of community services, whether under voluntary or governmental auspices.

3. Practical long-range goals for the improvement of community services, including broad priorities, in which all recommendations are related to community resources, should be established. These goals should be positive, and should represent an attack upon the causes of social problems. They should also be flexible and continuously reevaluated.

4. The Council has a responsibility to work for expansions, retrenchments, and changes to bring about a balanced, efficient community program.

5. Planning and financing go hand in hand; a close liaison between the two is essential.

6. Local conditions should determine organization and structure; no one master plan can be applied in all localities.

CONDITIONS FOR SUCCESS

Broad participation. . . . Top-grade leadership. . . . Good staff service. . . . Equal status for planning and financing. . . . Acceptance by the community of the value of planning.[16]

The following additional suggestions may be made as to the bases of an effective community welfare council.[17]

Underlying the council must be a basic spirit of good-will and a *desire to cooperate* on the part of citizens and agencies. Cooperation must be desired or it will not be achieved. A successful council cannot be superimposed upon unwilling agencies or individuals; the council is only a means of achieving something that they already recognize — however dimly — as desirable.

The council should have a *program* which is adapted to the needs of the community and which is changed as is necessary to keep pace with conditions. Such a program involves: (a) intelligent joint planning; (b) the setting up of long-range objectives and also short-range objectives for a current year or other period; (c) inclusion in the program of services and projects related to vital needs; (d) the establishment of "priorities" as to needs which are more and less important; (e) an emphasis on "timing" and alertness in taking advantage of openings and opportunities for constructive action. The council should seek to restrict itself to what it can do well. It should also lay special emphasis upon proceeding from study and discussion to action.

The council should give the member agencies and the community only those *services that can be given most effectively by a central federated body*. Normally the council should not administer direct services to consumers or clients.

The *emphasis* of the council should be on *initiation, planning, and stimulation of the activities of member agencies and community groups,* rather than on the council's playing a dominant part in the carrying out of such activities.

The council should be *the common voice of the social welfare forces of the community*. It should be also the technical planning organization through which the community effects continuous planning and action for social welfare.

[16] "What Makes a Good Council?," *Community*, Vol. 28, March 1953, p. 126.
[17] Some of this material is adapted from *Some Desirable Standards for Community Welfare Councils*, a draft document prepared by a seminar on the community welfare council at the School of Social Work of the University of Michigan, 1948.

The council should be *alert and sensitive to new needs and developments,* and it should preserve flexibility in its program and organization.

The council should provide *dynamic and creative leadership* for the forces of social welfare in the community. The council should be not merely a clearing house, a recipient of suggestions from without, or a piece of machinery to be used by community groups when desired. The council should have a life and personality of its own; it should be a positive force in promoting community progress.

L

ALTERNATIVES TO THE COUNCIL

The community welfare council is not the only possible form of central local coordinating and planning agency. Some possible alternatives are discussed below.

1. It is possible to dispense with a council as such and to *lodge the planning function in the chest.* Many organizational variations are possible; they range all the way from a simple chest Committee on Social Planning to a more or less elaborate council structure, with a board, functional divisions, and committees, all ultimately advisory or tributary to the chest board.

There are two objections to such plans. (a) They make coordinating and planning subordinate to fund-raising and joint-financing. Under any such plan the exigencies of fund-raising are too likely to become paramount in decisions regarding community welfare programs and policies. (b) Such plans fail to give democratic representation to all interests concerned, and particularly to governmental agencies, which form the basic pattern in American social welfare. The groups of control in the chest are normally the contributors and the *chest agencies* (all of them voluntary agencies, of course); even if the governmental agencies are given some kind of associate status, they do not have the same status or the same close relationship to the chest as the financially participating agencies.

2. Another alternative to the council as the central agency for community welfare organization would be *a local governmental agency concerned primarily with health and welfare planning.* The Office of Civilian Defense during World War II included this function, although there was frequently close cooperation between the OCD and the community welfare council, where such a council existed. There were those who advocated the continuance in peacetime of a governmental coordinating and planning agency for social welfare.[18] Such

an agency would be inclusive in the sense that government represents all the people; it could be established in every county or city, if desired; it would probably succeed more easily than a council in enlisting the active participation of other governmental agencies; it might have greater prestige than a voluntary council; it would have the financial stability of support from tax funds; and it would have whatever authority was vested in it by law.

Logically, a strong case can be made for a governmental health and welfare planning agency; but the available evidence suggests that as a matter of taste, Americans — or at least those who think about the matter at all — prefer to have the job done by a voluntary agency.

Another related possibility in respect to governmental organization for health and welfare planning may be mentioned. State and local planning boards may give an increasing emphasis to health and welfare planning as part of their total programs. If this should happen, there would be a need for a close and effective liaison between such boards and local community welfare councils; but it is doubtful that the planning boards would desire or find it practicable to take over the variety of activities that are now carried on by councils.

Today there appears to be no general demand and practically no advocacy of a local governmental welfare planning agency. The reason is probably found in the traditional emphasis in American democracy on the autonomy and freedom of voluntary groups of all kinds, including voluntary social welfare agencies. Under the impact of war, the people of the United States accepted a fairly high degree of control over individual and group life. In peacetime, however, the average thoughtful and informed citizen would probably be slow to approve the setting up of a governmental agency with any real power of coordination and planning affecting the family service society, the child placing agency, the settlement, and the hospital. If it be urged that this governmental agency could proceed chiefly by enlisting voluntary cooperation and with little reliance upon compulsion, the same informed citizen would probably shrug his shoulders and reply, "But that's the way the chest and council do it now, isn't it? In that case, why have a government agency do the job? Besides, it might get into politics!"

[18] See Thomas Devine, "Community Organization Under Public Auspices: From the Federal Viewpoint," NCSW, 1944, pp. 402–409; C. Ellis Henican, "From the Community Viewpoint," *ibid.*, pp. 411–414. See also McMillen, *Community Organization for Social Welfare*, p. 635.

3. Another alternative which was suggested in at least one large city was the creation of *a small independent committee of outstanding lay leaders* to do basic coordinating and planning for the field of health and welfare. It has been argued that such a committee might make for simplicity of organization and operation, less emphasis on vested interests, and the enlistment of more high caliber lay participation and perhaps more neutral parties in the planning process.

However, such a plan would obviously lodge a tremendous amount of responsibility and power in the hands of a small number of persons, without any adequate guarantees that the membership of the committee would be (or would continue to be) sufficiently informed, disinterested, and objective in their decisions.

Furthermore, regardless of their wisdom and ability, they would have no administrative authority over the many agency units and organizations in the community. A small group of planners might develop excellent plans for appropriate action, but nothing much would be likely to happen unless the organizations which would have to put such action into effect were convinced of the wisdom of the proposed action and accepted it as part of their own plan. Moreover, changes in the health and welfare programs happen largely as a result of the *process* of study, discussion and participation, rather than as a result of formal reports and recommendations.

There is another difficulty with this proposal, related to the question of who would appoint the committee. If it was self-appointed, the organization would of course be essentially undemocratic and the committee would be irresponsible in the sense of not being accountable to any representative group. If the committee was appointed by a community trust or local foundation, its status would still be paternalistic rather than democratic. If the committee was appointed by the community chest membership or board, this would be merely another variation of a social planning committee of the community chest. If the committee was appointed by some sort of assembly of citizens and agency representatives, this would approximate the present community welfare council.

4. The effectiveness of some of the statewide citizens welfare associations tempts one to consider the possibility of *a local "citizens association for community welfare"* as a health and welfare planning agency. Membership might be composed of persons who paid membership fees direct to the Association, plus all chest contributors who elected to belong to the Association. Presumably the major financial support would come from the community chest.

Such an association might have somewhat more independence and aptitude for social action than many councils have had. On the other hand, it would probably be difficult, without exceptionally able leadership, to enlist and build up a sufficiently large and strong citizen membership for an agency concerned primarily with planning. Moreover, local community organization, much more than statewide community organization, is intimately related to a large number of agencies and programs; and a citizens association would be planning for rather than with the agencies, unless the agencies had formal membership and representation in the association. This is again a return to the community welfare council pattern of citizen-members-plus-agencies, although perhaps with more emphasis on a broad citizen membership.

This discussion of alternatives to the community welfare council suggests these conclusions: (1) Among the alternatives explored — planning by the community chest, a governmental planning agency, an independent laymen's committee, and a citizens association — there is none that is at the same time obviously superior to the council and likely to prove acceptable to those concerned. (2) It is entirely possible that, through experimentation and experience, some pattern for health and welfare planning may evolve which will be superior to councils as we have known them in the past. (3) While most councils have not attained their full potentialities in the past, it is possible for modern community welfare councils, enlisting real citizen participation and applying the principles suggested in the foregoing section, to be highly effective in furnishing leadership in local community welfare organization.

Along with whatever changes and developments there may be in structure and function of local health and welfare planning agencies, we may see increasingly, in large communities as well as small, the establishment of some form of planning and coordinating council, committee, or organization that will represent all the major aspects of the community — economic life, education, housing and physical planning, as well as health, welfare, and recreation. While it is convenient to isolate social welfare organizations and services for certain purposes, yet it involves an artificial segmentation of community life, and there are many occasions when planning and action must be as broad as community life if it is to be as deep as human need.

QUESTIONS AND PROBLEMS

1. What are the differences in function, membership, and organization between a community welfare council and a community chest?

2. Make a report on a specific council. Consider such matters as: history; organization; functions; functional divisions; common services; project committees; local geographic organization; current program; relationship to community chest; relationship to joint budgeting; policy regarding legislative promotion.

3. Which of the following activities would be appropriate for a community welfare council? Why? How do these activities relate to the six community organization functions (Chapter 5) (a) a study of recreational facilities in the community; (b) conducting a course for board members; (c) carrying on a demonstration service in work with teen-age gangs; (d) attempting to bring about the establishment of a child guidance clinic in the community; (e) passing on budgets, at the request of the community chest; (f) promulgating an inter-racial code and recommending its adoption by social welfare agencies; (g) enforcing the adoption of this code (how?); (h) holding an annual city conference of social work; (k) participation in a statewide campaign for public welfare reorganization; (j) endorsing a national bill to establish health insurance; (k) making a recommendation to the mayor regarding the appointment of a City Welfare Director?

4. What are the strengths and weaknesses of an organization which is a "federation"?

5. To what extent ought a council membership to include not only operating "health and welfare agencies," but also citizens' organizations with a "civic" interest, such as associations, churches, veterans organizations, service clubs, women's clubs, etc.? To what extent should a council have individual members?

6. How can councils obtain more active and vital participation from (a) governmental agencies? (b) lay persons?

7. Try to give a convincing five-minute presentation to a lay group (choose your group!) on "Why We Have (or Need) a Community Welfare Council."

8. What should the council do about a situation where there is a large and powerful group work agency, (a member of the council and of the chest), with an autocratic executive who has held his job for fifteen years, largely untrained staff personnel, poor standards of work, and a complacent board?

9. You (as the council executive) are consulted by an attorney for an elderly and highly respected citizen who wishes to put into his will a bequest of $300,000, the income from which shall be used for some form of child welfare work. (There is no child caring organization in the city at present.)

The donor is uncertain whether to provide for an orphans' home, describing the eligibility requirements, organization, location, etc., carefully in his will, whether to provide for a children's aid society, or whether to make some other provision. The donor and the attorney would like some expert advice from you.

SUGGESTIONS FOR READING

Several of the articles on councils in various issues of the *Social Work Year Book* are excellent summaries.

Much of the material on councils has been published by Community Chests and Councils of America (now United Community Funds and Councils of America). To the references below should be added the periodical, *Community,* which contains many articles on councils.

Several of the references at the end of Chapter 11 relate to both chests and councils.

Two items on social action by councils are noted in the bibliography for Chapter 6.

Angell, Stephen L., "A Three-Dimensional Approach to Health and Welfare Planning." *Social Service Review,* Vol. XXVIII, September 1954, pp. 308–317. The approach to the Health and Welfare Council of Philadelphia, Delaware and Montgomery Counties.

Birt, Charles J. "Apples Plus Oranges Equal —?" *Survey Midmonthly,* Vol LXXIV, Nov. 1948, pp. 330–31. Discusses the importance of more "power to act" by community welfare councils.

"Code of the Chest and Council Movement," *Community,* Vol. 28, April 1953, pp. 160–161.

Community Chests and Councils of America:

Community Planning for Social Welfare: A Policy Statement (New York, 1950, 15 pp.).

Evaluating the Effectiveness of Councils (New York, 1955, mimeographed, 59 pp.). Report of the 1954 Research Workshop — contains papers on several aspects of evaluation.

Miracles Every Other Tuesday (New York, 1953, 47 pp.). A collection of true stories answering the question: "What do community welfare councils do?" Case illustrations of council operation and accomplishments.

Public-Agency-Council Relationships (New York, 1946, 47 pp.).

Teamwork in Our Town: Through a Community Welfare Council (New York, rev. ed., 1954, 31 pp.). The best available descriptive pamphlet on the community welfare council — brief, simple, readable.

A Volunteer Bureau Handbook. (Bulletin 168, New York, rev. ed., 1952, 82 pp.).

What Councils of Social Agencies Do. (New York, 1939, 57 pp.). Digest and Analysis of Council of Social Agency Programs over a Fifteen-Month Period in Twelve Selected Cities.

Devine, Thomas, "Community Organization under Public Auspices. I. From the Federal Viewpoint," NCSW, 1944, pp. 402–409. The possibility of a local governmental social welfare planning agency.

Dunham, Arthur and associates, *Teamwork for Community Service in New York City* (New York, The Greater New York Fund, 1948, 30 pp.). A study of the Welfare Council of New York City.[19]

Mayo, Leonard W., "Community Planning for Health and Welfare," NCSW, *Social Welfare Forum,* 1952, pp. 220–231. The outlook on councils and their tasks in 1952.

Pfeiffer, C. Whit and Gilmore, Otto T., "Problems of Administration in Community Organization," NCSW, 1941, pp. 577–596. "I. Selection of Projects and Participation of Public Agencies," C. Whit Pfeiffer. "II. Definition, Planning, Direction, and Timing of Projects," Otto Gilmore.

COUNCIL ORGANIZATION AND RELATIONSHIPS

Community Chests and Councils of America, *Constitutions and By-laws:* (a) Combined Community Chest and Council (New York, 1949, 11 pp.). (b) Community Welfare Council (New York, 1952, 3 pp.).

Johns, Ray, "Critical Issues of Council-Agency Relationships," NCSW, *Social Welfare Forum,* 1951, pp. 323–334.

Johnson, Arlien, "The Obstacle of Limited Participation in Local Social Planning," NCSW, 1940, pp. 425–435. Thoughtful discussion of some basic problems of council organization and operation.

Lefferts, Robert, "The Struggle of Structure," *Community,* Vol. 31, September 1955, pp. 6–8. Project committees versus functional divisions in councils.

Pfeiffer, C. Whit, "A Vote for Separate Councils," *Community,* Vol. 29, February 1954, pp. 103–106. "Los Angeles chooses Legal Separation of Planning and Fund-raising."

Sieder, Violet M., "The Relation of Agency and Community Welfare Council Structure to Community Organization." In Howard, Donald S. (ed.), *Community Organization, Its Nature and Setting* (New York, American Association of Social Workers, 1947), pp. 10–18.

Toward Improved Chest-Council-Agency Relations (New York, Association Press, 1951, 36 pp.).

DISTRICT AND NEIGHBORHOOD COUNCILS

Community Chests and Councils of America, *Neighbors Unite for Better Communities: A Handbook on District Community Councils.* (New York, 1956, 36 pp.).

[19] Studies of councils and chests are frequently included in social welfare surveys of large cities; e.g., Boston, Milwaukee, Pittsburgh.

Dillick, Sidney, *Community Organization for Neighborhood Development — Past and Present* (see bibliography, ch. 7). The history and present status of neighborhood community organization.

Lynde, Edward D., "Two-Pronged Approach to Community Planning," NCSW, 1951, *Selected Papers in Group Work and Community Organization*, pp. 104–107. Centralized and district planning.

Sieder, Violet M., "Solving Health and Welfare Problems through Neighborhood Participation", NCSW, *Social Welfare Forum*, 1951, pp. 311–322.

II.

COMMUNITY CHESTS AND UNITED FUNDS

———

THE COMMUNITY CHEST HAS many distinctions among community organization agencies. It is the community organization agency which is best understood and which enlists the widest degree of participation. The Chest's Red Feather, adopted only a few years ago, is already a well-known symbol. The chest is one of the most striking inventions in the way of social welfare machinery. In many urban communities the chest has been unquestionably the most powerful local force for community welfare organization. No other local voluntary welfare agencies have ever handled such large funds as have the chests and united funds, nor exercised such wide discretionary powers in the spending of these funds and consequent shaping of welfare programs and policies. Finally, the chest has played the most striking part in certain major developments and transformations in social welfare — particularly voluntary social welfare — in many communities.

WHAT IS A COMMUNITY CHEST?

UNITED COMMUNITY FUNDS AND Councils of America (UCFC) — formerly Community Chests and Councils of America (CCC) — the national agency representing community chests and community welfare councils, thus defines a community chest:

A Community Chest is a cooperative organization of citizens and welfare agencies. It has two chief functions: (1) It raises funds for its affiliated agencies, through a community-wide appeal and distributes them according to a systematic budget procedure. (In

160

time of war or other emergency it may also raise war relief and emergency service funds.) (2) It promotes cooperative planning, coordination and administration of the community's social welfare, health and recreation services. The direct responsibility for this function may be carried by a Community Welfare Council.[1]

The chest, through a single annual campaign, raises the money to be used by the member organizations for whatever part of their current operating expenses must be obtained by contributions. The contributor to the chest is usually held to be "immune" from individual solicitations by member organizations. The funds raised by the chest are distributed in accordance with budgets prepared by the member-organizations and approved by the chest. Continuous year-round interpretation is usually carried on by the chest, supplementary to such activities by individual member organizations. Through budgeting, allocation of funds, and other methods, the chest seeks to promote joint planning, coordination and the utilization of the community's resources to meet its social and health needs effectively.

ADVANTAGES AND DISADVANTAGES

Some of the major arguments frequently advanced for and against the community chest plan are the following: [2]

In favor of joint financing, it is argued that: (1) More money is raised through a joint campaign than through separate money-raising efforts. (2) More people contribute to social welfare services. (3) The cost of financing social welfare agencies is reduced. (4) The time and energy of agency board members and executives is released from a year-around struggle for finances, and they are better able to concentrate on the service program of their agencies. (5) The contributing public is relieved of a continuous round of appeals. One campaign is substituted for many. (6) The chest makes it easier for the contributor to measure his community responsibility and to give with the assurance that his gift will be used effectively. (7) Proper budgeting and accounting promote efficiency in social welfare undertakings. (8) Joint budgeting means an annual review of the programs and budgets of all chest agencies, by a representative community committee, and joint planning of social welfare programs.

[1] *Organizing and Operating a Community Chest* (New York, CCC, Bulletin 143, rev. ed., 1952), p. 3.
[2] Based partially on *Organizing and Operating a Community Chest, op. cit.,* pp. 3–5.

(9) The enlarged educational and publicity program spreads more widely the knowledge of and interest in social welfare. (10) The chest, as a joint-fund-raising agency, gives practical encouragement to joint planning and action, coordination, improvement of standards, and sound and equitable development of the community's welfare program. Chests have largely supported community welfare councils and many central services, as machinery for coordination and joint planning. (11) The chest stands for cooperation rather than competition in social welfare. It means "together instead of separately." Joint financing is the acid test of the ability of the social welfare agencies of a community to work together.

Against the chest plan, it has been argued that: (1) The chest involves dangerous centralization of power and loss of freedom by the individual agency. (2) A chest may be a purely fiscal operation, dominated by leaders who are interested primarily in money, and who know and care little about social welfare. The chest may lose the spiritual motivation of social welfare. (3) The chest plan tends to diminish the interest of the contributor in the specific causes or agencies to which he contributes. It depersonalizes the contributor's relationship to social welfare. (4) It deprives the giver of much of his freedom of choice in giving. Practically, if he contributes, it is to all the agencies in the chest, even if he disapproves of some and has little interest in others. "Designation" of contributions is of little or no practical value. (5) The chest may become autocratic and interfere with the program, policies, or administration of a member-agency. (6) The chest plan penalizes strong agencies by pooling their resources with weak ones. Strong agencies might expand more rapidly and substantially on their own initiative. (7) When a chest campaign fails, all the member-agencies may be crippled. If the individual agencies were on their own, some of them might achieve their goals. (8) Pioneer efforts to establish new services may be difficult under the chest plan. It is hard to finance a new local agency outside the chest, and this may give the chest something of a monopoly in voluntary social welfare in the community. (9) In its anxiety not to antagonize contributors, the chest may become a defender of the status quo in social welfare and may oppose or discourage social action or other controversial activities on the part of councils of member-agencies. (10) The chest plan tends toward the coercion of employees to contribute — through "payroll deduction plans," pressures for "one hundred per cent giving" in an industrial concern, department, etc. Much community chest giving tends to become almost an extra-legal tax, paid without real interest or willingness. (11) In entering a chest, an agency burns its bridges behind it. If the agency should ever want to withdraw, it must start from scratch in building up a contributor list and fund-raising machinery.

HISTORICAL DEVELOPMENTS

The establishment of the first modern community chest in Cleveland, in 1913, and the early years of the chest-council movement have been described in Chapter 7.

After the United States entered World War II the principle of one wartime campaign was generally accepted. War funds were organized in many cities, to include both war-related appeals and appeals for the community chest and other local agencies. Organized labor threw its weight behind the war chest.[3]

During 1942 and 1943, state war chests were established in all the states. Campaigns remained in the hands of local communities, but the state chests stimulated local organization on a county basis in order to cover small towns and rural areas.

On the national front, a federal agency, the President's War Relief Control Board, was established to control solicitations, receipts, and distribution for war-connected purposes.

To reduce confusion and promote cooperation among national agencies in fund-raising, CCC created a National Budget Committee for War Appeals. In 1943, the National War Fund was organized, in response to local demands for the federation of war appeals, and upon recommendation of the President's War Relief Control Board. The Fund resembled somewhat a "national community chest," but from the first it sought to have its appeal handled in the local community and war chest campaigns. The Fund was active during 1943–1946.[4]

Since the end of World War II there have been at least four major developments in respect to joint financing: (1) The increasing pressure of "multiple appeals" in local communities, and the development of "united funds" and "extended federation campaigns." (2) The national defense program. This brought about the establishment of the United Defense Fund (1950–1955), a joint financing operation involving some 25 national agencies, and United Community Defense

[3] See Wayne McMillen, "Wartime Developments in Federated Financing of Social Work," in Helen R. Wright (ed.), *Social Service in Wartime* (Chicago, University of Chicago Press, 1944).
[4] Harold J. Seymour, *Design for Giving* (New York, Harper, 1947).

Services (1950–1956), a federation of 14 national agencies to assist communities to cope with defense-created health and welfare needs. (3) The National Budget Committee has been re-established, with a National Quota Committee, to review budgets of national agencies and to report to communities on such budget requests as are submitted for review. (4) Postwar statewide funds have developed in Michigan, the Carolinas, and some other states, after most of the war chests ceased to exist.

The most impressive evidence of the growth of the chest movement is found in the increase in the number of chests and in the amounts raised.[5] The 39 chests of 1920 had become 632 chests in 1942, at the outbreak of World War II. This number had risen to 798 by 1946. But the really phenomenal increase has been during the past twelve years—from 798 to 1961 campaigns for 1957. The amounts raised rose from $19,000,000 for 1920 to $84,000,000 for 1931 and $101,000,000 for 1932, declined to $69,000,000 for 1935, then began to climb again so that $90,000,000 was raised for 1941. With the entry of the United States in World War II, the amounts raised increased from $104,000,000 for 1942 to $221,000,000 for 1945. During the next five years the amounts varied between $197,000,000 and $168,000,000. In 1951, with the beginnings of the united fund movement, the amount raised reached $212,000,000, and since that time it has increased by nearly 80 per cent, so that the highest amount yet recorded, $378,000,000, was raised for 1957.

AGENCY MEMBERSHIP

The financially participating agencies in a community chest are voluntary health and welfare agencies — those that raise money through appeals to the public for voluntary contributions. Governmental or public agencies are members of community welfare councils but are not financially participating members of chests. The typical chest usually includes agencies concerned with casework, group work, health services, and institutions of various types.

Agencies under religious or sectarian auspices may usually be admitted to chests if these agencies carry on substantial programs of social service. Practice differs as to the inclusion of Catholic and Jewish agencies, and as to the relationships between community chests and Catholic and Jewish federations, where such federations exist.

[5] *Trends in Giving, 1957* (New York, UCFC, 1957), Table 15, Total Raised by All Recorded Community Chests and United Funds, 1920–1957, p. 14.

Certain national agencies have had definite policies of separate fund-raising and of non-participation in community chest campaigns.

Agencies whose programs are vitally concerned with essentially controversial issues are usually not included in chests, on the theory that the chests must be able to appeal to virtually the entire adult population for support. Such agencies include those concerned with economic change and control, labor legislation and basic changes in economic standards, voluntary parenthood, political reform, promotion of good government, and perhaps even governmental research.[6]

Agency membership in a chest usually implies a formal, contractual relationship between the agency and the chest. The agency is ordinarily admitted by vote of the board of the chest, after investigation by an admissions committee and probably by the community welfare council, if there is one.

The chest member-agency is expected: to forego direct solicitation of funds (except by special arrangement with the chest); to accept its budget as approved by the chest, after full consideration and conference; to maintain a responsible management, with an active board; to cooperate with other agencies; to undertake new services or expand its program only with the approval of the chest; to keep proper accounts; and to submit reports to the chest.[7]

The chest, on the other hand, is expected: to set a campaign goal reasonably adequate to the needs; to make every effort to meet this goal; to cooperate with the agencies in maintaining a fair and democratic procedure for determining agency budgets; to maintain a democratic form of organization and responsible management; to maintain appropriate health and welfare planning machinery; to cooperate with the member-agencies but to avoid infringing upon their essential autonomy; and to cooperate with the agencies in interpreting their needs and maintaining good public relations.

CHEST ORGANIZATION

Two basic questions in connection with the organization of a community chest are: (1) Who elects the members of the Board of Directors? These electors, whoever they are, are the group of ultimate

---

[6] See Norton, *Cooperative Movement in Social Work*, pp. 154–172, for a discussion of the whole problem of agency membership.

[7] *Sample Constitution and By-Laws for a Separate Community Chest*, (1952); also a similar statement in *Sample* [Constitution and By-Laws] *for Combined Community Chest and Council* (New York, CCC, 1949, mimeographed).

control. In the last analysis they can determine the chest's program and policies; although in practice most basic decisions are usually left to the Board. (2) What is the organizational relationship between the chest and the community welfare council?

Many variations in organizational structure may be found in chest history and in current practice. In some chests all or most of the members of the Board have been elected by the contributors. This makes the chest, in effect, a givers' association; the chest agencies, in this case, are "beneficiaries" rather than equal partners in the enterprise. The opposite of this arrangement, where all or most of the members of the Board are elected by social agencies belonging to the chest or the council, is no more satisfactory, for it leaves out of account the contributing public whose gifts make possible the existence of the chest and the continuance of the agencies and their services. A third type of chest organization, in which the Board is self-perpetuating or is elected by a group of self-perpetuating members of the corporation, is of course completely undemocratic. Such a form of organization affords no guarantee that the Board will be responsive to the desires of either the contributors, the agencies, or the community as a whole.

Under the plan of organization suggested by UCFC for a separate community chest (that is, a chest that is not combined with a community welfare council), two types of membership are established: (1) Individual members, including contributors and volunteers who agree to give service through the organization. (2) Institutional members — agencies financed through the chest. Each agency may appoint five delegates to represent it at meetings of the membership.

The Board consists of 21 members, serving for overlapping terms of three years, plus the chairmen of the three committees on Campaign, Budget and Admissions, and Publicity.

Board members are nominated by a committee representing the Board, the institutional delegates, and the individual membership. The Board elects a President and other officers; it appoints committees on Campaign, Budget and Admissions, and Publicity; and it may employ an executive secretary.[8]

This plan of organization is simple; it gives representation to agencies, contributors, and volunteer workers; and it seeks to assure that the board shall be representative.

[8] *Sample Constitution and By-Laws for a Separate Community Chest* (New York, CCC, 1952).

THE COMBINED CHEST AND COUNCIL

The various types of organizational relationships between community chests and community welfare councils have been described in Chapter 10. The only one to be further considered here is the combined chest and council.

A plan of organization for such a federation, as suggested by UCFC, provides for two types of membership:[9] (1) organizational members, financially participating (the chest member agencies) and financially non-participating (governmental and voluntary non-chest agencies), each agency having two delegates; and (2) individual members — at least as many as the organizational members — elected by the members, for three-year overlapping terms. This membership body is similar to a delegate assembly for a modern community welfare council.

The Board of Directors consists of twenty-one directors, elected by the members, and serving for three-year overlapping terms, plus the chairmen of the Social Planning, Campaign, and Budget committees and the chairman of the public relations department steering committee.

The functions of the Social Planning Committee are similar to those of a community welfare council; indeed, the committee corresponds, in many ways, to a council board, except that the Committee is responsible to the board of the Federation rather than to the membership. The Committee has the power to create standing divisions and appoint committees, as required.

The Board has the power to establish departments to deal with such functions as research, public relations, social service exchange, and volunteer service bureau. There is a steering committee for each such department.

The plan as a whole is an ingenious one for mingling the functions of a chest and a council in one organization. The question as to whether it is better to have the chest and council combined or separate has been discussed in Chapter 10.

THE CAMPAIGN

The community chest makes a single, united, personal appeal to the community each year to secure the support from contributions

[9] See *Sample* [Constitution and By-Laws] *for Combined Community Chest and Council.*

needed by its member agencies. This is the annual chest campaign.

This campaign, in its outward manifestations, is the best-known aspect of the community chest. It is a major community event, each year; a large proportion of the people of the community participate in it, either as workers or contributors; a still larger number know that it is happening and have at least a general idea of what it is all about.

Norton says that the campaign is based upon five general principles: (1) Skilled planning and direction. (2) The compilation, efficient distribution, and constant control, of a sufficient number of prospect cards. (3) The organized use of large numbers of volunteer solicitors. (4) The largest amount of publicity possible. (5) A short specified time at the end of which the work is to be completed — somewhere between four days and two weeks.[10]

The campaign involves personal solicitation of prospects at their places of business or their homes, and group solicitation for large numbers of employees. In the case of larger and medium-sized contributions, the effort is to secure a pledge, payable at intervals throughout the year, and representing what the contributor is able to give for the whole year, rather than to obtain a smaller cash contribution.

The chest attempts to secure as complete coverage as possible of all persons in the community who are likely to be able to contribute. This includes: larger givers and corporations, who may be approached by a "special gifts" division, or otherwise, in advance of the public campaign; medium-sized contributors, approached individually at their places of business or their homes; and industrial, commercial, public utility, and governmental employees, canvassed through group solicitation at their places of employment.

The actual public campaign is a short, intensive high-pressure effort. The ideal length is probably a week to ten days, though a longer period is frequently necessary in some communities. Most chest campaigns are held in the fall.

The campaign is carried on under citizen leadership and with participation of a large number of volunteers as solicitors, speakers, members of committees, and so on. Selection of the campaign chairman is a matter of crucial importance. He should be an outstanding citizen, who commands public confidence, is a dynamic leader, willing to work, and able to enlist persons of like qualities to head up the various divisions of the campaign.

An effective campaign requires skilled executive direction. The chest usually has a full-time executive, who should be trained or ex-

[10] Norton, *Cooperative Movement in Social Work*, pp. 195–207.

perienced in campaign strategy and management, as well as general health and welfare work. Larger chests, of course, have staffs of various sizes, with a variety of specialized jobs. In a few instances chests employ commercial money-raising concerns to take charge of the executive direction of the campaign.

Setting the campaign goal is always a difficult problem. Shall it be based upon the social welfare needs of the community as expressed in agency budget requests, or upon the amount that it seems reasonable to think can be raised? In practice, the goal is usually a compromise between what is believed to be needed and what it is thought can be raised. The budget committee and the campaign committee should both be parties to the discussion, and the chest board of directors should make the final decision.

CAMPAIGN OPERATION

The campaign is a highly organized undertaking. The accompanying chart indicates how personnel, prospect cards, and publicity are all focused upon the period of personal solicitation of prospects. In all of this, timing is of the essence. The prospect cards are a vital factor in the campaign. The cards of at least larger potential contributors must be individually "rated," by a rating committee, on the basis of past history as a contributor and estimated ability to give. Cards must be assigned to teams; each card of a larger contributor must be assigned to the person who is most likely to be successful in securing the desired amount.

During the actual campaign period there is ordinarily an opening campaign meeting, a series of report meetings (usually luncheons), and a closing meeting. Along with this must go the daily receipt and auditing of returns from divisions and teams, and rapid and accurate accounting for pledges and cash received.

A contributor to the chest will usually not be solicited by chest agencies for operating expenses during the year. Membership campaigns by chest agencies, for more or less nominal membership dues, are frequently permitted. In addition the contributor is of course not "immune" to solicitation by organizations outside the chest.

The contributor may ordinarily "designate" all or part of his contribution to a particular agency or agencies. However, designation appears to have little practical significance. Few contributors avail themselves of this privilege, so that rarely, if ever, would there be designations amounting to an agency's total budget. If this should

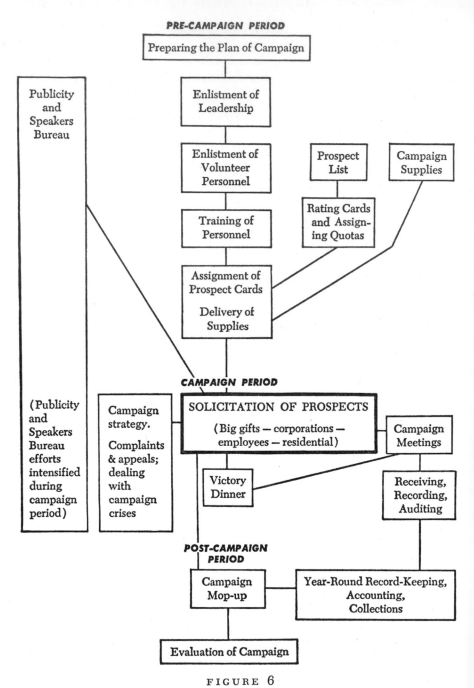

Preparing the Plan of Campaign

Publicity
and
Speakers
Bureau

Enlistment of
Leadership

Enlistment of
Volunteer
Personnel

Prospect
List

Campaign
Supplies

Rating Cards
and Assign-
ing Quotas

Training of
Personnel

Assignment of
Prospect Cards

Delivery of
Supplies

CAMPAIGN PERIOD

(Publicity
and
Speakers
Bureau
efforts
intensified
during
campaign
period)

Campaign
strategy.

Complaints
& appeals;
dealing
with
campaign
crises

SOLICITATION OF PROSPECTS

(Big gifts — corporations —
employees — residential)

Campaign
Meetings

Victory
Dinner

Receiving,
Recording,
Auditing

POST-CAMPAIGN
PERIOD

Campaign
Mop-up

Year-Round Record-Keeping,
Accounting,
Collections

Evaluation of Campaign

FIGURE 6

FLOW CHART—COMMUNITY CHEST CAMPAIGN

happen, the usual rule is that the "over-designation" would revert to the chest's general fund.

CAMPAIGN RESULTS

UCFC publishes each year a bulletin dealing with trends in community chest giving. This is an invaluable tool for chest campaigners and administrators.

A few highlights from *Trends in Giving, 1957* indicate some of the kinds of material available as an index to chest campaigns and their results in community giving.

In campaigns for 1957 the "average" community chest (excluding united funds) received approximately 38% of its funds from employee and executive gifts, and 37% from firm gifts.

The average per capita amount raised for 473 cities was $2.91. (For united funds including Red Cross the per capita was $4.18.) The number of contributors for the chests was about 25 per 100 population.[11]

INTERPRETATION AND PUBLICITY

The community chest carries on a program of interpretation and publicity on behalf of its member agencies, and, more broadly, on behalf of all social and health work in the community. Publicity efforts reach a climax during the annual campaign, but in a well-conducted chest the campaign publicity is only part of a year-round program of interpretation.

In its program of interpretation, the chest (or the chest and council jointly) must try to interpret the social and health needs of the community, the services of social welfare agencies, the need for voluntary financial support, and the values of the chest plan and of a cooperative approach to financing and health and welfare planning. This interpretation aims not only to educate the public and to create a general climate of acceptance; but also to awaken a vital concern over the needs presented, and to arouse the emotions to the point of *action*, through financial contributions and, if possible, personal service and participation in social welfare undertakings.

The interpretative program of the chest involves: close and continuous cooperation with the member agencies of the chest and council, from whom most of the raw material for publicity must be derived;

[11] *Trends in Giving, 1957* (New York, UCFC, Bulletin 197, 1957).

producing publicity and carrying on directly many kinds of interpretative efforts; and consulting with and assisting member agencies in carrying on their own interpretative and publicity programs, since it is intended that the chest program shall supplement and not supplant the efforts of the individual agencies.

In carrying out this program, the chest is likely to use a great variety of media of interpretation. Newspaper publicity of all sorts, paid advertising, printed leaflets, campaign emblems, window exhibits, public speaking, radio, television, movies, trips to agencies, outdoor scoreboards or indicators, pageants and parades are among the possibilities. Still other devices, such as house organs, leaflets inserted with the contributors' bills, and special letters, may be used in connection with the year-round program.

The large community chest has a full-time publicity director, perhaps with one or more assistants. In the smaller chest the interpretative function is carried by the chest executive. In the many small chests that have no paid service, the interpretation program, like other functions of the chest, is carried on by volunteers.

BUDGETING

Joint budgeting is the method by which funds are equitably distributed by a community chest among its member agencies.

The budget is an agency's fiscal work-plan for the year. The estimate of income and expense, for the coming year, is an expression, in financial terms, of the agency's program and plans. It is basic to program development and administration. Almost any important change of program or policy will be reflected in the budget. The opening of a new department or district, a change of location, the addition of a new worker, a change in salaries, an increase in publicity or a decrease in office supplies, all will produce changes in budget figures.

Federated budgeting is focused on the community as a whole and "on maintaining a service program which will best serve the total community." Through it the hopes and plans of agencies are viewed against the background of the attitudes of the contributing public, the programs of other agencies, and the unmet needs of the community.[12] The budgets of all the chest agencies, taken together, are even more important than the sum of the individual units. The

---

[12] *Budgeting: A Manual on Policies and Procedures* (New York, CCC, Bulletin 180, 1955), p. 7.

budgets as a whole represent the programs of most of the voluntary agencies in the community; that is, they represent a highly important segment of the total social welfare services and resources available in the community.

"Although budgeting is concerned with efficiency and economy of operation, its most difficult and important task is to make choices as to what services shall be financed. For this reason, 'budgeting is the crossroads at which planning and fund-raising meet. . . .' Federated budgeting is essentially an attempt to arrive at a work program for a given year which is mutually agreed upon by the Chest and the agencies, in the light of available resources." [13]

Joint budgeting by chest agencies causes every such agency to make an annual review of its program and finances and to plan definitely and realistically for the coming year. Moreover, the budget must be submitted not merely to the agency's own board but to a budget committee representing the community as a whole. This is a wholesome procedure. For a group of agencies, each with its own needs, interests, points of view, and aspirations, to be willing to submit their budgets to authoritative action by a representative community body is a striking demonstration of the workability of federation. Joint budgeting is an acid test of cooperation by health and welfare agencies.

PRINCIPLES OF JOINT BUDGETING

Chest budgeting is ordinarily based upon the following principles.[14]

1. The chest appropriates funds to an agency for the year's current operating expenses only — not for new buildings or other capital investments.

However, since the capital plans and undertakings of an agency are of concern to the chest, the chest has a right to prescribe general policies regarding capital expansion and to have access to information regarding the agency's capital account.

Agency building campaigns must be timed so that they will not conflict with the chest campaign. Moreover, such matters relating to capital expansion on the part of an agency must be a matter for joint decision by the agency and the chest.

[13] *Ibid.,* pp. 8, 10.
[14] *Budgeting: A Manual on Policies and Procedures.* See also: *Budgets in a Community Chest.* (New York, CCC, Bulletin 112, 1953; partial reprinting of edition of 1942).

2. The chest's allocation to its member-agencies is made for a fiscal year identical for all agencies — usually the calendar year.

3. The chest's allocation to its agencies is in the nature of budget balancing or "deficit financing": that is, the chest allocation is the difference between total expenses and income from other sources.

Agencies may receive income from other sources than the chest. Four principal sources of additional income are:

(a) Earnings — fees, camp, visiting nurse service, etc.; payments for room and board of children from relatives; payment for services given through dormitories, cafeteria, etc.; sale of products by a sheltered workshop; and so on.

(b) Memberships and direct contributions to the agency for operating expenses.

(c) Payments from tax funds. It is desirable that any such funds should be payments for specific services — room and board for specified children in foster homes, for example.

(d) Interest on investments.

Agency budgets differ greatly in the amounts and proportions of their income which they receive from sources other than the chest.

An exception to deficit financing is frequently made in the case of hospitals, where the chest in effect buys a certain amount of free service instead of attempting to balance the hospital budget.

4. The chest's allocation to an agency is based upon (a) a budget which includes detailed estimates of receipts and expenditures for the coming year, and (b) the records of the agency's actual receipts and expenditures during at least the last ended fiscal year and the current fiscal year, to date.

5. The Budget Committee of the Chest is the body which reviews agency budget requests and makes recommendations regarding chest allocations. Sometimes the budget committee is formally a committee of the chest only, sometimes of the chest and council jointly, and sometimes the chest delegates the whole budgeting function to the community welfare council.

Opinions differ as to whether budgeting should be done by the chest or the council. On the one hand, it is urged that the council is the body that best knows agency programs and needs and that therefore it is the logical body to pass on budgets. On the other hand, it is urged that the chest, in its function of joint-financing, is responsible not only for fund *raising* but for fund *disbursement;* that the chest as such should be in close touch with program needs and problems, and not become a mere campaign mechanism; and that the chest should properly do the budgeting itself and not delegate it to any other body, even the council. It may be argued also that assigning budgeting to the council puts the council in an undesirable authoritative or "Santa Claus" role and that it builds up a "we and it" instead of a "we" psychology in the minds of the agencies.

It would seem that budgeting *is* inherently a chest function, but that it should be carried on by the chest with the active cooperation, consultation, and assistance of the council. A joint chest-council committee, technically under the sponsorship of the chest, is one way of achieving this. Another is to provide for close interplay between the council divisions and the budget committee or sub-committees.

In a larger chest, the budget committee usually appoints sub-committees or panels from the various functional fields, such as family welfare, health, etc. These sub-committees may correspond to the functional divisions of the council, and the secretaries of the divisions may render consultant or other services to the sub-committees.

6. Agencies are normally not permitted to build up individual surpluses or reserve funds. An agency surplus at the end of the year reverts to the chest general fund. It is part of the logic of federation to have one "family reserve fund," available for use when and where it is most needed, rather than 30 or 130 funds in the treasuries of specific agencies.

If an agency deficit is incurred, the chest usually feels under no obligation to meet it unless it has been incurred with the approval of or at least after consultation with the chest. Most deficits can be prevented, and almost all can be foreseen. A prospective deficit is a matter for mutual consideration and planning by the agency and the chest.

The chest usually provides standardized budget forms for recording in detail the necessary financial data regarding receipts and expenditures.

Much of the success of the budgetary process depends upon the staff service given by the chest executive, budget secretary, or whoever is assigned to this task. A competent and experienced budget secretary attains a knowledge of the agencies' needs and problems and comparative conditions and situations which may be invaluable both to the budget committee and to the agency.

The usual course in the production, consideration, and approval of the agency budget is illustrated in Figure 7.

One of the most important steps in the process is the budget conference, between the Budget Committee and representatives of the agency, including the agency executive and representation from the agency's officers, finance committee, and board. The chest budget

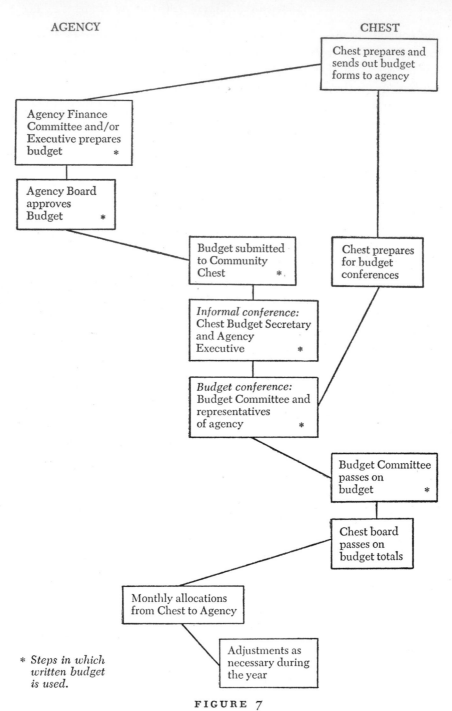

AGENCY   CHEST

Chest prepares and
sends out budget
forms to agency

Agency Finance
Committee and/or
Executive prepares
budget   *

Agency Board
approves
Budget   *

Budget submitted
to Community
Chest   *.

Chest prepares
for budget
conferences

Informal conference:
Chest Budget Secretary
and Agency
Executive   *

Budget conference:
Budget Committee and
representatives
of agency   *

Budget Committee
passes on
budget   *

Chest board
passes on
budget totals

Monthly allocations
from Chest to Agency

Adjustments as
necessary during
the year

* *Steps in which
written budget
is used.*

FIGURE 7

FLOW CHART—COMMUNITY CHEST BUDGETING

secretary is usually present as the technical adviser of the committee. The committee reviews the budget in as much detail as it thinks desirable, and makes its recommendation to the Chest Board.

Where the budgeting process is well done, this conference does not mean an unfriendly cross-examination of the agency or an attempt to beat down its budget estimates in the traditional spirit of the watchdog of the treasury. Rather, it is a friendly and objective, though searching, mutual consideration, by representatives of the community and of the agency, of the agency's estimate of its needs, in the light of other related community needs. A budget committee sometimes has occasion to suggest increases in certain items over the amounts included in the agency's estimate.

In the early days of the chest movement the principle of budgeting *before* the campaign was generally accepted. The theory was that the agencies submitted their budget requests; and that the sum of the approved requests (plus certain general expenses) determined the amount of the campaign goal. However, when a chest failed to attain its goal, precampaign budgeting caused complications. Agencies had been notified of the amounts of their approved budgets; but the chest's failure to reach its goal now meant reviewing the budgets again and making the cuts necessary to bring them within the amount of the funds available.

Even aside from any question of a possible failure to meet the goal, it is obviously easier for a committee to budget when it knows exactly how much money there is to be spent. Then, too, as chests have matured and gained experience, they have tended to set campaign goals earlier in the year. If pre-campaign budgeting were united with early goal-setting, it would mean early budgeting (probably in the summer — a bad time for committee meetings and conferences) with less current experience to go on and less realism in estimates and decisions. But the chest with several years of experience is no longer so dependent upon *detailed* final budget figures in fixing the campaign goal. The chest can ask for budget estimates from the agencies in the summer and work from these, rather than from the approved budgets, in setting the campaign goal, reserving detailed budget review, conference with agencies, and decisions until after the campaign. For these and perhaps other reasons, the present tendency, at least in larger cities, is toward post-campaign budgeting. More and more, also, budgeting is regarded as a year-round process rather than a seasonal manifestation.[15]

[15] *Budgeting: A Manual on Policies and Procedure*, pp. 18–20. *Guides for Community Chest Budgeting in the Smaller Community* (New York, CCC, Bulletin 155, 1950), p. 3. *Budget Administration: A Year Around Process* (New York, CCC, 1950).

THE ALLOCATION OF THE BUDGET

THE TOTAL BUDGET APPROVED by the chest includes all or most of the following elements:

1. Budgets of local chest member-agencies.

2. Central finance and planning — campaign expense, publicity, and year-round administration of the chest, community welfare council, social service exchange, and any other common services.

3. An allowance for "shrinkage" — that is, for failure to collect 100 per cent of the campaign pledges, by reason of deaths, removals from the city, financial reverses, and other reasons.

4. Sometimes an allowance is made for a reserve or contingency fund or both. A contingency fund is used to meet unforeseen requirements during the year. A reserve fund is ordinarily a larger fund, carried forward from year to year, for meeting major emergencies. UCFC notes that "many Chests are experimenting with the provision of a special fund or reserve for major repairs and emergency replacements." [16]

An analysis of the distribution of chest funds for 90 community chests showed the following: [17]

Agencies		84.8%
Family-children's service and general dependency	30.1%	
Recreation services	37.5	
Health services	14.9	
Care of aged, community organization and miscellaneous	2.3	
Chests and councils		12.4
Shrinkage allowance		2.8
		100.0%

There may of course be wide variations among individual chests and cities of different sizes in the proportion of funds allocated to the various types of agencies.

COLLECTION AND ACCOUNTING

Since most of the chest subscriptions secured at the time of the campaign are in the form of pledges rather than cash, the chest must

[16] *Budget Administration: A Year Around Process*, p. 8.
[17] *Budgeting for 1957* (New York, UCFC, Bulletin 196, 1957), p. 1. These figures are for chests other than united funds. Allocations for reserves and contingency funds are not shown in this publication.

make collections throughout the year. This involves cooperation with industrial concerns in handling payroll deductions where this form of contribution has been accepted by workers and management; sending out bills for payments on individual pledges on the dates due; receiving payments; and following up delinquent accounts.

The normal collection record of community chests is high. The "shrinkage" allowance, for failures to collect, is only 2.8% in the figures given above. For united funds the shrinkage may be somewhat higher.[18]

Community chest accounting has the function of accounting for the pledges made at campaign times; payments on pledges during the year, together with other financial receipts; and all chest disbursements. This requires a carefully planned accounting system, adapted to the specialized needs of the chest; some technical bookkeeping or accounting service; and a close working relationship between the collection and accounting functions.

One of the most important records is the contributor's permanent record card for an individual or corporation, which may show a history of pledges for a period of ten to thirty years, with certain details regarding the solicitor, the unit in which the solicitation was made, etc.

THE CHEST AND HEALTH AND WELFARE PLANNING

Where there is a community welfare council in a community, the council, rather than the chest, usually carries the primary responsibility for health and welfare planning, except in connection with budgeting, where the chest is directly and vitally involved in the planning function. Sometimes, where there is no council, the chest may have a "social planning committee" or some similar body which attempts to render services in health and welfare planning somewhat similar to those of a council. The chest also, in the adoption of its operating policies, often finds itself dealing with basic issues of health and welfare planning.

CHEST ACCOMPLISHMENTS

The community chest has played an immensely important part in American social welfare work since World War I. Among the major accomplishments of the chest are the following:

In less than 50 years the chest plan has become *the accepted method of raising funds for most local voluntary welfare agencies* in practically

[18] *Ibid.*, p. 1.

all large cities and in many smaller communities in the United States.

The record of the chests in money-raising has been extremely impressive. As shown previously, the almost two thousand campaigns for 1957 raised $378,000,000. The chests as a whole have usually raised 90 per cent or more of their campaign goals. The cost of raising the money is low: perhaps 4 to 5 per cent of the amounts raised.

Chests have not only raised much more money than individual agencies, but they have *enlisted the contributions of a larger number of givers,* and thus broadened the base of support. The figure of 25 gifts per 100 persons in the population is a striking one, when one takes into account the number of children, old people, and other dependents in our communities.

Chests have *enlisted a type of lay leadership and an amount of volunteer service,* particularly from business men in the community, which was almost unknown before the days of federation. This in itself is a vital contribution to social welfare.

Chests have established the method of *cooperative budgeting* for their member agencies.

By reason of the nature of joint budgeting and fund-raising, membership in chests has fostered a substantial amount of *practical cooperation among member agencies.*

Chests have made a substantial contribution toward *greater uniformity in personnel standards and practices* and toward job and salary classification in voluntary social welfare agencies.

Joint fund-raising has *relieved agency boards and executives of primary responsibility for money-raising.* Relieving them from the continual pressure of fund-raising has tended toward better board and executive service in relation to agencies' service programs.

To a considerable extent, chests have developed *a community-wide point of view* and community-wide financial policies in reference to at least voluntary social welfare services.

Chests have been the *main source of support for community welfare councils and central services* such as social service exchanges and volunteer bureaus. Without chest support most councils would be small and much less able to perform their functions adequately.

Chests and councils together have made substantial contributions to *improving social welfare services,* through strengthening existing programs, establishing new services, improving community patterns of social welfare organization, raising standards, and promoting better teamwork. Many of these advances could not have been made without the help and participation of the chests.

SOME MAJOR PROBLEMS

ALONG WITH THIS IMPRESSIVE record of positive accomplishments, there are certain problems which are connected with the community chest plan and its practical workings. These differ in incidence and importance in different communities.

The chest is big business in its financial operations; it must and does enlist business leadership on the board and in the campaign organization. Sometimes individual chests have become so identified with business that they have lost sight of the fundamental aims of social welfare and have become nothing much more than fiscal organizations. However efficient the money-raising machinery may be, no chest-supported program is safe under these conditions.

Individual chests are sometimes undemocratic in organization and unrepresentative of the community as a whole. Self-perpetuating chest boards or corporations, where they exist, are undemocratic devices which place the control of the organization outside of any democratic or widely representative group. Such forms of organization rightly arouse suspicion and such chests diminish their claim to community support.

Some chests have given evidences of *over-centralization of authority,* autocracy, and undue interference with the freedom of action of individual agencies in respect to their determination of policies, handling of cases, and so on. Some sacrifice of complete freedom and self-interest are inherent in the idea of federation. The values gained through cooperation are assumed to be worth some surrender of unrestricted freedom. However, the idea of essential self-direction in policy-making and operation is also inherent in financial federation; and when a chest begins to direct the internal affairs of an agency, it is exercising a centralized control which is in conflict with all our traditions of voluntary social welfare and which has yet to be demonstrated as being desirable.

In some cases chests, or groups primarily interested in finance, have made or *sought to make community welfare councils subordinate to chests.* This is an ominous development from the standpoint of the integrity of health and welfare planning and of community welfare as a whole.

The executive leadership of chests has sometimes been inadequate to the exacting requirements of the job. This is true of many other social agencies as well; but the chest executive is in a unique position of influence in relation to the health and welfare services in the community. Schools of social work, with few exceptions, have been backward in providing professional education and training needed by chest and council executives. Too often young men, with school of social work training but with no agency experience, and without even field work in direct-service agencies, have come into positions of responsibility in chests or councils which they were in no way fitted to assume. Even more disturbing is the number of chest executives without either training or experience in social work.

Occasionally a chest executive is found who has developed a cynical attitude toward social welfare principles and who derides professional ideals as "class-room theories." This type of person usually embraces a power-philosophy: you have to deal with practical realities, you have to go along with the people that run the town. Where this kind of chest executive exists he is a dangerous person as far as the welfare of the community is concerned. Obviously, the chest executive must understand the realities of community life, leadership, and power structure, but if he has any personal integrity he will not sell out social welfare to selfish interest groups.

Membership groups in agencies which belong to chests have in many cases dried up, and have left the agencies with no constituency groups and with self-perpetuating boards — an undemocratic and generally unsatisfactory pattern. This has been avoided by some agencies, such as Y.M. and Y.W.C.A.'s, where membership means something more than financial contributions; but, particularly with non-group-work agencies, the former contributor-members to individual social agencies have often been merged with the larger number of chest contributors. The chest group is larger but more impersonal; and, if the agency has a self-perpetuating board, it is remote from control by any community group other than the chest. No adequate solution has been found for this problem. Further experimentation is needed to see whether agency memberships and constituencies can be revived on a new and vital basis, or whether some entirely new approach must be made to the problem.

The chest is necessarily a majority agency — it must appeal to the majority of the people in the community for support. It therefore has a *tendency toward the preservation of the status quo;* it may be antagonistic to or timid about controversial programs and proposals; and it may have an over-cautious or even reactionary attitude as far as vigorous social action by social agencies or social workers is concerned. Also, because of the "coming campaign," the chest may be understandably loath to antagonize any actual or potential contributor.

As a matter of fact, one cannot expect the chest itself to be a social action agency. The federative form of organization is scarcely compatible with social crusading. Social action must usually be carried on by a compact minority group, precisely because the majority are not convinced; so it is scarcely reasonable to expect the active participation of a "majority agency" in such social action.[19] However, if the chest itself is not adapted to social action, some of its agencies are; and there is need from the chest leadership for broad tolerance of differences, for some receptiveness to the social action function of agencies, and for courage of outlook in respect to social change and community development.

Chests have sometimes connived at or *acquiesced in pressure upon wage-earners* to contribute. This is a violation of the whole idea of services supported by voluntary contributions. The increasing participation of organized labor in chest operations is the strongest safeguard against any such tendency.

The riddle of chest interpretation and publicity has not been adequately solved in most communities. How shall the chest interpret the total program of its member-agencies without being so superficial that it will do an inadequate job in respect to the interpretation of any one agency? Campaign publicity operates, necessarily, within definite limitations; perhaps it is inevitably more or less superficial. The more agencies there are in the chest, the less individual emphasis can be given to each of them, at least at campaign time. Probably the answer to this problem lies in the improvement of year-round publicity, so that in the course of the year there may be, through the partnership of the chest and the agencies, something approaching adequate interpretation of each agency.

One dilemma which the chest faces is the familiar question: *How much social welfare can the community afford?* From another angle, the problem lies here: voluntary social welfare agencies, if they are alert to the needs of the community, are likely to see, from time to time, new and enlarged opportunities for service through their agency programs. Pressure develops for the expansion of voluntary agency programs — that is, an expansion of agency budgets. On the other hand, there seem to be plateaus of giving in communities; and the question may be asked whether the chest will sooner or later reach a ceiling, or maximum amount that contributors in the community are disposed

[19] For a different point of view, however, as regards councils, see Violet M. Sieder, "The Community Welfare Council and Social Action," NCSW, *Social Work in the Current Scene*, 1950, pp. 22–41.

to give to voluntary social welfare agencies, even with highly effective leadership, campaign organization, and interpretation.

Probably the most important problem facing community chests and the contributing public, at the present time, is the *problem of multiple appeals.*

MULTIPLE APPEALS

The community chest originated in the desire to substitute co-operative financing for competitive financing — one campaign in the place of many. In communities where the chest had the widest coverage, it came to be thought of as *the central* financial effort in behalf of voluntary social welfare services, including almost all agencies except perhaps the American Red Cross, Tuberculosis Association, and a few others.

Within recent years there has been a new growth of national agencies concerned with specialized diseases — infantile paralysis, heart, cancer, and so on. The new national agencies usually did not apply for admission to the local community chests, and it is not certain that they would have been welcomed by all chests if they had applied. With the end of World War II, the war chests, with their inclusion of national war-related appeals, reverted again to peace-time community chests with mainly a local emphasis. Inflation increased, money was harder to raise; and capital-fund campaigns, dammed up during the war period, now showed signs of deluging the community. So, gradually, it became evident in most communities that the community chest was a major project, but only one of several annual fund-raising efforts.

Multiple appeals were again a community problem. In addition to the community chest drive each fall, there were the Red Cross membership campaign, the sale of tuberculosis Christmas Seals, the sale of Easter Seals for crippled children and adults, the March of Dimes for infantile paralysis, campaigns for organizations concerned with heart disease, cancer, and other drives, at various times throughout the year. Once more, as in the days before the community chest, contributors and volunteers were bewildered and sometimes irritated with the numbers of fund-raising campaigns. Again, the question arose: what can be done about these "multiple appeals"?

It might seem that an obvious answer would have been: incorporate these appeals in the community chest. But even if the chest was willing, several of the national agencies in question were not. Many chapters of the Red Cross had been member-agencies of chests in earlier days, but this policy had changed, and there had been no Red Cross-Community Chest affiliation in any community in recent years. Other national organizations that conducted large campaigns usually independent of chests were the American Cancer Society, National Foundation for Infantile Paralysis, National Society for Crippled Children and Adults, and National Tuberculosis Association. Some of the organizations had special money raising methods or devices which were of unique value in raising funds.

The proponents of more inclusive federation pointed to the values of the community chest plan, the phenomenal growth of the chest movement, and the successful history of the chests in many communities. They stressed the irrationality and the wastes of competition in fund-raising, the annoyance to contributors of multiple appeals, the desirability of joint budgeting and of an orderly community process for allocating community gifts among both local and national agencies. They sometimes raised questions as to whether certain national agencies did not receive more money than they needed, merely because of the effectiveness of their respective money-raising appeals and devices or the emotional factors involved.

The opponents of more inclusive joint financing demanded a continuance of freedom in welfare fund raising; they protested against "compulsory joint fund-raising" and "coercion." The health agencies declared that vital health education — personal involvement in a cause — could be accomplished only through separate appeals. They maintained, moreover, that a number of appeals, spaced throughout the year, were more effective in raising money than one highly-organized appeal; they pointed out that different people were interested in different programs and types of agencies; they defended the right of national agencies to set their own goals individually, and they derided the idea that any health agency had more money than it needed to do the things that needed to be done. Most statements in behalf of the "independent" national organizations did not attack "voluntary" financial federation by local agencies, in community chests, but made it clear that these organizations did not wish to be included in federated drives.[20]

---

[20] *The Case for Freedom in Welfare Fund Raising* (Washington, American National Red Cross, 1949). Robert Keith Leavitt, *Common Sense About Fund Raising* (New York, American Book, Stratford Press, 1949), pp. 7–8. American Heart Association, *The Heart Fund Story* (New York, 1955, 4 pp.).

This conflict came to a head in Detroit. Wayne McMillen has summarized what happened there:

In 1949 under the leadership of Henry Ford II and with the support of the labor unions, a drive was organized in which national fund-raising agencies were asked to participate. The campaign was limited to in-plant solicitation, and notice was given that no other drive would be permitted within the factories . . . Some of the national health agencies refused to join the drive and subsequently declined preferred shares in the proceeds. A compromise permitting the pledge card to afford opportunity for a separate subscription resulted in partial participation by the Red Cross. The ensuing campaign, in the fall of 1949, evoked fresh battles. National headquarters of the American Red Cross threatened withdrawal of the Detroit Chapter's charter if it entered the federated drive. An arrangement was finally devised, however, whereby in the single drive a separate gift could be made to the Red Cross accompanied by . . . a membership card. A comparable plan was also accepted by the National Foundation for Infantile Paralysis (March of Dimes).[21]

The conflict of ideas continued in various communities. Other "united funds" began to develop. In some cases, where national health agencies did not participate, these united funds raised funds for "causes" that represented the diseases or fields of interest of such agencies.

PLANT LEVEL FEDERATION

In some communities a plan called "plant level federation" was developed. Under this plan the employees of a plant or an industry raise money which is distributed among the chest or united fund and other beneficiary organizations, at the discretion of the plant level committee. Under a variation of this plan, the plant level organization is sometimes a "chapter" of the united fund and channels its giving through that organization.

Community chest leaders differ in their reactions to plant level federation. Some encourage and promote it; others accept it reluctantly, as a necessary means to increased contributions; still others oppose it. Some see in it a dangerous threat to the principle of joint budgeting.

It has been suggested that a plant level federation plan should

[21] Wayne McMillen, "Financing Social Work," SWYB, 1954, p. 222.

embody the following practices: (1) There should be year-round pay-roll deduction, rather than deduction for a limited period of weeks. (2) Deductions should be based on a percentage of earnings; there should not be flat deductions, the same for employees earning $3600 and $15,000. (3) Participation in the plan should not be made a condition of employment. Solicitation each year rather than at the time of employment seems desirable. (4) The plan should be sponsored and administered by a joint labor-management committee in the plant. (5) There should be year-round official liaison between the community chest and the plant labor-management committee.[22]

THE UNITED FUND

At the present time the united fund is an increasingly important aspect of the picture of community welfare organization.

A united fund is:

an autonomous, non-profit corporation formed for united community action toward eliminating duplicate campaign efforts and more adequately financing essential voluntary health and welfare services. It is designed to provide for national as well as local services, and the dominant and immediate purpose is that of bringing about one combined fund-raising campaign to take the place of many separate drives. Which causes are to be combined varies from city to city and is a matter for local negotiation and determination.[23]

Several different types of organization structure have been used in the establishment of united funds. These include the following: (1) Beginning anew, dissolving the Community Chest and building from the ground up. (2) Creating a new organization in which the Chest becomes a participating member. (3) Retaining the Chest as it is, and forming a new United Health Fund to consolidate the several previously separate national appeals into one joint campaign held in the spring. (4) Using the existing Chest organization with possibly a new name, such as "United Community Chest." [24]

The number of united funds has increased annually for the last eight years. The figures reported by UCFC are as follows:

[22] See *Experiments with More Inclusive Federation.* Part III, *Plant Level Federated Funds* (New York, CCC, 1951).
[23] *Organizing a United Fund* (New York, CCC, Bulletin 165, 1953), p. 5.
[24] *Ibid.*, p. 10.

NUMBER OF UNITED FUNDS KNOWN TO UCFC,

1950–1957

Campaign Year	Number
1950	106
1951	161
1952	276
1953	424
1954	572
1955	707
1956	864
1957	951

These united funds raised more than two-thirds of the total raised by all federated campaigns for 1957.

The American Red Cross is included in more than three-fourths of the campaigns. The inclusion of causes represented by the "Big Six" in these 951 campaigns was as follows:

Cancer	452
Crippled children	147
Heart	474
Polio	112
Red Cross	727
Tuberculosis	53

It is reported that in most cities where cancer, heart, and crippled children are included, the local unit of the national organization agrees on participation. Polio and tuberculosis, however, are frequently included as "causes" without agreement of the local unit of the national organization.[25]

During 1955–1957 the American Cancer Society and American Heart Association adopted revised policies prohibiting any new participation of their local affiliates in federated financing. The Cancer Society has provided also that its local affiliates shall not participate in united funds after 1959.[26]

The Heart Association has provided that:

Heart Associations already participating in a federated fund shall withdraw as soon as it is deemed advisable by the Board of Directors

[25] *1957 Experience in United Funds* (New York, UCFC, Bulletin 193, 1957), pp. 1–5.
[26] American Cancer Society. News release, March 17, 1955. Division Circular Letter, *Memorandum on the New Fund-Raising Policy of the American Cancer Society,* November 6, 1957.

of the American Heart Association, or of the direct affiliate, or both, after consultations with the Board of Directors of the affiliate and the chapter involved.[27]

Both national agencies cited statistics to prove that the increase in contributions had been greater in the cases of their affiliates which were outside of financial federations than in the cases of those which were within such federations.

Various arrangements are worked out in the agreements between the united funds and the American Red Cross: for example, "Red Cross" is sometimes used in the campaign name; the Red Cross usually reserves the right to determine its budget, although there may be variations in actual procedures; and it is frequently provided that persons from whose contributions the Red Cross receives one dollar or more receive Red Cross membership cards.

Obviously federated financing is in a transition stage today, but there appears to be decided movement toward the organization of united funds and extended federated campaigns. How inclusive these funds will ultimately become is still in question.

A national leader of the chest movement has made this appraisal and prediction:

> Federated financing has again demonstrated its enormous adaptability and its vitality . . . It becomes more and more clear that it will continue to grow geographically until every corner of the country is covered, and many more agencies and causes — national as well as local — will be united in the annual appeals.[28]

The commitment of the national organization to the united fund idea is further emphasized by the association's recent change of name to United Community Funds and Councils of America.

QUESTIONS AND PROBLEMS

1. Make a report on your local community chest or united fund. In this connection, see entry in *Directory of Community Chests and Councils.* Obtain from your local chest copies of the Chest's annual report and other literature, if possible. Consider such points as: history; organization; territory and population covered; number of member-agencies; for last campaign — dates, goal, amount raised, number of contributors, contributors per 100

---

[27] American Heart Association. *Fund Raising Policy in Respect to United Appeals.* Adopted October 26, 1955; amended December 10, 1955. See also *The Heart Fund Story,* published by the Association, 1955.

[28] Ralph H. Blanchard, quoted in *Community,* Vol. 30, March 1955, p. 126.

population, per capita contribution, number of solicitors, types of campaign publicity; joint budgeting — budget conferences before or after campaign, composition of budget committee, what participation by council in budgeting; relation of chest to council; how inclusive is chest or united fund — does it include Red Cross, national health agencies, etc.; if so, on what basis; has "plant-level federation" developed?

2. What points are covered in the agreement between your local chest and its member-agencies?

3. Plan one of the following: a chest campaign slogan, a campaign poster, or a window exhibit for a particular agency.

4. Deliver a five-minute fund-raising campaign speech to an assumed audience — service club, labor union, church women's guild, a high school social service club, or the workers in a plant.

5. Stage a solicitation interview in a chest campaign. Consider the techniques employed and the problems encountered.

6. When is budgeting done by your chest? Who does the budgeting? How is the Budget Committee made up? What is the budget procedure? Obtain a set of budget forms, if possible.

7. (Group project). A class may hold a *budget conference*, following as closely as possible the local chest's budget procedure. The instructor may prepare a "case problem" embodying a brief description of a fictitious agency, a statement of some major problems involved in the consideration of the agency's budget and a set of the financial figures for the agency (such as would be furnished to the Budget Committee). Four or five members of the class should be assigned to serve as representatives of the agency. The remaining members of the class should serve as the Chest Budget Committee; one of them should act as Chairman of the Committee, others may be assigned various citizen roles. The instructor, or possibly an advanced student, may serve as the budget secretary and resource person at the conference. Let the agency representatives present the agency's budget and the case for it; let the Budget Committee discuss the budget and make its decisions.

8. A chest has failed to reach its goal. The total funds available for agency budgets will be about 10 per cent less than last year. Budgets will have to be cut. How shall the Budget Committee proceed?

9. What major fund-raising campaigns have been held in your community during the past year? What have been the dates, goals, and amounts raised?

10. (Group project) Assume that you are a committee to study the problem of multiple appeals, methods of improving the situation and whether or not a united fund should be organized in your community. Assign roles representing the Chest, Council, various agencies from the "big six," management, labor, contributors and other interest groups. What action would you propose? If there are irreconcilable divisions, what are the issues and positions involved?

SUGGESTIONS FOR READING

United Community Funds and Councils of America (formerly Community Chests and Councils of America), 345 East 46th Street, New York, has issued a large number of technical publications on chests and councils; these include several annual or biennial statistical publications, an annual *Directory* of chests and councils, and the periodical, *Community*. UCFC's Publication List may be obtained on request to that organization.

The logical starting points for the study of chests are the *Social Work Year Book* articles and the CCC pamphlet, *Organizing and Operating a Community Chest*.

Several references at the end of chapter 10 refer to chests as well as councils.

Andrews, F. Emerson, *Attitudes Toward Giving* (New York, Russell Sage Foundation, 1953, 145 pp.).

———— *Corporation Giving* (New York, Russell Sage Foundation, 1952, 361 pp.). See also NCSW, *Social Welfare Forum*, 1952, pp. 251–261.

———— *Philanthropic Giving* (New York, Russell Sage Foundation, 1950, 318 pp.). A scholarly study of the various aspects of giving to and fund-raising for social welfare programs and services.

Atwater, Pierce, *Problems of Administration in Social Work* (Minneapolis, University of Minnesota Press, 1940, 319 pp. OP). Chapter 16 includes a vivid commentary on the nature of the chest campaign.

Community Chests and Councils of America:

Constitutions and By-Laws. Samples — mimeographed — for (a) Combined Chest and Council (New York, 1949, 11 pp.), (b) Separate Community Chest (New York, 1949, 5 pp.).

Friends and Relations: The Community Red Feather Services and the Public (New York, 1947, 22 pp.). Chest public relations.

Helpful Hints for Campaigners (Bulletin 148, New York, 1950, 15 pp. and exhibits). Campaign handbook.

Organizing and Operating a Community Chest (Bulletin 143, New York, 1952, 17 pp.). Basic descriptive pamphlet on the community chest.

Danstedt, Rudolph T., "Current Conflicts in the Approach to Community Organization," *Social Service Review*, Vol. XXIV, March 1950, pp. 67–73.

McMillen, Wayne, "Wartime Developments in Federated Financing of Social Work," in Wright, Helen R. (ed.), *Social Service in Wartime* (Chicago, University of Chicago Press, 1944, 201 pp.), pp. 144–168.

Massachusetts Community Organization Service, *Toward Solving the Puzzle: A Manual for the Appraisal of Community Resources and Social Services* (Boston, 1954, 88 pp.). An important experimental manual for chests and councils in appraising a community's fiscal ability and social welfare resources.

Norton, William J., *The Cooperative Movement in Social Work* (New York, Macmillan, 1927, 373 pp. OP). An authoritative volume on the community chest and the chest movement to 1927. Much of the author's discussion is still relevant and of practical current use.

Seeley, John R. and others, *Community Chest: A Case Study in Philanthropy* (Toronto, University of Toronto Press, 1957, 593 pp.). An intensive case study of the Community Chest of Indianapolis in the early 1950's.

Seymour, Harold J., *Design for Giving: The Story of the National War Fund, 1943–1947* (New York, Harper, 1947, 182 pp., OP) Chapter V contains a stimulating discussion of the fund-raising campaign.

MULTIPLE APPEALS AND UNITED FUNDS

American National Red Cross. *The Case for Freedom in Welfare Fund Raising* (Washington, 1949, 24 pp.). The case for "independent," non-federated fund-raising.

Blanchard, Ralph H., *The Future of Federation* (New York, CCC, 1949, 14 pp.). The outlook for the chest-council movement.

Community Chests and Councils of America:

Experiments with More Inclusive Federation (New York, 1951). Three bulletins: Part I, A Sound Approach, 6 pp. Part II, Summary of Community Experience, 18 pp. Part III, Plant Level Federated Funds, 12 pp.

Organizing a United Fund (Bulletin 165, New York, 1953, 35 pp.).

"Somebody Ought to Do Something . . ." (New York, 1950, mimeographed, 19 pp.). The problem of multiple appeals.

Leavitt, Robert Keith, *Common Sense About Fund Raising* (New York, American Book-Stratford Press, 1949, 64 pp.). Arguments in favor of "independent" as against federated fund-raising.

I2.

STATEWIDE AGENCIES[1]

THE STATE SETTING FOR community organization is radically different from that of the local community. The differences stem from geographic area and distance. The state contains a variety of communities and types of territory: large cities, small cities, towns, villages, and open country. Topography and climate vary. The total population of the state, unlike that of the local community, *does not dwell in contiguous territory.*

Distance is of physical, sociological, and psychological importance. Distance breeds sectionalism as isolation breeds provincialism. There may be the perennial struggle between east and west or north and south — or between the large city and rural upstate or downstate. A mountain range may divide the state and intensify the rivalry between two cities. Rivalries may exist between several large cities of almost the same size.

Statewide organization is much more difficult than local organization. It is harder to hold meetings, both of committees and of larger groups. It is difficult, time-consuming, and expensive for people representing all sections of the state to get together for a committee meeting. A state organization must depend far more upon the written word and far less upon first-hand contacts than a local organization. Many first-

[1] Substantial portions of this chapter are reproduced or adapted from a paper by the author, "Statewide Community Organization Comes of Age," which was presented at a meeting of Community Chests and Councils of America, at the National Conference of Social Work, 1950, and was published in the *Social Service Review*, Vol. XXIV, December 1950, pp. 484–492; copyright, 1950, by the University of Chicago. Used by permission of University of Chicago Press.

hand contacts can be made only through staff travel, which is expensive and time-consuming. Moreover, the statewide organization's constituency is usually larger, more widely distributed, and more diverse in experience and points of view.

Nevertheless, statewide community organization is of great importance. Governmentally, the state is the basic unit of the nation. The state possesses a large degree of autonomy; even in time of war or economic depression, when federal centralization is increased, most social legislation is state legislation. The state stands midway between the nation and the community. Legally, the county and municipality are creations of the state.

Moreover, the basic pattern today in the field of social welfare is public welfare. The state plays the leading part in the public social services, especially in programs of categorical public assistance, treatment of the physically handicapped, mental health, corrections, and frequently in child welfare and general assistance. Most public welfare programs today involve state legislation, administration, leadership, supervision, or support.

It is virtually impossible to reach most rural areas with social services except by means of statewide programs. Left entirely to their own resources, too many rural counties would have neither the vision, the leadership, the cohesiveness, nor the financial resources to develop social welfare programs adequate to their needs. With statewide programs and leadership, there is far more chance of developing something like adequate services to the rural counties.

One important characteristic of statewide community organization is the promotion of legislation. All public welfare programs rest upon a statutory basis, and many other social relationships of concern to social welfare agencies are affected by legislative provisions: for example, marriage, adoption, domestic relations, education, public health provisions, inheritance, and many criminal proceedings.

THE BACKGROUND OF STATEWIDE COMMUNITY ORGANIZATION

STATEWIDE COMMUNITY ORGANIZATION for social welfare, as we think of it today, is a fairly recent development. In the field of governmental services we may trace it back to the first "state central authority," the Massachusetts State Board of Charities, in 1863, the precursor of our modern state welfare departments. On the side of voluntary organization, we may go back to the founding of the New York State Charities Aid Association in 1872 and the organization of the Wisconsin Conference of Social Work in 1881. By 1940, state conferences had spread to almost all the states; and a number of these conferences had become year-round "action" bodies, with full-time executives. Statewide citizens associations had grown up in a few states; councils of statewide agencies had been organized in a number of states in the 1920's, but did not survive; and a large and uncounted number of statewide promotional and community organization agencies had come into existence in such fields as tuberculosis control, social hygiene, crippled children and adults, and mental health.

Since about 1940, it has been widely recognized that the community organization process — in spite of the local sound of its name — may be practiced on any geographical level or between any geographical levels, including, of course, the state level. This idea is a natural corollary to the conception of community organization as an attempt to bring about and maintain an adjustment between social welfare needs and social welfare resources. The term "statewide community organization," is of course here interpreted broadly enough to include not only "overall health and welfare planning" but also the programs in specific fields, such as crippled children or mental health, where there is a large promotional component in the job.

Since 1940, there have been new and important developments in the area of statewide community organization. The number of state conferences with full-time executives has increased. All states have or have had statewide commissions or other planning bodies for various aspects of social welfare — children and youth, health, the aging, recreation, alcoholism, etc.

During World War II, the state war chests swept the country. Since the War, there has been some movement toward statewide joint-fund-raising in certain states.

In 1949, a Directory of certain statewide agencies, published by CCC listed 194 statewide planning and coordinating agencies concerned primarily or partially with social welfare.

The Directory omitted most state public welfare agencies and agencies dealing with specific problems such as tuberculosis, mental health, etc.

An analysis of the 194 agencies listed in the Directory yields the following classification into 13 categories:

FIGURE 8

TYPES OF STATEWIDE AGENCIES LISTED IN CCC DIRECTORY (1949)*

Associations of chests and councils	9
State chests and review boards	6
State citizens' councils	5
Commissions and associations for children and youth	40
State conferences on social welfare	47
Development commissions	19
Health councils and associations	19
Planning boards	16
Recreation commissions and associations	9
Statewide citizens' welfare associations	5
Legislative councils	6
Community organization service (Mass.)	1
Other	12
Total	194

* Based on *Directory of Statewide Agencies,* published by Community Chests and Councils of America, 1949.

The following chart summarizes the major types of contemporary statewide agencies with programs related to community organization, including those omitted from the 1949 Directory. The chart gives four kinds of information about each type of agency: (1) Whether the agency is governmental or voluntary. (2) What is its area of interest — social welfare in general; some special aspect of social welfare; or some other field, such as economic development. (3) Whether it is primarily or only secondarily concerned with social welfare. For example, a state conference on social welfare is interested primarily in social welfare; a state planning board is concerned with it only secondarily. (4) Whether the agency's concern with community organization — planning, coordination, program development, and so on — is primary or secondary. The statewide citizens welfare association is primarily a community organization agency; the state welfare department or a statewide client service agency has other primary duties, and its concern with community organization is secondary.

A review of this chart indicates several facts about these statewide agencies: first, eleven of the fourteen types of agencies are voluntary; all except two are concerned primarily with social welfare; all except two are concerned primarily with community organization.

The total number of statewide agencies represented in all these

FIGURE 9

CLASSIFICATION OF MAJOR TYPES OF STATEWIDE AGENCIES WITH PROGRAMS RELATED TO COMMUNITY ORGANIZATION

NO.	TYPE OF AGENCY	AUSPICES — GOVERN-MENTAL OR VOLUNTARY	AREA OF INTEREST	RELATION TO SOCIAL WELFARE — PRIMARY OR SECONDARY	COMMUNITY ORGANIZATION FUNCTION — PRIMARY OR SECONDARY
1.	State public welfare agencies (departments of mental health, corrections, etc.)	G	Public welfare in general or special aspects of public welfare	P	S
2.	State commissions and other planning bodies — for children and youth, recreation, aging, alcoholism, etc.	Usually G	Special aspects of social welfare	P	P
3.	State planning boards and state development commissions and associations	Usually G	Physical and social planning; economic and social development	S	P
4.	State conferences on social welfare	V	Social welfare — general	P	P
5.	Statewide citizens' welfare associations	V	Social welfare — general	P	P
6.	State health councils and associations	Usually V	Health	P	P
7.	Statewide community organization service	V	Local community organization	P	P
8.	Statewide associations of chests and councils	V	Chests and councils	P	P

CLASSIFICATION OF MAJOR TYPES OF STATEWIDE
AGENCIES WITH PROGRAMS RELATED TO
COMMUNITY ORGANIZATION (continued)

NO.	TYPE OF AGENCY	AUSPICES — GOVERNMENTAL OR VOLUNTARY	AREA OF INTEREST	RELATION TO SOCIAL WELFARE — PRIMARY OR SECONDARY	COMMUNITY ORGANIZATION FUNCTION — PRIMARY OR SECONDARY
9.	State chests, united funds and related organizations	V	Federated financing	P	P
10.	State citizens' councils	V	General welfare of state	S	P
11.	Legislative councils	V	Social welfare legislation	P	P
12.	Statewide agencies dealing with specialized problems (tuberculosis, crippled, mental health, infantile paralysis, probation and parole, corrections, association of public welfare or public assistance officials, etc.)	V	Specialized	P	Usually P
1ʳ.	Statewide consumer service agencies (child-placing, etc.)	V	Specialized areas (child-placing, etc.)	P	S
14.	Statewide associations of special types of local consumer-service agencies — family service, Y.M.C.A., etc.	V	Special types of consumer service	P	P

categories is unknown. According to the *Public Welfare Directory,* published by the American Public Welfare Association, there are about 100 state public welfare agencies (excluding institutions), besides those listed in the CCC Directory. On the basis of a conservative estimate of seven specialized agencies per state (categories 12 and 13) there would be 336 such agencies; adding these to the 100 public welfare agencies, and the 194 agencies in the Directory, the total is 630 agencies. Probably there are not less than 700 statewide agencies concerned with community organization to a greater or lesser degree, and it is possible that the total may exceed a thousand.

Five groups of agencies are most important for statewide community organization as a whole. These are: state public welfare agencies; state commissions; state conferences of social work; statewide citizens welfare associations; agencies concerned with statewide joint financing or with chests and councils.

STATE PUBLIC WELFARE AGENCIES

Every state has one or more statewide public welfare agencies. In some states there is an integrated state welfare department, carrying on all or most of the necessary state public welfare functions; in other states there are separate state departments of social welfare, mental health, and corrections; in still others there are different patterns of organization.

A state public welfare agency is usually concerned primarily with certain administrative functions (licensing, supervision, allocation of funds), and with direct care programs, such as public assistance, child placement, or institutional programs. In addition to these services, most state public welfare agencies carry on a variety of community organization activities. These may include the development of a state program for the blind; the promulgation of minimum standards of public assistance, and the efforts of a field staff to translate these printed standards into the daily practice of county agencies; visitation, consultation, and assistance to private child care organizations; the development of a program of classification in the state prisons; and publication of educational leaflets for parents regarding child training and mental health.

The assets and liabilities of the state public welfare agency's use of the community organization process may be thus summarized:

Among its assets are: (1) Its authority as part of the state government. There is a statutory basis for its activities. (2) Its prestige. If the department has a history of effective service and has reasonably good public relations, its prestige is likely to be greater than that of any statewide private agency. (3) The agency usually has a fairly well-developed organization and staff. (4) It is likely to have a fairly large budget; in spite of the inevitable pressures upon even the most generous budgets, there will probably be some leeway for studies, publications, travel, group conferences, and public addresses. (5) As a public agency, it has access to the resources of the state government, and it probably has close cooperative relationships with the Administration, certain legislative committees, and other administrative departments.

There are, however, some counter-balancing liabilities: (1) It is, to some extent at least, a part of the state administration, and thus it is never entirely free. This is true even if it has a directive board at the head of it rather than a single executive immediately responsible to the governor. As an administrative agency of the state government, it usually does not have a free hand in formulating or promoting legislation. It operates within rather definite limits. A public administrative agency is not designed primarily to be a social action agency. (2) The agency often operates within a limited field, and ordinarily it cannot plan or act outside of that field. For instance, if there is a separate state agency for corrections or mental health, the state welfare department cannot take the lead in community organization in those fields. (3) The department must operate within the limits of its statutory powers. It is often inhibited by legal restrictions from taking action that it might think desirable. (4) The department may be politically dominated or controlled. (5) The leadership and staff of the department may be more competent for public welfare administration, their main job, than for community organization, which requires somewhat different emphases, outlooks, and skills. (6) The department may have engendered criticisms and antagonisms because of matters relating to public assistance policies, state supervision of local agencies, or other activities; these antagonisms may carry over into opposition against other social welfare organization programs sponsored by the department.

There is much that the state welfare department can accomplish in community organization; but probably it can do more with studies, education, and the development of standards than with broad-scale planning, program development, or the promotion of highly controversial legislation.

STATE COMMISSIONS

State commissions for social welfare go back at least as far as the Ohio Children's Code Commission of 1911. These bodies represent a rather common approach to statewide problems which have gained widespread public recognition. A governmental commission, created by law or action of the Governor, is appointed to study the problem and the needs of the group involved, to make recommendations, and in some cases to plan and develop a coordinated program.

There are state commissions on children and youth in 46 states, plus the District of Columbia, Alaska, Hawaii, Puerto Rico, and the Virgin Islands. There have been study commissions on the aging in some 25 states; and nine states have permanent bodies with financial support. At least thirteen states have had commissions on alcoholism.[2] State recreation commissions were reported in the 1949 Directory as existing in some nine states.

Many of these state commissions have a broad range of duties. Practically all of them are concerned with exploring designated problems (juvenile delinquency, aging, etc.) and making reports for the guidance of legislative bodies and administrative officials. Some carry out other functions, such as education, planning, promotion, coordination, stimulation of local communities and interested groups, clearinghouse service, consultation, and improvement of programs, personnel, and facilities in the fields in which they are interested.

STATE CONFERENCES ON SOCIAL WELFARE

A state conference on social welfare is a statewide voluntary organization, made up chiefly of individual members, which is concerned primarily with the field of social welfare, and which holds, as a primary element in its program, an annual (or sometimes biennial) statewide conference open to all persons interested.

State conferences are one of the oldest and most widespread statewide voluntary agencies concerned with social welfare. They exist in all 48 states; 18 of them have full-time executives and 9 employ part-

[2] U.S. Department of Health, Education, and Welfare. *National Council of State Committees for Children and Youth.* A directory. Washington, 1957, mimeographed. Clark Tibbitts, "The Aging," SWYB, 1957, p. 98. Raymond G. McCarthy, "State Action on Alcoholism," *State Government,* Vol. XXVII, December 1954, pp. 240–244, 259.

time executives.[3] A few have additional professional staff members. The conferences go by a variety of names, including social work or social welfare conference, association, council, league, and forum.

Broadly, there are two types of state conferences. One is the forum-type which focuses its activities on the annual forum meeting. The other is the so-called action-type, which goes beyond the forum function, undertakes various community organization activities, and is sometimes active in promoting social legislation.

THE ANNUAL CONFERENCE

The annual meeting or conference is a primary function of any state conference. The conference is usually held in the fall or the spring, and it ordinarily lasts two or three days. As in the National Conference, there may be general sessions of the whole conference, business sessions, section meetings, smaller group meetings, and meetings of associate groups and similar organizations. The prevailing pattern in meetings of the state conferences is usually the reading of formal papers and the making of prepared addresses. These may be followed by supplementary presentations by designated discussants or by open discussion from the floor. Other types of program devices may include: the symposium; the panel; the "clinic" for the discussion of problems, types of publicity material, and so on; the round table or group discussion; and occasionally, perhaps, a formal debate. Conferences in social work serve as opportunities for social workers and laymen interested in social welfare to share experiences; consider current problems; report accomplishments and undertakings; submit the results of studies and research; raise questions and offer ideas, suggestions, and recommendations; and sometimes to formulate platforms, endorse specific proposals, and engage in more or less vigorous social action.

Conferences mean different things to different people. Many conference attendants are most interested in the larger meetings with their prepared addresses by leaders in the field of social welfare. Others find greater value in some of the smaller meetings where there is opportunity for personal participation in the informal give-and-take of group discussion. Some social work leaders, including executives and field representatives of national and state agencies, may attend few

[3] Association of State Conferences of Social Work. *Directory of State Conferences of Social Work.* (Columbus, National Conference of Social Work, 1957, dittoed). The Directory lists 17 states with full-time executives, incorrectly omitting Texas.

formal program meetings, except where they have individual responsibilities, but they may have a full schedule of interviews, committee meetings, and conferences with small groups. Such a worker
may be able to accomplish, in one crowded conference week, the
equivalent of several weeks' work in the field. Many an attendant
finds a conference an opportunity for personal consultation of one
sort or another — about employing or being employed, securing
further professional training, about the services offered by some
national or state agency, or about some special agency or individual
problem. The conference attendant has also an opportunity to check
up on new publications at the book tables, to look over the exhibits,
and sometimes to visit local institutions or agencies of special interest.[4]

Some conferences publish proceedings or selected papers from
their programs. Other functions sometimes assumed by the forum-
type conference include: institutes, or brief study courses for limited
groups of registrants, at the time of the annual meeting; regional conferences, which draw attendance from many who would not travel
longer distances to statewide meetings, and publication of proceedings, bulletins, or newsletters.

HEALTH AND WELFARE PLANNING FUNCTIONS

The most vital problem which the state conference has faced
in the past thirty years is the question: Shall the conference restrict its
function to that of the forum, or shall it enter the area of planning,
legislative promotion, and social action in general?

The vast increase in the development of statewide public welfare
programs since 1929 has underscored the importance of having some
kind of a voluntary agency concerned with statewide programs and
standards, particularly in the field of the public social services. Few
states have citizens' welfare associations, and in an increasing number
of instances the state conference has seen itself as the logical organization to serve as a clearing house on legislative proposals relating to social welfare, and sometimes to engage actively in legislative
promotion and to take on other community organization functions.

It was reported in 1949 that at least 37 conferences endorsed,
initiated, or promoted legislation.[5] A number of conferences have

[4] Arthur Dunham, "Conferences in Social Work," SWYB, 1945, pp. 100–101.
[5] Jane Chandler, "Conferences of Social Work," SWYB, 1949, p. 140. Later
comparable figures appear not to be available.

standing committees concerned with legislation; and several report legislative news in special publications or in their regular bulletins.

Other activities which have been carried on at various times by individual conferences include: studies and surveys; publication of statewide directories; operation of speakers bureaus; sponsorship of voluntary registration of social workers; provision of consultation service to local communities and agencies; assistance in recruiting students for schools of social work; attempts to promote the establishment of needed programs and facilities; educational and interpretative activities; participation in long-range planning for social welfare.

Although state conferences of the action type are doing a substantial amount of health and welfare planning, few of them have sufficient financial support to develop adequate year-round planned programs.

Most state conferences are clearly interested in the broad process of community organization, and most of them are expanding their programs. A few conferences (such as Michigan, Missouri, Texas, and Wisconsin) today resemble statewide citizens welfare associations more closely than they resemble the traditional type of state conference, even though they still retain the conference forum function. There is a tendency toward a blurring of lines between the two types of organization.

STATEWIDE CITIZENS WELFARE ASSOCIATIONS

The statewide citizens welfare association usually has these characteristics: (1) It is a continuously operating statewide, voluntary agency with at least two full-time professional staff members. (2) It has a membership of citizens or citizens and organizations. (3) Its support usually comes primarily from individual memberships and contributions, and grants from community chests. (4) Its officers and board members are primarily laymen. (5) It is primarily a community organization agency; it normally provides no direct consumer-services. (6) Its main interest is usually problems and programs in the field of public welfare and closely adjoining fields such as public health. (7) Its program usually includes services concerned with at least factfinding, education, and legislation; and there is ordinarily a strong emphasis upon analyzing, reporting, and promoting social legislation.

An additional negative characteristic may be noted: none of the citizens associations has an organic connection with the state conference in its state. Presumably it has been felt that the conferences, as forum bodies, should not be organically related to the citizens associations as action bodies, with legislative programs to promote. On the other hand, an increasing number of state conferences have had no difficulty in combining their original forum function with legislative promotional programs.

Statewide citizens welfare associations are few in number, but they are among the most interesting and important community organization agencies in existence. The three organizations which are always included in this category are the New York State Charities Aid Association, the Pennsylvania Citizens Association for Health and Welfare; and the Ohio Citizens Council for Health and Welfare. The Massachusetts Community Organization Service is sometimes regarded as belonging to this group.[6]

The citizens associations resemble community welfare councils in the breadth of their community organization programs; but they have usually been thought of as associations of individual citizens rather than federations of agencies; as citizens associations, they parallel the various state public welfare programs; and they have a major concern with social legislation.

The State Charities Aid Association (SCAA) of New York, the oldest and largest of the statewide citizens associations, was founded in 1872 by Louisa Lee Schuyler. The SCAA has grown in 80 years to be the largest voluntary state health and welfare agency in the United States, with volunteer committees in every county of the state, thousands of individual supporters, and an annual budget of about $900,000. The Association has its offices in New York City. Its program is carried out through the State Committee on Tuberculosis and Public Health; the New York Heart Assembly; the Child Adoption Service (a direct-service agency); the New York State Society for Mental Health (an autonomous but cooperating agency); the State Committee on Children and Public Welfare; the New York City Hospital Visiting Committee; the Legislative Information Bureau; and the Public Information Department. The Association serves also as secretariat for the State Association of Councils and Chests. Each of the volunteer committees in the various counties is concerned with one or more of the Association's fields of activity. The statewide units

---

[6] New Jersey had a Charities Aid Association from 1886 until at least 1917. See Paul Stafford Tutt, *State Welfare Administration in New Jersey* (Trenton, New Jersey Department of Institutions and Agencies, 1934). New Hampshire had a Citizens Council for the General Welfare for a few years following 1945.

concerned with Tuberculosis and Public Health, Heart, and Mental Health are affiliated with the respective national organizations in these fields.

Homer Folks, executive of the Association for 53 years, once observed that the things which the SCAA has undertaken to aid public charities had ranged . . .

> from establishing the first Training School for Nurses in a general hospital in America, to reporting to the hospital authorities that on Ward 33 there were no safety pins available on September 13th at 3:00 P.M., and no more in the storeroom; from organizing State-wide support for a bond issue for $50,000,000 for State Hospitals, or for $60,000,000 for emergency relief, to initiating and organizing the prevention of tuberculosis which has already saved several times over the cost of the insane and the poor; from securing a modern public health law, to reporting a minor violation of the Sanitary Code; from placing 6,000 children in homes for adoption, to advising one bewildered mother where she could get advice.[7]

In one legislative session the Association's Health and Welfare Legislation Bureau followed 1225 bills and resolutions. It reported 1160 of these in bulletins which were distributed to public officials, voluntary agencies, citizens groups, and community leaders.

The Pennsylvania Citizens Association for Health and Welfare (PCA), formerly the Public Charities Association of Pennsylvania, was organized in 1912, at the instance of the state conference on social welfare.

The PCA has over 3,000 individual members and an annual budget of about $135,000, most of which is derived from allocations from community chests. The Association has standing committees on Child Welfare, Public Assistance, and Corrections. The former Mental Health Division became a separate but closely cooperating agency in 1952. The headquarters of the PCA are located at Harrisburg and active regional offices are maintained at Philadelphia, Pittsburgh, Harrisburg, and Wilkes Barre. The Association, in recent years, has emphasized the development of a decentralized program, with an organization structure representing various geographical sections of the state.

Over the years, the PCA has been active in connection with many surveys, including studies of problems and services relating to delinquency and corrections, in particular counties and communities; it

[7] Homer Folks, *The Central Purpose of the State Charities Aid Association* (New York, SCAA, 1942).

has analyzed, reported on, and promoted legislation; it has carried on mental health education, through many channels, and has worked for adequate institutional facilities for the mentally handicapped, children, and adult offenders. It cooperated closely with the state unemployment relief agency during the depression of the 1930's, and played a leading part in bringing about the abolition of Pennsylvania's archaic system of poor relief and the establishment of a modern integrated system of public assistance; it has worked for increased appropriations for public assistance; it sponsored the cooperative planning of a ten year program of child welfare for Pennsylvania and it has studied the child welfare problems of particular counties. It has played an active part in relation to a State Health Survey, the organization of a State Health Council, and efforts to improve the health services of the Commonwealth; it has cooperated and maintained liaison with many governmental agencies; and it has been active in promoting reorganization of state and local health and welfare services.

The Ohio Citizens Council for Health and Welfare was reorganized in its present form, in 1945, as a successor to the Ohio Institute, originally established as a governmental research agency in 1913. The Council has a board of about 120 persons and an individual membership of about 2000. Some 50 community chests and united funds contribute support to the budget of about $70,000. The Council's headquarters are in Columbus, the state capital.

The Council is concerned with the fields of public health, mental health, child welfare, juvenile delinquency, the aging, public assistance, and rehabilitation. The services of the Council include research, consultation, field service, education, and planning and coordination. Consultation to local communities on community organization and health and welfare problems has received increasing emphasis in recent years. The Council has had a major concern with the problems of the aged and with possibilities of rehabilitation of physical and mental patients. The Council organizes and promotes regional conferences to discuss local and statewide issues in health and welfare. The Council works in close cooperation with state departments and local community welfare councils in Ohio.

The statewide citizens associations are of special interest for several reasons: (1) They have demonstrated impressive results achieved by effectively organized and soundly financed voluntary statewide agencies. (2) They illustrate what can be done by a citizens agency, made up primarily of lay citizen members, as contrasted with a federation of agencies or a membership made up primarily of social workers. (3) They exemplify the effective use of social action (particularly legislative action) as a major part of their programs. (4) They demonstrate an enormously important aspect of democracy: a citizens association — non-partisan, non-political, untrammeled by administrative commitments, free to support, defend, criticize, or attack — interested in and paralleling the governmental services concerned with health and welfare.

STATEWIDE JOINT FUND-RAISING

Since World War II a number of states have made various experimental approaches to statewide federated financing. State services have ranged all the way from conference and exchange of information to the operation of a state fund for state or national appeals, or both. At the close of 1956 state funds were operating in ten states: Iowa, Michigan, Minnesota, New Jersey, North and South Carolina (represented by a joint fund), Oregon, Pennsylvania, Texas, and Virginia. Michigan raised $2,500,000 for 1956; other amounts raised ranged from $960,000 in Pennsylvania to about $124,000 in Virginia.[8] For the country as a whole the future of statewide joint fund-raising is at present uncertain.

The Massachusetts Community Organization Service, established in 1947, is not a state fund, but it lays special emphasis on consultation to local communities regarding problems of joint planning and joint financing. It conducts a legislative clearing house, and it has produced a unique workbook for local communities interested in appraising local services and in determining the community's fiscal ability to support health and welfare programs.[9]

In a number of states there are associations of chests and councils which confer regarding common problems and sometimes engage in a measure of joint planning. Sometimes the statewide citizens association or state conference serves as a secretariat for such a group.

THE TASKS OF STATEWIDE COMMUNITY ORGANIZATION

IN STATEWIDE COMMUNITY ORGANIZATION we may apply the general principle that *getting certain functions performed is more*

[8] *The State Approach to Joint Fund-Raising* (New York, CCC, 1953). *Facts on State Fund Raising Organizations* (New York, UCFC, Dec. 1956, mimeographed).
[9] *Toward Solving the Puzzle* (Boston, Massachusetts Community Organization Service, 1954).

important than the precise agency patterns or forms of organization used to do the job.

Leaving out of account the promotional organizations in specialized fields, there appear to be nine major functions of over-all statewide community organization.[10]

1. *Conference.* The conference and open forum function of the state conferences is of basic importance for the exchange of experience and ideas, for education, for the improvement of standards, and for the development of a sense of unity among social workers and laymen concerned with social welfare. The United States is too big for one national conference to do all that is needed; on the other hand, a conference should represent ideas and experience from beyond the limits of any one community. So the traditional open forum function is still important.

2. *Fact-finding* is basic to any sound planning for social welfare. This should include the regular collection and dissemination of needed data in respect to needs and resources, the making of special surveys and studies, and the development of a comprehensive long-range plan of research into which specific fact-finding projects can be fitted.

3. *Coordination* and integration of effort is required — first among the statewide agencies, governmental and voluntary, and second between statewide bodies and national and local organizations. For voluntary statewide agencies one prime requirement is the constant maintenance of an adequate liaison with state governmental agencies in the same or related fields.

4. *Joint planning and action* on statewide problems is the acid test of much community organization effort. This activity sometimes reaches a climax in the planning and execution of a long-range statewide program in a particular field such as public assistance, child welfare, health, rehabilitation, etc.

5. *Education* and interpretation is an essential aspect of the community organization process on the statewide level as on the local and national levels.

6. *Legislative analysis, reporting, and promotion* is an immensely important function. Every state needs competent analysis and prompt reporting of social welfare bills during every legislative session; every

[10] This list corresponds, to a considerable degree, with the similar analyses in Lyman S. Ford, *Planning for Health and Welfare of the State,* address at the Nebraska Welfare Association, May 13, 1948; mimeographed; and the memorandum, *Community Organization for Health and Welfare on a Statewide Basis* (New York, CCC, 1946; mimeographed).

state needs, moreover, a rallying point for promotion of or opposition to specific legislative proposals.

7. *The enlistment and mobilization of citizen participation* in social welfare is a test of the vitality of the community organization process in a democracy. The statewide citizens welfare association and any other agency that attempts a dynamic program of health and welfare planning in a state stands or falls with the effectiveness of its performance of this function.

8. Probably certain functions in respect to *joint financing and allocation of funds for voluntary agencies* should be performed on the state level. The benefits of joint financing are not likely to be gained for smaller communities or counties with scattered populations without some statewide joint financing organization. State chests or similar agencies may also play a part in working out the difficult problems of fund-raising for certain national agencies.

9. *Consultation and assistance to local communities* in reference to health and welfare planning, joint financing, and program development in specific fields is a state function of great potential importance. There is a rich field here for experimentation in cooperation between national and statewide agencies in respect to field service and the most effective ways of channeling consultation and help to local communities.

GUIDEPOSTS TO STATEWIDE COMMUNITY ORGANIZATION

IT WOULD SEEM THAT THE FOLLOWING principles might serve as guideposts to the future of statewide community organizations:

1. All or nearly all of the nine functions listed above are needed in every state. These functions, then, ought to be covered in each state by some agency or agencies.

2. A state department of public welfare can and should perform certain community organization functions. But the state welfare department, as a governmental administrative agency, cannot properly and should not be expected to take the lead in most controversial matters of legislative promotion and social action.

3. *Every state needs a strong and well-equipped voluntary organization concerned with broad health and welfare planning.*

4. The exact form of this voluntary agency is a matter of secondary importance. But whatever its form, the agency ought to meet the following specifications for any state with a population of 1,000,000

or more: It should be a continuous, year-round "going concern," with a broad citizen membership and a board composed chiefly of laymen. It should have a skilled staff with at least two professionally qualified workers; it should have a budget of at least $35,000; and it should perform the major functions among those listed above.

5. In any state with a population of over 3,000,000 there is a *prima facie* case for a statewide citizens welfare association or something closely resembling it.

6. In a smaller state, the action-type of state conference will probably have to give the major leadership in community organization. It is possible that in some smaller states a voluntary citizens council, or similar organization (like those of Georgia and Kentucky, for example), with health and welfare planning as one aspect of its program, may give adequate leadership in statewide health and welfare planning.

7. The interests and so far as possible the program of the state health and welfare planning agency should be as broad as the whole field of health and welfare. Ideally, this would include general public welfare organization, social insurance, public assistance and family welfare, child welfare, mental health, programs for the physically and mentally handicapped, corrections, public health, housing and planning, and recreation. It is doubtful that any existing agency covers all this ground, but such coverage seems a desirable objective. In the interests of integration and economy of effort, it would seem that all practicable community organization in a specialized field should be carried on through a division of the central statewide health and welfare planning agency or a closely related agency rather than through a completely separate agency.

8. Every statewide health and welfare planning agency which has not done so within the last five years should make an inventory of the needs and resources in each of the fields in which it is active. Needs would include those in the areas of fact-finding, education, legislation, and administration. Resources would include the laws, the governmental and voluntary agencies, the adequacy and quality of employed personnel, and current budgets and appropriations. This inventory would be a basis for examining relative needs in various fields and for establishing program priorities.

9. Every state needs a comprehensive, long-range statewide program for the development and improvement of its total public welfare programs and services. Where a state has more than one state public welfare agency, each such agency usually feels limited to its own field in planning. Even where there is a single integrated state

welfare department, it may not have either the leadership or the freedom from political or administrative commitments to draft bold, far-reaching plans. Any sound long-range public welfare plan must be a product of joint thinking and cooperation, and the statewide health and welfare planning agency will frequently be in a strategic position to take the initiative in developing such a plan.

10. Finally, we need more research in the history, objectives, programs, methods, and accomplishments of statewide community organization. We need also a working literature, beginning with a practical and down-to-earth workbook or guide to statewide health and welfare planning.

RECENT DEVELOPMENTS

IN RECENT YEARS THERE HAS BEEN a gradually increasing recognition in the field of social welfare of the importance of statewide community organization.

Since 1924, there has been an Association of State Conferences (originally under another name), for which the National Conference on Social Welfare has served as the secretariat. For some years also there has been an informal national group of State Planning Executives in the fields of health, welfare, and recreation. This group includes representation from the statewide citizens' associations, certain of the state conferences, and the state agencies concerned with joint financing. UCFC serves as the secretariat for this group.

In December, 1955, a conference of representatives of statewide agencies was held under the joint auspices of the National Social Welfare Assembly, United Community Funds and Councils of America, and the National Conference on Social Welfare. This conference emphasized the importance of a statewide health and welfare planning agency in each state; and it authorized the appointment of a committee which has been exploring the possibility of a consultative staff service to state agencies under the auspices of the three national agencies named above. Such a development could materially increase the effectiveness of community organization in the important but frequently neglected area of the state.

QUESTIONS AND PROBLEMS

1. Compile a list of statewide organizations concerned with health and welfare in your state. What are the general functions of each?

2. Prepare a descriptive report on a particular statewide agency having a major concern with community organization. Use the Outline for a Descriptive Report on a Social Welfare Agency, in Appendix C, as far as it seems applicable.

3. Prepare a chart of the principal statewide agencies concerned with community organization in your state. Cover such points as: name, location, governmental or voluntary, type of agency (see chapter), year of establishment, functions, organization.

4. What are the functions of the state conference on social welfare in your state? Attend an annual meeting of the Conference, if possible. What are your impressions of the Conference?

5. To what extent does the state welfare department in your state engage in community organization activities?

6. What agency in your state seems to give the most active leadership in overall statewide health and welfare planning? What is its program?

7. What are some of the major problems of community organization in your state?

8. Report on some current or recent statewide community organization project: why it developed, its history, present status, who is carrying it on, what methods have been used, what problems have been encountered.

9. Which of the tasks of statewide community organization, as mentioned in the chapter, seem to be performed in your state, and by what agencies?

10. Where does your state stand in reference to the suggested guideposts for statewide community organization?

SUGGESTIONS FOR READING

The literature on statewide community organization is sparse. The best general discussions are in recent issues of the *Social Work Year Book* and some of the texts on community organization. (See Basic References.) The publications of statewide organizations are an important source of information.

Association of State Conferences. *Bulletin,* issued irregularly, mimeographed. *Directory of State Conferences of Social Work,* annually. (Columbus, National Conference on Social Welfare.)

Benjamin, Paul L., "State-wide Community Organization" (NCSW, 1946, pp. 139–148).

Community Chests and Councils of America, *Directory . . . of Statewide Planning and Coordinating Bodies Operating Either Totally or Partially in the Broad Field of Social Welfare* (New York, 1949, 48 pp. No later edition).

———— *The State Approach to Joint Fund-Raising* (New York, 1953, 12 pp.).

Dunham, Arthur, *Pennsylvania's Ten Year Program for Child Welfare* (New York, Association Press, 1949, 38 pp.). A case record of a statewide program in the 1930's.

Gunn and Platt, *Voluntary Health Agencies: An Interpretive Study*. (See bibliography, Ch. 8.)

Sanders, Irwin T., *Making Good Communities Better: A Handbook for Civic-Minded Men and Women* (Lexington, University of Kentucky Press, 1950, 174 pp.). A state approach to community organization in local communities.

13.

NATIONAL AGENCIES

NATIONAL WELFARE AGENCIES are an essential part of social welfare in America. They exert enormous influence through their leadership in fact-gathering, education, programs and policies, developing personnel, coordinating effort, building and maintaining standards. Their activities form a network throughout the nation; there is hardly a community that is not in some way influenced by these national agencies.

An excellent statement of reasons for the existence of national agencies is given in the following paragraphs:

Today our national and international responsibilities are becoming part of our local responsibilities. This results inevitably from the basic social, economic, and technical changes taking place. National agencies in the field of health and welfare are all part of the whole enterprise which has been built up in this country to serve the people — all the people. They cannot be separated from local agencies and local services.

Effective service in one community inspires similar service in another and another until there is a chain of similar services across the land. Services are provided the other way too. Some services — such as fundamental research, or developing effective programs and standards within special fields — are beyond the resources of most communities. Consequently, many communities, counties, and states pool their resources in support of national agencies, which can do certain things better and more economically than the supporting communities individually could do them.

National health and welfare agencies exist to do those things which can be done best by this particular teamwork approach.

The national agency comes into the picture because: (1) a number of local agencies in the same field need the coordination, development, stimulation, and support that a national association can give them; (2) some general needs affecting almost all communities, can be best met by a national approach.[1]

Most national agencies are community organization agencies. Few give direct service to consumers; most are concerned with bringing about a better adjustment between needs and resources in some specific functional field — family service, service to children, health, recreation, corrections, etc. Thus, a national agency such as the Family Service Association of America, whose local member-agencies all give casework service, is not itself a casework agency but a community organization agency.

This chapter will consider briefly some historical developments; the number and types of national welfare agencies; their functions, methods, and organization; some national agencies which are of particular interest from the standpoint of community organization; and some of the current problems, trends, and developments in the area of national agencies.

SOME HISTORICAL DEVELOPMENTS

THE UNITED STATES PUBLIC HEALTH SERVICE had its origin in an act of Congress in 1798, which authorized marine hospitals for the care of American merchant seamen. This is probably the earliest American national social welfare agency. The American Seamen's Friend Society, established in 1828, seems to be the earliest American national voluntary social welfare agency of those recorded in the *Social Work Year Book, 1957*. National voluntary social welfare agencies have greatly increased in numbers and importance since World War I; of 217 such agencies listed in the 1957 *Year Book*, 137 or 63 per cent were established (or in some cases reorganized under their present names) since 1919.

Cooperative organization among national agencies dates back to the 1920's. The National Health Council was created in 1921; the National Social Work Council was organized in 1922, and was succeeded by the enlarged and strengthened National Social Welfare Assembly in 1945. National joint-financing enterprises have included

---

[1] *Manual, National Budget Committee* (New York, 1952), p. 1. Compare this with the statement by George W. Rabinoff in "National Organizations in Social Welfare," SWYB, 1954, p. 360.

the National War Fund (1943–1947), the United Defense Fund (1950–1955) and the contemporary National Budget Committee. Another striking cooperative development among national agencies is the United Service Organizations: a joint operation of seven national agencies, to serve the needs of members of the armed forces and workers in defense industries.

NUMBER AND TYPES OF NATIONAL AGENCIES

THE SOCIAL WORK YEAR BOOK, 1957, lists 59 federal agencies and 354 national voluntary agencies.

The central federal agency concerned with social welfare is the Department of Health, Education, and Welfare which was created as a cabinet department in 1953, succeeding the Federal Security Agency, established by presidential action in 1939. The Department's operating units are the Social Security Administration, Public Health Service, Office of Education, Office of Vocational Rehabilitation, Food and Drug Administration, and St. Elizabeths Hospital. The subordinate bureaus of the Social Security Administration are the Bureau of Old Age and Survivors Insurance (a consumer-service agency which administers this completely federal program of social insurance), the Bureau of Public Assistance, the Children's Bureau, and the Bureau of Federal Credit Unions.

Other federal agencies listed in the *Year Book* include units in eight cabinet departments and sixteen other agencies.

Of the 354 national voluntary agencies listed in the *Year Book*, about 217 are concerned primarily with social welfare; others, such as the American Civil Liberties Union, League of Women Voters, National Education Association, and Public Administration Service, have only a secondary or incidental relation to social welfare.

The following paragraphs relate to the 217 national voluntary social welfare agencies.

There are at least three ways of classifying these agencies. By *auspices*, they may be classified into non-sectarian, Catholic, Jewish, Protestant, denominational (under the auspices of a single Protestant denomination). Sometimes there are other special auspices such as organized labor. The great majority of the agencies are in the non-sectarian group.

The second method of classification is by *field of service:* the total field of social welfare, family service, mental health, etc.

The third classification is by *function*.

FUNCTIONAL TYPES OF AGENCIES

National voluntary agencies are of five functional types: (1) service, planning, and promotional agencies; (2) vocational associations; (3) conferences; (4) foundations; (5) federated groups.

The *service, planning and promotional* agency operates a service program for individuals, agencies, or geographical entities. A few such agencies conduct consumer-service programs, but most are concerned with factfinding, planning, program promotion and development, improvement of standards, and other aspects of community organization, usually in reference to a specialized field, problem, or aspect of social welfare.

This is of course the typical national agency. Examples include such agencies as the Boy Scouts and Girl Scouts, Child Welfare League of America, United Community Funds and Councils of America, Family Service Association of America, National Probation and Parole Association, and Young Men's and Young Women's Christian Associations. Some agencies, such as the American Public Health Association, American Public Welfare Association, and National Recreation Association, represent broad fields of operation, and a great diversity of state and local agencies.

A *vocational association* brings workers together for joint action in behalf of their mutual professional, economic, or other interests, or provides services to them. The vocational associations are of at least five varieties: (1) The *professional association* open to all social workers who meet the membership eligibility requirements as to professional education. The National Association of Social Workers represents this category. (2) In an *association of workers in a special type of agencies,* the primary eligibility requirement is usually employment by that type of agency, although there may be basic educational and experience requirements as well. Examples are: the American Recreation Society, National Association of Girl Scout Executives, and National Association of Jewish Center Workers. (3) The *labor union* including social workers in its membership constitutes a third type of vocational association. An example is the American Federation of State, County and Municipal Employees, AFL-CIO, and its affiliate, Community and Social Agency Employees Conference. (4) A *personnel service agency* provides services to employed personnel, in connection with employment, retirement, etc. Examples include the Social Work Vocational Bureau and the National Health and Welfare Retirement Association. (5) Finally, there is the national *association of volunteers,* such as American Women's Voluntary Services and the Association of Junior Leagues of America.

A *conference* has as a primary function the planning and conducting of an annual or other periodical meeting for its own membership and for the public. The National Conference on Social Welfare is the prime example; others include the National Conference of Jewish Communal Service, National Conference of Catholic Charities, and Church Conference of Social Work. In some cases these conference agencies also have certain service and promotional functions. Conversely, many service and promotional agencies hold national or regional conferences, annually or otherwise, as integral parts of their programs.

The *foundation* is a non-governmental, non-profit organization having a principal fund of its own, established to maintain or aid social, educational, charitable, or other activities serving the common welfare.[2] The Carnegie Corporation, Commonwealth Fund, Ford Foundation, Russell Sage Foundation, and Rockefeller Foundation are examples. National and other foundations have made enormous contributions to the development of social welfare programs in the United States.

The *federated group* is an organization of national agencies which band together to accomplish some common objective or objectives.

Four types of federated groups may be distinguished: (1) the *council of national agencies* is an organization which brings together for joint planning and action those national agencies which have certain common interests. The National Social Welfare Assembly and the National Health Council are examples. (2) A *common service* is an organization created by national agencies to provide some service in behalf of these agencies. Cooperative for American Remittances to Everywhere (CARE) and the Family Location Service are examples. (3) A *cooperative operation* is a federation of national agencies for the purpose of conducting a specific program. The United Service Organizations and the former United Community Defense Services are examples of this type of federated group. (4) *Joint financing agencies* are federated groups for the purpose of conducting joint fund-raising efforts or joint budgeting. The former National War Fund and United Community Defense Services were joint fund-raising operations; the National Budget Committee provides a joint budgeting service for those national agencies which wish to use it.

[2] Shelby M. Harrison and F. Emerson Andrews, *American Foundations for Social Welfare* (New York, Russell Sage Foundation, 1946), p. 11.

FUNCTIONS OF NATIONAL AGENCIES

Voluntary national agencies are concerned with all of the six basic functions of community organization. (See Chapter 5.) More specifically, most service-planning-promotional voluntary national agencies perform four major functions. *First,* the national agency is a reservoir of knowledge and experience, a clearing-house, and a co-ordinating agent for its field. *Second,* it is concerned with the development of program and the improvement of standards in its local agencies. *Third,* it usually provides certain specific services for its field and its member-agencies, such as agency surveys, research, publication, and consultation. *Fourth,* it represents the national "movement" in its field, in terms of official representation and relationships to other national bodies; it may engage in social action; it supplies national leadership and, at best, social statesmanship; it is active in grappling with special problems and in standing by its member agencies in times of difficulty, in crises and emergencies.

METHODS OF WORK

In carrying out these four functions, national agencies employ the following major methods:

Research and study may include the compilation of statistical material; formal research projects; study committees which draw upon the experience and creative thinking of the field in attacking particular problems; and the making of surveys of member-agencies, on request, and participation in broader community welfare surveys. A number of national health agencies engage in extensive research programs.

Planning includes the formulation of national policies, the mapping out of a kind of overall strategy for the national movement, and detailed planning of local program operation, procedures, record forms, and reports.

Publication is, of course, the easiest way of reaching the whole field. Journals, periodicals, house organs, or newsletters are commonly published; there are also descriptive and popular interpretative materials, handbooks, technical monographs, and special bulletins, annual reports, program aids, and a variety of other published materials. The furnishing of *supplies and equipment* may be an important service, especially in fields concerned with group work and recreation. National agencies may furnish also interpretative and publicity material and audio-visual aids. The national agency also frequently provides the machinery for the *exchange of materials* published by member-agencies.

Conferences, institutes, workshops, and meetings, either national or regional, are frequently held. Many national agencies are "associate groups" of the National Conference on Social Welfare, and hold meetings at the time and place of the Conference.

Services in relation to *personnel* are often of major importance. The national agency is frequently concerned with the problems of recruiting; promoting professional education; placement; in-service training; job classification; and personnel standards and practices, including salary standards. These services may range all the way from informal consultation to a special personnel department with a well-developed placement service, continuous personnel records, and special in-service institutes or courses for executives, workers, and sometimes board members.

Consultation may be given in person, at the agency's headquarters or branch office, through correspondence, or through field service. *Field service* is one of the ways through which the national agency makes itself felt most personally and vitally in the local community. In its field service the national agency ceases to be physically remote; its representative actually comes into the local communities where its local agencies carry on their services.

Representation of the agency's field may take place in all sorts of ways; in contacts with other national agencies or federal departments, in the activities of the National Social Welfare Assembly or other councils of national agencies, in service on inter-agency committees, in other cooperative inter-agency efforts, and in appearing at legislative or other formal hearings.

ORGANIZATION OF NATIONAL AGENCIES

The organization of national voluntary agencies varies greatly. Little precise information is available about the subject, for national agencies in general; to obtain adequate information for specific agencies it would be necessary to study not only their constitutions and by-laws but also other written and unwritten indices of practice.[3]

[3] Some suggested organizational classifications of national agencies will be found in Ray Johns, *The Cooperative Process Among National Social Agencies* (New York, Association Press, 1946), pp. 192, 198, and in the various SWYB articles on national agencies.

Certain key questions may be used to determine the organization of any specific national agency.

1. Does the national agency have local agencies as affiliates, does it have individual members only, or does it have both agency members and individual members? Agency members are ordinarily local operating agencies (Y.M.C.A.'s, family service societies, etc.), while the individual members are usually primarily financial supporters and perhaps the group of ultimate control.

Many national service-planning-promotional agencies have local agency members only (e.g., Child Welfare League of America and United Community Funds and Councils of America); others, such as the Family Service Association of America and American Public Welfare Association have both organization and individual members, and in varying proportions; while still others, such as the National Child Labor Committee, have only individual members.

2. What is the group of ultimate control for the agency? The group of ultimate control is normally the group that elects the board of directors of the national agency. If this group is composed of individual members or agency members, or both, then control of the agency rests finally with the membership, if they choose to exert it. If the board is self-perpetuating, then the board itself is the group of ultimate control. Sometimes, as with the American National Red Cross, the board is made up of members elected or appointed in several different ways.[4]

3. If there are local member-agencies or affiliates, what degree of centralization of authority is found in the national agency? The relationships between the locals and the national may range all the way from practically full local autonomy to a high degree of centralization in which the national exerts virtually complete authority over the locals. Some of the keys to determining the degree of centralization are: Does the national "charter" the local agency? The American National Red Cross and the Boy Scouts of America, for example, charter local groups; the Family Service Association of America (FSAA) does not. Any local group may set itself up as a family service society, without any charter, and without seeking or receiving approval from the FSAA; it may become a member of the FSAA, however, only upon measuring up to certain rather exacting membership standards. This leads to another question: What membership

[4] *U.S. Government Organization Manual*, 1957–58, p. 532. However, of the 50 members of the Board of Governors of the Red Cross, 30 are elected by the Chapters.

standards are required of the local for admission to the national? For example, the standards of the FSAA relate to the nature of the program (the basic service must be family social work); the existence of a responsible lay board; competent paid staff; joint participation of board, executive, and staff in agency planning; a sound financial policy, with major support from non-governmental sources; and a lay constituency.[5] Finally, we need to inquire, what degree of control does the national exert over the actual program and operation of the local? There are various ways of exercising this control, such as the issuance of detailed manuals and regulations, the requirement of periodic reports, the requirement of approval of certain actions, controls over personnel standards or employment of personnel, and the power to revoke the charter or terminate membership of the local. A high degree of centralization, as in the military-type of organization found in the Salvation Army, normally produces a high degree of uniformity; less centralization and more autonomy will give greater freedom and flexibility to the locals, while it may also produce a greater diversity in program and standards.[6]

NATIONAL AGENCIES OF SPECIAL INTEREST FROM THE STANDPOINT OF COMMUNITY ORGANIZATION

While almost all national agencies are primarily community organization agencies, each agency is usually concerned with one specialized area — mental health, crippled children and adults, recreation, child care and protection, etc.

Some national agencies, however, are of special interest to practitioners and students of community organization — because either they are concerned with the whole area of social welfare, including community organization; or their interests relate to some special aspect of community organization; or they are federated groups of national organizations. Among these agencies are: the American Council of Voluntary Agencies for Foreign Service, Association of State Conferences, National Budget Committee, National Conference on Social Welfare, National Health Council, National Information Bureau, National Publicity Council for Health and Welfare Services, National Social Welfare Assembly, United Community Funds and

---

[5] Clark W. Blackburn, "Family Social Work," SWYB, 1957, p. 249.
[6] Compare Leonard D. White, *Introduction to the Study of Public Administration* (New York, Macmillan, 4th ed., 1955), pp. 168–171.

Councils of America, and United Service Organizations. Information regarding specific agencies will be found in the *Social Work Year Book* and the references at the end of the chapter. One agency, however, the National Social Welfare Assembly, requires further mention here.

THE NATIONAL SOCIAL WELFARE ASSEMBLY

The National Social Welfare Assembly (NSWA) is the central federated group of national agencies. In many ways the Assembly resembles a community welfare council, except that it operates on the national level. The Assembly regards its program as being based on a three-fold partnership of government and voluntary agencies, national and local, laymen and professionals.

The program is carried out through some twenty standing conferences and committees, plus several *ad hoc* committees. The Conference on Individualized Services and the Education-Recreation Conference bring together agencies concerned with these types of services, somewhat as do a local council's divisions on family and child welfare and recreation. In the area of health services, the National Health Council operates as an autonomous organization, although it is an associate group of the NSWA. The Young Adult Council represents 24 national agencies; it has held national conferences of young adults, has furnished United States representation in the World Assembly of Youth, and has expressed the interests of young adults in respect to international problems and developments.

The NSWA's National Committee on the Aging may serve as an example of the Assembly's service in one important area. A book entitled, *Flexible Retirement,* a report of a project on utilization of older workers, was published during 1957. An architectural competition for plans for a home for the aged was conducted with the cooperation of two periodicals, *Architectural Record* and the *Modern Hospital.* Reprints of a study of buildings for the aged, published in the *Architectural Record,* have been widely distributed. Plans have been made for a volume on Planning and Building a Home for the Aged. A report on *Standards of Care for Older People in Institutions* has run into a third printing; about 3000 copies were sold in the third year after publication. The Committee's documentary film, "A Place to Live," has had 114 prints in circulation and has been seen by about a million persons during the past year. This film has received several awards for excellence. The Committee conducted a spring meeting at Indianapolis on "Maintaining Independence in Old Age." The program at the annual meeting emphasized the health of older people, as seen from various viewpoints. The Committee has received a foundation appropriation of $500,000; it is to be used over three to five years for carrying on its program and maintaining a national information and consultation service.

Other subjects represented by Assembly committees — all of concern to national agencies — range from international social welfare and broad national social issues to such specific topics as education by television, field service, national agency financing, and the presentation of social welfare ideas through the National Comics Publications, reaching some 20,000,000 children. A number of the Assembly's projects are carried on under the joint auspices of the NSWA and other organizations, particularly UCFC.

The Assembly has a membership of about 200 individuals, most of them nominated by the 68 federal and voluntary affiliate organizations and the rest chosen as members-at-large. There is a professional and technical staff of about seven persons, plus some part-time workers. The total expenditures were $264,000 for 1956, including $80,000 for separately financed special projects. The support of the NSWA comes primarily from affiliate national organizations; local chests, united funds and councils; and contributions from individuals, foundations, and corporations, largely from the New York City area.[7]

DEVELOPMENTS AND PROBLEMS

Some of the most important recent major problems in the field of national social welfare agencies are the following:

Federal leadership in social welfare. The Social Security Act of 1935 marked the federal government's acceptance of a role of long-time participation, support, and leadership in the field of public welfare. The creation of the Federal Security Agency in 1939 brought into being a central federal agency concerned with the public social services. Its reorganization in 1953 as the Department of Health, Education and Welfare is another important landmark. The Department is undoubtedly the strongest and most powerful single organization concerned with social welfare in the United States today. Today the nation has a clear commitment by the federal government to a broad interest in the public social services, and a department of cabinet rank to express federal concern and leadership in this area.

[7] National Social Welfare Assembly, *Serving Organizations and People: 1956 Annual Report*, New York, 1957. National Budget Committee, *Local Support of National Health and Welfare Agencies: 1958 Reports* (New York, 1957), pp. 113–116.

The place of voluntary national agencies. National voluntary agencies have become one of the most powerful forces in social welfare in the United States. Several hundred of them are in existence. The National Information Bureau investigates 600 national agencies each year. Probably a majority of these agencies are concerned with social welfare in one way or another.

These national agencies furnish a vast amount of leadership and exercise an immense influence, particularly in the areas of social welfare programs and standards. They perform invaluable services as clearing houses and coordinating centers. They make hundreds of studies and inquiries each year; they employ several thousand workers, and their boards and committees engage the services of another several thousand volunteers; they publish millions of pieces of literature each year; they carry on an astronomical volume of field visits, interviews, meetings, informal conferences, and correspondence.

Individual national agencies may be progressive or reactionary, dynamic or static; they may be characterized by alertness and creative leadership or by a heavy traditionalism and an immovable attachment to the past. National agencies present at the same time an enormous potential for progress and some of the most difficult problems to be found in the field of social welfare.

There is a lack of adequate and readily available information about national voluntary agencies as a whole. The general literature is still scanty, although some notable additions have been made to it within the last 15 years. The directories mentioned at the end of the chapter are basic sources of information. National agencies publish a vast amount of material, yet it is not always easy to get a clear-cut statement of the functions, organization, and program of a particular agency. Some highly respectable national agencies do not issue annual reports, and some of those that are issued are more promotional than informative. Some national agencies violate an elementary rule of administration and publicity by issuing undated pamphlets and leaflets.

The number and variety of national agencies inevitably raise questions. Are all these agencies needed? To what extent do the present patterns of national agency organization approach a rational allocation of functions and reasonable coverage of fields, and to what extent do they represent a crazy-quilt of unrelated and competing efforts?

The authors of the Gunn-Platt study remarked that, "If one could imagine a group of America's outstanding health leaders being given the assignment to set up *de novo* an effective plan of voluntary health agency organization, certainly they would not recommend the disjointed chain that has developed."[8] This comment is applicable to other areas of national social welfare effort. It is likely that efforts at greater unification of agencies would encounter the same obstacles indicated in the Gunn-Platt study; although the consolidation in 1950 of three separate agencies into the National Association for Mental Health, and the 1955 merger of the seven professional associations into the National Association of Social Workers, are demonstrations of positive action toward unification.

It would seem highly desirable that the major sectors of the field of social welfare should be covered, gradually, by a series of studies which might cut across the areas of national, state and local effort, but which would serve the purpose, among others, of evaluating the programs and services of national agencies and of suggesting desirable directions of development.

The development of more effective cooperation among national agencies has been a marked trend in recent years. Ray Johns has pointed out that these cooperative experiences include: discussing common problems; conferring with governmental officials; interpreting needs and services jointly; joint fund-raising; establishing inter-agency understandings; providing coordinated consultative services to local communities; working together on personnel matters; defining standards of workmanship; providing common headquarters services; and planning and operating local services together.[9]

These are important, because historically national agencies have had much less experience than local agencies with outside control and cooperative organization among themselves.

During the last three or four decades thousands of local agencies have been members of community chests and have been accustomed to submitting their budgets — their basic annual fiscal working plans — to community budget committees. Even more agencies have been subject to the democratic self-discipline of belonging to and participating in community welfare councils as central planning and coordinating bodies. A single local agency may belong to a local council and community chest, may be licensed by the state welfare department, and may be subject to the membership requirements and standards of a national agency.

Compared with the local agencies, national agencies have had much

[8] Gunn and Platt, *Voluntary Health Agencies*, p. 193; see also pp. 194–200.
[9] Johns, *The Cooperative Process Among National Social Agencies*, pp. 34–60.

more freedom and much less control. The National Information Bureau has operated as an endorsement agency since 1918 and has set up certain minimum standards for national agencies. The President's War Relief Control Board exercised certain federal controls during 1942–1946; its successor, the Advisory Committee on Voluntary Foreign Aid, is now a part of the International Cooperation Administration. Many national agencies have voluntarily undergone the discipline of submitting plans and budget requests to foundations; but frequently these requests deal with proposals for expansion and special projects rather than ordinary operating costs; and usually, and quite properly, even their approval by foundations does not imply any general supervisory relationship.

Until recent years the main external control over most national agencies has been the ultimate power of the purse exercised by local communities through local affiliates of the nationals, community chests, and individual contributors. But these controls are much more dispersed and remote and much less imminent than the local agency's relationships with a single centralized community budget committee having power to approve or disapprove the items of the regular operating budget.

The evidences of cooperative organization and operation among national agencies are therefore of major importance — the establishment of the various councils of national agencies and particularly the organization of the National Social Welfare Assembly; the development of cooperative program sessions at the National Conference on Social Welfare; the experiences of the United Service Organizations and the American War-Community Services; the experience with joint financing through the National War Fund and the United Defense Fund; and the establishment and continuation of the National Budget Committee. There are still many national agencies outside these various cooperative arrangements; much remains to be done in strengthening, extending, and improving the various methods of cooperation; but national agencies have already made impressive gains toward more effective integration of effort.

One service which seems to be lacking in the national field is a *central social welfare survey service* under some inter-agency auspices. There have been joint community welfare surveys carried on through the cooperative efforts of several national agencies, sometimes under the leadership of UCFC; and Community Research Associates, organized in 1949, has made valuable contributions in this area.

However, there is so much work to be done in the field of surveys and studies that there still would be substantial value in a central survey service, under cooperative national agency auspices, and therefore divorced from direct organizational connection with any one agency. It might perform such functions as: (1) Provide or organize the technical direction and staff for community and state surveys, where these were desired under independent auspices. (2) Give consultation and advice to agencies and groups (local, state, or national), on request, regarding planning, organizing, executing, and getting results from surveys. (3) Refer or steer requests for surveys to appropriate national agencies. (4) Maintain, so far as possible, up-to-date indexes of current and completed social welfare surveys and studies, together with a library of survey literature and reports. (5) Maintain a file of competent persons available for temporary survey service. (6) Promote the study and formulation of principles, methods, and standards for social welfare surveys and studies.

Such a service might operate with a relatively small permanent staff, drawing service from national agencies, research agencies, schools of social work, and elsewhere as required. It could be extremely useful, however, as an independent clearing house on social work surveys and studies, maintaining close touch with national agencies and cooperating closely with them.

National agencies have recently come into *more active participation and leadership in the field of social work education*. The National Council on Social Work Education, organized in 1946, included representation of not only the associations of schools of social work but of professional organizations and national agencies. An important study of social work education was made under the auspices of this Council; and the reorganized Council on Social Work Education is now operating as a central, widely representative organization in the field of social work education. These developments are important in their implications for the future of social work education and therefore for the services of social work to the nation.

The *relationships of national agencies and local communities* has long been a subject for discussion.

In 1920, William J. Norton recounted an extreme instance of a national agency representative "with a full-fledged plan in his handbag, written at national headquarters, which was just the thing to replace the [local] plans so painfully evolved." Some local workers inquired of this representative: " 'Suppose the delegates of all our social agencies, representing all our social work are called together and after listening to you, they ask you to leave, will you go?' 'No,' said he, 'I have orders from national headquarters to Americanize you.'" [10]

In 1942, Leonard W. Mayo proposed the following tests of the extent to which national agencies are actually participating in community organization in a given locality:

1. Do national agencies work with and through local chests, councils, and other federated groups and with public agencies?

2. Do they press their local members or affiliates to keep in constant touch with the total over-all picture of community needs and to study their responsibilities in regard thereto?

3. Do they differentiate between those localities which particularly need their services and those which do not?

4. Do the field staff of the executives of national agencies meet to discuss the problems of a given geographical area or locality with local representatives?

5. Do national agencies encourage their constituency to work jointly with other community agencies in meeting urgent needs rather than lobbying for projects to be run under their own auspices?

Mr. Mayo added:

While there are exceptions, the general pattern of . . . . national agency work would not at present allow affirmative answers to these queries, in the sober opinion of this observer. The community organization idea, procedure, and machinery are in our minds, as representatives of national agencies, on our lips, and in our literature, but not as yet in our muscles.[11]

Probably a good deal of progress has been made in these directions since 1942, though we lack satisfactory means of measurement. Certainly many national agencies have been seriously concerned with the problem. The National Social Welfare Assembly has consistently stressed the idea of the local-national partnership; and Robert E. Bondy, the Director of the Assembly, has given this realistic and forward-looking point of view:

National agencies are rooted deep in local soil. They were created as national movements to meet the needs and serve the interests of

[10] William J. Norton, "The Growing Demand for Co-ordination of National Social Work." NCSW, 1920, p. 31.
[11] Leonard W. Mayo, "Community Organization at the National Level," NCSW, 1942, pp. 234–235.

people in their home communities. It is fallacious to think of them existing, remote and aloof in some national fastness of their own. For their origins, their purposes, their services, their constituencies, and their support all stem from local roots. And these roots have been growing a long, long time.[12]

The *financing of national agencies* is a perennial problem. The exact total of the funds which national voluntary agencies administer is unknown. "It was estimated that $245,000,000 was raised by thirteen major national health agencies in 1955, including the American Red Cross, while the 32 national agencies which report to the National Budget Committee raised $23,400,000 for their national programs in the same year." [13]

The funds of national voluntary agencies are derived chiefly from payments by local affiliated organizations, allocations from community chests and united funds, individual memberships and contributions, interest on invested funds, and earnings from fees, sales of publications and goods. Proportions differ among various nationals. Obtaining support from local communities is complicated by the geographical remoteness of the nationals and the frequent lack of local understanding of the nature and value of the nationals' services.

The National Budget Committee (NBC) is one constructive approach to the problem of financing national voluntary agencies. Use of the NBC by nationals is voluntary. The operation of the NBC differs from that of a local chest budget committee. The local budgeting is closely related to a local campaign; the national budgeting is not. The NBC is not part of any fund-raising machinery. It passes on the requests of agencies which submit their budgets, and *recommends* to community chests, united campaigns, and the contributing public the budget figures which the NBC believes represent the legitimate program needs of these agencies. The recommendations of the NBC constitute approval of the agencies' budgeted requests and support plans. These recommendations are not binding upon any chest or community, but they are available as guides and they carry substantial weight with many local budget committees.

The NBC has about 100 members, who represent nearly three-fourths of the States. Members serve as individuals and not as representatives of agencies, groups, or special interests.

[12] Robert E. Bondy, "National Roots in Local Soil," *Community*, Vol. 22, May 1947, p. 168. See also Rabinoff, SWYB, 1954, p. 369.
[13] George W. Rabinoff, "National Organizations in Social Welfare," SWYB, 1957, p. 386.

The Committee reviews the budgets of national or international health and welfare agencies which meet certain established criteria. After budget conferences between the Committee and representatives of national agencies, the Committee approved 1958 budget estimates for 32 agencies for a total of about $25,700,000.[14] Most of the support of national agencies comes from communities where there are chests or united funds.

The National Quota Committee, a sub-committee of the NBC, prepares national quota data, which may be used as desired by national agencies, state and local chests and united campaigns. The basis of these data is the relative giving ability of each state as indicated by a series of economic and social indices, plus previous fund-raising experience through federated financing. State quotas are further broken down among the community chests and united campaigns within the respective states.[15]

The National Social Welfare Assembly has a Committee on National Agency Financing which is giving continued study to this problem. The Committee has formulated a Code of Fund-Raising Standards, which has been endorsed by the boards of a number of agencies.

National agencies represent one of the frontiers of community welfare organization — one of the areas where the greatest change, development, and movement are taking place. With modern communication, national agencies are closer to local communities than they have ever been in the past. They represent an area with which every social worker should be acquainted, and the community organization worker needs, as part of his professional equipment, both an understanding and practical working knowledge of this important aspect of American community welfare organization.

QUESTIONS AND PROBLEMS

1. Prepare a report on a specific national social welfare agency, governmental or voluntary. Use Outline I in Appendix C, as far as it seems applicable. Consider the various sources of information which may be available; note directories referred to in the bibliography at the end of this chapter, the annual report and other publications of the agency, the periodical published by it, etc.

[14] National Budget Committee. Summary Listing from Reports of the National Budget Committee for 1958. Unpublished memorandum, 1957.
[15] See *Manual, National Budget Committee, Part Three, Basic State and Community Percentages and Agency Support Plans Built Upon Them* (1954); see also 1958 *Reports*.

2. Find out about the current program of the local chapter of the National Association of Social Workers. Do any of its activities relate particularly to community organization? If possible, attend and report on an open meeting of the chapter.

3. Interview a representative of a local agency which is affiliated with a national agency. What seem to be the major characteristics of the relationship between the national and the local in respect to: services and help given by the national to the local; control and direction of programs and policies; finances? What degree of national centralization or local autonomy seems to obtain?

4. Attend the National Conference on Social Welfare, if you have an opportunity! If not, look over the program of the last Conference, and talk with someone who attended it. What do you think are the chief values of the Conference (1) for a social work student or a younger social worker, (2) for an executive or a social worker with a good many years of experience, (3) for the field of social welfare as a whole?

5. What are some major contributions which national agencies have made in your community during the last two or three years?

6. What have been some of the major recent activities of the National Social Welfare Assembly as indicated by its last annual report?

SUGGESTIONS FOR READING

The best general sources for information about national agencies are the *Social Work Year Book* (articles and directories) and, for federal agencies, the annual *U. S. Government Organization Manual*. The publications of individual national agencies are of major importance as sources.

Andrews, F. Emerson, *Philanthropic Foundations* (New York, Russell Sage Foundation, 1956, 459 pp.).

Glenn, John M.; Brandt, Lilian; and Andrews, F. Emerson, *Russell Sage Foundation, 1907–1946* (New York, Russell Sage Foundation, 1947; 2 vols.). The history of a foundation which has played an important part in social work.

Gunn and Platt, *Voluntary Health Agencies: An Interpretive Study.* (See bibliography, Ch. 8.)

Johns, Ray, *The Cooperative Process Among National Social Agencies* (New York, Association Press, 1946, 290 pp.). One of the most important recent studies of national agencies.

Lee, Porter R.; Pettit, Walter W.; and Hoey, Jane M., *Report of a Study of the Interrelation of the Work of National Social Agencies in Fourteen American Communities* (New York, National Information Bureau, 1922, 157 pp.). An early report of historical importance.

McMillen, Wayne, "The War Relief Agencies," *Social Service Review*, Vol. XVII, September 1943, pp. 303–319.

McMillen, Wayne, "Wartime Developments in Federated Financing of Social Work." In Wright, Helen R., (ed.), *Social Service in Wartime* (Chicago, University of Chicago Press, 1944, 201 pp.), pp. 144–168.

Marquette, Bleecker, *Some Aspects of the National Health Situation* (New York, United Community Funds and Councils of America, revised 1957, 59 pp. plus exhibits).

Mayo, Leonard W., "Community Organization at the National Level," (NCSW, 1942, pp. 229–237).

National Budget Committee, *Manual, National Budget Committee* (3 parts. New York, 1954, variously paged).

I4.

INTERNATIONAL AGENCIES

INTERNATIONAL SOCIAL WELFARE as we know it today is largely a development of the last 40 years, although the International Red Cross dates back to 1864. Large-scale social welfare programs developed rapidly during World War I. Following the war, the League of Nations (1920–1946) sponsored programs relating to labor, health, and certain other aspects of social welfare. The International Conference of Social Work was organized in 1926, and the first conference was held in Paris in 1928.

The desperate plight of refugees and the need for overseas aid to oppressed groups were acute international problems in the years preceding World War II. During the war vast programs of international social service were in operation. The United Nations Relief and Rehabilitation Administration (UNRRA) functioned from 1943 to 1948. In 1945, the United Nations (UN) was established, and the social aspects of its program and those of the related specialized agencies have steadily developed during the past decade. The United Nations Expanded Program of Technical Assistance and the United States Technical Cooperation Program (Point Four), now administered by the International Cooperation Administration (ICA) were initiated in 1951.

The particular focus of interest in this discussion is community organization in relation to international social welfare. The following topics will be discussed: (1) certain developments in international social welfare; (2) the United Nations and community organization for social welfare; (3) some current issues and problems.

DEVELOPMENTS IN INTERNATIONAL SOCIAL WELFARE

THE ESTABLISHMENT AND GROWTH OF THE UNITED NA-
TIONS itself is, of course, the one overshadowing development. The
UN has accepted responsibility for inter-governmental leadership in
the field of international health and welfare, and it has implemented
that acceptance in its organization and program. Back of the newspaper
headlines and the publicized meetings of the General Assembly and
Councils is the Secretariat, with its corps of carefully recruited and
hard-working employees, among whom are a substantial number of
competent specialists in community organization and a still larger
number in social welfare.

Several of the *specialized agencies* connected with UN are carrying
on programs that relate, primarily or incidentally, to social welfare.
These include the World Health Organization (WHO), Food and
Agriculture Organization (FAO), International Labour Organisation
(ILO), and United Nations Educational, Scientific and Cultural Organization (UNESCO). Like national agencies, these international
organizations are primarily community organization rather than direct-
service agencies.

For the nations of the Western Hemisphere there is an *Organization
of American States,* whose charter was signed in 1948. The Pan American Union, established in 1890, is its permanent organ and secretariat.
The Organization has an Inter-American Economic and Social Council,
and the Union has a Division of Labor and Social Affairs, with sections
on Social Security, Social Work, Labor and Migration, and Cooperatives.[1]

A beginning has been made in *obtaining basic facts* about problems
and resources in the field of international social welfare. The UN reports on the World Social Situation (1952 and 1957) are important
examples of such research. This fact-gathering is leading to an increasing awareness of the appalling poverty and problems of sub-
sistence, health, sanitation, and education which are faced by a large
proportion of the world's population.

Exchange of information and personnel between nations has become a well established custom and an important feature of international social welfare today. These activities have been carried on
under the UN Expanded Program of Technical Assistance, the United
States program of Technical Cooperation, and by voluntary agencies.

[1] *U.S. Government Organization Manual, 1957–58,* pp. 551–552. Irving Jack
Fasteau, "International Social Welfare," SWYB, 1957, p. 317.

These programs have included exchange of social work personnel; opportunities for students of social work to study in countries other than their own; consultation and assistance to various countries by specialists from other nations; and regional seminars, such as the Social Welfare Seminars for Arab States and a Latin American seminar on rural welfare. There has been considerable emphasis on surveys, demonstrations, and assistance in developing personnel, through schools of social work and otherwise. Actually, the key to any sound effort in technical assistance is helping a country to develop its own indigenous social welfare patterns, programs, leadership, and personnel.

The International Conference of Social Work is increasingly important as a world-forum on health and welfare. It provides an unparalleled channel for communication, for the sharing of ideas and experience, and for the building of world-opinion among leaders of health and welfare in various countries. Its *Proceedings* are more and more an important addition to the literature of social welfare, for use in all countries. The Conference has held seven meetings, between 1928 and 1956. The next meeting is scheduled for Tokyo in 1958.

In spite of the development of UN and other governmental and intergovernmental services, voluntary or *non-governmental organizations* still play a most important role in international social welfare.

Voluntary agencies, in the international sphere as elsewhere, operate with more freedom and flexibility (though with less resources) than governmental agencies; they are particularly helpful in the bridging of the gap between need and governmental provision to meet need, in conducting experiments and demonstrations and in engaging in social action. A single type of program, like the voluntary work camps developed by the American Friends Service Committee and other voluntary agencies, may have far-flung implications for social service, for education, and for the nurturing of democracy.

The American Council of Voluntary Agencies for Foreign Service, established in 1943, and composed of 40 national agencies, has thus stated the case for international voluntary social welfare agencies:

> There are certain situations, certain conditions under which governmental action and assistance may be inexpedient, inadvisable, impossible or even unacceptable. In these situations the voluntary agency, maintaining itself and its operations outside of the political arena, frequently in cooperation with indigenous voluntary groupings, is often able to fill the gap, to provide vitally-needed aid, to point the way to new forms of service.

Despite differences, the principle of voluntaryism is basic to each agency. Each of them provides a way for people to express their goodwill freely and directly and to contribute personally, even at a sacrifice. And because this concept is deeply rooted in American democracy and in the minds and hearts of the people of America, the voluntary agency will continue to exist so long as there are those in need of aid and others determined to help them.[2]

Particularly important to those interested in community organization is the establishment of the concept and practice of *community development*, particularly in reference to newly developing societies. This subject is discussed in the next chapter.

THE UNITED NATIONS

THE CHARTER OF THE UNITED NATIONS manifests its concern with social welfare, both in the establishment of the Economic and Social Council (ECOSOC) and in the provisions that:

With a view to the creation of conditions of stability and well-being which are necessary for peaceful and friendly relations among nations . . . the United Nations shall promote:

a. higher standards of living, full employment, and conditions of economic and social progress and development;

b. solutions of international economic, social, health, and related problems; and international cultural and educational cooperation. . . .[3]

This concern is further expressed in the Universal Declaration of Human Rights adopted by the General Assembly of UN in December, 1948. The Declaration includes, among others, the following statements which are pertinent to social welfare.

Article 1. All human beings are born free and equal in dignity and rights. They are endowed with reason and conscience and should act towards one another in a spirit of brotherhood.

Article 16, (3). The family is the natural and fundamental unit of society and is entitled to protection by society and the State.

[2] *Voluntary Agencies in Service Programs Abroad.* A Position Paper by Agencies Associated in the American Council of Voluntary Agencies for Foreign Service, Inc., New York, 1954.
[3] *Charter of the United Nations,* Chapter IX, Article 55.

Article 21, (2). Everyone has the right of equal access to public service in his country.

Article 22. Everyone, as a member of society, has the right to social security and is entitled to realization, through national effort and international cooperation and in accordance with the organization and resources of each State, of the economic, social and cultural rights indispensable for his dignity and the free development of his personality.

Article 23, (1). Everyone has the right to work, to free choice of employment, to just and favourable conditions of work and to protection against unemployment. (3) Everyone who works has the right to just and favourable remuneration insuring for himself and his family an existence worthy of human dignity, and supplemented, if necessary, by other means of social protection.

Article 25, (1). Everyone has the right to a standard of living adequate for the health and well-being of himself and of his family, including food, clothing, housing and medical care and necessary social services, and the right to security in the event of unemployment, sickness, disability, widowhood, old age or other lack of livelihood in circumstances beyond his control. (2) Motherhood and childhood are entitled to special care and assistance. All children, whether born in or out of wedlock, shall enjoy the same protection.

Article 29, (1). Everyone has duties to the community in which alone the free and full development of his personality is possible.[4]

The UN's concern for international social welfare is implemented in its organizational structure by various bodies and organization units. The principal organs of the UN are few in number, but the total organizational structure of the UN in general and of the Secretariat in particular are extremely complex.

Of the 49 major organization units of the United Nations,[5] at least 19 are, in the judgment of the author, concerned to a substantial degree with some aspect or aspects of social welfare. These are:

COUNCILS
1. Economic and Social Council (ECOSOC)
2. Trusteeship Council

[4] *Our Rights as Human Beings* (New York, UN, Sales Number 1951·1·13), pp. 25–30.
[5] United Nations. *Organs of the United Nations. Organization chart.* (New York, Presentation No. 031257)

UNITS RELATED TO GENERAL ASSEMBLY

3. UN Relief and Works Agency for Palestine Refugees in the Near East

4. UN Korean Reconstruction Agency

5. Committee on Information from Non-Self-Governing Territories

UNITS RELATED TO GENERAL ASSEMBLY AND ECOSOC

6. United Nations Children's Fund (UNICEF)

7. Office of United Nations High Commissioner for Refugees

COMMISSIONS RELATED TO ECOSOC

8. Commission on Human Rights

9. Social Commission

10. Commission on the Status of Women

11. Population Commission

12. Commission on Narcotic Drugs

OTHER UNITS RELATED TO ECOSOC

13. Administrative Committee on Coordination

14. Technical Assistance Board

SPECIALIZED AGENCIES, RELATED TO ECOSOC

15. International Labour Organization (ILO)

16. Food and Agriculture Organization of the United Nations (FAO)

17. United Nations Educational, Scientific and Cultural Organization (UNESCO)

18. World Health Organization (WHO)

SECRETARIAT

19. Certain units of Secretariat: particularly Department of Economic and Social Affairs, Technical Assistance Administration, and Department of Trusteeship and Information from Non-Self-Governing Territories.

In the UN Secretariat, the Bureau of Social Affairs, in the Department of Economic and Social Affairs, is most directly concerned with social welfare problems.

The Bureau operates under the direction of the Economic and Social Council (ECOSOC) and certain of its commissions, such as the Social Commission and Population Commission.

The Bureau of Social Affairs has three branches, or major operating units, on Population; Housing and Planning; and Social Welfare; and it has two staff "groups" on Social Policy and Research and Community Development. The Bureau has relationships also with three regional units: the Regional Social Affairs Office for the Middle East, the

Division of Social Affairs in the Economic Commission for Asia and the Far East, and the Division of Social Affairs in the Economic Commission for Latin America.

The Social Welfare Branch has two sections: on Social Service and Social Defense (crime and delinquency). The Social Service Section works in close cooperation with UNICEF, and with certain non-governmental organizations. It has been concerned with such subjects as the training of social welfare personnel, organization and administration of social welfare services, family and child welfare, welfare of special groups such as youth and the aged, rehabilitation of the handicapped, and social aspects of migration. Here, as in other units, research, publication, conference, and direct assistance to governments are among the major methods used.

The Population Branch, as its name suggests, is concerned with research, estimates, and forecasts of population.

The Housing, Building and Planning Branch seeks to aid governments in matters relating to city, town, country, and regional physical planning and housing, particularly for low-income groups.

The Community Development Group is the unit in the Bureau whose program relates most closely to community organization. This unit was established in 1952 following a resolution by ECOSOC providing for a study of "community welfare centers." As the study proceeded, it became clear that the community welfare center was only one facility or approach in effecting improvements in community conditions; the study and the concern of the unit was therefore broadened to the much more comprehensive subject of community development.

SOME CURRENT ISSUES AND PROBLEMS

A PUBLICATION BY THE NATIONAL SOCIAL WELFARE ASSEMBLY stresses certain principles basic to an approach to international social welfare problems. Four of these seem especially important:

1. Interdependence among nations and people has become a part of daily life and must be accepted as an essential in all we plan and do . . .

2. Foreign policy must reflect a concern for the well-being of all peoples . . . Economic and social development [should] go hand in hand.

3. Peace cannot be secured by military means. Nations, through

their domestic programs, their independent international efforts, and their collaboration within the United Nations, must apply themselves energetically toward improving the social conditions of their people. . . .

4. Advancing the well-being of all peoples requires collaboration from many fields. The social welfare specialists contribute to the development of health and welfare programs to help people to help themselves.[6]

This same NSWA publication points out some current important issues and problems in international social welfare, from the standpoint of the United States.[7] All of these problems have a relation to international community organization.

United States participation in the United Nations. The UN is the strongest organized international force working for a peaceful world and for improved standards of living. It is of crucial importance that the United States should give adequate support to the UN and its organs and specialized agencies which are concerned with social welfare.

This in turn calls for *more effective education regarding the UN* and international social welfare issues, through both governmental and voluntary channels. The National Social Welfare Assembly, National Conference on Social Welfare, National Association of Social Workers and many voluntary agencies and citizen groups have parts to play in such educational efforts in the field of social welfare.

The United States Technical Assistance Program should be recognized as a necessary long-range program. Technical assistance should be a clearly identifiable program of economic and social aid — an integral part of foreign policy. "Friendly peoples abroad should see that technical assistance is a sharing of accumulated skills, a way of voluntarily developing their own countries, [and] participating with other nations in advancing peace and security." The social aspects of the program should parallel the economic elements. Competent social welfare personnel are essential for the social services. The federal government should utilize the experience and skill of voluntary agencies and business in planning and supplementing the government's programs.

The Department of State's former *social welfare attaché program,*

---

[6] From: National Social Welfare Assembly, *International Social Welfare Issues — 1955* (New York, 1955, mimeographed), p. 1.

[7] See *ibid.*, pp. 2, 4, 5–8.

now discontinued, should be reinstated on the ground that it is in the political interest of the United States and that the program has been of service to friendly peoples abroad.

International exchange of persons. The International Educational Exchange Program has been an effective means of increasing understanding among peoples. Adequate appropriations for this program and more adequate inclusion of social welfare personnel are needed.

Immigration and refugee relief. Immigration and refugee problems are still acute. Among the desirable approaches to this problem are revisions in the U.S. immigration laws and procedures, encouragement by the United States of more UN activity on problems of refugees and surplus population, and support of the UN Refugee Fund for the permanent settlement of refugees.

QUESTIONS AND PROBLEMS

1. Prepare a report on an international agency concerned with social welfare. Use the Outline I in Appendix C, as far as it seems applicable. Consider the various sources of information which may be available: bibliography items, the annual report and any other publications and periodicals issued by the agency.

2. *Visit the United Nations!* Every social worker and social work student ought, if possible, to visit the United Nations Headquarters in New York. It will be worth while to take the guided tour, ask questions, explore the public portions of the buildings, look at exhibits, browse in the bookstore, and attend whatever meeting may be in progress and open to the public. What indications do you get as to the UN's concern with social welfare? In addition the social work visitor to the UN may wish to visit some of the non-governmental organizations located in the Carnegie Endowment International Center, 345 East 46th St., New York, across the street from the UN. Pending an actual visit to the UN, one may get a great deal of insight and information about it through reading, lectures, discussions, slides, and motion pictures.

3. With what international social welfare problems have the NASW chapter or local agencies in your community been concerned during the past year? What has been their relationship to or action regarding these problems?

4. What is the present status of the international social welfare problems mentioned near the end of the chapter?

5. Talk with a foreign student who is studying in an American school of social work. What are some of the major similarities and differences between social welfare and community organization in his country and in

the United States? What does he see as the values and problems in getting the most out of social work education in this country?

6. If an American social work student wants to prepare himself for service in international social welfare or for such service in a foreign country, what sort of training and preparation should he obtain?

SUGGESTIONS FOR READING

There is no one comprehensive volume on international social welfare. The articles in the *Social Work Year Book* for 1957 and 1954 and a chapter in Friedlander's *Introduction to Social Welfare* (see bibliography, ch. 1) are the best starting points and brief guides to the subject.

The publications of the United Nations, the Proceedings of the International Conference of Social Work (see Basic References) and the publications of specific international agencies are basic sources.

American Association of Social Workers, *Promoting Social Welfare through Self-help and Cooperative Action in the United States* (New York, 1954, processed, 51 pp.). U.S. Committee report on the theme of the International Conference of Social Work, Toronto, 1954.

———— *The Role of Social Service in Raising the Standard of Living* (New York, 1952?, mimeographed, 41 pp.). Working papers prepared by the Committee for U.S. participation in the International Conference of Social Work, Madras, India, 1952.

Howard, Donald S., "The Common Core of Social Work in Different Countries" (NCSW, *Social Welfare Forum*, 1951, pp. 19–36).

———— "Fifty Years of Social Work in the World." In *Fifth International Conference of Social Work* (Paris, 1950, pp. 26–81).

Myrdal, Alva; Altmeyer, Arthur J.; and Rusk, Dean, *America's Role in International Social Welfare* (New York, Columbia University Press, 1955, 109 pp.). Three lectures, by the respective authors, on A Scientific Approach to International Welfare (Myrdal); Training for International Responsibilities (Altmeyer); and Peace, Freedom, and Social Welfare (Rusk).

Pickard, Bertram, *The Greater United Nations.* (New York, Carnegie Endowment for International Peace, 1957, 86 pp.) An essay concerning the place and significance of non-governmental organizations.

Wilensky and Lebeaux, *Industrial Society and Social Welfare.* (See bibliography, ch. 1.)

United Nations, New York. Publications. Documents may be purchased through International Documents Service, Columbia University Press, 2960 Broadway, New York 27, New York. The UN issues an annual catalogue of publications. See also: *Ten Years of United Nations Publications — 1945 to 1955 — A Complete Catalogue.* (ST/DPI/SER. F/7. 1955, 271 pp.)

Annual Report of the Secretary-General on the Work of the Organization.

Everyman's United Nations, 1954–1955. 5th ed., 1956, 444 pp. A reference book to the structure, functions and work of the United Nations and related agencies during the ten years, 1946–1955.

Preliminary Report on the World Social Situation, (E/CN.5/267, 1952, 180 pp.). *Second Report, 1957,* 198 pp.

Progress Made by the United Nations in the Field of Social Welfare During the Period 1 January 1955—31 December 1956 and Proposals for the Programme of Work 1957–59. Report by the Secretary-General. (Social Commission, Eleventh Session, Agenda Item 8. E/CN. 5/326, 1957, 119 pp. plus annexes).

Training for Social Work: An International Survey. Lake Success, N.Y., 1950, 248 pp.

15.

COMMUNITY DEVELOPMENT

———

THE TERM "COMMUNITY DEVELOPMENT" has been used with various meanings. As sometimes employed in the United States, it is roughly the equivalent of "community improvement." As applied to rural communities in newly-developing (or technically less-developed) countries, *community development may be defined as organized efforts to improve the conditions of community life, primarily through the enlistment of self-help and cooperative effort from the villagers, but with technical assistance from government or voluntary organizations.*[1]

Community development implies: (1) a planned program with a focus on the total needs of the village community; (2) technical assistance; (3) integrating various specialties for the help of the community; and (4) a major emphasis upon self-help and participation by the residents of the community.

Community development is closely related to but is not synonymous with community welfare organization. The two overlap. Community development is concerned with economic life, roads, buildings, and education, as well as health and welfare, in the narrower sense. On the other hand, community welfare organization is concerned with adjustment of social welfare needs and resources in cities, states, and nations as well as in rural villages.

[1] For other definitions see: United Nations, *Social Progress Through Community Development* (E/CN.5/303/Rev. 1, New York, 1955), p. 6. UN, *Report on Concepts and Principles of Community Development and Recommendations on Further Practical Measures to be Taken by International Organizations* (E/CN.5/325, New York, 1957), Annex II, p. 1. "The Community Development Guidelines of the International Cooperation Administration," *Community Development Review*, December 1956, p. 3.

A recognition of the conditions that obtain in many of the villages of newly-developing countries comes as a shock to the average Westerner. A few years ago it was pointed out that more than half the people of the world earn less than $100 a year; that millions of people are chronically hungry and live under the threat of famine and starvation; that seven out of ten people in newly-developing countries are chronically ill; that eight or nine out of ten persons are illiterate; that there are ghastly losses due to infant and maternal mortality and preventable diseases; that the life expectancy in one vast country was 27 years, as against 63 years (at that time) in the United States.[2]

The beginnings of community development may be traced back to isolated projects under governmental and voluntary auspices, to work by missionaries, and to the Gandhian movement for village improvement in India; but community development as we know it today is largely a product of the last ten or fifteen years.

National programs of community development are found today in various forms and under different names, in a considerable number of countries in the Near East, Asia, Africa, Latin America, and parts of Europe. A UN report includes references to the welfare-through-employment program in Greece, for promoting simple local public works through national funds; planned communities for landless squatters and farm laborers working on sugar plantations in Puerto Rico; rural welfare centers in Egypt, staffed, typically, by an agricultural social worker, doctor, health and social welfare nurse, and youth leader; rural development societies in Ceylon; the "Better Village Approach" in Jamaica, including cooperatives, community education, cottage industries and mobile cinema units; mass education and development teams with a multi-purpose program of village reconstruction, in Burma; the Village AID (Agricultural and Industrial Development) Program in Pakistan; and India's nationally aided self-help program of community development.[3] More fundamental than any specific concrete accomplishments in any of these programs is the arousing of the people to a sense of their own power to achieve better standards of living through cooperative effort.

[2] Charles E. Hendry, "The Contribution of Community Organization to the Raising of Standards of Living in Under-Developed Areas of the World." In *Social Service and Standards of Living* (Proceedings, International Conference of Social Work, 1952; the Conference, Bombay, 1952), p. 119.

[3] See *Social Progress Through Community Development,* especially Chapter III.

COMMUNITY DEVELOPMENT AT WORK

TWO ILLUSTRATIONS MAY HELP to give further insight into the workings of community development.

A handful of seed, offered by a government worker, was the beginning of a revolution in the life of one hunger-stricken village. One farmer cautiously agreed to try the new seed on half a field. It produced almost half again as much as the old seed. The next season more than half the fields were planted with the new seed. A new plow was introduced — with two handles instead of one and an iron share instead of wood. The village's idle Cooperative revived and began to sell seed, plows, harrows, fertilizer. Old wells were cleaned to gain more water for the fields during the dry season. The cows were bred with better bulls and bore stronger calves.

Brick houses began to replace mud huts. The women learned to weave cloth and make baskets, to be sold through the Cooperative Union in the cities. With the threat of hunger lifted, the villagers and the village council agreed that the next need was for knowledge. A school house was built with voluntary gifts of money and labor. At night, after work, grownups attended classes so that they too might learn to read and write. A house was established as a village center: it contained books, papers, magazines, and an exhibit of village products. The villagers began work on roads and bridges to other villages so that people could travel easily, exchanging goods and friendship. The Cooperative acquired a tractor, which each cultivator could rent for a few days for a small sum.

Life became happier for both parents and children. For the first time the villagers looked to the future with hope. Fairs were held — festivals were celebrated with prayers and songs and plays. At a great social day to honor those who had helped the villagers, the priest spoke for the people: "Hunger and fear are being driven from our district. . . . We, the people, are masters of our lives and of our land. May all . . . Asia . . . may all the world heed the lesson you have taught us . . . the lesson of what a man can do with knowledge, work and love." [4]

The Burmese Mass Education Organizer (community development worker) receives a salary of 200 kyats ($45) per month. He must provide his own food, lodging, clothing, and travel, except when he

[4] Adapted from Arthur Goodfriend, *What Can a Man Do* (New York: Farrar, Straus and Young, 1952). Used by permission of the publishers, Farrar, Straus, and Cudahy.

travels more than five miles from his base. Sometimes the villagers get together and build a house for him.

Working through a village committee, the MEO works toward the building of a community center and related recreation facilities. The center is used for committee meetings and usually has a reading room. A village medicine chest is located there, and in the evenings the center is often used for lectures, drama, or cinema. The Mass Education Council provides some books. Villagers collect money to get others. Sub-committees for agriculture, animal husbandry, child welfare, kitchen gardens, resettlement, recreation, etc. are also stimulated, and help is requested from other Ministries in planning and carrying out work in these areas. Lady organizers make home visits to teach housekeeping and sanitation.

"Through the central village committee, in some cases, complete village resettlement (village rebuilding) projects are organized. The entire village, section by section, is torn down, replanned on the basis of a survey to secure an orderly street plan, improved drainage, better location of facilities, etc. Gutters are dug along the sides of the street and village streets are surfaced. Other than the help in surveying and planning, and the construction of culverts where necessary, the villagers receive no help from the government except through the services of the Mass Education Organizer." [5]

INDIA'S PROGRAM OF COMMUNITY DEVELOPMENT

The largest national program of community development is found in India. While no two national programs are exactly alike, an examination of the Indian program may give some insight into the organization, problems, and accomplishments of other community development programs.

India has a population of some 377,000,000 people (more than twice the population of the United States), living in an area of about two fifths the size of the continental United States. The relation of population to food supply and agricultural productivity is a major problem. Eighty-five per cent of India's people live in 550,000 villages. The villages may vary in size from a hundred to several thousand people. A typical village is a collection of mud huts with thatched roofs. The houses are clustered together along irregular, winding dirt "streets," and the fields lie round about the village.

[5] J. Sheldon Turner, "Community Development in Burma," *Community Development Bulletin* (ICA), September 1956, pp. 52–53.

Community development has been one of the most important aspects of India's first Five Year Plan (1951–1956). About a fourth of the villages have been touched by the program during that period, and during the Second Five Year Plan it is hoped to extend the program to all of the half million villages.

The Community Development program is organized on the national, state, "block" and village levels. The block is an administrative unit of about 100 villages; the block program is under the direction of a Block Development Officer (BDO), a generalist with whom are associated "subject-matter specialists" representing such fields as agriculture, animal husbandry, public health, education, cooperatives, home economics, youth organizations, and so on.

The program places basic reliance upon a multi-purpose worker — the Gram Sevak or Village Level Worker (VLW), who serves five to ten villages. The VLW is usually a "matriculate" or high school graduate. He frequently comes from a village background himself. He goes through a rigorous process of selection and training. He lives in a village and has daily contacts with the villagers in the communities which he serves. In many ways, the VLW is the key to the actual operation of the community development program in India.

The Government has developed a training program for VLW's, BDO's, "social education organizers," and various types of specialists. There is continuing evaluation of the community development program by an Evaluation Unit which is separate from the administration of the program.

There are substantial evidences of concrete achievements in many of the villages of India. Since the increase of agricultural productivity is a basic problem, much emphasis has been laid upon improved methods of planting and cultivation, the development of new crops, the use of improved seeds, fertilizer, compost pits, weed and pest control; the encouragement of kitchen gardens, to introduce more varied diets; and the construction of bunds (dams) and irrigation ditches. Agricultural research is being carried on continuously as a basis for further advances. In the related field of animal husbandry, an artificial insemination program has been initiated; efforts are being made to improve the breeds of cows, bullocks, and chickens; and veterinary services have been introduced.

In the area of construction there have been some improvements in housing; bathing rooms have been introduced, and in some cases, latrines; and smokeless chulas (ovens) have provided improved means of cooking. Panchayat (village council) houses, cooperative buildings and information centers have been built. Roads have been constructed to connect villages with highways and other villages; streets have been paved and drains and soak pits (for waste water) have been constructed.

In the area of health and medical care, wells have been dug, providing water supply purer than the traditional village "tank" (artificial lake), used indiscriminately for drinking and cooking water, laundering, and bathing of human beings and animals. "Primary health centers" and dispensaries have been established; mobile clinics have been put into operation; the training of midwives has been undertaken; and health education has been developed for both children and adults. The Government has been concerned with a program of family planning.

In the area of education, additional school buildings have been built, "basic education" — education functionally related to life in the village — has been encouraged, literacy classes have been organized, and many kinds of adult education have been carried on, including the use of demonstrations, films, and various audio-visual methods.

Training has been given to some of the villagers in certain crafts (carpentry, tailoring, tinsmithing, weaving, etc.) so that village industries may supplement the inadequate earnings of the cultivators. Women's associations have provided opportunities for women to come together for limited periods to obtain training in sewing and other domestic activities.

In addition, youth clubs — somewhat like our 4-H clubs — have been organized; "libraries" and information centers, with pictures, magazines, and radios have been established; and village meetings, recreational, religious and "cultural activities" have been encouraged.

In carrying out this program, one of the chief operational problems has been the necessity of coordinating many specialized services into one integrated program. Another difficulty is the reluctance of the villagers to change traditional habits of life. In the last analysis, the success of any community development program depends at least as much upon changing basic attitudes as upon specific concrete accomplishments. There have been difficulties in engendering the real spirit of self-help and in discovering and developing sufficient progressive village leadership.

The recruitment of an adequate number of properly qualified personnel has been difficult. The training of personnel has been another problem: in the main, too much content must be given too rapidly to the trainees. The program has encountered the basic problem of enlisting and holding sufficient creative and imaginative leadership within the somewhat rigid hierarchical structure of a large government program. The program has faced the dilemma of setting up concrete administrative "targets" and adequate institutional controls, and yet preserving the freshness, flexibility, creative quality, and enthusiasm of a new movement.

India is engaged in the most far-reaching program of community development in the world's history. Whether or not it all works out according to the details of the present plan, one is deeply impressed by the actual accomplishments to date, the social statesmanship implicit in the program, and the sheer audacity of this overwhelming modern humanitarian undertaking.

CONCEPTS AND PRINCIPLES OF COMMUNITY DEVELOPMENT

SEVERAL ATTEMPTS HAVE BEEN MADE to state the underlying principles of community development.[6] These principles relate, broadly, to the community program, outside help from government or other sources, personnel, self-help, and public relations.

There has been relatively little crystallization of thinking about these principles.[7]

Without attempting to review these principles in detail, we may note that from experience with community development certain concepts have emerged which are of major importance to those interested in community organization.

The first is *a new emphasis on the unity of community life* and the corollary that *community organization should be used in behalf of the total life of the community* and not applied to some segment arbitrarily labeled health, welfare, or recreation.

The second concept is *the importance of a team approach* to community development. This is more than "multi-professional": it is really "multi-vocational," for it may include some sub-professional as

[6] UN, *Social Progress Through Community Development*, pp. 8–13. ICA, *Report on Community Development Programs in India, Iran, Egypt and Gold Coast by Team III* (Washington, 1955), pp. 7–8. George M. Foster, "Guidelines to Community Development Programs," *Community Development Bulletin*, Vol. VIII, March 1957, pp. 32–38.

[7] A student of the subject who analyzed the three statements referred to above identified 41 separate statements of principle on 32 different subjects, with only one item appearing in all three sets of principles and only five in two of the three sets. Mya Thi Dar, *Community Development and Social Welfare in Technically Less Developed Countries*. Ann Arbor, University of Michigan, School of Social Work, Master's thesis, 1957.

well as professional services. The social worker is logically one member of the community development team.

The third concept is *the need for the multi-purpose worker* on the village level. On his return to the United States from the International Conference in Madras, in 1952, an American social work leader commented on this point:

> Our emphasis in recent years has been placed more and more upon specialization, with casework as the solid base upon which all training is founded. In Asia, Africa, and in most countries of Latin America the principal need is not for the caseworker, nor even for the casework approach. The need is for the multi-purpose community worker — not the community organization specialist, but the social worker who is able to work in the community on the jack-of-all-trades basis.
>
> There should be no difference in the basic philosophies held by social workers, whether in under-developed or highly developed areas. In one sense there is no difference in their basic skills, for those skills are fundamentally the ability to analyze social conditions, understand psychology, work with people and get people to work with each other.[8]

A fourth concept relates to the necessity for an *understanding of the cultural pattern* of the village by persons from other countries who participate in bringing technical assistance to newly-developing societies. This problem goes to the heart of community development, where the basic emphasis is upon education, self-help, group process, and cooperation.

Most important of all is the concept of *self-help.* Community development is to be carried on not *for* but *with* and so far as possible *by* the residents of the community. The program should start with the "felt needs" of the villagers and should involve the participation of as many people as possible. The skilled worker is an enabler and a helper; it is not his function either to dictate courses of action or to "take over" the community's problems and relieve the people of the community from finding their own solutions. The development of local leadership and of village councils or other devices for democratic discussion and action are among the most important aspects of a community development program.

[8] Lester B. Granger, "Passage to India," *Community,* Vol. 28, April 1953, p. 157
The question arises as to whether this multi-purpose community worker is or should be a social worker.

THE UN AND COMMUNITY DEVELOPMENT

The UN Community Development Group is an international center for research, education, consultation, and assistance in respect to community development.

This unit has issued two of the most important documents on the nature and principles of community development.[9] It has published "country monographs" on community development in various countries and has made regional surveys of selected community development programs and experiments in the Caribbean area and Mexico, the Middle East, South and Southeastern Asia, and Africa.

The unit has produced study kits available for training purposes; they have been published in English, French, Arabic, and Spanish. The exchange of technical literature between governments has been encouraged and stimulated.

International and in some cases national seminars and study tours have been conducted. The unit has participated in the selection, briefing and supervision of experts, made available to various countries through the Technical Assistance Administration, who assist by way of consultation and participation in planning and in training programs.

Current subjects for research by the Community Development Group include: organizational structure of national and local agencies dealing with community development; the relationship of community development and cooperatives to the industrialization process; the financing of community development programs; training of personnel; and evaluation of programs.

In many cases the work of the Community Development Group involves cooperation with other units of UN, with the specialized agencies, and with non-governmental organizations. For example, the Fifth Social Welfare Seminar for Arab States, which dealt mainly with community development, was organized under the sponsorship of the UN and the Arab League; but in addition it included representatives of United Nations Children's Fund, UN Relief and Works Agency for Palestine Refugees in the Near East, ILO, FAO, WHO, and UNESCO, as well as observers from five non-Arab countries, including the United States and United Kingdom, and observers from the Near East Foundation and a number of national social welfare agencies.[10]

[9] *Social Progress Through Community Development* (1955) and *Report on Concepts and Principles of Community Development* . . . (1957).
[10] UN, *Progress Made by the United Nations in the Social Field During the Period 1 January 1955—31 December 1956 and Proposals for the Programme of Work*

COMMUNITY DEVELOPMENT AND SOCIAL WORK

ONE OF THE MOST DIFFICULT problems in community development programs is the working out of effective team operation. Questions arise as to what professions or vocations should be represented; what should be their roles, functions and relationships; how can generalists and specialists be best used; how can the problem of leadership best be worked out; what should be the relationships between the team members and indigenous community leaders and residents?

Closely tied in with these questions is the problem of *what should be the role and contribution of social work in community development*. The available evidence suggests that in many newly-developing countries social workers have not thus far played an outstanding part in community development programs. This is due partly to the scarcity of qualified social workers in these countries; but it is due also to the fact that, for the most part, neither the social workers nor anyone else has been very clear or articulate about the nature of the contribution which the social workers should make.

It is suggested here: (1) That social work, as we know it in the United States, does have a positive contribution to make to community development. (2) That this contribution applies to the program as a whole, rather than to a specialized area of knowledge and skill, comparable to public health, agriculture, or literacy education. (3) That community organization is the process of social work which is most closely related to social work's contribution to community development.

It seems clear that social work has a potential contribution to make to community development. Both are concerned with enabling people to live wholesome and abundant lives. Both deal with problems of individuals, groups, and communities. Much of the knowledge and many of the skills and attitudes of social work are directly applicable to community development.

However, the contribution of social work is not the communication of a body of knowledge and skills in a specialized area of community life, as is the case with the specializations of public health or home economics, for example. There is a rather definite set of public health standards and practices which the public health worker hopes will be adopted by a community and its residents: personal hygiene, provision

1957-59. (Report by the Secretary-General to the Social Commission, E/CN.5/326, New York, 1957), Ch. III, "Community Development."

of pure water supply, pure food, sewage disposal, and so on. The same thing is true with home economics. But there is really no equally definite and specialized body of social welfare standards and practices which the social worker may claim as his specific domain and which he hopes will be embodied in the life of the community. The social worker is concerned with a great variety of aspects of community living: family life, child care, group process, recreation, community institutions, and programs, and so on. If the social worker has a unique contribution, it relates to the program as a whole rather than to any one sector of community life.

This contribution to the total program may draw upon all the processes of social work. Casework can help the social worker better understand the behavior of the individual, and develop skill in interviewing, and in inter-personal relationships. From group work he may draw an understanding of group process and skill in group participation and leadership; from research he may borrow the emphasis upon the scientific approach and the importance of facts as a basis for planning and action. From the philosophy of social work in general he will derive: respect for and acceptance of individuals; recognition of the right of self-determination for individuals, groups, and communities, within the limits of the society in which they exist; the need to help people to solve their own problems; and the desire to enlist maximum participation and cooperation in problem-solving and in social undertakings.

It is to community organization, however, that the social worker will turn particularly for concepts, methods, and principles that can be used in community development. The community organization worker's skill in the *development of social welfare programs* is directly applicable or adaptable to community development, with all that programming implies in factfinding, community surveys, analysis, planning, conference, committee operation, consultation, organization, and recording. An American social worker, with broad generic community organization training and experience, ought to be able to make an exceptionally valuable contribution to community development if he understands the cultural pattern and can adapt his knowledge and skill to its requirements.

So much for the American social worker; but what about the student from a newly-developing country who comes to the United States for professional education? In general, it seems doubtful that contemporary American social work as a whole is readily exportable in its present form to countries with widely different cultures or patterns of development. Foreign students may gain much that is of great value to them from American social work; but they may not get what they most need within the framework of traditional American social work degree programs. American schools of social work may need to make more or less substantial adaptations or modifications of their curricula and their usual requirements, to work out certain cooperative arrangements with other schools and departments of the universities, and to explore new possibilities in field work placements, if the needs of foreign social work students are to be met most effectively.

PROFESSIONAL EDUCATION FOR COMMUNITY DEVELOPMENT

Closely allied to this topic is the problem: *What type of professional education is needed for leadership in community development?* More and more, we may suspect that perhaps we need a new kind of professional that does not exist today, or at least does not have a recognized discipline. We may need a *specialist in general community development.* Paradoxical as it may sound, actually he would specialize in being a generalist! Such a generalist would need much of the equipment of the adult educator. He would require a good part of the knowledge and skill of a well-qualified community welfare organization worker — including the skills mentioned above. In a sense, this worker would be a specialist in community organization and educational methods. He would also need to know a good deal more than probably either the social worker or adult educator usually knows, about special aspects of community life and areas of content as different as agriculture, public health, public education and public administration. We are familiar with the idea of multi-purpose village workers in less developed areas. Are we here describing a multi-purpose professional? Is this a contradiction in terms? Obviously this person cannot become an expert in half a dozen content areas; but he might learn to find his way around in each of them; to understand basic concepts, objectives, and resources; to be able to give directly certain types of help and consultation, to recognize situations which are beyond his competence, and in those cases to help community residents connect up with other more technical resources. It is at least conceivable that social work, adult education, public health, and a number of other disciplines might unite in exploring the possibilities of a real inter-departmental program for training a new type of professional consultant in community development.[11]

Community organization and community development are inextricably intertwined. International community development is one of the most exciting social frontiers in the world today. The challenge of community development has been thus stated:

> [The community development] approach is based on the belief that all people have the capacity to grow and develop, to take responsibility, to raise their own standards of living if given the opportunity and technical help required. The approach proposed relies upon the power of democracy to call forth man's best creative energies. It offers a practical means of reaching hundreds of millions of people quickly in ways that will turn their frustration and unrest into faith in themselves and their fellowmen. As the late Henry Garland Bennett said when he spoke at the 1951 Food and Agriculture Organization Conference in Rome: "By joining hands together we can win this fight in this generation . . . to live together in peace, to feed and clothe and house and educate and bring health to all people everywhere." [12]

QUESTIONS AND PROBLEMS

1. Compare and contrast the conception of community development with: (a) the conception of community welfare organization with which you are familiar; (b) the conception of general community organization or rural community organization suggested by some of the writers on these subjects. (Biddle, Sanderson and Polson, Ross, etc.)

2. Prepare a report on community development in one newly-developing country. Consider such matters as: the country, total population, rural population, economic bases, form of government; designation of community development program; history of the program; content and emphases of the program; national, regional, and local organization; training and personnel; problems encountered in the operation of the program.

3. What kind of background and training would be desirable for (a) a regional administrator, (b) a multi-purpose village worker, in a community development program in a newly-developing country?

4. Review the three statements of principles of community development

[11] Adapted from a statement by the author, in connection with a symposium on "The Role of Adult Education in Community Development," *Adult Education*, Vol. VI, Autumn 1955, pp. 20–21.
[12] U.S. Interdepartmental Committee on International Social Welfare Policy, *An Approach to Community Development* (Washington, Federal Security Agency, 1952, mimeographed), p. 4.

referred to in footnote 7. What general similarities and dissimilarities do you find among them? Which do you think you would find most useful if you were going to work in a community development program? Why?

5. Review critically the UN *Study Kit on Training for Community Development* (1957). Which of the ideas suggested are similar to social work concepts? Which of the suggestions, if any, might be applied to social work practice or administration? How and where might they be applied?

SUGGESTIONS FOR READING

Under Basic References, see Ross, *Community Organization, Theory and Principles,* and the Proceedings of the International Conference of Social Work, 1952 (Madras) and 1954 (Toronto).

Goodfriend, Arthur, *What Can a Man Do?* (New York, Farrar, Straus, and Young, 1952, 128 pp.). A vivid, largely pictorial, popular interpretation of community development.

Hendry, Charles, "The Contribution of Community Organization to the Raising of Standards of Living in Under-Developed Areas of the World." In: *Social Service and the Standards of Living,* Proceedings, International Conference of Social Work (Madras), 1952, pp. 115–138. See also the author's shorter paper, "Teamwork in Rural Communities," in NCSW, *Social Welfare Forum,* 1953, pp. 266–278. Stresses the oneness of community life and the importance of the multi-purpose worker in undeveloped communities.

Kurukshetra: A Symposium on Community Development in India (1952–1955) (New Delhi, Government of India, Community Projects Administration, 1955; 525 pp.). Contains a large number of articles, case illustrations, etc. relating to the history, operations and aspirations of the community development program in India.

Mead, Margaret (ed.), *Cultural Patterns and Technical Change.* A manual prepared by the World Federation for Mental Health (Paris, UNESCO, 1953, 348 pp.). Discusses: the international setting of technical change; studies of four cultures; cross-cultural studies of aspects of technical change; specific mental health implications of technical change; principles involved in developing mental health during technical change.

Paul, Benjamin David, (ed.), *Health, Culture, and Community: Case Studies of Public Reactions to Health Programs* (New York, Russell Sage Foundation, 1955, 493 pp.). Sixteen cases are presented under the headings, reeducating the community, reaction to crises, sex patterns and population problems, effects of social segmentation, vehicles of health administration, and combining service and research.

Spicer, Edward H., (ed.), *Human Problems in Technological Change: A Casebook* (New York, Russell Sage Foundation, 1952; 301 pp.). Fifteen cases affording examples of attempts to bring about change in various cultures. In each case, the problem, the course of events, and relevant factors are described; the student is then asked to attempt to answer the questions presented, before proceeding to the final sections on the outcome and analysis.

United Nations, *Progress Made by United Nations in the Social Field During 1955–1956 and Proposals for the Programme of Work, 1957–59* (Report by the Secretary-General to the Social Commission, E/CN.5/326, N.Y., 1957, 119 pp. plus annexes). Includes a chapter on community development.

———— *Report on Concepts and Principles of Community Development and Recommendations on Further Practical Measures to be Taken by International Organizations* (Report by the Secretary-General to the Social Commission, E/CN.5/325, N.Y., 1957, processed, 160 pp. plus annexes). An important report. Discusses the principles of community development enumerated in *Social Progress Through Community Development* (1955) and the observations of member states regarding them; surveys current projects in various parts of the world; and proposes a long-range program for community development.

———— Bureau of Social Affairs. Series on Community Organization and Development. Includes monographs on community development in various countries, reports of surveys, etc. For detailed list see *Social Progress and Community Development* (listed below), Annex II.

———— Bureau of Social Affairs. *Social Progress Through Community Development* (New York, 1955, 120 pp.). The most valuable general discussion available regarding community development — its nature, principles, methods, the operation of local and national programs, the training of employed personnel and local leaders, etc.

———— Department of Economic and Social Affairs. *Study Kit on Training for Community Development* (New York, 1957, 69 pp.). A valuable general discussion of the subject is supplemented by a variety of illustrative materials from various countries.

United States, Foreign Operations Administration (now International Cooperation Administration). *A Selected Bibliography on Community Development* (Washington, 1955, 22 pp.).

———— Interdepartmental Committee on International Social Policy. *An Approach to Community Development* (Washington, Federal Security Agency — now Department of Health, Education, and Welfare — 1952, processed, 8 pp.). Contains excellent illustrative case material on early community development in Egypt.

Witte, Ernest F., "Community Development in Selected Countries," *Social Work*, Vol. 2, January 1957, pp. 7–16. The nature of community development — discussed against the background of the author's experience as a member of an ICA team visiting India, Iran, Egypt, and the Gold Coast. For a more detailed discussion, see the author's paper in *Community*

Organization in Social Work: Its Practice in Old and New Settings (New York, Council on Social Work Education, 1956, 68 pp.).

PERIODICALS

American Council of Voluntary Agencies for Foreign Service, Technical Assistance Clearing House, New York. *Technical Assistance Quarterly Bulletin.*

Community Development Bulletin (Community Development Clearing House, University of London, Institute of Education, Malet Street, W.C.1, London). Published quarterly.

United States, International Cooperation Administration. *Community Development Review.* Published quarterly.

III.

Community Organization
at Work

16.

SOME FOUNDATIONS OF PRACTICE

PART III OF THIS BOOK IS INTENDED as a guide for those practicing community welfare organization.

The chapters will deal with: some basic factors in the practice of community organization; personnel; records; methods; committees; and principles of community organization.

These chapters necessarily contain a great deal of material on methods, techniques, and various aspects of administration. If people are to be served more effectively community organization practitioners must subject themselves to professional disciplines. But the community organization worker must master techniques, not be mastered by them. He must keep clear his underlying objectives and the practical necessities of situations. In short, the practitioner must always make sure that the spirit rather than the letter of community organization is expressed in his service.

BASIC FACTORS IN THE PRACTICE OF COMMUNITY ORGANIZATION

THIS CHAPTER DISCUSSES SIX basic factors of community organization practice: the problem, as the starting point of community organization; the classification of community organization activities; steps in using the community organization process; the nature of the community organization agency; the agency's program; and supervision in community organization.

THE PROBLEM IN COMMUNITY ORGANIZATION

Community organization always begins with a problem. "Community organization begins when someone says, 'Isn't it awful? Come on, let's do something about it.'"[1] Obviously, unless there is some kind of a problem, there is no need of going to the rather considerable trouble of doing community organization.

The community organization problem presents a social welfare need or difficulty. Etymologically, the word problem is derived from a Greek verb meaning to throw or lay before. The problem presents a situation and throws down a question before concerned persons: What should be done about this situation? A problem involves alternative choices, if only the choice between yes or no, between taking action or doing nothing. An immediate, concrete, simple-looking problem may raise issues that go far beyond the immediate situation. For example:

> A chest budget committee was asked to pass on an item of a few hundred dollars for the continuance of ballet classes in a small community center. Before the committee finished its discussion, it found itself involved in such questions as these: What activities are appropriate for a community center of this size? Who should decide its program and activities? How should priorities be decided in the budgets of the various recreational agencies in the city? How should priorities be decided between different types of agencies — family and child welfare, health, recreational, etc.? What is a minimum size and optimum size for a community center? Is it an efficient and economical expenditure of funds to continue operating a small community center with a budget of less than $15,000?

Community organization problems vary greatly in importance. Some problems may be called casual or incidental; they arise (or sometimes explode) incidentally in the course of other activities, and frequently they must be dealt with on the spot. Often the whole problem and the response to it may be encompassed within a few minutes. Some examples may make this clearer.

A family caseworker is asked by a minister: "Just what does your agency try to do? I've always wondered about this: if the ministers were really trained properly for their jobs, would we need casework

[1] Clarence King, *Organizing for Community Action*, p. 5.

agencies — at least for church members? I'd be interested to know
what you think."

A community chest has failed to reach its goal by $20,000. At a
meeting of the chest Budget Committee, a member of the committee (himself a fairly large giver and a hard worker in the
campaign) suddenly observes, "I'll tell you one way to save about
$10,000. Cut out this confounded community welfare council and
get rid of the council assistant and his secretary. The council never
does anything but talk, anyhow, as far as I can see. For my money, it
isn't worth $10,000 or $1,000." The Chairman of the committee turns
to the chest-council executive. "What do you say to that, Bob?" the
Chairman inquires. In this case, while there must be an immediate
response to a potential crisis situation, that situation is really a
symptom of a more basic problem of interpretation to which the
council and chest-council executive had better direct their attention!

A lawyer, close to organized labor, telephones the executive of a
statewide citizens welfare association shortly after the election of a
new Governor, largely by the labor vote. "Look, Tom," says the
lawyer, "I've just had an invitation to sit in on a conference with the
Governor, tomorrow morning at nine. I'm leaving for the capital
on the five o'clock train. I've heard you sound off a couple of times
about this idea of a county welfare department that you think we
ought to have in each county. I always thought it made sense, but
politically it never had a chance. Well, it might have a chance with
this new man. He's pretty much interested in welfare as well as
labor, I guess. I'll tell you — I was wondering whether you could
dictate a little memo of your idea for this county welfare plan?
It's three-fifteen now — do you suppose you could get it over to
me by four-thirty?" Obviously this request may eventually lead to a
major legislative project — or it may lead nowhere.

From the standpoint of duration and the amount of staff time spent
on them (though not necessarily from the standpoint of their inherent
importance) these incidental problems contrast with major problems.
A community organization agency is likely to respond to a major
problem by developing a project or other substantial service, if this is
possible within the limits of the agency's resources.

CLASSSIFICATION OF PROBLEMS

Community organization problems may be tentatively classified according to the content or central focus of the problem. Six of the categories correspond to the six functions of community organization agencies. In the following list these categories of problems are marked with asterisks.

A TENTATIVE CLASSIFICATION OF PROBLEMS IN COMMUNITY ORGANIZATION FOR SOCIAL WELFARE

(Under each category, one or more examples are listed.)

1. *Community organization in general.* Problems relating to the general adjustment of social welfare needs and resources.

A child welfare worker, after her first six months in a rural county, tries to decide which community child welfare needs are the most pressing, and where to begin trying to do community organization.

*2. *Factfinding.* Problems involved in: how to make a community welfare survey; how to study a specific agency; how to initiate the registration of social welfare statistics in a particular community; how to compile a social service directory.

*3. *Program development* — including also problems in relation to function, policies, and joint budgeting.

Should the family society and child-placing agency be merged? Should each county in the state have an integrated county welfare department? If so, with what functions and organization structure? What should be the year's program and objectives of: a national health agency; a community welfare council; a community or district council in one section of the city?

*4. *Standards.*

How can a chest-council raise the level of personnel in a small city where there are only four or five fully qualified social workers? How can a national agency promote better standards of service and community participation on the part of its local agencies?

*5. *Relationships and coordination.* This may involve relationships among individual agencies, functional fields, agencies under various auspices (governmental, voluntary, non-sectarian, etc.), social welfare and non-social-welfare groups, etc.

How far should the budgeting power of the community chest extend? Shall there be "line by line" budgeting? How much authority shall a national agency have over its state or local branches or affiliates? Shall the city welfare department and family service society work together on certain cooperative cases, or should one agency handle any specific case entirely?

6. *Conflict.* This is closely connected with problems of relationship, but it seems sufficiently distinctive to be listed as a separate category.

A planned parenthood league applies for admission to the community welfare council. Opponents of the league's program threaten to withdraw from the council if the league is admitted.

The Governor directs the Welfare Commission (as they interpret it) to "give one of their employees a hearing and then fire him." The members of the Commission resign.

7. *Auspices.*

Who should do the major child-placing job in a particular community? A governmental agency? City? County? State? A voluntary non-sectarian agency? Sectarian agencies? A combination of several of these types of agencies?

The leaders of a national labor union consider whether organized labor should follow a policy of developing special social welfare services under labor auspices, or should throw its weight in favor of governmental operation of welfare services, or support both governmental and voluntary agencies.

8. *Organization and control.* Some of these problems illustrate the mingling of community organization and administration content.

How can the control of social welfare agencies be made more democratic? How can we get away from self-perpetuating boards in community chest member-agencies which have no membership? Should consumers participate in the control and direction of social welfare agencies?

9. *Leadership.*

How shall a community welfare council develop better citizen leadership in its community councils and functional divisions? How shall a national agency raise the level of professional leadership in its field?

10. *Methods* (other than factfinding, education, and fundraising, which are covered elsewhere in this classification).

How can a national agency improve: conference and committee techniques in its field: consultation by the staff members of the national? How can a state conference improve the effectiveness of its legislative promotional efforts?

*11. *Education.*

What should be included in a plan for a year's program of interpretation and public relations for: a specific operating agency; a council; a chest; a national agency? In a specific community, how can the general level of understanding among board members be raised?

*12. *Support and participation.*

What should be the chest campaign goal? To what extent should it be determined by: social welfare needs (and how shall these be measured?); the amount that can probably be raised? What can be done about the large number of fund-raising efforts outside of the community chest? How can volunteers be effectively recruited for agency service?

13. *Other problems.*

What part should social welfare agencies play in a community program for dealing with unemployment or disaster? Should a national agency promulgate a suggested code on race relations for its locals?

ANALYZING A PROBLEM

The first step in handling any major community organization problem is, normally, the analysis of the problem. In making such an analysis, the basic questions — what, who, where, when, why, how — may be used to advantage. The following outline is suggested as a tool for analyzing a community organization problem. In the case of a major problem, a written analysis is usually desirable.

OUTLINE FOR THE ANALYSIS OF A COMMUNITY ORGANIZATION PROBLEM

1. *What* is the problem? Describe the problem-situation. How long has it existed? What is the setting and background — historical, economic, sociological, psychological, etc.?

2. *Who* are the persons or groups involved or concerned with the problem? What personality factors, attitudes, beliefs, prejudices, etc. are significant?

3. *Where* is the problem? What territory is involved? What relationships, if any, with other geographical units or levels are involved?

4. *When* is the problem? Is it immediate? Or is it in the future? Is it a temporary or a long-range problem? Is there a time limit for achieving or proposing a solution?

5. *Why* is this situation a problem? What would probably happen if nothing were done about the situation?

6. *How* may the problem best be approached?
   a. Who should take the initiative?
   b. What organization (agency, committee, association, etc.) or what organized effort, if any, will be involved?
   c. What personnel will be required?
   d. What existing resources can be utilized?
   e. What methods and procedures should be used?
   f. What will be the probable cost of the effort? How can this cost be met?

An analytical approach to community organization problems suggests various devices for problem accounting, with the recording of problems, action taken, and results. Pierce Atwater suggested a "social problem index," in looseleaf form, with a page or more for each major problem and notations of "every important occurrence in connection with the problem." [2]

A community organization agency or department may find it useful to list current major problems in such a form as the following:

Problem   What Should Be Done?   Who Should Do It?

A council executive in a small city once made an analysis of problems as they related to the various agencies in the council. He drew up a chart with three columns:

Agency   Problems   What the Council Can Do

The same idea might be utilized by a field representative of a national or statewide agency.

CLASSIFICATION OF COMMUNITY ORGANIZATION ACTIVITIES

In dealing with the problems suggested above, community organization agencies engage in a complex and bewildering variety of activities.

The term activity, as we are thinking of it here, is difficult to define. Obviously we are concerned only with *service activities;* that is, activities directly related to the giving of community organization service or the application of the community organization process. This

[2] Pierce Atwater, *Problems of Administration in Social Work*, pp. 214–215. Compare: Walter L. Stone, *Community Welfare Planning* (Nashville, Council of Community Agencies, 1941, mimeographed), pp. 22–32, for an analysis of the problems of a council.

excludes purely administrative activities. A community organization activity might be defined as a primary operation (1) which is carried out by an agency or worker using the process of community organization, and (2) which is separate and distinguishable from other operations in objective and content, not merely a subordinate part of some other operation.[3]

The activities of the community organization agency are extremely diverse. In most client-service agencies the major units of work are more uniform and more continuous than in the community organization agency. The casework agency has the case as its unit; the youth service agency has the leisure time group, plus perhaps certain mass recreation activities. A city recreation department may have such major operating units as playgrounds, community centers, beaches, skating rinks, etc.

Contrast this with the program of a community welfare council! The social service exchange and the section of the research bureau that deals with the registration of social statistics are probably the two chief subdivisions of the council that have uniform and continuous units of work — the clearing, in the case of the exchange, and the agency statistical report in the case of the research bureau. In the rest of the council all sorts of diverse activities may be in progress.

For example: the office of the executive is preparing for the annual meeting, and the executive is conducting delicate negotiations with the department of public welfare and the school of social work regarding certain problems of personnel and professional education. The Health Division is cooperating with the social hygiene society in promoting a special educational campaign among industrial establishments to prevent and decrease venereal disease. The Child Welfare Division is working with two institutions on plans for a merger; and the committee on boarding homes is seeking an increase in boarding rates from the city and county. The Family Division is trying to promote a visiting housekeeper service. The Recreation Division is making a study of recreational opportunities for older people. All the divisions are cooperating with the community chest in preparing for budget hearings. The six district councils are doing a great variety of things, separately, and are collaborating on plans for a city-wide Citizens Leadership Institute. The Social Service Exchange and Community Information and Referral Service are carrying on their daily services as usual.

Multiply these activities by a hundred or more things that are done in one week in a large council and we have an overwhelming and

[3] Compare Lane, "The Field of Community Organization," NCSW, 1939, p. 501.

chaotic collection of items — unless some rational method of classification can be devised. Some scheme of sorting out these activities is essential to bring like activities together, to grasp general patterns of operation; and thus to make possible intelligent recording, service accounting, and reporting of what is being accomplished; from this to move to better program direction and more effective service by the council.

Any system of classifying community organization activities must take account of two characteristics of the program of a community organization agency: first, this diversity of activities, and second, the fact that the different services or units of operation continue for varying lengths of time. A few, like the social service exchange, are continuous; some, like contacts with agencies or division meetings, are intermittent; others, like studies, educational campaigns, and negotiations, are temporary.

An ideal system of classification of community organization activities should possess these characteristics: First, it should be based upon some one constant factor. For example, if one is classifying activities by functional fields, that must be the sole or at least the primary basis of classification throughout. One may use some other method of classification, such as classification by objectives, but it must be a separate or secondary classification. In the second place, the classes should be mutually exclusive. There should be no doubtful cases. Third, the classification should be objective. Opinion, individual interpretation, and subjective judgment should not enter in. If five community organization practitioners, with equal knowledge and ability, undertook to classify a hundred activities, they ought to come out with the same results. Fourth, the classification should be simple, clear, and readily applied. Finally, the classification should have practical administrative utility for recording, service accounting, and program direction.

The following classification of community organization activities is suggested for tentative use, experimentation, and research. This may be called an operational or time-centered classification, since the method of classification is based upon the time-factor and is intended for use in connection with the day-by-day operation of community organization agencies. This classification is intended to relate primarily to community welfare councils, national agencies, and other diverse-program community organization agencies. Other classifications will probably be required for specialized agencies such as community chests (for which statistical recording has been well developed), social service exchanges, research bureaus, publicity departments, and legislative services.[4]

The primary basis of this classification is the time-span of the activity. One of the three major divisions may be further subdivided, on the basis of the nature of the activity.

The three major types of activities suggested are: (1) *continuous services,* (2) *projects,* and (3) *occasional services.* Administrative activities are not included in this classification.

CONTINUOUS SERVICES

Continuous services are usually expected to continue indefinitely. The continuous service usually deals with more or less standardized units of operation, and often the requests for the service are initiated outside the welfare council.

Examples are: operation of social service exchange; welfare information bureau; central referral service; volunteer bureau; registration of social statistics; budget department (as a year-round operating unit of a community chest); campaign service (year-round unit of a chest); central calendar of meetings and events; continuous collection of social data or social welfare materials; public relations service; distribution of literature.

PROJECTS

A project is a planned undertaking which has a specific community organization objective, which involves several successive steps and related activities, and which is expected to continue for a substantial but limited period of time.

Since the project is one of the most frequent, most important and most representative types of community organization activities, this definition should be examined more closely.

First, the project is an undertaking or enterprise of some kind. The nature of the project may vary enormously, as the following examples suggest: a survey or study; attempt to establish a new agency or service; merger of two agencies; formulation of a set of standards by and for a group of agencies; planning and holding of a study course, conference, institute, or exhibition; legislative campaign.

[4] For two other approaches to classification of activities, see *Stone, op. cit.,* pp. 22–23, and CCC, *What Councils of Social Agencies Do* (New York, 1939), p. 4.

Whatever the project is, if it is a community organization project it will have a community organization objective; that is, it will be concerned with one or more of the six community organization functions: factfinding, standards, coordination, program development, education, and support.

The project inevitably involves some kind of planning. There must be some attempt to project or determine in a general way action to be taken in the future. A live community organization project is usually either being planned, being carried into effect or carried to completion, or in a state of suspended animation.

The project is not a single activity like a speech or an isolated conference of the representatives of several agencies. It involves several successive steps and related activities.

A project normally continues for a substantial but limited period of time. As contrasted with the continuous service, the project is temporary or of limited duration; it has a beginning and end. A month might be arbitrarily suggested as the minimum for a project. No specific maximum length need be specified. A study of a small agency might conceivably be initiated, planned, executed, and reported on within a period of six weeks. On the other hand, a project for bringing about a reorganization of a state's public welfare resources, making a nation-wide study of public assistance, or planning, holding, and following up a White House Conference on Child Welfare might extend over several years.

Project control is close to the core of program direction for a community organization agency. Project control involves at least the following elements.[5] (1) Clear-cut identification and recognition of projects by the agency. Sometimes a considerable period may elapse before it becomes clear whether or not an agency is going to sponsor a particular proposal and accept it as a project. To meet this difficulty it may be necessary for the agency to recognize in its administration and record-keeping the existence of potential projects which are under consideration. (2) Formal adoption of a project as a part of the agency's program. This should usually be done by the governing board or an appropriate committee; sometimes by a competent executive authority. At the time of this action, the following points should be clear: the nature and content of the project, the objective, organization, personnel, and budgetary requirements. It should be decided

---

[5] In this connection see the discussion of Steps in the Community Organization Process, on pp. 278–279. See also: Comstock Glaser, *Administrative Procedure* (Washington, American Council on Public Affairs, 1941), pp. 76–82.

whether the project will be referred to some existing committee, whether a new committee shall be created, or whether it shall be carried on as a staff project, subject only to the oversight of the governing board or departmental committee.[6] (3) Periodic reporting and appraisal of the project, as it goes forward. (4) Concluding the project. The project should be brought to a definite and formal conclusion; it should not merely peter out. Concluding the project is the equivalent of "closing a case" in social casework. In general, the project may be closed because it is completed, more or less successfully; or as much has been accomplished as it is thought possible; or it is abandoned as impracticable or unsuccessful; or it is indefinitely postponed.

OCCASIONAL SERVICES

Occasional services are separate individual services which are not integral parts of either continuous services or projects. These may be of several varieties. A specific agency may of course use all or some of these subdivisions for purposes of record-keeping or it may lump them all together.

Recurrent activities occur at more or less regular intervals; some of them are definitely seasonal. The recurrent activity is not an isolated phenomenon; it has usually happened before and it is expected to happen again.

Examples include: biennial revision and publication of a directory of social agencies; legislative service of observation, reporting, and analysis at the time of the legislative sessions; consultation and assistance to the budget department of a chest, by a council staff member, during the period of agency budget hearings; work with the federal decennial census regarding census tracts; issuing occasional publications; annual review by a council committee or staff member of the city budget; meetings of the council or its divisions.

Intermittent relationship activities are contacts by the agency with organizations with which it sustains continuing relationships.

These relationships may be of at least three kinds: (1) The community organization agency may give advice, consultation or assistance — that is, it may have a helping relationship to another agency. (2) The community organization agency may itself seek advice or assistance from another agency. (3) The community organization agency may maintain liaison with another agency.

Examples are: office consultations with agency representatives;

[6] A suggested analysis blank for a project is given in Appendix C.

field visits; a statewide citizens welfare association keeps in close touch with the state welfare department.

Collateral activities are separate and miscellaneous occasional service activities not included under the foregoing categories. They are incidental to the main stream of the agency's service. Some of these may be activities of staff members which are general community or professional contributions, but not actually a part of the agency's program.

Examples include: assembling, by a staff member, of a brief report on a particular topic, requested by the executive of the agency; holding a special public meeting; making an analysis of a subject of interest to the agency; holding an interview with the mayor regarding the appointment of a director of welfare; writing a letter to a legislator regarding a current bill which the agency approves but for which it is not actively campaigning; furnishing information at the request of an outside organization; speaking to outside groups; serving on certain committees outside the agency; attending meetings of outside bodies.

The term collateral should mislead no one as to the extent or the importance of these activities. In the aggregate, *collateral activities take up a substantial portion of the average community organization worker's time* — perhaps as much as a third or fourth of it. It is folly for any community organization agency to lay its plans without making due allowance for these "incidental" services. One council executive, a former football coach, used to call these incidental services "defensive activities" and the planned services (including continuous services and projects) "offensive activities." How far one progressed on his own planned job was measured by his progress in respect to the offensive activities; the defensive activities one had to perform in order to continue with the job at all, but the general object was to get them done and "off the desk" as expeditiously as possible.

Nevertheless, *the collateral services given by a community organization agency are likely to be of vital importance,* not only for goodwill and public relations, but also from the standpoint of the actual services rendered. An interview with an eager young college student may lead to a career of outstanding professional service in social work; a public address to a service club or a ministerial association may present a community need with a vividness that stirs consciences and leads to action; faithful service as the chairman of an NASW chapter may bring about the stimulation and quickening of the professional life of the social workers of a community. The col-

lateral services, unsought and burdensome as some may be, cannot be indiscriminately brushed aside nor superficially glossed over.

STEPS IN COMMUNITY ORGANIZATION

While there are many variations in individual instances, certain steps are typical in the use of the community organization process. These steps are:

1. The *recognition of a problem* or need.

2. Some statement or *analysis of the problem.* In practice, the analysis may be prolonged or fleeting, thorough or superficial. Sometimes action seems to follow directly upon the presentation of the problem, without any real use of analysis or planning. Some situations may require this sort of immediate, active response; but, generally speaking, it is an advantage to know what one is trying to do and how one expects to do it before leaping into action.

3. *Factfinding.* In some instances this must be undertaken before further progress can be made. The factfinding may be limited or extensive, brief or prolonged.

4. *Planning.* This involves consideration of the action to be taken and the order of the various proposed activities, organizational requirements (committees, staff, etc.), methods and procedures, and finances.

5. *Official approval.* Unless the action to be taken is within the content of an accepted, ongoing program, such approval will probably be necessary at this point. The authority giving approval will usually be a group, such as an agency board or committee, although it may be an official, such as the director of the state welfare department. In any case, the authority will normally represent those who will supply financial support, either taxpayers or contributors.

6. *Action* in executing plans and initiating the service or project. The kinds of action will be infinitely varied, depending on whether the proposed service is a survey, an institute, a legislative campaign, the promotion of a merger, or some other type of activity. The action is likely to involve *cooperative or inter-group activities* of some sort.

7. *Recording and reporting.* A record of the undertaking should be kept in one form or another. At the end of the project, or periodically, if it is long continued, there should be reporting to the board or supporting constituency.

8. *Adjustments.* As the action proceeds, problems will be encountered, and usually certain adjustments will have to be made in the original plan.

9. *Evaluation.* At the end of the project, and also periodically if it is long continued, there should be evaluation of how effective the action has been and what has been accomplished.

Next steps to be taken, in the light of the evaluation may include the following possibilities: (a) Acceptance of the action taken as having solved the original problem. (b) Reformulation of the problem. (c) Recognition of a new problem. (d) Decision to continue the action, unchanged or modified. For example, if a bill to establish a state mental health department is defeated in the legislature, the State Conference board may decide that the bill shall be reintroduced in the next session, with certain changes from the present draft. (e) Abandonment of the effort to deal with the problem, for the present at least. It is obvious that in this list item b or c may mean the emergence of what is virtually a new problem, and this may start the community organization cycle again.[7]

THE COMMUNITY ORGANIZATION AGENCY

In many respects, the community organization agency is like other social welfare agencies. Its organization structure is similar: it is likely to have a board, executive, staff, departments or subdivisions, committees, and so forth. Most of its administrative problems are similar: it must deal with matters of personnel, physical plant, finances, office management, and public relations.

The major difference in the community organization agency is that it has a different kind of service program. As has already been demonstrated, it deals with a great diversity of problems and it engages in a wide variety of activities.

Because of the nature of its operations, the community organization agency has at least three special administrative needs: for ade-

[7] For other suggested formulations of "steps in community organization," see: Eduard C. Lindeman, *The Community*, pp. 119–138. Lindeman's "ten steps" are included also in Dwight Sanderson and Robert A. Polson, *Rural Community Organization*, pp. 223–224. Otto T. Gilmore, "Problems of Administration in Community Organization. II. Definition, Planning, Direction, and Timing of Projects." NCSW, 1941, pp. 590–591. Hertha Kraus, "Community Organization in Social Work: A Note on Choices and Steps." *Social Forces*, Vol. 27, October, 1948, pp. 54–57; Johns and DeMarche, *Community Organization and Agency Responsibility*, ch. 11.

quate self-analysis on the part of the agency; for a clearly-defined program; and for adequate program direction.

AGENCY SELF-ANALYSIS

Because community organization is more varied, less tangible, and less easily understood than casework or group work, it is especially important that the community organization agency analyze thoroughly just what it is trying to do and how it expects to do it.

Adequate self-analysis by an agency involves answering the following questions. After each item the type of document in which that particular information should be recorded is suggested. Much of this material belongs in the agency's office manual or organization handbook.

1. What are the long-range objectives of the agency? What is it really trying to do? (Constitution; Office Manual.)

2. What are the functions of the agency? What services and activities does it carry on, as means toward attaining its objectives? (Office Manual.)

3. What is the agency's current program? What is it doing or trying to do during the current year? (Work Plan; [8] Program.)

4. What progress is being made, during given periods, in carrying on the current program? (Work Progress Report.)

5. How is the agency organized? How are its organization units related to each other? What are the functions, current activities, internal organization, and personnel of each unit? What are the lines of authority, responsibility, and other organizational relationships? (Organization chart and textual material, in Office Manual.)

6. What committees does the agency have? What are their functions, assignments, organization, personnel, and activities? (Committee List or Index.)

7. What are the jobs in the agency? What are the duties of and the qualifications for each job? (Office Manual or separate collection of job specifications.)

8. What are the costs of operation, how are they allocated, and what are the sources of the agency's funds? (Office Manual and current financial records.) [9]

[8] The Work Plan and Work Progress Report, referred to in this chapter, are discussed in Chapter 18.
[9] For a more general and somewhat different approach to the process of administrative analysis, see Glaser, *Administrative Procedure*, pp. 17–48.

The foregoing information should be kept up-to-date and readily available for use by the executive, the staff, and the board.

THE AGENCY'S PROGRAM

A caseworking agency is mainly occupied in giving individual services to a succession of clients who apply or are referred to the agency. The clients remain with the agency for varying periods of time. In any case, the initiative, the requests for service, come usually from without; the agency responds to those requests.

With most community organization agencies, the situation is different. The community welfare council, for example, receives some requests for service — studies, consultation, etc. — from other agencies or groups. Even in respect to these requests, the council may exercise considerable selectivity. But in addition to these outside requests, *the council chooses, on its own initiative, to undertake certain current projects.* That is, the council has a relatively large degree of freedom in making up its program.

The council, then, should plan and formulate in writing a program for the year, setting down the activities which it definitely wishes to carry on, both for the council as a whole and for various divisions and departments. The program will probably never work exactly as planned; it will have to be modified, to some extent, as the year goes on; emergencies will arise, and there will be unforeseen requests for service which ought not to go unheeded. But if the council has its own basic plan, with some indication of priorities among projects, it will be able to make such departures and still keep the most important parts of the program in continuous operation.

It is the responsibility of the executive and staff to draw up a tentative program for the year. If a council is a large one, its program will include the various divisional and departmental programs plus the program projects and other activities of the council-as-a-whole.

In any case, the first step is to make up a tentative list of projects and other activities. The major sources of this list will be: (1) current activities of the council, not likely to be completed at the end of the current year, and (2) activities suggested by members of the council's board, committees, executive, and staff, delegates, member-agencies, and other persons or groups, inside or outside of the council.

Program suggestions, like budget requests, are likely to exceed available resources. If the suggested list looks considerably larger than what can be encompassed, an analysis of the suggested activities,

in chart form or otherwise, should be made. Such items as the following may be noted: (1) Designation and brief description of proposed
activity. (2) General nature of activity — study; meeting(s); legislative promotion; etc. (3) Suggested by whom? (4) New or carried
forward from current year? (5) Is there a commitment to continue?
(6) Assignable to what division or department? (7) Requirements in
terms of: (a) Assignment to a committee. Existing? New? Function of
committee: directive, advisory, other? (b) Staff time. (c) New staff
personnel. (d) Additional funds. Note any suggested special source of
such funds. (8) Relation to other activities of council? (9) Urgency?

On the basis of this analysis, the executive and staff may list their
recommendations as to acceptance, modification, or rejection of suggested items and as to priorities among them. In some cases it may be
better not to "pre-digest" the suggested program too completely by
way of definite executive recommendations, but to submit to the
board alternatives and arguments pro and con.

If the agency uses a Work Plan, the service program becomes the
heart of the work plan. (The other portions of the work plan deal
with administrative and extra-agency objectives and plans.)

In any case, either the work plan or the proposed service program
*should be formally submitted by the executive and acted upon by the
board,* or other governing authority, around the beginning of the working year. If the number of desirable projects is larger than can be undertaken with the resources of the agency, the board must decide which
program requests shall be approved and what shall be the major priorities among them. This is an important exercise of the board's power of
determining program and policy, it is a valuable educational process,
and it is likely to give the board members a clearer picture than they
would otherwise have of the resources of the agency in relation to the
needs and demands for service.

*A generous margin of time must be left in this program for in-
cidental activities and unforeseen emergencies.* This includes the
"collateral activities" discussed in the section on Classification of
Activities.

PROGRAM DIRECTION

Program direction means central control over and dynamic
leadership by the executive and the board in carrying forward the
agency's total service program. It is much more difficult to maintain

adequate program direction in a community organization agency than in the average consumer-service agency, where working units are more uniform and there is an automatic flow of established types of services.

Adequate program direction would seem to depend upon at least four factors: *Clear and logical lines of organization* are needed for effective coordination and central direction. *Intelligent and responsible central executive leadership* is necessary. There will be no real program direction unless the executive believes in it, wants it, and is willing to work to achieve it. *A working classification of activities* is required, for record-keeping, measurement of progress, and staff supervision. *Adequate records* are a necessary element in intelligent programming and effective service.

SUPERVISION

Supervision involves a "line" relationship: that is, it involves authority on the part of the supervisor and responsibility on the part of the worker. However much the supervisor may proceed by indirection and may encourage the worker to do his own thinking and to make his own decisions, nevertheless in the background there is necessarily an element of accountability and control. Supervision differs from consultation, which is an advisory or "staff" service. Supervision involves administrative control and direction.

In spite of what has just been said, the actual process of supervision is largely a teaching process. Guidance, stimulation, suggestion, helping the worker to work out the solutions to his problems should have a much greater place than merely giving orders, issuing instructions, or "giving the answers" to questions raised by the workers. The worker, at any stage of his development, should have as much freedom and self-direction as he can use productively.

The supervisor should obviously be a capable community organization practitioner himself; but he must also be competent to direct others; he must have some basic understanding of the process of supervision and the relationships and types of problems involved. The supervisor should have a greater degree of understanding of community organization and greater skill in its practice than the worker has. In the case of a council, the executive will probably know less about health than the secretary of the health division, less about recreation than the secretary of the recreation division. But the executive should have a broader knowledge and greater skill in respect to the total process and area of community organization than any of the staff members.

Among the methods of supervision which may be used are: (1) Regular supervisory conferences. (2) The review and discussion of completed work, work in process, or proposed activities, such as an agenda, a set of minutes, a plan for a project, or a draft of a leaflet. (3) The observation of the worker in action — for example in making a speech, conducting a group discussion, or participating in a conference. In this respect, the community organization supervisor has an advantage over the casework supervisor, who rarely has the opportunity to observe at first hand the caseworker's contacts with his clients. (4) The review and discussion, at regular intervals, of a basic administrative report such as the Work Progress Report. This report should be a tool of fundamental importance in supervision, comparable to the case record in casework or the group record in group work.

QUESTIONS AND PROBLEMS

1. List ten community organization problems. Try to classify them according to the classification suggested in the chapter; set up additional categories if necessary. What difficulties or problems do you encounter? What changes, if any, would you suggest in the classification? (A competent student of community organization could make a valuable contribution by analyzing and classifying several hundred community organization problems, representative of several different types of community organization agencies, but uniformly recorded as a basis for study. Such a study should yield not only a more complete classification of problems but also it should throw light on how the problems arose or were identified, the types of organizations and groups and the geographic levels involved, the actions taken and services required in response to the various problems, etc.)

2. Prepare a written analysis of a community organization problem, using the analysis outline suggested in the chapter. To what extent would an analysis of this sort probably be helpful in the practice of community organization? Would the analysis be worth the time it takes? Should it be used only in special cases or situations? What kind?

3. A social work executive objects that the council executive's chart of agencies and problems (page 271) represents improper procedure, indicates a paternalistic attitude toward the agencies on the part of the council executive, and is "full of dynamite." What do you think?

4. Apply the proposed classification of activities to the job of some community organization agency (or department) with which you are familiar;

or interview some community organization worker and get his estimate as to the extent to which he thinks the proposed classification would apply to his agency or his job.

5. Analyze a community organization project. Use the Outline for Analysis of a Community Organization Project, in Appendix C.

6. What are some of the similarities and differences between supervision in community organization and in casework, group work, and administration?

7. What are some of the methods of supervision used in a community organization agency in your community? Are there significant differences in supervision of community organization staff workers and students doing community organization field work?

SUGGESTIONS FOR READING

Little has been written on the administration of community organization agencies or on the specific topics discussed in this chapter. Some materials will be found in the various texts. (See Basic References.) Several of the references below are volumes on general administration.

Atwater, Pierce, *Problems of Administration in Social Work*. (Minneapolis, University of Minnesota Press, 1940, 319 pp., OP). Includes chapters on public relations, fund-raising, and the executive and politics.

Dimock, Hedley S. and Trecker, Harleigh B., *The Supervision of Group Work and Recreation*. (New York, Association Press, 1949, 280 pp.). Applicable in part to community organization.

Glaser, Comstock, *Administrative Procedure: A Practical Handbook for the Administrative Analyst*. (Washington, American Council on Public Affairs, 1941, 207 pp.). See especially chapters II–VI on analysis, organization, and planning.

Johns, Ray, *Executive Responsibility: An Analysis of Executive Responsibilities in the Work of Voluntary, Community Social Welfare Organizations*. (New York, Association Press, 1954, 258 pp.). Several chapters relate to various aspects of community organization.

Pfeiffer, C. Whit and Gilmore, Otto T., "Problems of Administration in Community Organization," NCSW, 1941, pp. 577–596. "I. Selection of Projects and Participation of Public Agencies," C. Whit Pfeiffer. "II. Definition, Planning, Direction, and Timing of Projects," Otto Gilmore. One of the few available discussions of council administration.

Stone, Walter L., *Community Welfare Planning* (Nashville, Council of Community Agencies, 1941, mimeographed, 93 pp.).

——— *A Manual on Community Welfare Organization* (Published by the author. Nashville, 1946, mimeographed, 109 pp.).

Street, Elwood, *A Handbook for Social Agency Administration* (New York, Harper, 1947, 434 pp.). Includes chapters on committees, public relations, finances, etc.

Tead, Ordway, *The Art of Leadership* (New York, London, Whittlesey House, McGraw Hill Book Company, 1935, 308 pp.).

Williamson, Margaret, *Supervision — Principles and Methods.* (New York, Woman's Press, 1950, 170 pp.). Much of this material is applicable or adaptable to community organization.

17.

PERSONNEL[1]

THE QUESTION, "Who participates in community welfare organization?" might be answered, "Practically all social workers — consciously or unconsciously, at one time or another — and many laymen!"

Citizen participation is of overwhelming importance in community organization. Laymen are needed as members of committees, which are essential in most community organization undertakings. In addition, service volunteers participate in surveys, make speeches and promote social legislation, solicit for fund-raising drives, and carry on hundreds of other activities. The importance of the volunteer is implicit in every chapter of this book.

This chapter, however, is concerned with *professional* social work personnel in community organization. Social workers may be classified into five groups on the basis of their practice of community organization:

1. Community organization *practitioners* — workers who devote themselves exclusively to the *practice* of community organization, in councils, chests, national and other agencies. Two groups of these practitioners should be distinguished: those who practice overall health and welfare planning, such as workers in community welfare councils, and those who are concerned with program development and promotion in specialized agencies, such as staff members of state or national mental health associations.

2. *Executives of community organization agencies,* such as councils or chests. The executive of the community organization agency

---

[1] This chapter has been adapted in part from a paper by the author, "What Is the Job of the Community Organization Worker?" NCSW, 1948, pp. 162–172.

combines administration and the practice of community organization. In a small council the executive may be occupied almost entirely with community organization practice; in the large national agency he may be engaged almost completely with administration.

3. *Executives and sub-executives of consumer-service agencies,* whose jobs are concerned primarily with administration and secondarily with community organization.

4. *Quasi-community-organization workers,* whose jobs are primarily client-service or administration, but who also spend a substantial proportion of their time and effort on community organization. Examples include child welfare workers under the Social Security Act; certain other rural workers; some settlement, community center, and "area" workers; and field representatives whose jobs combine administration and community organization.

5. *Consumer-service workers* who occasionally do some community organization as incidental to their client-service jobs. For example, a psychiatric caseworker in a child guidance clinic may interpret the function of the clinic to parents, teachers, ministers, and others, or may serve on an inter-agency committee.

We are concerned here especially with the first two of the groups listed above — community organization workers and executives in community organization agencies. The term "community organization worker" is selected deliberately in preference to "community organizer," which carries a subtle suggestion of promotion, manipulation, and wire-pulling in a local community.

The quality of professional personnel available is the most important single factor in effective community organization. We shall consider the major types and functions of community organization jobs; the roles of the community organization worker; the types of persons who hold community organization jobs; the equipment of the community organization worker; and some aspects of professional education for community organization.

TYPES OF COMMUNITY ORGANIZATION JOBS

EVERY COMMUNITY ORGANIZATION WORKER performs one or more of the six basic functions of community organization: fact-finding; program development; the establishment and improvement of standards; coordination and facilitating inter-group relationships; education and public relations; and enlistment of adequate public support and participation. The following discussion of community organization

jobs includes positions concerned with: research which is closely related to programming; public relations and interpretation; fund-raising
for individual agencies as well as joint financing; and social action, insofar as social action relates to social welfare objectives.

United Community Funds and Councils of America has made a job
analysis study of positions in community chests and community welfare councils. On the basis of this study, they have drawn up job specifications for 19 types of jobs in chests and councils.[2]

Three of these are non-social-work positions — Accountant, Comp-
troller, and Office Manager — and as such they are omitted from this
discussion.

Of the remaining sixteen jobs, several are generic types of community organization jobs rather than merely chest-council specializations. Among these are: District Community Council Secretary (a job
which might be called Neighborhood Worker in agencies other than
chests and councils), Research Director, Public Relations Director, and
Publicity Director. From the standpoint of most community organization agencies, we may consolidate the two latter chest-council jobs,
reducing the list to fifteen positions.

It seems possible to identify at least eight other types of community organization jobs outside the chest-council field. Thus we have
a suggested list of 23 community organization jobs.[3] In the table on
the following page, this list is compared with the UCFC list of chest-
council jobs.

This classification covers only executive or primary jobs.[4] In practice, one would find in many community organization agencies such
gradations as the following:

Executive. The administrative head of an agency such as a council, chest, national agency, etc.

[2] *Job Descriptions for Chests and Councils.* New York (Community Chests and
Councils of America, Bulletin 141, Revised edition, 1953).
[3] This classification is generally comparable with the classification of positions of
266 community organization practitioners by Robert Irving Hiller in *The Education and Work Experience of Community Organization Practitioners* (New
York, Association for the Study of Community Organization and CCC, 1949),
pp. 5–6, and with the classification in an exploratory study by Samuel Brown:
*An Inventory of Certain Community Organization Jobs as Reported by Thirty-One
National Agencies,* Master's Thesis, School of Social Work, University of Michigan,
1955.
[4] Job 15, Field Representative, is likely to be a senior or junior practitioner job,
but it seems sufficiently distinctive and "primary," because of its field service aspect,
to be set off in this list and distinguished from the hierarchy of community
organization jobs in the agency headquarters.

FIGURE 10

COMMUNITY ORGANIZATION JOBS AND CHEST-COUNCIL JOBS

JOBS WITHIN AND WITHOUT CHESTS AND COUNCILS	CHEST-COUNCIL JOBS (CCC, 1953)
	1. Accountant (non-social-work)
1. Budget Secretary	2. Budget Secretary
2. Bureau (or Department) of Community Councils Secretary	3. Bureau (or Department) of Community Councils Secretary
3. Campaign Director	4. Campaign Director
4. Campaign Division Secretary	5. Campaign Division Secretary
5. Chest Executive Secretary	6. Chest Executive Secretary
6. Chest and Council Executive Secretary	7. Chest and Council Executive Secretary
7. Community Development Worker	
	8. Comptroller (non-social-work)
8. Conference Executive	
9. Council Division Secretary	9. Council Division Secretary
10. Council Executive Secretary	10. Council Executive Secretary
11. District Community Council Secretary (or Neighborhood Worker)	11. District Community Council Secretary
12. Executive of national or international agency for coordination and broad health and welfare planning	
13. Executive of program promotional agency in a specialized field	
14. Executive of statewide agency for health and welfare planning	
15. Field Representative	
16. Financial Secretary	
17. Labor Representative	12. Labor Representative
18. Legislative Representative	
	13. Office Manager (non-social-work)
19. Public Relations Director (or Publicity Director)	14. Publicity Director 15. Public Relations Director
20. Research Director	16. Research Director
21. Social Service Exchange Director	17. Social Service Exchange Director
22. Volunteer Bureau Director	18. Volunteer Bureau Director
23. Volunteer Bureau Referral Secretary	19. Volunteer Bureau Referral Secretary

Sub-executive. Line assistant; staff assistant; head of department with substantial responsibility for supervision of other staff members.

Senior practitioner. A worker with established skill and substantial experience, working on a job which gives wide opportunity for initiative and self-direction, and which is concerned primarily with the practice of community organization rather than the supervision of other staff members.

Junior practitioner. A worker with limited skill or experience, working on a community organization job under fairly close supervision, with limited opportunities for initiative and self-direction.

The lines between senior and junior practitioners are not sharply drawn; the two categories tend to shade into each other.

In general, the job of the community organization worker — even that of the senior or junior practitioner — resembles the job of an executive or sub-executive of a consumer-service agency, in terms of its content and types of activities, more closely than it resembles the job of the casework or group work practitioner. This fact has important implications for the training, selection, and supervision of community organization workers.

The foregoing classification contains some borderline jobs which require further study to determine whether or not they are primarily social work jobs. The positions which seem to lie in this borderline area are: Budget Secretary, Campaign Director, Campaign Division Secretary, Community Development Worker, Financial Secretary, Legislative Representative, Public Relations Director, and Research Director. The question is whether the incumbents of these jobs should be primarily social workers, with community organization training, or whether we should expect to draw these staff members largely from other related professional or vocational fields such as accountancy, fund-raising, rural extension work, legislative promotion, public relations, and social science research.

Certain community organization jobs require knowledge of specialized areas of health or welfare as well as knowledge of and skill in community organization. The secretary of the health division of a community welfare council or a staff member of a national agency concerned with child welfare or youth service are examples.

The job of teacher of community organization is not included in the foregoing classification, since it is concerned primarily with education rather than community organization practice; but it is intimately related to the field of practice and there is a good deal of movement back and forth between teaching and practitioner jobs.

FUNCTIONAL SPECIALIZATIONS

From the standpoint of job content and the skills involved, we can distinguish at least 15 major areas of functional specialization in these community organization jobs:

1. *Budgeting.* This involves analysis and preparation of budget materials, and executive service to a budget committee in carrying out the function of joint budgeting.

2. *Campaigning* relates to the planning and direction of joint fund-raising activities.

3. *Community chest operation: joint financing.* The operation of a financial federation, including joint budgeting, publicity, campaign, collection and distribution of funds, and proper accounting, is an important and well-marked function.

4. *Conference administration* refers to the planning and direction of large forum-type conferences or conventions, such as the National Conference on Social Welfare or state conferences.

5. *Field service* is the representation, "in the field," of a national or state agency, in its relationship to local or other affiliated agencies. This type of field service involves primarily community organization relationships and voluntary cooperation rather than authoritative or administrative relationships.

6. *Fund-raising other than in financial federations.* Financial promotion for an individual agency is distinct from joint financing, which is a federative effort with emphasis on large-scale organization and a joint campaign. The fund-raiser for the individual agency may concentrate on mail appeals and the solicitation of a relatively small number of individual prospects. Since the widespread development of community chests, this function in the individual local agency has disappeared in many cases, but it is still an important function in national, state, and some local non-chest agencies.

7. *Health and welfare planning.* This term, commonly used by UCFC, denotes the "overall" community organization job. It is concerned with bringing about a better adjustment between welfare needs and resources, *in general,* in a community, state, nation, or other area. Manifestations of this function are found in community welfare councils, statewide citizens associations, "action-type" state conferences, and national agencies concerned with the whole field of social welfare, such as the National Social Welfare Assembly.

8. *Legislative analysis and promotion,* usually on the state or na-

tional level, appears to be a distinctive function of community organization.

9. *Liaison with organized labor.* This function is concerned with bringing trade union members and other workers into participation in health and welfare programs and financial support of such programs.

10. *Planning and promotion of program in specialized field.* This function is concerned with achieving a better adjustment between needs and resources in a specialized field (family welfare, child welfare, health, recreation, or the aging), or in behalf of a special religious, racial, or other group (Catholics, Lutherans, Jews, Negroes, or foreign-born). This function may appear on any geographical level.

11. *Promotion of general community improvement.* This is giving assistance and enlisting self-help in community development — that is, improvement of the life of a community — usually a village or rural area. The best examples of this function are community development programs in newly developing countries (see Chapter 15), although there are some more or less similar jobs in this country. The community development worker often deals with problems relating to the total life of the community rather than to social welfare in the narrower sense. Such a worker is sometimes a "multi-purpose worker" and sometimes primarily a representative of another vocation, such as agriculture. However, this type of job seems to involve enough use of community organization process to justify its inclusion in the present discussion.

12. *Public relations and interpretation.* The function of developing and maintaining sound relations with the general public or special groups is clearly distinguishable. As pointed out above, the CCC *Job Descriptions* distinguish two different jobs here — Public Relations Director and Publicity Director.

13. *Research.* This is factfinding in connection with community organization and program development. It does not include "pure" social science research, unrelated to social work practice.

14. *Social service exchange administration.* The exchange, as a central index and clearing house, is a unique piece of community organization machinery, and its direction is a distinctive community organization function.

15. *Volunteer bureau administration.* This includes the planning and operation of a community volunteer program. The CCC *Job Descriptions* include two jobs concerned primarily with this function — Volunteer Bureau Director and Volunteer Bureau Referral Secretary.

Appendix D contains a chart which presents, in tabular form, certain data regarding these various types of jobs and the functional specializations which seem to apply to them.

THE ROLE OF THE COMMUNITY ORGANIZATION WORKER

Kenneth L. M. Pray and others have emphasized that the community organization worker is essentially an "enabler" and not a manipulator.[5]

There is a basic truth involved here. If we follow any community organization job back far enough, we shall always find that the professional community organization worker is the agent of some group or aggregation of people — whether it is voters of the United States or the supporters of the local community chest — in carrying into effect some program which these people support by contributions, or active assent, or at least by acquiescence. It is in harmony also with the fundamental ideas of democracy that the practitioner enables the group to achieve its desires rather than commands or manipulates the group.

However, we must avoid over-simplifying this matter of the role of the community organization worker. If a community or a constituency group is substantially united in its thinking and knows what it wants to do, we have a rather simple situation where the community organization worker acts as the agent of the constituency in helping it attain its objectives. But often a constituency group or even a governing board is not united in its thinking and does not know what it wants, except in very general terms. For example, a group of agencies and citizens in a community form a community welfare council to improve the well-being of the community through better teamwork and joint planning and action. But they may have little idea as to how they may attain this result, or what should be their immediate program. Should they give priority to a recreation survey, an attempted reorganization of the municipal department of public welfare, raising standards among the child caring organizations, or interpreting social work to organized labor?

The community organization worker is not *merely* an enabler. His role must often be that of creative leadership. Ordway Tead's well-known definition of leadership is "the activity of influencing people

[5] Kenneth L. M. Pray, "When is Community Organization Social Work Practice?" NCSW, 1947, pp. 194–204.

to cooperate toward some goal which they come to find desirable." [6]
The community organization worker will usually give indirect rather
than direct, public, or official leadership. But he must bring to the
problems of his agency all the knowledge, imagination, resourcefulness
and creative craftsmanship that he can command. He must often
interpret, suggest and analyze alternatives, and enter fully as a dynamic
partner into a creative group process by which goals will be chosen,
decisions will be hammered into shape and translated into action. The
final decision, the "last word," will be with a lay group; but the community organization worker must be a creative partner and participant
in the determination of objectives as well as the expert in the application of the community organization process. The roles of community
organization workers on various jobs would probably run the whole
gamut from fact-finder, analyst, planner, catalyst, interpreter, educator,
conferee, negotiator, mediator, and consultant to organizer, agent,
executive aide, advocate, promoter, social actionist, militant leader,
and occasionally perhaps social statesman. [7]

WHO ARE THE COMMUNITY ORGANIZATION WORKERS?

In 1948, Robert Irving Hiller made a questionnaire study of 266
community organization workers, members of the Association for the
Study of Community Organization. [8]

Of the 266 workers, 62 per cent were men, 38 per cent women. The
average age was 42 years; the majority of women were over 45, while
about three-fourths of the men were 45 or younger, with 51 per cent
of all the men in the 31–40 group.

About 95 per cent of the group were college graduates. Of the
whole group of 266, 38 per cent had Master's degrees in social work —
44 per cent of the men and 29 per cent of the women. Among the men
all degrees were held by those under 51 years; 52 per cent of those
under 51 had Master's degrees in social work.

The 266 workers had held 1522 jobs, 83 per cent of them in social

[6] Ordway Tead, *The Art of Leadership* (New York, McGraw-Hill, 1935), p. 20.
[7] Murray G. Ross (in *Community Organization: Theory and Principles*, Chapter 8)
suggests that the community organization worker may act in the roles of guide,
enabler, expert, and (he seems to add somewhat tentatively) "therapist." The
first three terms are suggestive of broad types of roles, but the realities of practice in community welfare organization seem more complex than this.
[8] Hiller, *The Education and Work Experience of Community Organization Practitioners.* For later data on ASCO members, see Ernest B. Harper, "ASCO and
Social Work," *Social Work Journal*, Vol. XXXIV, October 1953, pp. 182–183.

work, an average of 5.7 positions per worker. The average length of time on a non-executive position was 2 to 3 years; on an executive position, about 4 years. Most of the years of social work experience were spent on community organization jobs, although a substantial per cent of the total was in casework and group work positions. More than two-thirds of these practitioners entered social work in casework or group work practice. The women had more total consumer-service experience than the men. The men showed a greater tendency to move into executive community organization positions, particularly in the older age groups.

A study by the federal Women's Bureau estimates that there were some 2500 community organization workers in 1949, about 70 per cent of whom were men. Probably more than half were employed in community chests and community welfare councils. The supply of qualified community organization workers is inadequate; the annual need for replacements is probably at least 83, whereas of the 2000 graduates of the schools of social work only about 50 have specialized in community organization. For the near future, a good many positions will probably "continue to be supplied by experienced social workers who have demonstrated their skill in community organization techniques while working on other types of positions." [9]

THE EQUIPMENT OF THE COMMUNITY ORGANIZATION WORKER

What should be the equipment of the community organization worker? The community organization worker derives his equipment for the job from four main sources: personal qualities, general education, graduate professional education, and experience. His professional equipment includes knowledge, skills, philosophy, and attitudes.[10]

A college education and two years of graduate professional education in an accredited school of social work, with some specialization in community organization, normally gives the best foundation for a practitioner of community welfare organization.

[9] U.S. Department of Labor, Women's Bureau, *The Outlook for Women in Community Organization in Social Work* (Women's Bureau Bulletin 235-5, Social Work Series, Washington, Government Printing Office, 1951), pp. 1, 8, 15–16. This bulletin is a valuable source of information regarding community organization personnel; and, in spite of its title, most of the content is almost as applicable to men as to women.

[10] Cf. Hollis and Taylor, *Social Work Education in the United States*, pp. 220–225.

There are six basic elements in the equipment of the community organization worker:

1. *First hand experience in dealing with people,* preferably in a consumer-service agency. It seems desirable that the community organization worker should have one or more years of staff experience (not merely field work) in a casework, group work or other consumer-service agency, or possibly a reasonable equivalent for such experience in a closely allied profession. Social work is concerned with serving people; its focus is on human needs and human relationships. The community organization worker should make his entrance into social work at the point of helping and working with people rather than at the point of committees, meetings, organization charts, plans, programs, surveys, or campaigns. Persons who are remote from the experience of direct service agencies, and who may tend to think of social welfare programs in abstract and impersonal terms, are ill-equipped for leadership in community organization.

2. *A working knowledge of the field of social welfare* and of social welfare resources on local, state, and national levels. In most community organization jobs, the worker must be a "generalist" rather than a specialist, in terms of knowledge of functional fields.

3. *A practical understanding of community organization* — its objectives, the types of problems encountered, types and functions of agencies, methods and principles; and also at least an elementary understanding of the subject of administration.

4. *Skill in the practice of community organization.* This element, above all others, distinguishes the practitioner of community organization from one who merely "knows about" it. Skill is likely to be gained primarily from properly supervised field work and from experience.

5. *Personal qualities.* The community organization worker needs the personal qualities of any social worker, and also many of those of an executive.[11] Among the qualities that are important for a community organization worker we should certainly include: integrity, courage, emotional balance and adjustment, objectivity, sound judgment, tact, sensitivity, adaptability, imagination, ability to work under pressure, an interest in and liking for people, and a deeply-held respect for human personality. One can hardly insist, in addition, that a sense of humor be mandatory, but the worker will have a rugged life without it!

[11] *Social Work as a Profession* (New York, Council on Social Work Education, 1953), pp. 9–10. Tead, *Art of Leadership,* pp. 82–114.

6. A *sound philosophy of community organization.* Such a philosophy would be rooted in democracy and oriented to its values of ultimate control by the people; the right of self-determination by the individual, the group, and the community; and cooperation and participation in the achievement of common goals.

PROFESSIONAL EDUCATION FOR COMMUNITY ORGANIZATION

Formal professional education for social work in the United States began with a summer session in New York in 1898. By 1904 there was a year-round school, now the New York School of Social Work of Columbia University. Courses in community organization seem to have made their appearance about 1917. In 1923, a short course for community chest executives was organized by Ohio State University and what is now UCFC. The School of Social Service Administration later established at Ohio State University has continued to emphasize specialized training in the field of chests and councils. Community organization came to be accepted as one of the basic subjects in the social work curriculum: this was confirmed by actions of the American Association of Schools of Social Work in 1932 and 1944, and of the National Council on Social Work Education in 1952. An introductory course in community organization has been offered in most schools since about 1939. A sub-committee on community organization, of the American Association of Schools of Social Work, was active from 1939 to 1943. It studied courses and teaching materials; prepared bibliographies; brought greater integration of thinking among community organization teachers; and achieved some agreement regarding the content of the introductory course. Community organization, like other areas of social work education, profited by the Hollis-Taylor study of social work education (1948–1951); [12] and the subject is included as an integral part of the current Curriculum Study of the Council on Social Work Education.

Some present tendencies that affect community organization as an aspect of social work education are the following:

It is generally accepted that community organization should be a required subject for all degree candidates in graduate schools of social work. The reasons for such a requirement are obvious. Social work is almost always practiced in a community setting; all agencies make some use of community organization; every social worker finds his job

[12] Hollis and Taylor, *Social Work Education in the United States.*

affected by community problems, patterns, resources, and attitudes; and every social worker needs to understand the community organization approach to problems which cannot be solved through casework or group work alone.

There is wide acceptance of the idea that social work education is concerned with the development of knowledge, skills, and attitudes on the part of the student. It is generally agreed also that the social work curriculum should be an integrated whole, and that it should provide knowledge and understanding of (1) the social services, (2) human growth and behavior, and (3) social work practice, including community organization.

There is much current study and experimentation in schools of social work in the attempt to work out more fully integrated curricula. Some of the reorganized curricula involve considerable redistribution of course material.

SPECIALIZATION IN COMMUNITY ORGANIZATION

Specialized training for community organization is offered by some schools of social work, within the limits of the two year Master of Social Work degree. Such students fulfill all general requirements for the degree, and their first year of training is about the same as for other students.

Entrance to this specialization is restricted by some schools to students who have had previous social work experience. Other schools are willing to admit to the specialization students without previous experience, but require such students to take field work in casework or group work before beginning field work in community organization. Some schools and some national agencies also encourage such students, upon graduation, to work first in a consumer-service agency before taking a community organization job. The practical difficulty with this plan is the lack of enough qualified community organization workers in the field, and the consequent tendency of community organization agencies to "snap up" graduates with specialization in community organization, whether or not they have had consumer-service experience.

A sound specialization in community organization should include among the minimum requirements: one or more advanced courses in community organization, beyond the introductory course; a course in social welfare administration; and field work in community organization. Much of the experience with field work in casework and group work may be applied or adapted to use in connection with community organization field work; for example, the principle of the "protected" work load; close supervision by a member of the school faculty or a field supervisor from the agency staff; practice in record keeping by the student; and careful evaluation of the student's performance. Placements may be made in councils and chests, sectarian federations, urban leagues, housing associations, state and city public welfare agencies, state commissions, organizations for improving inter-cultural relations, health promotional agencies, and so on.

One important type of advanced course in community organization is a technical, generic course, cutting across special agency settings, and focusing on the practice of community organization, with special emphasis on problems, methods, and principles, and with some attention to program direction and records.

Some of the topics which might lend themselves to treatment in special courses or institutes, and certainly to extended research are: (1) health and welfare planning in the local community; (2) the development of social welfare programs; (3) joint fund-raising; (4) interpretation and public relations; (5) the financing of social agencies, governmental and voluntary; (6) state, national and international aspects of community organization; (7) the development of programs in specific fields — family and child welfare, health, recreation, housing, race relations, etc.; (8) citizen participation and neighborhood community organization; (9) community development — community organization in small communities and rural areas; (10) community organization and the job of the executive; (11) governmental and voluntary agencies — their functions and relationships, and the relationship of governmental agencies to the process of community organization; (12) concepts, theory, and principles of community organization; (13) social action and legislative analysis, planning, and promotion.

QUESTIONS AND PROBLEMS

1. List ten community organization jobs. Check these against the list of types of jobs and functional specializations suggested in the chapter. Classify them also as to grade—executive, sub-executive, senior practitioner, junior practitioner, etc. To what extent does the suggested classification cover these jobs? What criticisms or suggestions have you in regard to the chart (in the Appendix) and classification suggested?

2. Prepare a written job description or job specification for a community organization job.

3. What qualities and skills seem most important for an executive or worker in a community welfare council?

4. Find examples of the roles of the community organization worker as shown in some current community organization project (perhaps a field work assignment) or in a community organization case record.

5. A student in a community organization seminar raised the question, "What is wrong with 'manipulation,' anyhow? Isn't it inevitable in certain situations? Isn't it a normal part of social action?" What do you think of these questions? What is manipulation? What is your conception of the proper role for the community organization worker? Check the list of suggested roles in this chapter. Which of them seem valid and appropriate?

6. Do you think a school of social work graduate, without previous social work experience, should go directly into a community organization job, or should he have consumer-service experience first? Why?

7. Suppose a social worker graduated from a school of social work six years ago, with specialization in group work. He is now assistant director of a small settlement. He would like to get into a community organization job but doubts that he is well prepared for it. What sort of plan might he work out in order to head in the direction in which he wants to go?

SUGGESTIONS FOR READING

The *Social Work Year Book* articles on social work as a profession, education for social work, and personnel standards and practices include references to community organization; the texts also include some pertinent materials.

Community Chests and Councils of America:
Job Descriptions for Chests and Councils (Bulletin 141, New York, rev., 1953, 23 pp.).
We Want an Executive. (New York, rev., 1947, 14 pp.). Duties and qualifications of the chest-council executive.

Hiller, Robert Irving, *The Education and Experience of Community Organization Practitioners* (New York, Community Chests and Councils of America and Association for the Study of Community Organization, 1949, 61 pp.). A study of the education and work experience of 266 members of ASCO.

Hollis and Taylor, *Social Work Education in the United States.* (See bibliography, ch. 1.)

Lynde, Edward D., "The Role of the Community Organization Practitioner," (NCSW, 1952, *Selected Papers in Group Work and Community Organization,* pp. 118–128).

Newsetter, Wilber I., "Teaching Community Organization in Schools of Social Work." In McMillen, *Community Organization for Social Welfare,* pp. 59–67 (See Basic References.) An early paper discussing the place of community organization and inter-group work in the curricula of schools of social work.

Pfeiffer, C. Whit, "The Community Organization Worker in Action." In *The Job of the Community Organization Worker* (New York, Community Chests and Councils of America, and Association for the Study of Community Organization, 1948, pp. 15–24.). Primarily a discussion of the community organization worker and committee process.

Portner, Faye, *Training for Community Organization* (New York, Association for the Study of Community Organization, 1952, processed, 31 pp.).

Sieder, Violet M., "The Tasks of the Community Organization Worker: The Professional Method Related to the Community Organization Process." NCSW, *Planning Social Services for Urban Needs.* (Papers on Community Organization, 1957), pp. 3–16.

Social Work as a Profession (see bibliography, ch. 1).

United States Department of Labor, Women's Bureau. *The Outlook for Women in Community Organization in Social Work.* Women's Bureau Bulletin 235–5, Social Work Series. (Washington, Government Printing Office, 1951, 41 pp.). One of a series of bulletins relating to the outlook for women in various areas of social work. The discussion is largely applicable to men as well as women.

Van Valen, Donald, "Community Organization, Manipulation or Group Process?" NCSW, *Social Work in the Current Scene*, 1949, pp. 325–342.

18.

RECORDS

A RECORD IS A DOCUMENT or other auditory or visual product, intended to be used primarily as a working tool by an organization or individual, and which performs one or more of the following functions: (1) it gives an account of something which has taken place; (2) it identifies some person, group, or thing; (3) it contains factual descriptions, analyses, instructions, directions, opinions, recommendations, or suggestions; (4) it sets forth plans for the future.[1]

This definition is intentionally broad.

A record may be not only a textual document, but it may be a chart, graph, map, blueprint, photograph, microfilm, micro-card, film, slide, recording, or other product intended to be seen or heard at some time in the future.

A record is intended as a working tool. It is usually unpublished and for use primarily within the organization or some other group, rather than for the use of the general public. Even when a record is published, as is the *Congressional Record*, its *primary* purpose is to serve members of Congress and other government officials in carrying on the operations of the federal government.

Records have four general functions:

1. To give an account of something that has happened. The record is a substitute for or an extension of memory. It provides an authentic and lasting written or other "recorded" account in place of

---

[1] Compare: Sidney and Beatrice Webb, *Methods of Social Study* (London, Longmans, Green, 1932), ch. 5, especially p. 100; Harleigh B. Trecker, *Group Process in Adminstration* (New York, Woman's Press, 1950), p. 296.

the uncertain and fading recollections of human beings. A case record, a day sheet, a set of minutes, and a ledger card are all examples of this function.

2. For identification. A social security card, a driver's license, army identification tags, and a social service exchange name card are examples of identification records.

3. To set forth factual descriptions, analyses, instructions, directions, opinions, recommendations, or suggestions. An organization chart, a job description, standard practice instructions or standard operating procedures ("SOP's"), a directive from an administrative superior to a subordinate, an opinion of the Attorney-General, an advisory memorandum from an administrative assistant, a memorandum of recommendations from a committee or staff member — all of these illustrate this function of records.

4. To set forth plans for the future. The agenda for a meeting, an agency work plan for the year, a time schedule for a community chest campaign, and a worker's plan sheet for the day or week are examples of these records which look to the future rather than to the past.

To the question, are reports records, the answer is that it depends on the nature of the report. The report normally has the function of *transferring* information or recommendations from one person or group to another. However, if the report is for use primarily within the agency, it is a record and should be reckoned as an integral part of the agency's system of records. If, however, the report is essentially a piece of publicity material, intended primarily for public consumption or for a broad group of members or supporters, the report is not a record.

WHY RECORDS?

Records are used in every area of organized human relationships — government, business, religion, education, social welfare, and so on. Community organization records are to be distinguished from administrative records (such as minutes, mailing lists, financial statements, etc.) which are maintained by community organization agencies in common with other social welfare agencies. Community organization records are specialized records relating to the practice of community organization, just as the case record is specifically adapted to the practice of social casework. The records discussed in this chapter are concerned primarily with recording the activities of the community organization agency. This does not include systems maintained by such agencies for recording the operations of consumer service agencies, such as records of service statistics.

Adequate records are an essential tool in carrying on community organization effectively. Record-keeping is an integral part of sound professional practice, and in the long run the community organization worker can no more practice effectively without records than can the engineer, the accountant, the administrator, or the case worker.

In social work, records have been most highly developed in the practice of casework. But in casework there is generally only one basic unit of service — the "case" of an individual or family. There is, consequently, one basic kind of record — the case record — which is kept for every case or unit of service. Moreover, the case record is recognized as an essential tool for doing casework. No one could do modern casework with any considerable number of cases, for any substantial length of time, without keeping a case record for each case.

In community organization there is no one unit of service, like the case. Projects differ all the way from surveys to fund raising and legislative campaigns. Consequently, there is no one type of record which is obviously applicable to all community organization services; no one record is generally recognized as an essential and basic tool in the practice of community organization. And, unfortunately for the development of professional practice, it is possible to practice community organization, after a fashion, without keeping any one basic type of record.

In casework a vast reservoir of recorded experience is available for use in current practice, for reference, for research, for supervision, and for teaching purposes. There is no comparable reservoir of records in community organization.

The development of group work records no doubt stands somewhere between casework records and community organization records. The "group record" is the central type of record in group work. Keeping a good group record is probably more difficult than keeping a good case record, because of the larger number of personalities and the more complex inter-relationships involved in the group; on the other hand, an individual group worker deals with fewer records than an individual case worker.

In the following pages the attempt will be made to outline the purposes of keeping records in community organization agencies; to suggest some types of records and certain minimum essentials in community organization record-keeping; to discuss the Work Plan and the Work Progress Report as basic tools for record-keeping and program control; and to outline certain principles underlying program control and record-keeping. These topics are discussed from the standpoint of community welfare councils, national agencies, and other organizations doing generalized community organization jobs, rather than from the standpoint of specialized agencies such as community chests or social service exchanges.

There are six main purposes for using community organization records:

1. To facilitate and improve the service of the agency. This is the basic reason for all social welfare records. Records promote accuracy and precision in performance. Action is based upon a sure foundation of recorded facts, opinions, and plans, rather than upon vague and uncertain recollections. With records it is infinitely easier to interpret developments and plans; to enlist the cooperation of other persons or groups, within or without the agency; and to transfer or reassign an activity from one staff member to another. It is almost impossible for a staff member to take over a job or a project and carry it on without great waste of time and effort if there are no adequate records. Records, then, improve the service of the agency by increasing the effectiveness and the efficiency of the members of the staff.

2. To facilitate and increase the effectiveness of executive control and supervision. It is doubtful that there can be effective executive control or supervision in a community organization agency without adequate records. No experienced executive would attempt to administer a government bureau, a school, or a business without appropriate records. The community organization executive is no exception. He may be able to supervise one assistant with few or no records; but with responsibility for supervising three or more subordinates, the executive must have adequate records or he will do an inadequate job of executive control and supervision. Vagueness about objectives and methods, "fuzziness" of thinking, and sloppiness in performance are an inevitable accompaniment of a lack of an adequate system of records.

3. To provide the material for interpreting activities, problems, and accomplishments, to higher administrative authorities, to boards and committees, and to the members of the constituency who provide moral or financial support for the program. Any community organization agency should have to justify its existence periodically. Adequate records are the only sound bases for such reports.

4. To provide an adequate historical record of the agency, its program, services, and accomplishments. If a community organization agency is doing anything worth while, a historical record of what has been done is important to the agency itself, to cooperating organizations, to the community, and to similar agencies and practitioners in other communities. Such an historical record is of the greatest importance also to an incoming executive or staff member, or to a committee or executive seeking to study or evaluate trends and developments over a period of years.

5. **To provide more adequate teaching material for use in training students, workers-in-training, and new and junior workers.** Providing professional education for social work is a cooperative venture for schools of social work and social welfare agencies. Agencies with sound standards expect to obtain most of their workers from the schools; so the agencies are vitally concerned with the freshness and adequacy of teaching material available to the schools. Teachers of community organization could do their work infinitely better if they could turn to an adequate supply of good record material in the agencies, for documentary source material, illustrative materials, case problems, and so on. Moreover, the agency itself could do a better job of orientation of new workers, in-service training, and staff development if it had a backlog of adequate records.

6. **To provide material for professional research.** Such research involves the analysis of problems and activities, and is a basis for the improvement of professional practice, methods, and standards.

ADMINISTRATIVE RECORDS

The community organization agency has the administrative problems of any other social agency and it uses many of the same administrative records. These are not specialized community organization records and will not be discussed in this chapter; but it seems worth while to identify some of them, and to distinguish them from community organization records.

Administrative records include: office manuals or organization handbooks; scrapbooks of newspaper clippings, etc.; subject files, containing material on agencies, geographical entities, problems, fields and types of service, and so on; resource files or indexes; organization charts; job descriptions and job specifications; personnel records; mailing lists; statistical and financial records; correspondence and office memoranda; subject memoranda; notices of meetings; agendas; minutes; [2] and many types of reports.

[2] Minutes are of great importance in community organization. They are discussed in Ch. 22, in connection with the subject of committees.

OPERATING AND TEACHING RECORDS

Community organization records may be divided into two broad classes: operating records and teaching records.

The function of operating records is to facilitate the service and operation of the agency. The great bulk of community organization records fall into this category.

Teaching records serve as teaching material in courses in community organization or elsewhere. These records are commonly called "community organization case records," but they are not altogether analogous to individual case records. The individual case record is usually an operating record, which may be adapted to teaching purposes. Like the individual case record, the community organization teaching record is an historical account. Sometimes the community organization record is based on one or more operating records. An example would be a teaching record based on the monthly and annual reports of a child welfare worker. Sometimes the teaching record is based on a special type of operating record which was originally kept with an eye to its later use for research or teaching purposes.[3] Sometimes a teaching record is written after the fact, as a paper or article, or expressly for teaching purposes.[4]

There are probably not more than 20 to 30 published and currently available community organization records. A larger number no doubt exists, in mimeographed form, in the possession of individual schools of social work and teachers. The instructor in community organization will be fortunate, however, if he finds more than half a dozen records that are really satisfactory for his purposes. A committee of the Council on Social Work Education is working on the production of more community organization teaching records and has issued several such records.

[3] For example, the published record by the author, *Pennsylvania's Ten Year Program for Child Welfare* (New York, Association Press, 1949) was based on a much longer "project case record" which was kept by the agency largely because it was believed that the project was unique and that there ought to be a historical record of it, available for future consultation and study, if not for publication.
[4] An example of this type of record is Spencer R. Gordon's *The Reorganization of the Winston County Unemployment Relief Board* (New York, Association Press, 1949).

PROCESS RECORDING

Process recording in community organization is a type of recording which may be applied to any diary or case-history type of record. The usual diary or case-history record is a "narrative record:" the major emphasis is on *what happened.* The process record attempts to incorporate the community organization process into the record; that is, it not only tells what happened, but it lays emphasis on *how and why* various things happened, and how the worker made use of the community organization process.

The following statement indicates the place of process recording in community organization records:

Both OPERATING RECORDS and TEACHING RECORDS may employ the *case-history* or *diary* type of records, among others. Any case-history or diary type of record may be a *narrative record* or a *process record,* depending on whether the emphasis is mainly on what happened (narrative) or also on why and how the community organization process was used as it was (process record). There may also be mixed narrative-process records, where process-recording is done in certain portions of the record.

Advantages and disadvantages claimed for process records may be summarized as follows:

Advantages:

1. The process record is more complete than the ordinary narrative record, and it therefore gives the reader better understanding of what happened and why and how it happened.

2. It lays special emphasis upon the social-psychological aspects of community organization and upon individual, group, and intergroup relationships. These basic factors are likely to be ignored or treated superficially in narrative records.

3. The process record reveals much more adequately than the narrative record the role of the professional worker as a community organization practitioner — what problems he encountered, what relationships were involved, why and how he did what he did and with what results. The process record is therefore much more useful than the narrative record for purposes of self-study by the worker, supervision, teaching, and research.

Disadvantages:

1. Process records are usually extremely long. Process-recording is therefore exceedingly time-consuming and expensive. There is no clear

evidence that process records as regular operating records are worth what they cost.

2. The selection of material for process recording seems to be highly subjective. Among hundreds of details, which should be recorded and which should not? Unless some fairly objective criteria can be evolved, process recording may be a more or less intuitive and esoteric exercise, of doubtful value as a method of professional practice.

3. Process records sometimes contain a large amount of trivial and irrelevant material, including guesses, surmises, hunches, and sometimes psychologically half-baked interpretations of actions, motivations, and attitudes. They contain so much detail that the central narrative may be obscured; it is actually difficult, sometimes, to find out the simple objective facts as to what really happened.

4. Habitual process recording may tend to make the worker introspective and too much absorbed in his "role" and the details of relationships and practice. The worker should not become so enmeshed in the analysis of process that he loses the spontaneity and creative quality which should characterize the professional community organization worker.

These issues remain to be answered. There are also certain related questions: When and for what kinds of records should process recording be used? Should process records be regular operating records, kept continuously even by workers of long experience, or are they useful chiefly for purposes of special research, for recording certain new and experimental programs, for teaching, and for learning and supervision in the case of field work students and less experienced workers? [5]

A STUDY OF COUNCIL RECORDS

In the study of council records by Gene Wallace,[6] questionnaire replies were received from 127 community welfare councils having employed executive staff. Some of the major findings of the study may be thus summarized.

[5] In respect to process records, see: Gloria Roman, "A Perspective on Process Recording," in *Evaluating the Effectiveness of Councils: Report of the 1954 Research Workshop* (New York, CCC, 1954?), p. 44. Campbell G. Murphy, *Community Organization Practice*, pp. 299–301, Anne W. Lindsay, *Group Work Recording: Principles and Practice* (New York, Woman's Press, 1952), pp. 1, 97–99. Trecker, *Group Process in Administration*, pp. 301–306. Some examples of published process records are noted at the end of the chapter.
[6] Gene Wallace, *Community Organization Operating Records in Community Welfare Councils*. Master's thesis, University of Michigan, School of Social Work, 1954.

The types of records kept by various numbers of councils were as follows:

RECORD	COUNCILS REPORTING RECORDS
Minutes	127
Correspondence	119
Newspaper Clippings	112
Agenda	94
Memo-to-the-files	73
Program record	60
Progress report	57
Other reports	49
Project case history	49
Committee case history	37
Committee face sheet	37
Agency face sheet	24
Record of supervisory conference	18
Project face sheet	18
Agency case history	14
Worker's log	9
Agency log	5

Ninety-six councils replied as follows to a question as to what records (aside from minutes, agenda, and correspondence) they considered most important:

TYPE OF RECORD	NUMBER OF COUNCILS
Reports other than progress reports	24
Progress reports	22
Project case histories	15
Memos-to-files	10
Agency face sheets	8
Process records	7
Committee case histories	6
Worker's log	5
Miscellaneous (records mentioned less than five times: included membership records, community resource files, committee face sheets, reference material regarding state and national agencies, etc.)	46

Of 121 councils commenting on whether they considered their present record systems adequate, 60 per cent regarded them as inadequate. Major deficiencies reported in current record systems were: records incomplete in content (the need for more "community organization process" in records was most frequently mentioned in this connection); additional types of records needed (narrative records were mentioned by nine councils); records lacking uniformity and integration; and, in one case, records too voluminous.

Among the problems encountered in respect to records, 101 out of 115 councils replying mentioned insufficient staff time, and 67 reported insufficient clerical assistance. Other problems were: uncertainty regarding record forms (30), difficulty in selecting material (26), lack of dictating equipment (19), staff not interested in recording (8), filing problems (4), and lack of recording skill (2).

TYPES OF OPERATING RECORDS

Most operating records may be classified within the following six categories:

1. "Stream records" (diaries, logs, day sheets, etc.)
2. Face sheets [7] and analysis blanks
3. Community organization case histories
4. Work plans and programs
5. Administrative reports
6. Historical analyses and summaries

Under each of these headings several possible types of records are described below. Probably no one agency would use more than a few of these records.

STREAM RECORDS

A stream record is a chronological record of the "stream of events" or developments in relation to a job. The material is presented chronologically rather than topically.

The diary is a day-by-day narrative record kept by a worker. This is probably both the most comprehensive and the most flexible type of stream record. Particular events may be described in much or little detail, and entries may be confined to objective factual items or may include the worker's interpretations and comments. Generally speaking, the more free and uninhibited a diary is, the more valuable it is as

---

[7] The term "face sheet" is borrowed from casework usage, where the family face sheet gives basic facts about a family, such as composition of family, relatives, previous employment, and previous addresses.

a picture of the way the worker sees the job. If the diary is subject to review by a supervisor, the worker's freedom of comment may be somewhat lessened.

There is no standard form for social work diaries. They may be written in the first or the third person. Diary entries should be written in complete sentences rather than in disconnected phrases. The diary should be written up daily and kept up to date. Some extracts from social work diaries are available in published form, but the whole subject presents a rich field for exploration and study.[8]

The diary is the most detailed and theoretically the most valuable form of stream record; the one serious objection to it is the amount of time it takes. The diary seems particularly appropriate for students doing field work in community organization, and for workers on new or experimental jobs; but it would be desirable if more experienced workers could keep diaries, over certain periods at least, for purposes of analysis and study.

A *day sheet* provides an instrument for a kind of shorthand stream-recording of the day's activities of the worker. It is brief, compact, easily recorded and reviewed. It does not lend itself to process recording.

One day sheet for community organization and administrative workers is mimeographed on 8½ × 11 inch paper, with the long edge at the top, and with the following column headings (Figure 11). The methods of making entries are, briefly summarized, as follows:

1	2	3	4	5	6	7	8	9
From	To	Hours	Activity	Person or Group	Subject	Place	Assignment	Remarks

FIGURE 11

DAY SHEET

[8] For examples of diaries or material based on diaries, see: Walter W. Pettit, *Case Studies in Community Organization* (New York, Century, 1928), "Dale County." Benjamin Glassberg, *Across the Desk of a Relief Administrator* (Chicago, American Public Welfare Association, 1938). Margaretta Brereton, *The General Secretary of a Community Y.W.C.A.* (New York, Woman's Press, 1940?), pp. 172–184. Murray *et al, Group Work in Community Life* (New York, Association Press, 1954).

Columns 1–3 are used only if the day sheet is to be used also as a time sheet. Enter the time of beginning and ending a specific activity, counting to the nearest quarter of an hour; thus: 9:00, 9:15, 9:30. In column 3, the total time of the activity may be entered in hours and decimal fractions of hours: thus, 1.75 hours. In column 4 enter an abbreviation indicating the *type of activity*, without reference to its function or purpose: e.g., interview, conference, meeting, dictation, telephone conversation, handling incoming or outgoing mail, planning, reading and study, travel, etc. In column 5 enter person or group concerned, if any — name of interviewee, committee, etc. In column 6, enter subject of activity, if desired — particularly, subject of interview, conference, planning, etc. Under column 7, enter place if other than headquarters office. In column 8, enter a letter or number abbreviation to indicate the "asignment," or *functional division of the job* (that is, the purpose) to which this activity relates. Thus a small-city council executive might have certain general assignments indicated by letter abbreviations, such as: administration (A); agency consultation and assistance (C); participation in joint budgeting (B); public relations (PR); chest-council relationships (CC); etc.; and the various projects in the council program might be indicated by numbers, thus: 1, developing program for aged; 2, Youth Center Study; 3, attempt to establish child guidance clinic; etc. Column 9 gives a place for miscellaneous notes, comments, or remarks.

An agency log is a daily (or possibly weekly) narrative record of important developments. It differs from a diary in that the log is selective rather than comprehensive. Only special and significant developments are "logged." Appropriate items might include: changes in program projects; organizational and administrative developments (changes in structural organization, committees, personnel); meetings held; publications; and important developments in inter-agency relationships.

The Scrapbook of Publications is not strictly a community organization record, but an administrative device. It is included here because it does not seem to be widely used, although such a record is particularly important for a community organization agency which issues many pieces of material. The Scrapbook should contain a sample of every piece of printed or mimeographed material issued by the agency, including record forms as well as publications, but excluding minutes and agendas. Items are entered in chronological order and given serial numbers. An analytical table of contents provides a key to the information in the Scrapbook. This Scrapbook, if it is kept complete and up to date, is a valuable reference book and administrative tool as well as an important historical record.

FACE SHEETS AND ANALYSIS BLANKS

The community organization face sheet is a type of record that gives, in itemized form, the identifying information about some one entity — a committee of the agency, a project, or an agency, community, county, or state. Some of these records include enough analytical information so that they may properly be called analysis blanks.

The committee face sheet, a card or page in a looseleaf book, gives identifying information about the organization and functions of a committee.

The project face sheet gives basic information about the nature, purpose, and organization of the project, and the dates of its beginning and end.

A *project analysis* goes beyond mere descriptive information and presents analytical data on the basis of which some evaluation of the project may be made.

Agency, community, county, or state face sheet or analysis. The unit of recording would depend upon the unit with which the community organization agency had its major contacts. A community welfare council might wish to keep such a face sheet for each member agency; a national agency might keep either state or community face sheets, or both, depending upon how its local units were organized; a state welfare department might be more interested in county face sheets. A community face sheet would include some information as to population, area, location, type of community (economic basis, etc.), and social welfare resources. For an agency, the face sheet might include such items as name, location, auspices, function, organization, plant, budget, and possibly certain service statistics.[9]

CASE HISTORIES

The case history is a chronological narrative record of developments, contacts, problems, etc., in respect to some one entity — an

[9] The Outline for the analysis of a Community Organization Problem and Pierce Atwater's Problem Index, both referred to in Chapter 16, are not listed here as formal records. Both are tools for analysis and are related to the analytical records discussed above.

agency, a project, etc. Such a record is analogous to a case record for a family or individual.

Agency, community, county, or state case record. The record should refer to minutes, correspondence, and reports, but usually these should not be included in full in the body of the record. Summaries of long records may be needed. Such case records are important where a community organization agency has continuing relationships with member agencies, as in the case of a council, chest, or national agency; or where it has a continuing supervisory or consultative relationship, as is often the case with a federal or state public welfare agency.

A project case record relates to a single project of the community organization agency.[10]

Conceivably, agencies might keep such a record on every project; but this appears to be a "counsel of perfection." In practice, it is doubtful whether any agency with many projects would find such a practice feasible in view of the time and expense entailed. It would be desirable, however, for each agency to keep full case records on one or two particularly significant projects. This would be at once a contribution to the agency's records, to professional practice, and to the accumulation of more adequate teaching materials.

WORK PLANS AND PROGRAMS

The work plan is a written plan of operation for an agency over a year or other specified period. It is discussed in detail later in the chapter.

A program is a list of projects and other service activities planned for a given period, or a list of activities which are in progress or accepted as current obligations at a given time. The program relates only to service activities: it is less inclusive than the work plan, which includes also the areas of administration and extra-agency developments.

ADMINISTRATIVE REPORTS

Many kinds of administrative reports are possible. The basic type of report suggested is a Work Progress Report, to be compiled

---

[10] See: Frances Goodall, *A Narrative of Process in Social Welfare Organization* (St. Louis, Washington University, 1948). Arthur Dunham, *Pennsylvania's Ten Year Program for Child Welfare* (New York, Association Press, 1949). Murphy, *Community Organization Practice* (1954), pp. 300–301.

monthly or at other regular intervals. The Work Plan and the Work Progress Report are here regarded as the keys to the whole system of records for a community organization agency.

The *work progress report* is an administrative report prepared at the end of a month, quarter, or other period, by the chief executive, a departmental executive, or a worker. Its purpose is to review the activities of the report-period, giving a picture of the present situation, and indicating the next steps. The work progress report is made against the background of the work plan. This report is discussed below.

Administrative reports of various kinds have been developed by community organization agencies. In the cases of some national agencies, recording has probably been more highly developed for the field staff than for the agency as a whole.

Administrative reports may be statistical, textual, or both. Few administrative reports of community organization agencies appear to attain the standards suggested below for the work progress report.

HISTORICAL RECORDS

Many of the types of records listed above contain historical material. The records referred to under this heading are historical summaries over longer periods.

Narrative histories are usually written for special purposes — sometimes for publication and sometimes for administrative use. Such a document may cover the history of an agency, a special type of service (such as licensing and supervision of child caring organizations by a state welfare department), a project, a demonstration, and so on.

Analytical Summaries of Projects. Projects are the heart of the programs of most councils and many other community organization agencies. A summary of the projects of such an agency over a year or several years gives important insight into the nature and emphases of the agency's program. Such a summary may be of great value in appraising past activities and planning future programs. An extract from such a summary study of a council is shown in Figure 12.[11]

[11] Virginia S. Shenefield, *The Program Projects of a Council of Social Agencies . . . 1940–1944.* Detroit, Master's Thesis, Institute of Social Work, University of Michigan, 1945. In the illustration, the column designated "Objective" refers to the six community organization functions. The column "Major Methods" proved less useful than the other items of analysis, partly because the original records were not always such that the methods could be deduced with accuracy or completeness.

FIGURE 12

EXTRACT FROM SUMMARY OF COUNCIL PROJECTS

No.	Designation & Description of Activity	Dura-tion	Organizational Unit	Functional Field or Other Area	Objective	Major Methods	Results
1	Made study of local living costs in relation to minimum family budget requirements	Feb. 1944 to May 1944	Joint Committee of Family and Children's and Health Sections	Family Welfare	Standards	Fact-finding Analysis Planning Education	Published report on "Suggestions for Family Budgets in Low-Income Group" for use as agency guide
2	Camp school held to train new people for camp staffs	May 1944 to June 1944	Committee of Group Work Section	Recreation	Standards	Planning Education Operating inter-agency service	Provided help for camps not able to secure experienced staff
3	Made study of proposed changes in State Children's Code, and carried on campaign of education about Children's Code. Made recommendations to State Commission (See Project #2–1943)	1943 to June 1944 Oct. 1944 to 1945	Committee of General Council	Child Welfare	Education	Analysis Planning Education Conference Promotion of legislation Exerting social pressure	Created interest among community leaders and legislative delegation for adoption of proposed legislation

No.	Designation & Description of Activity	Duration	Organizational Unit	Functional Field or Other Area	Objective	Major Methods	Results
4	Christmas giving was planned and Christmas Clearing House was operated under auspices of Social Service Exchange	Nov. 1944 to Dec. 1944	Committee of General Council	Family Welfare	Coordination	Planning Education Organization Operating inter-agency service	Coordinated work of several groups participating in Christmas giving

FIGURE 13

SUMMARY OF COMMUNITY CHANGES AND COUNCIL ACTIVITIES*

Name of Council: New Haven Council of Social Agencies   *From January 1, 1937, to April 1, 1938*

| | COUNCIL ACTIVITY IN EACH FIELD | | | | |
| *Significant Community Changes by Fields of Service* | *Description of Activity* | *Classification by Function* | | | |
		Education	*Action*	*Administration*	*Coordination*
CARE OF CHILDREN Juvenile court bill failed. Has more extensive backing in present legislature.	Correspondence with Legislators re state-wide juvenile court bill.		x		
Guardianship bill failed. New bill proposes unification of guardianship under county commissioners, with state standard setting.	Correspondence with Legislators in support of bill to unify guardianship of dependent and neglected children in state.		x		
Girls' Service League discontinued work with unmarried mothers and guidance cases. One orphanage closed. New case supervisor for principal children's agency. Staffs of two largest children's agencies strengthened.	New Haven Study (with general committees on Bibliography, Seminars, Personnel, Executives, etc.)	x	x		

Significant Community Changes by Fields of Service	Description of Activity	Classification by Function			
		Education	Action	Administration	Coordination
Better assignment of responsibility for unmarried mothers' cases.	Committee on Unmarried Mothers and Guidance Work.		x		x
Provision of domiciliary care to take the place of the Girls' Service League.	Committee on Future Study in the Field of Child Care.		x		
Budget reduction in Leila Day Nursery.	Research project: Cost Analysis, Leila Day Nursery.			x	
Increasing day nursery care for children with behavior problems.	Day Nursery Committee's review of the cooperative arrangement between the Nursery and the Family Society.				x
Case conference assuming responsibility for much wider range of cases than those originally denominated.	Case Conference Committee (meeting weekly to consider all cases in which children are to be committed or in which Department of Charities is being asked to assume financial responsibility).				x

* From: *What Councils of Social Agencies Do* (CCC).

Summary of Community Changes and Council Activities. An historical summary, under this title, made for the New Haven Council of Social Agencies, is appended to *What Councils of Social Agencies Do*, published by CCC. This record is particularly interesting in that it starts with significant community changes and then attempts to determine the relation of council activities to these changes. (See Figure 13.)

As we have suggested, these general categories and types of community organization records certainly do not exhaust the possibilities. This area of practice is one where a great deal of research, experimentation, and reporting of results is needed.

Each community organization agency must build up its record system to meet its own needs. But there are two basic, interlocking records which it is believed should be used by all community organization agencies. These are the Work Plan and the Work Progress Report. These seem to the author to constitute a minimum for community organization record-keeping, and to be worth discussing in some detail.

THE WORK PLAN

A work plan is a written plan for the operation and development of the service program, administration, and extra-agency relationships of a social welfare agency (or an organization-unit thereof), for a year or other specified period.[12] Its objectives, content, and operation may be outlined as follows:

OBJECTIVES

The objectives sought in the use of a work plan are:
1. To improve the service of the organization. This is the basic underlying purpose.
2. To increase the agency's effectiveness, efficiency, and economy of operation.

[12] The Federal Social Security Administration has used work plans as basic instruments in program and administration. See: Charles Miller, "The Work Plan Story," *Oasis* (publication of the Bureau of Old Age and Survivors Insurance), Volume 1, April 1955, pp. 12–13. The present author is indebted to the Bureau of OASI for providing helpful material regarding the use of work plans by the Bureau. The *rationale* of work planning is set forth by Solem Arnie, in "Work Planning in Government," *Advanced Management*, Vol. VII, July–September and October–December 1942.

3. In respect to the employed and volunteer personnel of the agency:
   a. To promote their understanding of what the agency is trying to do and how it expects to do it.
   b. To enlist, to the fullest degree possible, their active participation in the planning and carrying out of the plans of operation.
   c. To increase their satisfaction in their service to and association with the agency.
4. To provide for periodic and systematic stock-taking, self-evaluation, and comparison of objectives and plans with accomplishments on the part of the agency.
5. To provide factual information regarding the agency's program, plans, and operation, as a basis for extra-agency reporting and interpretation.
6. To contribute to the building and preservation of an adequate historical record of the agency and to make available appropriate material for professional research and education.

CONTENT

The work plan should be a comprehensive plan for the year. Its content should include three broad aspects of the agency's operation:
1. Its service program. This is, of course, the reason for the agency's existence.
2. Its administration. This includes the activities which are not a part of the service program as such but which are necessary and incidental to the carrying on of the service program.
3. Its extra-agency relationships. These include relationships with overhead authorities, with other agencies, organizations, and groups; and with the public.

In general, the work plan should indicate for each activity which it includes:
1. *What* is to be done? Describe briefly the nature of the activity.
2. *Why* is it to be done? What is the purpose of the activity?
3. *Who* is to do it? Indicate the department, organization unit, geographic branch, committee, etc., which is to be in charge of the activity. If a volunteer committee is in charge, indicate the staff position of the person designated as the staff aide, to the committee.
4. *Where* is it to be done? This should be included if the agency has districts, branches, or other geographical units.
5. *When* is it to be done? Note the methods to be used, if significant.

(For example, it might be indicated that a certain inquiry would be made through a questionnaire study of agencies.) Note any special budgetary provisions. (For instance, a particular project may be carried out under a special budgetary grant from a federal agency, foundation, etc.) A related question is sometimes *how much* should be done. It is desirable, wherever possible, to estimate the number of professional and clerical man-days required during the year for an activity.

The following checklist may be used in determining the content of the work plan. Those who prepare the plan should consider what items, if any, should be entered under each of the following headings:

1. *Service program.* What are the major functions of the agency? What are the major divisions or aspects of its service program?

It is assumed that the agency may carry on three types of activities: continuous activities, projects, and occasional activities.[13] *Continuous activities* may be described in detail in the first work plan issued by the agency, but may be merely referred to by name in subsequent work plans, unless there are changes expected in the nature or quantity of service. Each current or proposed *project* within the work-plan period should be listed and adequately described in the work plan. This description should include the project number (if any), designation of the project, organization unit and worker in charge of it, date of initiation of the project, and present status. Where *occasional activities* can be planned or foreseen in advance (such as major meetings, hearings, etc.), they should be described in the work plan. In respect to other miscellaneous unplanned but inevitable "collateral activities," their nature may be indicated in a descriptive paragraph, and an estimate may be made of the staff time which they will probably require.

2. *Administration.* What activities should be noted in respect to any of the following aspects of administration?

a. General administration
b. Organization structure and relationships — general overhead organization, internal organization, committees
c. Personnel administration
d. Plant, equipment, and maintenance
e. Fiscal administration
f. Office administration

[13] See Ch. 16, Classification of Activities.

3. *Extra-agency relationships*
   a. Relationships to overhead authorities
   b. Relationships to agencies on same geographic level
   c. Relationships to agencies on other geographic levels
   d. Relationships to the public or to special groups (public relations)

PREPARING THE WORK PLAN

Methods of preparing the work plan will vary with the nature and organization of the agency, but the following outline may be suggestive:

1. In some cases, it may be desirable for the chief executive, after conference with the major sub-executives, to prepare a background statement concerning "work emphases," in the light of economic, social, legislative, and political factors that may be expected to affect substantially the agency's program.
2. Each department, division, branch, or other organization-unit should prepare a work plan.
3. These work plans should be reviewed, summarized, and revised as necessary, through conferences of the executive and sub-executives, and usually through full staff meetings; and eventually the departmental work plans, plus any agency-wide activities, will form the basis for the agency work plan.
4. The agency work plan, as formulated by the agency executive, should be submitted for approval or revision to the board of the agency, if the agency has a directive (policy-determining) board, or to any overhead authority to which the agency is directly responsible.
5. The work plan should be closely related to the agency's budget, which is essentially a fiscal work plan. The work plan year should be the fiscal year.

The compilation of an agency's first work plan will of course be more difficult than the preparation of any subsequent plan, because there is no previous plan to serve as a guide.

THE PLAN IN OPERATION

The work plan should ordinarily be given wide distribution among the agency's board and staff members.

Any modifications of the work plan, during the year of its operation, should be arrived at in the same manner in which the original plan was formulated, and the revisions should be given the same distribution as the original work plan.

An experimental work plan for a large-city Urban League, following substantially the outline above, gives a clear, lively, but concise picture of an active organization.

Among the continuous activities of the Community Services Department the following appear:

1. The attainment and effective execution of an open-occupancy policy of placement in local public housing projects.

2. A program in cooperation with other community activities to provide more adoptive and foster homes for Negro children.

Special projects include the following:

1. Organization of a community Dads' Club.

2. Further organization and development of neighborhood groups in a particular district.

3. Development of the Urban League Guild.

Occasional activities include: cooperation with the police in reference to a Youth Club; participation as resource consultants on a city Committee on Youth; and consultative service to a day nursery.

The administrative portion of the plan emphasizes preparation of the annual budget; work on a salary scale; and action by the Board on a draft of a personnel practices manual prepared by the staff.

Public relations items include plans for the annual report and annual meeting, work on a film, and a Christmas calendar project.

THE WORK PROGRESS REPORT

The Work Progress Report is primarily a tool to facilitate more adequate program operation and control, and therefore better service by the agency. The report is written against the background of the agency's Work Plan; it normally follows the general outline and headings of the Work Plan.

GENERAL CHARACTERISTICS

The Work Progress Report has three specific functions:

1. It reviews what has happened during the past report-period.

2. It gives a picture of the present situation.

3. It indicates next steps.

The unique value of this type of report lies in the following characteristics:

1. The Report covers the total operation of the agency, including service program, administration, and extra-agency relationships. It is based on the classification of service activities into continuous services, projects, and occasional activities. The Report thus makes provision for covering all types of activities, and not merely projects.

2. The Report covers major developments in respect to organization, personnel, and administration.

3. The Report provides a standardized type of record which lends itself to continuity and ease in recording, to interpretation, and comparison of records.

4. It is a report to be produced at regular intervals. It provides for a continuing documentary record of the agency's work.

5. The Report is designated specifically as an instrument of professional practice and program direction; and it lays special emphasis upon the initiation, direction, and closing of projects.

6. The Work Progress Report is an administrative report. It is for use primarily by the executive and staff in carrying on the program and administration of the agency. In some cases it may be submitted in its original form to the board of directors or a departmental committee; in other cases it may be condensed, simplified, or summarized. In any case, this report is not intended as a piece of publicity for the general public or for a lay constituency. It is likely to be too long, too formal, and too technical, and it may be too confidential for such a purpose. The report does, however, provide the basic factual material from which a report for the public or a lay constituency may be prepared.

The Work Progress Report is intended particularly for community organization agencies engaging in a variety of activities, such as councils, national agencies, statewide citizens associations, state conferences, promotional agencies in special fields, etc. It may be adapted for use in reporting the community organization activities of agencies which combine community organization with consumer service or other functions. Any agency may of course need to make special adaptations of the report to fit its particular needs.

A Suggested Outline for Work Progress Report is included in Appendix C. The Report may be worked out either as a textual document, with appropriate headings and sub-headings, or as a series of charts or tabular sheets. The headings suggested in the Appendix may be applied to either form of arrangements.

USES OF THE PROGRESS REPORT

The basic purpose of the Progress Report is, of course, to improve the agency's service. Among the specific uses to which the report may be put are the following:

1. As an instrument of administrative control and direction over the program of the agency.
2. As a means of increasing administrative efficiency.

    For example: many thoughtful executives of community organization agencies have been concerned about the question of what are reasonable work loads (the equivalent of case loads for case workers) for community organization workers. A series of Work Progress Reports would at least begin to provide factual material as to actual current work loads and accomplishments of various organization units and workers.

3. As an aid to supervision. The report forms a basic document for use by both supervisor and worker in supervisory conferences and otherwise.
4. As a record of what has happened during the past report period.
5. As a source of reference regarding past events and developments.
6. As a basis of comparison with previous periods.
7. As a basis for a report to a board, committee, or constituency.
8. As a basis for critical review of the agency's program and progress.
9. As a guide to future action.
10. As supporting material for budget requests, or material to be used in interpretation and defense of the agency when questions are raised as to what it is doing and why.
11. As a means of orientation for a new executive, worker, or volunteer officer, board or committee chairman.
12. As a link in a chain of work progress reports which, taken together, present a developmental history of the agency.

A Yearly Work Progress Report should be compiled from the monthly, quarterly, or other reports, thus providing an administrative review and analysis for the year.

A progress report, covering a four-month period, was prepared by a suburban branch Council and Chest, connected with a metropolitan Chest-Council. It began with a section called Summary and Highlights. Six projects were then reported: development of a Teen-Age Club; institutes for volunteers; Case Study Committee; Committee on Public Financing of Social Services; Committee on Day Camping;

and community organization in two school districts. Recurrent Services included various activities in connection with the Community Chest Campaign. Occasional Services included meetings of the Family Welfare Division and Group Work and Recreation Division. Administrative meetings included meetings of the Board, Nominating Committee, and Budget Review Conferences. Major contacts were noted with two agencies: the Girl Scouts and a school community center. Other sections dealt with Collateral Activities, Publications, Administrative Developments, and Major Current Problems.

QUESTIONS AND PROBLEMS

1. Try to find out what community organization records are actually kept by a community organization agency in your community. To what extent do they correspond with the various categories suggested in the chapter?

2. What community organization records do you think should be kept by a community welfare council with one professional worker; a council with three professional workers; a child welfare worker in a rural county; a field representative of a national agency?

3. Analyze one record which is used by an actual community organization agency. Try to cover these points: agency; name of record; purpose; form (printed, etc.); size; classification (does it fit into any category suggested in chapter?); brief description — content, arrangement, etc.; how and by whom is the record used — try to trace it from origin to final disposition; do you see any ways in which the record or its use might be improved?

4. If you are working on a community organization job or a community organization field work assignment, undertake one or more of the following: (a) keep a diary or day sheet for a month; (b) prepare a work plan for the agency or department; (c) prepare a work progress report for the agency or department.

5. Make a critical analysis of a community organization teaching record, using the following outline so far as it seems to apply. Name of record; bibliographical citation (author, title, publisher, city, year of publication, pages); brief description — what is it about; narrative or process record; actual or fictitious names; locale; types of organizations, groups, persons chiefly concerned; time period; summary of contents; aspects of community organization emphasized — problems, situations, methods, relationships, process, results, other; form and style — first or third person, personalities and characterizations; use of documents; evaluation — strengths, weaknesses, suggestions.

SUGGESTIONS FOR READING

There is little available published material on community organization records, and most of it has been produced within the last few years. The most substantial general discussions of the subject are in Murphy's *Community Organization Practice* (pp. 19–20, 23, 299–301; see Basic References) and in the Los Angeles report on *Recording*, noted below.

Published teaching records are referred to in the bibliography for ch. 8. Green's *Social Work Practice in Community Organization* (Basic References) and Goodall's *A Narrative of Process in Social Welfare Organization* furnish examples of community organization process records.

Barry, Mildred C., "Community Organization Process: An Approach to Better Understanding," *Social Work Journal*, Vol. XXXI, October 1950, pp. 157–163.

Cockerill, (ed.), *Social Work Practice in the Field of Tuberculosis*. (See bibliography, ch. 3.)

Recording in Community Organization in Social Welfare Work. A report by the Los Angeles Chapter of ASCO. (Community Organization Materials No. 2, ASCO, Detroit, 1951; mimeographed, 16 pp.).

Roman, Gloria. "A Perspective on Process Recording." In: *Evaluating the Effectiveness of Councils: Report of the 1954 Research Workshop*. (New York, Community Chests and Councils of America, 1954, processed, 59 pp.), pp. 43–53.

Trecker, Harleigh B., *Group Process in Administration*. (New York, Woman's Press, 2nd ed., 1950, 330 pp.), ch. 16.

Webb, Sidney and Webb, Beatrice, *Methods of Social Study* (New York, Longmans Green, 1932, 263 pp.), ch. 5.

19.

METHODS

———

THE *aim* OF THE COMMUNITY organization process is to bring about and maintain a progressively more effective adjustment between social welfare needs and resources in a geographical area or a special field of service.

In seeking to achieve this aim, community organization agencies and workers perform certain *functions:* (1) to secure and maintain an adequate *factual basis* for sound planning and action; (2) to initiate, develop, modify, and terminate social welfare *programs* and services; (3) to establish, maintain, and improve social welfare *standards,* and to increase the effectiveness, efficiency, and economy of operation of social welfare agencies; (4) to improve and facilitate inter-relationships and to promote *coordination* between organizations, groups and individuals concerned with social welfare programs and services; (5) to develop better *public understanding* of social welfare needs, resources, objectives, programs, methods, and standards; and (6) to develop adequate *public support* of, and public participation in social welfare activities. These functions may be thought of also as channels through which the aim is carried into effect.

The aim of community organization indicates *why* community organization is being carried on; the method indicates *how* this is being done.

A method of community organization is *a distinctive way of applying the process of community organization;* that is, a distinctive way of helping to bring about adjustment between social welfare needs and resources.[1]

[1] There is a lack of uniformity in the use of the terms "process" and "method" in social work literature. The author regards process as the more inclusive term.

Let us take a simple illustration. A murder committed by three teen-agers has deeply shocked a community and brought to a head its concern with juvenile delinquency.

A conference of public officials and citizen leaders is called by the mayor, at the request of the community welfare council, to consider what to do about this problem. In the course of the conference, five different approaches are suggested. Each of these represents one or more different methods of community organization.

A social scientist advocates a *survey* to get the basic facts about the problem: let's get the facts first, he says, and then plan on the basis of the facts. A business man, a member of the Board of Education, suggests a *Citizens Committee on Juvenile Delinquency*, to serve as a planning and coordinating body representing all groups interested in the problem. An editor and a minister stress the necessity of *educating the community* and arousing the people to the seriousness of the problem; any action, to be effective, they say, must be based upon public understanding. A militant attorney is for vigorous *social action,* including the passage of a curfew ordinance, enlarging the powers of the police over juveniles, and demanding an end to the "coddling of these young criminals." A housewife, who is the vice-president of the community welfare council, emphasizes the necessity of *expanding the city's public recreation program and enlarging the county's appropriation to the Juvenile Court,* so that the Judge can obtain the three additional probation officers which are needed.

In other words, the specific methods suggested by members of the conference group include factfinding, planning, organization, education, legislative promotion, and financial promotion. Of course, no one of these approaches alone is the "right" or complete answer; each is one road to bringing about the better adjustment of needs and resources in order to meet the problem.

A CLASSIFICATION OF METHODS

It seems possible to identify at least 14 distinctive methods of community organization, or ways of approaching the job of adjusting needs and resources.[2] These 14 methods fall into four broad categories, as indicated in the following outline:

In this volume, casework, group work, and community organization are considered processes of social work, and each process has certain subordinate methods. Some writers reverse this usage and speak of casework, group work, and community organization as methods, with each method having subordinate processes.
[2] Other analyses of methods may be found in several of the publications listed at the end of the chapter.

METHODS OF COMMUNITY ORGANIZATION

A. PROGRAMMING
1. Factfinding
2. Analysis
3. Evaluation
4. Planning

B. COORDINATION AND INTEGRATION
5. Conference
6. Consultation
7. Negotiation
8. Organization

C. EDUCATION AND PROMOTION
9. Education
10. Legislative promotion
11. Non-legislative social action

D. FINANCING
12. Fund-raising
13. Federated financial campaigning
14. Joint budgeting

SOME GENERAL COMMENTS ON METHODS

Some general comments may be made on these methods of community organization, as a group.

Most of the primary methods may be broken down into secondary methods. For example, making a survey or study is a secondary method under the primary method of factfinding.

Primary and secondary methods may be still further broken down into specific techniques. The word "technique," from the Greek word meaning art, skill, or craft, carries the connotation of "skill" and may be used to denote these detailed applications of community organization methods.

A particular method sometimes appears in relative isolation, but more often the various methods appear in varied combinations and intricate relationships. These methods resemble chemical elements more than building blocks or the tiles of a mosaic.

A survey or study falls primarily under the general method of factfinding; but it will probably involve the use of analysis, planning, conference, organization, consultation, evaluation, education, and perhaps other methods, before it is completed.

Most of these methods require group or inter-group activity of some sort (conference, organization, fund-raising, legislative promotion, and so on); some may be used by either an individual or a group (for example, factfinding, analysis, evaluation, planning, education).

Since the committee is so important in community organization, there may be some question as to why the outline does not include "committee operation" as a method. A committee is not "a method" — it is an instrument for getting something done — a type of organization unit which may itself employ a number of different methods — conference, of course, but also factfinding, analysis, evaluation, planning, education, fund-raising, joint budgeting, social action.

The committee might be called a "tool" of community organization, since a tool is an instrument for performing or facilitating an operation. (Committees are discussed in ch. 22.) The term "tool" might appropriately be extended to some quite different types of "instruments" — for example, interviews and meetings as tools of communication, and records as tools of administration.

Many methods of community organization are used also in other areas — administration, public education, publicity, politics, commercial fund-raising, and so on. Federated financial campaigning and joint budgeting are unique in that they are used exclusively or primarily in the field of social welfare.

The practice of community organization ordinarily requires the use of a relatively large number of widely different methods rather than the intensive use of a few. In this respect, community organization resembles administration much more than it resembles social casework, for example. The caseworker uses relatively few basic methods, but he uses them intensively and in an infinite variety of situations. Probably few community organization workers use any one method as intensively as the average caseworker uses the "psycho-social study," for instance.

No one will ever learn to practice community organization merely by learning about the nature of separate methods in themselves. Methods are interwoven and adapted in response to actual situations and problems which always involve human beings. As Arlien Johnson says, "If community organization in social work is a process, as is casework and group work, then we may conclude that its content is the interaction of people in defined situations where a professional service is offered by a social worker."[3] More fundamental than any single method is the understanding of individual and group behavior and the inter-personal, group, and inter-group relationships involved in community organization.

[3] Arlien Johnson, "Community Organization in Social Work," SWYB, 1945, p. 93.

SKILLS

Skill implies not only knowledge but the ability to put the knowledge to practical use; it connotes competence, ease and precision of execution, dexterity, efficiency and effectiveness in performance. We may speak of skill in driving a car, in swimming, in making a survey, in leading a conference group. Skill has been called "the ability to do a thing right the first time." Skill is concerned primarily with *doing* rather than with either knowing or feeling.

At least three different kinds of skills are involved in the practice of community organization. First, there are skills which are basic to the practice of any kind of social work and to the use of any of its processes. Establishing rapport with individuals or groups is among such common skills. Second, there are skills connected with the use of each of the methods of community organization — factfinding, conference, consultation, etc. We have already noted that the term "techniques" (detailed application of methods) carries the connotation of skill. Third, there are broader community organization skills that cut across and transcend specific methods. Arlien Johnson suggests some of these: (1) "the maintenance of many relationships with individuals and groups, simultaneously and often independently of one another"; (2) "timing the drawing into contact of these relationships"; (3) "the skill involved in knowing where to take hold and when to let go of a project." [4] Perhaps some other general community organization skills are: skills in dealing with "intergroups" ("social intergroup work" in Wilber Newstetter's phrase); skill in the selection, combination, and application of methods in a particular situation; and skill in applying general principles of community organization (involving value judgments) to particular situations.

Campbell G. Murphy has suggested that perhaps "the most important skill used by any social worker in community organization is *professional discretion* . . . The worker's professional discretion is involved in knowing when to use which methods, and in knowing through what groups to work in using the method selected." [5]

[4] *Ibid.*, p. 95. See also Hollis and Taylor, *Social Work Education in the United States*, p. 223, for a list of skills expected of all social workers.
[5] Murphy, *Community Organization Practice*, p. 25.

PLAN OF REMAINING DISCUSSION OF METHODS

Chapters 20 and 21 are devoted to brief discussions of the various methods of community organization. In each case the method is defined or described, some secondary methods are usually referred to, and the use of the method is illustrated. Beyond this, no one rigid pattern of presentation is followed. In some cases, as with education, there is an extensive literature available; in other cases little has been written about the subject. In two instances the methods have been discussed in previous chapters.

QUESTIONS AND PROBLEMS

1. Consider critically the suggestions from the various authors cited in the first paragraph under Suggestions for Readings, below, as to the major methods of community organization. Which of these outlines seems to account most adequately for the phenomena of community organization?

2. Criticize the outline and classification of methods suggested in this chapter. What changes would you suggest in this outline?

3. Try to identify some of the techniques in connection with a particular method of community organization.

4. What do you think are some of the major skills needed by a community organization practitioner? How do these compare with skills needed by the caseworker or group worker?

5. Apply the following analysis to one of the methods discussed in this or the following chapter: (a) Read critically the discussion in the text. Do you agree with the definition or description of this method? If not, how would you modify this statement? (b) Do you have other criticisms of the statement in the text? (c) Give some illustrations of community organization situations in which the method has been or would probably be used. (d) Illustrate some of the uses of this method in the practice of community organization. (e) Can you suggest ways of studying further the nature and use of this method? (f) What would be the best ways of training a field work student or a new community organization worker in the use of this method? (g) What other comments or suggestions have you regarding this method?

SUGGESTIONS FOR READING

Classifications of methods of community organization (though sometimes designated by other terms) are included in the Basic Reference items by Green (ch. III, IV, V), Johns and DeMarche (pp. 150–156), Lane (pp. 501–502), McMillen (p. 26), Murphy (pp. 287–306), and Stroup (pp.

303–545), and in the references below under McNeil, Mayo, Murphy, Newstetter, Sieder, and *What Councils of Social Agencies Do.*

Some of the best insights into the application of community organization methods to specific problem situations will be gained from community organization case records (see bibliography, ch. 8) and from King's *Organizing for Community Action* (Basic References).

Johnson, Arlien. "Community Organization in Social Work," (SWYB, 1945, pp. 93–97). A stimulating and suggestive discussion of process, methods, and skills.

McNeil, C. F. "Community Organization for Social Welfare," (SWYB, 1951, especially pp. 124–125; SWYB, 1954, especially pp. 123–125).

Mayo, Leonard W. "Community Organization in 1946," (NCSW, 1946, pp. 129–138; especially pp. 132–134).

Murphy, Campbell G. "Community Organization for Social Welfare." (SWYB, 1957, pp. 182–183).

Newstetter, Wilber I. "The Social Intergroup Work Process." (NCSW, 1947, pp. 205–217).

Sieder, Violet M. "The Tasks of the Community Organization Worker." (See bibliography, ch. 17).

What Councils of Social Agencies Do (New York, Community Chests and Councils, 1939, 57 pp.), p. 4.

20.

PROGRAMMING AND COORDINATION

PROGRAMMING

FOUR METHODS — factfinding, analysis, evaluation, and planning — are included under the category of programming. The development of programs and projects is a central aspect of community organization; and these methods, while they may be used in other situations also, are basic to programming. Typically, factfinding, analysis, and evaluation lead up to planning, which is the essence of program development.

FACTFINDING

Factfinding includes activities designed to aid in the discovery, ascertainment, assembling, compilation, and recording of facts. Factfinding is here conceived of as a broader term than "research." It includes the techniques of formal scientific research; but, as used by community organization practitioners, factfinding includes also certain more informal activities which are of practical importance but which could not be dignified by the name of "research." Factfinding implies an attitude of objectivity and open-mindedness and a conscious effort to free one's self from bias or emotional attitudes and to go where the facts lead. No attempt is made here to discuss the broad subject of social research. It has a literature and methodology of its own. It is assumed that an understanding of the basic concepts, methods, and tools of social research is necessary to the community organization practitioner who engages in any considerable amount of factfinding. Some specific aspects of factfinding, which may be of special concern to the community organization practitioner, are noted below. Major emphasis is laid upon the survey or study.

The central recording and analysis of social data are carried on by many community organization agencies. Many community welfare councils carry on monthly registration of service statistics from the consumer-service agencies in the community. Councils may also assemble and maintain social and welfare data by census tracts.

The compilation or revision of a directory or handbook is another manifestation of factfinding. Councils, for example, quite commonly publish social service directories for their communities.

The formal "hearing" is a method of factfinding when its purpose is primarily that of assembling facts rather than reaching a judicial decision, as in the case of a "fair hearing" on a public assistance appeal. The inclusion of subjective opinions on the part of those who testify at such hearings does not necessarily vitiate the hearing as a factfinding device, as long as the opinions are recognized as being opinions. One of the objects of the hearing may be to find out how representative citizens think on a particular issue or proposal.

Example: A state commission to study the revision of the laws relating to children holds hearings to consider certain legislative alternatives.

Experimentation, under controlled conditions, is a method of factfinding. A project may be undertaken to *find out* whether a certain program will work or how effective a particular type of program or organization will be — for example, the provision of specially qualified group workers to work with teen-age gangs. Such experiments are sometimes inaccurately called "demonstrations." Properly, "demonstration" carries the connotation that a project is to show or prove something of which its sponsors are already convinced; and it is thus an educational rather than a factfinding device.

Some other less formal activities which are at least related to factfinding are: (1) A community organization agency maintains a reservoir of factual data — a collection of documents, indexes or files of information. (2) A community organization worker gathers information about a specific subject, quickly, for a particular purpose. (3) Every community organization must keep abreast of new developments and new information in regard to certain subjects.

THE SURVEY OR STUDY

From the standpoint of community organization, the survey or study is probably the most frequently used and most important aspect of factfinding.

The terms "survey" and "study" are used here in a general sense, and not in the more specialized meaning which is sometimes given to the term "social survey" or "community welfare survey." [1] A social welfare survey or study, as the term is here used, means simply a specific systematic inquiry or investigation in respect to social welfare phenomena, with the purpose of applying the results to social welfare practice.

This definition embraces three elements: (1) The study is a specific and systematic inquiry; it is not merely a vague, casual, or random collection of data. (2) It relates to social welfare phenomena. The focus and scope of particular studies differ enormously. A specific study may be concerned with: a single agency; a group of agencies — for instance, the child caring agencies of a community; it may be concerned with one or more problems or practices — recreation for older people in a community, family budgets in low-income families, personnel practices of group work and recreational agencies; or it may extend to a more or less complete community welfare survey of a metropolitan area. (3) Presumably the social welfare study is always undertaken with the purpose of *using* the findings in some way; that is, of applying the results to the practice of social welfare. The survey or study is not "pure research"; it has an involvement with more or less immediate, practical issues and problems.

CLASSIFICATION OF SURVEYS

There are various ways of classifying surveys, according to their geographical scope (neighborhood, community, state, nation, etc.); their subject-matter; their methods; whether they are "self-surveys," studies by specialists, or mixtures of the two; and so on.[2] A classification on the basis of the over-all purpose of the survey, which is useful from the standpoint of community organization, divides studies into

[1] Cf. Pauline V. Young, *Scientific Social Surveys and Research* (Edgewood Cliffs, N.J., Prentice-Hall, 3rd ed., 1956), pp. 17–18.
[2] See: *Shall We Make A Survey?* (New York, National Social Welfare Assembly, 1949), pp. 8–10. *Social Surveys — A Guide for Use in Local Planning* (New York, Council of Jewish Federations and Welfare Funds), pp. 2–5.

(a) reconnaissance or pilot studies, (b) descriptive studies, (c) analytical or evaluative studies, and (d) pathfinder studies.

A *reconnaissance or pilot study* is a brief preliminary and exploratory study to determine whether a larger study should be made or what would be involved in such a larger study.

If it were proposed to make a study of social welfare problems and services in a city of a million population, it would obviously be good sense to make a preliminary "reconnaissance" or "spying out of the land" to see what problems would probably be involved in the proposed study, what data and other survey reports are readily available, what should be the scope of this study, how long it would take, how large a staff would be needed, how much it would cost, and so on. In some cases, limited "test" or "pilot" studies might be made to help answer certain of these questions. If the proposed study was likely to cost from $75,000 to $200,000, it might be worth while to spend perhaps one to five percent of this amount on a reconnaissance study, to obtain a sound basis for planning the larger survey.

A *descriptive study* seeks merely to describe — to present objective factual data, with a minimum of interpretation and without evaluative comments. The purely descriptive study is rather rare in the field of social welfare — usually the makers or the sponsors of the study seek more than description — they want analysis or evaluation as a guide to action.

The *analytical or evaluative study* not only describes; it also analyzes and interprets the data. It may also evaluate performance and appraise an agency's program, standards, operation, or administration. Most social welfare studies are at least analytical, if not actually evaluative.

The *pathfinder study*, historically, was one which was used extensively by Francis H. McLean, in the earlier years of his association with what is now known as the Family Service Association of America. It has been used also in defense communities, during and since World War II. The pathfinder survey, usually made in a smaller community, is a brief "sizing up" of the general situation in the field of social welfare and a pointing out of general directions of desirable advance. It is really a form of analytical study, but it is quicker, admittedly less thorough, and it confines itself to questions of general program and policy rather than detailed evaluation of standards or performance. This type of study obviously requires a well equipped social welfare "generalist," and even then it can be applied most effectively only to a relatively small community.

Any study worth making is worth planning carefully. The only safe way of planning a study is to reduce the plan to writing. The written plan forces the surveyor and the group interested in the study to come to grips with practical questions: Why do you want a study? Just what do you hope to get out of it? What is to be the scope? How extensive and intensive is it to be? What methods are to be used? Who is to do the study? How long will it take? How much will it cost?

Because community organization workers are so frequently involved in studies, a suggested outline of a plan for a study is presented below. This outline, with variations, has been used, over a period of years, in connection with many studies of different types, and it has proved a tool of great practical value.[3]

OUTLINE OF A PLAN FOR A SOCIAL WELFARE SURVEY OR STUDY

1. *Designation:* What is the designation of the study?

2. *Purpose:* What is the purpose of the study? (The purpose of a study is always to discover, to ascertain, to test, to find out something — never to "prove" some preconceived idea. Frequently it is worth while to append to the general statement of purpose a list of specific questions to be answered.)

3. *Scope:* What is the scope of the study as regards:

a. Subject matter or field to be covered? (This may be expressed in terms of topics, subjects, problems, questions, organizations, etc.)

b. Geographical area? (Neighborhood, community, state, nation, etc. — or it may be a study of an agency or a department of an agency.)

c. Time — period of time or point in time? (It may be desired to study the trends in public assistance over five years or some other period of time. On the other hand, it may be desired to make a population study of certain state institutions as of the first day of the year or some other specified date.)

4. *Sources of information:* What are the chief sources of information to be used in the study? Are they available for study?

[3] For the basic ideas underlying this outline the author is indebted to some lectures by Professor George B. Mangold, in St. Louis, many years ago. The outline in its present form has evolved and been modified over the years, in the light of the author's experience. The portions of this material which are in parentheses are explanatory notes and are not part of the substantive outline.

5. *Methods:* What methods are to be used in the study? For example: study of documents, published and unpublished; interview, based on (a) schedule, (b) outline, (c) "free interview"; observation; "participant observer"; [4] schedule filled out by interviewer or observer; questionnaire filled out by recipient; statistical analysis; case analysis; experimentation or tests; other.

6. *Auspices:* Under what auspices is the study to be conducted? (Council? Agency? Committee?)

7. *Organization and personnel.*

a. Who is to make the study? (Is it to be a "self-survey," a study by a specialist, or a mixture of the two?)

b. To whom will the "surveyor," or director of the study, be responsible? (Survey committee, council or agency board, etc.)

c. Will there be a study committee? Who will be the members of it? Will the committee be a directive or advisory body?

d. What personnel will assist with the study? Paid or volunteer? Appointed by whom? What will be their functions?

e. Will there be any cooperating bodies? What will be their relationship to the study?

8. *Time schedule:* What time schedule is to be followed in making the study? Enter the estimated dates covering the beginning and end of the following processes:

a. Planning

b. Organization

c. Fact-gathering — obtaining the data

d. Interpretation of data and preparation of report

e. Submission of draft report

f. Review, return, and revision of report

g. Submission of final report

h. If report is to be published: (1) preparation of "printer's copy" — putting manuscript in final form for printing. (2) submission of proofs by printer; correction and return of proofs; (3) publication.

i. Interpretation and discussion of report

(The foregoing items suggest the main steps in planning and carrying through a study. The assistance of a specialist will probably be needed in estimating the time required. It is vitally important to *allow enough time for the preparation of the report.* The temptation is to think of the fact-gathering as the essence of the job and the "part that will take the time." Actually, the field work or fact-gathering may

[4] See Eduard C. Lindeman, *Social Discovery* (New York, Republic Publishing Co., 1924), ch. VIII, "Observation and the Participant Observer."

occupy 50 per cent or less of the total time required for the whole survey, including in this total the time for preliminary planning and organization, preparation and interpretation of the report, etc. The best basic unit for computing the time for a study is the number of *staff working days*. If it is estimated that a particular study will require 100 staff days, this means, theoretically at least, that one worker could do the job in 100 working days, 2 workers in 50 days, or 4 workers in 25 days.)

9. *Budget:* What expenses will be required for the study? What sources of income will be utilized to meet these expenses? (Again, the help of a specialist will be needed in arriving at the budget. Fundamentally, the budget will be based on the time schedule. Some of the main items are likely to be salaries, travel, maintenance — if this is paid for any members of the survey staff, — supplies, and sometimes rent, cost of publication of report, etc. It is important to leave some leeway in the budget to allow for unexpected additional items to be studied, unforeseen delays, and so on.)

10. *Reports*

a. What reports are to be made?

b. Are these reports: (1) Merely to present the facts, without stating conclusions as to the meaning of the facts? (2) To contain conclusions or interpretations as to the facts? (3) To contain recommendations?

c. To whom are the reports to be submitted?

d. Is the final report to be officially the report of the study committee or of the staff? (This and the following question are important, although they are often overlooked in survey planning. If the report is to be the report *of the study committee,* official commission, or whatever the body may be, then the staff executive is primarily a consultant, technical adviser, and agent, but he does not have the major responsibility for the contents and especially the recommendations of the report. If, however, the report is the report *of the staff, to the committee,* the case is entirely different.)

e. In case of difference of opinion between the committee and the staff, in reference to conclusions and recommendations, what course is to be followed? (If the report is the report of the committee, then obviously the committee decides what shall go into the report. If the report is the report of the staff, the report as such cannot properly be altered without the approval of the staff. The committee or the agency sponsoring the study may, of course, do as it likes about following or rejecting the recommendations, but a technical staff report, as a report, should stand as submitted, unless the staff members who wrote it are convinced that it should be changed. If such a report is published, there is no reason why the committee might not indicate, in footnotes, an attached document, or otherwise, the points on which it differs from the staff.[5])

f. What is to be the form of the final reports? Typed? Mimeographed? Printed? Is the report to be published? The entire report? Portions of it? A summary only? To whom are the reports to be distributed? How widely are the reports to be circulated or made available for use or reference?

SOME SUGGESTIONS REGARDING SURVEYS

The following factors, among others, should exist before a survey is undertaken: (1) A clear understanding of why the study is wanted. (2) Willingness — and, if possible, active desire — on the part of the agencies to be studied. (3) An attitude of reasonable open-mindedness on the part of the group sponsoring the study. (4) Satisfactory local auspices. (5) Readiness to meet the cost.

The surveyor, the survey committee, and the agencies should, so far as possible, move along together throughout the course of the survey. "No surprises in the final report" is a sound principle. In some cases, certain recommendations may actually be put into effect before the final report is submitted.

The report is the permanent record of the study. It should reflect the survey adequately; it should be clear, sufficiently detailed, forthright, and readable. It should come to conclusions and should afford a basis for action in solving problems.

The real test of the value of a survey is what use is made of it afterwards. To speak of a "good survey, but with no perceptible results" is not much better than, "The operation was successful — but the patient died."

A survey will not build programs or advance social progress of itself. A survey is a *tool* which must be intelligently used if it is to yield results in health and welfare planning.

As in any other aspect of community organization, the relationships involved in a study are likely to be more important than any

[5] For an example of this procedure, see *Greater Boston Community Survey*, pp. 130–131.

other one aspect. A social welfare study deals with people and groups, and in the last analysis it must be judged and measured as a cooperative undertaking — a venture in human relations.

ANALYSIS

Analysis lies midway between factfinding and planning. It is the *breaking up* of a problem, situation, or collection of data, and the exploring of the content and the examining and setting forth of various aspects, issues, and relationships involved. The purpose of analysis is to gain insight and understanding, particularly, to understand the content better, by dividing it up on some logical basis; and to understand the relationships involved in the content. The outline, the chart, the written statement, the "brief," are among the methods of recording and presenting the results of an analysis.

Analysis is the one most typical method of dealing with a problem in community organization. No complicated problem can be intelligently attacked wholesale. It must first be resolved into its elements or into a number of more specific problems.

For example, the problem, what shall be done about older people in our community of 100,000, needs to be broken down into specific questions, such as the following: What do we mean by "older people"? How many of them are there? What ages? Where do they live? What are their basic needs in respect to income maintenance, housing, health, employment, recreation, and so on? What are the resources available for dealing with these problems? Answering some of these questions may involve factfinding, but even if all the facts are readily available, some analysis of the problem must precede any intelligent or effective planning.

Analysis is closely related to both factfinding and planning. However, we may have factfinding without analysis. Statistics may be merely "collected" without ever being analyzed; data may be gathered and left in undigested masses without being subjected to the analytical processes which would reveal their real meaning.

Planning can scarcely exist without analysis. The two are complementary. Analysis is the breaking up of the problem; planning is the synthesis, the putting together of proposals for future action. A sound plan normally implies that the planner has the facts and that the facts and the problem have been analyzed as a basis for the formulation of the plan.

The following suggestions may indicate some of the possibilities as to ways of using or applying analysis.

Probably the most important single key to analysis is *the application of the six basic analytical questions:* what, who, where, when, why, how? Some suggestions regarding the use of these questions in analysis, and the relation of these questions to substantive factors in planning, are presented below, under planning.

The *definition of terms* is an obvious basis to any clear thinking or planning.

Classification is another way of using analysis. For example, a large community welfare council must classify its member agencies to obtain a picture of the resources in various functional fields in the community.

Comparison is another way of applying analysis. Comparisons of case loads, service statistics, and per capita costs come readily to mind. The Social Security Administration has used the comparative descriptive tabulation as a means of analyzing and comparing the laws of various states on a particular subject, such as adoption or a type of categorical assistance.

Analysis of the meaning of the text of a formal document, such as a legislative bill, is frequently necessary in community organization. One of the simplest methods of analyzing such documents is the underlining of the key words, phrases, and sentences which state the basic propositions. Where the text is definitely ambiguous, the formulation of specific queries as to the meaning of certain passages is helpful in indicating just what needs to be clarified.

Annotation of a document with explanatory notes, questions, interpretations and comments is often of value.

In a conflict situation or in the case of a controversial proposal the *clarification of issues* is often a major need. Closely related to this is the *statement of alternatives* as to possible courses of action, proposals, etc. It may sometimes be worth while to analyze in writing a complicated community organization situation, setting up four vertical columns headed: Alternative, Probable Results, Advantages, and Disadvantages.

Chronological analysis is frequently useful in untangling a complicated situation — listing the various steps taken and their dates. Chronological analysis may look toward future plans as well as past history.

Organizational analysis and job analysis may have application to community organization as well as administration.

A *checklist* of questions or points to be considered is frequently valuable. Checklists have been suggested at various points in this book; they may be used in reference to such subjects as problems, committees, projects, surveys, and meetings.

Financial and *statistical analysis* are two other familiar forms of analysis, which are of great importance in the areas of research and joint budgeting.

The validity of analysis, like the validity of factfinding, depends largely upon the objectivity of the process. Where a writer undertakes in the same document to present an objective factual analysis and to submit more or less subjective interpretations and opinions, it is usually highly desirable to make clear what is objective and factual and what is subjective.

In some early case studies, published in pamphlet form by the Judge Baker Foundation, the objective tests and other data of the case record were presented on the left-hand pages and the comments of the worker, or the author or compiler of the pamphlet, were entered at appropriate points on the right-hand page. The same effect can of course be obtained by the use of two parallel columns.

This distinguishing sharply between fact and opinion is the reverse of advocacy or promotion, where fact and argument may be woven together into the presentation of a persuasive case. Analysis should have no tincture of promotion. Analysis should be clear, incisive, and — one is tempted to say — almost ruthlessly objective.

EVALUATION

Evaluation or appraisal is closely related to both analysis and planning, but it has a distinctive aspect. The essence of evaluation is the *making of value judgments* in regard to certain phenomena. Thus evaluation goes a step beyond analysis but not necessarily as far as planning.

Evaluation is constantly used by community organization practitioners. Examples come readily to mind. A community chest committee to select a campaign chairman evaluates several persons proposed for the job . . . A chest budget committee, with total budget requests of $620,000 and only $480,000 to allocate, evaluates the relative importance of various agency requests.

The evaluation of staff personnel is not discussed here, since that is an administrative procedure; but it is one with which the community organization practitioner should be familiar, since he may at times need to apply the principles of personnel evaluation to the performance of committee chairmen, committee members, and other volunteers.

The essence of evaluation is the *comparison* of actualities or proposals with certain standards or assumed values. Sometimes these values or norms are expressed in written formulations — statutory provisions for characteristics of a state plan, licensing standards for child caring agencies, or membership standards for a national agency. More often the standards of judgment are not definitely formulated in writing. They may be implicit in the philosophy, convictions, general professional standards, or experience of the evaluators. They may be vague, and they may be colored by subjective factors. In general, no social welfare evaluation that involves judgment or discretion is better than the capacity or equipment of the evaluator.

Evaluation implies selection or ranking. We will choose *these* projects to include in the program of the Recreation Division, this year. Sometimes evaluation provides the basis for the establishment of priorities. Thus a budget committee may have ten valid requests for budget increases, but only a few of them can be financed at this time. The committee will probably have to establish priorities and rank the requests in order of importance, at this particular time, and under these particular circumstances.

Although evaluation is grouped, in this classification of methods, along with factfinding, analysis, and planning, under the general heading of Programming, yet in practice evaluation may come either before, during, or after a project. Thus, a group may evaluate the methods *to be used* in a forthcoming campaign, or it may evaluate *what was done* in the campaign that has just been concluded. Of course, in one sense, even evaluation-after-the-fact looks forward to the use of the evaluated experience in some possible future action.

PLANNING

Planning, in the sense in which it is here used, means determining an intended or proposed future action or course of action, or determining methods, procedures, forms of organization, or instruments to be used in the future. Planning has been described as "going through a job in imagination, beforehand."

Essentially planning is the formulation of coherent ideas calling for and describing action in the future. It has to do with rounded recommendations, proposals, and suggestions of courses of action to be followed. Since these are a thrust into the future, they always introduce elements of risk and uncertainty. Such proposals and suggestions seem more acceptable when each phase of them has been examined and weighed by people who have had experience with the subject of the planning operation and who have given thought and study to it and when knowledge and experience are synthesized. But knowledge and even experience are not the whole story. Planning implies capacity to invent new ways of accomplishing purposes and deliberately to adapt old ways to new circumstances.[6]

Planning appears to involve at least the following elements:

A factual basis. Sound plans should be based upon facts. If planning does not involve the finding of fresh facts it will rest upon the use of facts already found.

Analysis. Analysis and planning are complementary.

A synthesis of various elements. Planning is a process of putting together, to form a balanced and rational whole, just as analysis is the process of breaking up a whole in order to understand more clearly its nature and parts.

In many instances, where planning relates to a new organization or an extensive project, it may be necessary for the plan to take into account at least *six substantive elements,* which correspond to the six "key questions" in the analysis of a problem. The following outline suggests the relationships between these factors in analysis and planning. This outline is a practical working tool; and the preparation of a written analysis or plan will frequently clarify the situation as nothing else can do, and will ultimately save time, money, and effort.

Planning involves evaluation — *a choice among alternatives,* and the establishment of priorities.

Imagination is one of the prime requirements of planning. Planning is not an obvious or routine procedure; it should never be a dull mechanical type of activity; it calls for a creative quality, for insight, invention, a sense of values, and a degree of artistry.

Planning involves the *formulation* of the proposals in some coherent, rational, systematic form. A written plan is desirable where the subject is complex or far-reaching.

[6] Neva R. Deardorff, "Areas of Responsibility of Voluntary Social Work During Period of Changing Local and National Governmental Programs," NCSW, 1936, p. 315.

RELATIONSHIP BETWEEN ANALYSIS AND PLANNING IN THE PLANNING OF AN ORGANIZATION PROJECT

ANALYSIS SEEKS TO ANSWER THESE QUESTIONS:	THE PLAN SHOULD EMBODY THE FOLLOWING ELEMENTS:
1. *Why* is the project being undertaken?	1. *Objectives* of the project
2. *What* is the nature of the project? What is to be done?	2. *Program,* functions, services, activities
3. *Who* are to perform the activities? What relationships are they to have to each other?	3. *Organization structure* and *personnel*
4. *Where* is the project to be carried on?	4. *Territory* of operation
5. *When* is the project to be initiated and carried on?	5. *Time schedule* (chronological planning)
6. *How* is the project to be carried out? Under what general policies? By what methods? How is it to be financed? Also, how well is the job to be done — what standards will be observed?	6. *Policies* *Methods* *Budget* *Standards*

Planning involves *decision.* There must be a final focus on one road, one way of proceeding.

Planning is normally the *key to action.* The better the planning, the less the fumbling and trial-and-error, when action begins. Yet, at the same time, it is necessary to strike a balance between planning and action. Time and deadlines require action; one can't go on planning forever, so he must frequently compromise by planning as well as he can in the time available.

Some types of planning which may be involved with community organization are the planning of: extensive or long-range programs; specific projects, services, and activities; a course of action (e.g., campaign strategy, program alternatives); an organization, reorganization, merger, or federation; a budget; a time schedule (for a survey, a fund-raising campaign, the establishment of a new agency, etc.); and procedures (for example, joint budgeting procedures); also the formulation of an agency work plan, and the planning or formulation of standards or criteria.

Planning calls for the collaboration and participation of many specialists and many kinds of people. Social welfare planning is not a far-off process to be carried on in some remote "ivory tower"; sound planning grows out of practical experience and intimate knowledge of day by day problems and practice.

Planning is one of the most difficult jobs in social work. It requires knowledge of the facts; analysis of problems and difficulties; experience, imagination, and inventiveness. Planning is essentially creative — it projects something new into the future. The good planner must be a realist, with a knowledge of the past; but he must also be an adventurer, with the spirit that breaks new trails, ventures into the unexplored, and occasionally attempts and accomplishes the impossible.

THE SOCIAL WELFARE PROGRAM

Planning, as a method of community organization, reaches its climax in the social welfare program. In the sense in which this term is here used, a social welfare program is a plan of related activities, intended to be carried into effect over a period of time, to achieve one or more social welfare objectives.

A social welfare program usually has at least five characteristics: [7]

First, there must be *concerned people*. A program is not merely a written plan; it is a living, active, growing *movement* of individuals and groups. There must be a constituency, a group of participants and supporters; and from the participants must come the necessary citizen leadership.

Second, the program needs *a clear objective* or objectives. It must be more than just a movement; it must be a movement that is going in some specific direction. The leaders and participants must know what they are trying to accomplish.

Third, a program implies conscious and deliberate *planning* as to who should do what, and when and where and how.

Fourth, a program must include a number of *related projects or activities*, and must continue over *a substantial period of time*. A program is more than a single speech, a single meeting, a single report, or even a single project. The project and continuing activities are the normal units of operation of the program. The program may have several projects in operation at the same time or it may take up one project at a time.

A program normally involves some form of *organization*. Organization usually flowers into committees; ordinarily it requires some kind of

[7] Adapted from a paper by the author, "Initiating and Developing a Program of Community Improvement," in *Strengthening Our Communities Through Social Welfare* (Denver, Colorado, Conference of Social Welfare, 1954), pp. 13–15.

a budget; and frequently a continuing, active organization finds that it needs skilled staff services.

Social welfare programs originate in various ways. One common way is for a group — or even a concerned individual at the outset — to start out to deal with one problem, one need. The group attacks this need, then moves on from this need and this project to other related needs and other projects, which gradually build into a more or less logical program.

Sometimes a program takes shape from the more or less miscellaneous activities of an existing organization. For example, a council may develop a variety of activities, on an opportunistic basis, without any logical over-all plan. But gradually the council begins to get a general picture of needs, resources, and priorities; and out of the hodgepodge of activities the outlines of a rational and balanced program begin to emerge.

Again, a survey report may contain a series of recommendations which present the outline of a program for the area or functional field which has been studied.

In still other cases a growing concern by various groups over a broad problem — juvenile delinquency, safety, poliomyelitis, or mentally retarded children — may bring these groups together for joint planning and programming.

The social welfare program is a major challenge to social welfare forces — to the focusing of their insights and imagination and planning ability, their skills and their resources. In a real sense, an effective health or welfare program is a supreme test and a climax of community organization.

COORDINATION AND INTEGRATION

Four methods are included under the heading of coordination and integration; conference, consultation, negotiation, and organization. All of them have the common objective of producing cooperative or joint action.

CONFERENCE

The term, conference, as it is here used, means informal group discussion, by three or more persons, with the object of carrying on open-minded exploration and usually of achieving agreement or integration of thinking in regard to a subject or problem.

This definition of the term involves these factors:

Conference is carried on by a *group*. A group is here regarded as three or more persons. There is a substantial practical difference between an uninterrupted conversation on the part of two persons and the discussion between a larger number, where participation by any one person is a smaller proportion of the whole discussion, and where more relationships and more complex relationships are involved.[8]

Many different groups use the conference method: committees, boards, divisions of community welfare councils, study groups, and informal groups, such as a conference of representatives from three or four agencies discussing a mutual problem.

Conference normally involves a *face-to-face* meeting of the group. We communicate but we do not "confer" by correspondence. A three-way telephone system would enable three persons to "confer," after a fashion, but the values of face-to-face discussion (physical presence, expression, gesture, etc.) and much of the feeling of cohesion would be lost.

Conference uses *informal group discussion* as its basic way of proceeding. There may be pauses or even deliberate periods of silence, but the fabric and the underlying pattern of the meeting is that of discussion. This discussion is carried on informally, rather than under the frequently useful but always artificial and formal procedure of parliamentary law.

Conference also implies *general participation*. A group of seven persons do not achieve a conference if two do all the talking and the other five merely listen.

A conference normally has someone who assumes the role of *leader*, whether or not he is formally designated as such. The functions of a recognized discussion leader are quite different from those of a presiding officer in a parliamentary assembly.

The conference has some definite *subject* for discussion — the group does not engage merely in casual conversation.

The underlying aim of the conference is to *explore* a subject open-mindedly and usually *to achieve agreement or integration of thinking.* The general interest of most of the members must be in reaching consensus if we are to be justified in calling the gathering a conference. If all or most of the members come merely to make speeches presenting their points of view — for reasons of ego-satisfaction, "for the

[8] Luther Gulick and L. Urwick, (eds.), *Papers on the Science of Administration* (New York, Columbia University, Institute of Public Administration, 1937). V. A. Graicunas, "Relationship in Organization," pp. 183–187.

record," or to reach some outside audience — the purpose of a conference will not be achieved.

A classic description of the method of conference or "group thinking" is found in Mary P. Follett's book, *The New State*. Miss Follett believed that democratic progress was bound up with group action, the group consisting of individuals accustomed to taking counsel together and understanding what is meant by doing group thinking and having collective ideas. She said:

> The object of a committee meeting is first of all to create a common idea. I do not go to a committee meeting merely to give my own ideas. If that were all I might write my fellow-members a letter. But neither do I go to learn other people's ideas. If that were all I might ask each to write me a letter. I go to a committee meeting in order that, all together, we may create a group idea, an idea which will be better than any one of our ideas alone — moreover which will be better than all of our ideas added together. For this group idea will not be produced by any process of addition, but by the interpenetration of us all. . . .
>
> The majority idea is not the group idea. Suppose I belong to a committee composed of five — A, B, C, D, and myself. According to the old theory of my duties as a committee member I might say: 'A agrees with me; if I can get B to agree with me that will make a majority, and I can carry my point.' That is, we five can then present this idea to the world as our group idea. But this is not a group idea, although it may be the best substitute we can get for the moment. To a genuine group idea every man must contribute what is in him to contribute. Thus even the passing of a unanimous vote by a group of five does not prove the existence of a group idea if two or three (or even one), out of indifference, or laziness, or prejudice, or shut-up-ness, or a misconception of their function, have not added their individual thought to the creation of the group thought. No member of a group which is to create can be passive. All must be active, and constructively active.[9]

Conference or group thinking is characterized by "give-and-take" and by a constantly changing situation. A group discussion resembles somewhat a game of doubles in tennis. A serves the ball; B must deal with the situation as created by A's serve; B returns the ball; C must now deal with the situation created by A's serve plus B's return; and

[9] M. P. Follett, *The New State* (New York, Longmans, Green, 1920; first edition, 1918), pp. 24, 27–28.

so on. Effective group discussion means participation by all the members of the group.

Group discussion is not a "safe" method which assures that the group will come out with some preconceived "right" answer. Conference is, in fact, no safer than democracy. Conference is a joint exploration, a group adventure. It is perhaps the most truly creative of all the methods of community organization.

Conference or group discussion is radically different from conventional parliamentary procedure. *Voting is a device for recording division* and differences of opinion; group discussion is a method of attempting to arrive at agreement. Voting is often essentially divisive; conference should be a creative and unifying process. Parliamentary procedure actually represents a high degree of social evolution, and it is of great value as a method of orderly procedure, particularly for large assemblies or those sharply divided into interest groups. Nevertheless, there is an increasing awareness on many sides that parliamentary procedure has been somewhat overrated by Anglo-Saxons, and that it is not the only way nor is it necessarily the best way for groups which are seeking unity and integration of thinking.[10]

In some meetings of boards, committees and other bodies, part of the business is transacted by conference or consensus, and other parts by parliamentary procedure. In other cases, the real process of discussion and arriving at decisions may be accomplished by conference, but decisions thus arrived at may be confirmed and ratified by formal motions and votes.

Obviously group discussion will not work as the basic method for an assembly, such as a legislature, made up of warring factions, each of which is primarily concerned with "putting over" a program or gaining certain ends. It may be noted, however, that even in such an assembly a surprising volume of business is often transacted by "unanimous consent." But in any case, there are few instances of such bodies in social welfare. No social welfare agency which is a "house divided against itself" is likely to stand for any considerable length of time; or, if it does remain standing, it will not be likely to give effective service.

It is usually believed that group discussion is not appropriate to "large" bodies, but there is considerable question as to the exact point

[10] See Malcolm S. Knowles, "Move Over, Mr. Robert," *Leader's Digest: The Best from Adult Leadership, Volume No. 1* (Chicago, Adult Education Association of the U.S.A., 1954), pp. 40–42. Article reprinted from *Adult Leadership*, June 1952.

at which size eliminates the conference method. This whole subject is in need of further research and exploration.[11]

Bruno Lasker believes that effective "group discussion must pass methodically from (a) a situation that gives concern, to (b) an analysis of the conflicting attitudes about it which are voiced or reported by members, hence to (c) a scrutiny of suggested ways of dealing with the situation, in (d) the light of circumstances or larger values not at once evident when the matter was first raised, and so if possible to (e) some final solution." [12]

This is a helpful analysis, though perhaps a bit too neat and orderly to fit all the infinitely varied facts of life in regard to conference.

Research in "group dynamics" is seeking, through scientific methods, to gain an understanding of group behavior. The results to date are impressive and they suggest that community organization and other areas of group operation may increasingly look to this field for valuable help in conferences and other group activities.

Some of the concepts of group dynamics are of great potential value for community organization: for example, the concept of three types of leadership — autocratic, laissez-faire and democratic; the concept of certain recognizable individual roles in groups (e.g., information seeker, orienter, energizer, encourager, harmonizer, aggressor, etc.), and the fascinating ideas of the "hidden agenda," [13] and the "deep freeze" (a cooling-off period when the group abstains from discussing a controversial question). Some of the techniques of the researchers can be applied to advantage in many community organization groups. Some of these techniques and devices, which group dynamics researchers have invented or used, are:

The observer — a person who observes critically what is taking place in the group, from the standpoint of group behavior. He may make comments to the group on what he sees, from time to time, or at the end of the meeting.

[11] Members of the Society of Friends (Quakers) have, for three hundred years, conducted their business meetings on the basis of consensus or "sense of the meeting," rather than by voting. This method is used successfully even with Yearly Meetings where several hundred persons may be in attendance, with the right of full participation. To be sure, Friends present a special case, because of the close bond of religious fellowship which unites them, and because of the close relationship between collective worship, "on the basis of silence," and their business meetings.

[12] Bruno Lasker, *Democracy Through Discussion* (New York, Wilson, 1949), pp. 291–292.

[13] See ch. 22.

The post-meeting reaction sheet (*PMR*). A questionnaire for getting at the group members' reactions to a meeting.

The "buzz-group." The term is an unsatisfactory one, but it is surprisingly difficult to come up with a better one. "Work group" is one possibility. This technique involves breaking up a large audience into small face-to-face groups of about five or six, which meet for a short period — perhaps five to fifteen minutes — consider a specific assignment (what topic do you most want discussed, what approach to this problem have you found most effective, etc.), and report back to the main group. The name is, of course, derived from the "buzz" that arises from a meeting room when fifteen or twenty of these groups are in action. Such groups are useful in drawing everyone in a large audience into participation and in tapping the suggestions of the audience as a whole rather than those of a few vocal members. Buzz-groups will be most useful, in community organization at least, if they are used in moderation and do not become epidemic.

Role-playing — that is, acting out assigned roles, spontaneously or with some preparation, in an assigned situation involving group relations.

The "feed-back." This involves a member of the group who records what goes on in the group and "feeds it back" to the group at the end of the meeting. There may also be a tape recording of an entire session.

Probably the best test for the use of any of these devices is: Can it be assimilated by the group so that it becomes a natural and helpful part of the group process? If it makes the group self-conscious, if it seems a mere mechanical gadget, a ritual observance, or an artificial control imposed from without rather than a creative aid, the group will probably be better off without it. It is of primary importance to preserve spontaneity in group process.

To almost all who have any part to play in community organization, the "art of conference" is of major importance. To the average community organization practitioner, who normally spends a large portion of his waking hours in committees and conferences, the understanding of groups and their behavior and skill in using the method of conference are central factors in his professional equipment.

CONSULTATION

Consultation, as the term is here used, means the giving of counseling, advice or assistance to an organization, group, community or other unit, by a person or team of persons with specialized knowledge, skill or other technical qualifications. Consultation, as a method of community organization, implies an advisory relationship, and is to be distinguished from supervision, which is an administrative relationship and which involves authority. Occasionally consultative and supervisory functions are mingled in one job; this is likely to pose delicate problems for the consultant, and to complicate relationships.

Consultation is frequently given by staff members of community welfare councils and community chests, state and national agencies, and sometimes other agencies.

For example: A field representative of a state welfare department consults with the representatives of an integrated county welfare department: he discusses with the executive and supervisor a plan for staff development for the coming year; he discusses with the county welfare board the implications of recent amendments to the state law; and he meets with a staff committee which is undertaking a thoroughgoing revision of the department's manual of policies and procedures.

Rudolph T. Danstedt calls "consultation and advice" one of the major activities of a community welfare council. He says:

A large part of a council's activities is a day-by-day consultation by letter, telephone, and personal conference with laymen and staff on a wide variety of agency administrative problems and community problems. Such consultations frequently precede the organization of a formal study and are important factors in informal evaluation of agency programs and community needs. When institutes are established around special areas, these are essentially a form of group consultation and can be important factors in introducing new concepts or practices into agency programs.[14]

Since consultation is advisory, it is not likely to be of much value unless the "consumer" or consultee wants it. Consultation, then, is ordinarily given only at the request or desire of the consultee. Where there seem to be valid exceptions to this rule, it will probably be found that some authoritative relationship is involved.

Geographically, personal consultation is likely to be given either in the local community where both agencies (the consultant and the consultee) are located; at the headquarters of a national or state agency giving the service; or by a field representative of a national or state agency, traveling to a local community and giving consultation to an agency or group in the community. While we usually think of face-to-

[14] Rudolph T. Danstedt, "Councils in Social Work," SWYB, 1954, p. 144.

face consultation, through an interview or conference, consultation may be given also by letter or telephone.

"Field service" is here regarded as a type of job and not a method of work. The field representative uses the method of consultation, but he may also use other methods of community organization, such as factfinding, planning, evaluation, education, etc. A field representative's job may be focused primarily on either community organization or administration, or it may combine elements of both. Field service is vital to the national agency's service to local communities. The field representative interprets the national program to the local agency and its community, and in turn brings back to the national agency an interpretation of the local program, situation, and points of view.[15] While there are many facets to the job of the field worker, one of his most common and most useful roles is that of a traveling consultant.

The equipment of the consultant should include at least the following elements:

A technical knowledge and understanding of any specialized field or content concerning which he is attempting to give advice — whether this be public assistance, recreation, public health nursing, or some other area of service.

A knowledge of resources — literature, agencies, etc. This is especially important for the council staff member, who cannot be an authority on all the problems about which he is likely to be consulted.

An understanding of his role as a consultant and the self-discipline to limit himself to that role.

Skill in teaching. Consultation sometimes requires some of the same qualities that are needed by a field work supervisor or a teacher in a seminar course.

An understanding of individual and group behavior, of social welfare in general, and of the nature and situation of the consultee agency and its community.

An ability to enter into a helping relationship, with emphasis upon helping the consultee to arrive at his own decisions and to solve his own problems.

The ability to put aside the consultee's problem, after the consultation is over — even though it may be taken up again later. The consultant, particularly the field representative, cannot, in justice to his total job, stagger around under the accumulated weight of the problems of all his consultees. He may share the consultee's concern over

---

[15] *Resource Book on Field Service Administration* (New York, National Social Welfare Assembly, 1952), p. 6.

the problem, at the time of the consultation, and he will give his best efforts in trying to help the consultee; but he must not take away the consultee's problem and make it his own. Growth for the consultee does not lie in that direction.

The consultant may give several kinds of help: helping the consultee to analyze his problem; jointly exploring a problem or situation with the consultee; providing information; suggesting and referring the consultee to other resources and sources of help; interpreting and clarifying material (for example, certain standards and policies of the national agency); helping the consultee to gain new insights, new awareness, or greater perspective; counseling and making suggestions; giving the consultee a sense of the interest, concern and support of the consultant organization; and sometimes, doing a kind of "teaching demonstration" job. Examples of this last type of activity would be helping a young executive to make out his first budget, or aiding a supervisor in drafting job specifications for a specialized casework job.

Sometimes consultation leads to an extended process of helping an agency or community to work out certain problems. There seems to be more than a superficial parallelism between such "agency casework" and at least that type of social casework with families and individuals which deals mainly with environmental adjustments.

The Board of Belmont House, a small settlement, appealed to the executive of the community welfare council for advice concerning the future of the House. The secretary agreed to collaborate with a member of the Board of the settlement in making a self-study. From the study emerged a plan which seemed revolutionary to the Board. It was recommended that Belmont House become the Belmont Community Center; that the Board should be reorganized and strengthened; that the House be sold and that the new community center program should be carried on at the well-equipped public school, with the cooperation of school and playground authorities.

There were tense moments at the Board meeting where the Board member and the Council executive retraced their vivid experiences in the study and led up, step by step, to their conclusions and recommendations. However, at the end of two hours of discussion, the Board unanimously adopted the proposed program.

The council executive, as he later analyzed what had happened, identified these common elements in this community organization process and in social casework: understanding the problem; focusing resources; interpretation; re-education or rehabilitation; achieving the spirit and reality of teamwork between the client and the worker.[16]

In the light of more recent thinking about social casework, one might emphasize also the relationship between the council executive and the agency as a central factor in this consultation or "agency casework" situation.

It is, of course, desirable to keep adequate records of consultative service, particularly if there are continuing or intermittent contacts with consultees. Some national and state organizations have developed what are essentially agency or community "case records" covering their contacts with and services to local agencies and communities.

NEGOTIATION

Negotiation means communicating or carrying on dealings with a view to coming to terms. In some instances negotiation may result in real integration of thinking; but usually it has the connotation of bargaining, on the part of groups or individuals. An attempt is made to reach an agreement, by compromise if necessary, but the desire on the part of each party is to gain certain points or to safeguard certain interests or values.

Examples might include the following:

The legislative committee of a state conference on social welfare negotiates with the commissioner of the state welfare department and a legislative leader regarding certain bills to be introduced in the legislature. . . . Two institutions which are considering a merger negotiate as to the use of their respective buildings and equipment and the employment of their respective staff members. . . .

Leonard W. Mayo points out that:

In all aspects of negotiation, the necessity for understanding people and their motives and objectives is paramount. In negotiation with a political group, a women's club, a church organization, or the representatives of a union it is essential to know the purposes and functions of the group as well as the pressures under which the members find themselves if support is to be gained for one's project.[17]

Three aspects of inter-agency relationships, which lie somewhere within the areas of integration or bargaining, may be noted briefly.

[16] Arthur Dunham and Esther S. Dunham, "The Transformation of Belmont House." *Survey Midmonthly*, Vol. LIX, October 15, 1927, pp. 91–92.
[17] Leonard W. Mayo, "Community Organization in 1946," NCSW, 1946, p. 134.

The making of more or less formal *inter-agency agreements* between two or more groups is a familiar method of effecting inter-agency cooperation.

Example: An agreement between the Juvenile Court and voluntary child placing agencies regarding the rate of board for children placed by the agencies on behalf of the court.

Among the steps which may be involved in effecting such agreements are: clarifying objectives, positions and issues; getting the facts; analyzing areas and points of agreement and disagreement; seeking to resolve the points of difference through integration, compromise, or a change of position by one party or the other; hammering out the substance of the agreement; drafting the formal agreement; providing for the translation of the agreement into practice; and following up and evaluating the agreement in terms of its results.

Another approach to inter-agency cooperation is *to effect* (or attempt to effect) *concerted action, on the part of two or more organizations,* in reference to such matters as general policies, emergency situations, coordination of services, and day-by-day activities.[18]

For example: a council works out a plan for concerted action on the part of social and health agencies in the event of disaster; ten agencies agree to request their workers to report violations of the housing code to the Housing Association.

An attempt to bring about a *merger* of two or more social welfare agencies is an ultimate test of negotiation. A proposal for a merger calls for, first, an analysis of the advantages and disadvantages involved; in addition, the practical carrying out of the merger involves working out problems in relation to such factors as the following: The name for the merged agency, the basic administrative document (law, charter, constitution, etc.); the agency's functions; organization structure; officers and board members; executive and staff personnel (who shall hold what positions, seniority and status in relation to retirement and other benefits, personnel policies, etc.); housing and equipment; finance; extra-agency relationships — to the community welfare council, community chest, state or national agency, etc.; steps required during the period of transition, consummating the merger, and mutual assimilation.

Kurt Peiser has pointed out that, however a merger originates:

[18] Compare Persons, *The Welfare Council of New York City,* pp. 24–26.

It should not mean a sledge-hammering of agencies. Rather must it involve a thinking through of the changes with joint participation of all elements concerned. The *final* action is an agreement democratically arrived at on the basis of an acceptance of the values which the merger is to bring.[19]

ORGANIZATION

Organization may be defined as the establishment and allocation of functions and relationships, and the integration of effort for the achievement of a central purpose. Organization has two aspects, which may seem antithetical but which are really complementary — breaking up the job, and seeing that the parts, thus established, operate in unity to achieve the common purpose. Organization always implies the conscious integration of human effort.

The definition given above is broad enough to cover a great variety of forms of human association, from the very simple and informal to the most formal, elaborate and complex. Formal organization may involve such factors as: definition of purpose; determination of functions; establishment and modification of organization structure; establishment of lines of authority and responsibility; distribution of tasks, including departmentalization and establishment of line, staff, and auxiliary functions; and coordination.[20]

In addition to formal organization, there is the more elusive but no less important realm of "informal organization." As Chester I. Barnard has observed, " 'Learning the organization ropes' in most organizations is chiefly learning who's who, what's what, why's why, of its informal society." [21] The understanding of informal organization may be of special importance to the community organization worker, who must often deal with situations which elude formal organizational definition. Examples would include understanding and working with the realities of political organization and community power structure. Often one of the most valuable assets of the community organization worker is his knowledge of human resources within special organizations — to whom to turn for particular facts, advice, cooperation or help.

[19] Kurt Peiser, "The Place of Mergers in Community Planning." In McMillen, *Community Organization for Social Welfare*, pp. 143–152.
[20] See James D. Mooney, *The Principles of Organization* (New York, Harper, rev. ed., 1947). L. Urwick, *The Elements of Administration* (New York, Harper, 1944), pp. 35–76.
[21] Chester I. Barnard, *The Function of the Executive* (Cambridge, Harvard University Press, 1938), p. 121.

Organization is usually thought of as an aspect of administration, relating primarily to agency structure and to intra-agency relationships. It is, also, however, one of the essential ways of using the process of community organization, where it often involves extra-agency relationships, inter-group situations and federative enterprises. Some specific aspects of organization, when used as part of the process of community organization, relate to: the creation and appointment of committees; organizing a new agency, program or service; expanding, contracting or otherwise modifying the organization of an existing agency, program or service; reorganizing an agency, program or service; effecting a merger of two or more agencies; and organizing inter-agency bodies.

There is an extensive literature on organization, as an aspect of administration, and it seems unnecessary here to enter into a detailed discussion of its various ramifications. Two aspects of organization, however, should receive special comment.

One of these is Clarence King's suggestion of the *"snowball technique."*

> You begin by rolling a *small* snowball. All depends on that central, cohesive core . . . But once that small snowball begins to attract other particles to itself the trick is half done. Given a sufficient expanse of snow and a steep enough slope, you could give the ball a push and it would go on without you, enlarging itself indefinitely. So it is in community organization . . .[22]

Liaison service is an important but frequently overlooked aspect of organization. The essence of liaison service is keeping in close touch with another organization; keeping abreast of developments in that agency; keeping open and using channels of information, communication, and possible assistance and cooperation. Liaison service obviously has a public relations aspect, but it is more than public relations — it has to do with the actual development and maintenance of cooperative working relationships between agencies. Much that is written of the job of the "staff officer" or "staff executive" has a bearing upon the use of this method of liaison service.[23]

> Examples: A representative of a statewide citizens welfare association makes it a point to keep in touch with the commissioner and various bureau heads of the state welfare department; a chest executive maintains a close liaison with the executive of the Jewish Federation and the director of the Catholic Charities.

[22] Clarence King, *Organizing for Community Action*, pp. 14–15.
[23] See Albert Lepawsky, *Administration: The Art and Science of Organization and Management* (New York, Knopf, 1952), ch. 10, "Staff and Line Organization."

Among the aids to liaison service are: reading materials issued by the agency with which liaison is being maintained, and attending meetings held under its auspices; service on inter-agency committees; holding joint meetings or conferences of selected board or staff members; and particularly, frequent visits to the agency and interviews and conversations with staff members. In general, most liaison contacts should probably be on an informal basis.

Organization should be conceived of in dynamic rather than mechanistic terms. Organization is essentially people cooperating, in an orderly way, to achieve a common objective. The nature of organization as a *cooperative undertaking* is more basic than all the machinery, charts, and formal arrangements. In particular, this is the most important point about organization for the community organization worker, since voluntary cooperation is the key to effective community organization.

QUESTIONS AND PROBLEMS

1. What steps are involved in the registration of *social statistics* in your community? How are the data thus collected used?

2. Analyze critically the report of a *social welfare survey* or study. What points in the outline suggested in the chapter are covered in the report? What seem to be the strengths and weaknesses of the report?

3. Prepare an outline for a plan for a specific social welfare study.

4. Illustrate the use of the method of *analysis* in current community organization practice in your community.

5. What would be some of the major criteria which you would use in *evaluating* the following: a community welfare council; a community chest; a state conference on social welfare?

6. Assume that you are the executive of a community welfare council. Outline a *plan* for action in one of the following community organization situations: (a) There are ten institutions for dependent children in your community. Several of them are not filled to capacity most of the time. Half of them do not have qualified casework service. Four of the institutions are backward in almost every way. (b) The Executive Committee of the council has voted "that the council, as one of its major objectives during the coming year, seek to develop close and effective cooperation with the 27 churches of the community; and that the executive secretary be asked to submit at the next meeting a plan of action looking toward this end." (c) A community survey has been completed. One major recommendation is for the merger of the family service society, a child placing society, and a protective agency into a single caseworking agency to be called the Family and Child Welfare Association. No one has expressed any open opposition; but the

agencies involved are all noncommittal and are playing a game of "watchful waiting."

7. Analyze a current or recent social welfare *program*. Consider: the reasons for its development; its objectives, content, organization; major problems encountered; accomplishments; strengths and weaknesses; present status.

8. Observe a meeting in which the method of *conference* is used. What were the strong and weak points of the meeting?

9. Compare parliamentary procedure and conference method with respect to purpose, methods of procedure, methods of reaching decisions, functions of the member, and functions of the chairman or leader.

10. What are some of the practical applications that can be made to community welfare organization from research in group dynamics?

11. If practicable, interview a member of a community welfare council staff: To what extent do members of the council staff give *consultation?* In what sorts of situations? In their experience, what are some of the criteria for sound consultation service?

12. If practicable, interview an executive of a local consumer-service agency. What kinds of consultation and field service does his agency receive from the national or state agency in its field? In what sorts of situations or regarding what kinds of problems? What are some of the practical values of such service?

13. If possible, identify some recent social welfare or other situation in your city or state that has required *negotiation*. Who were involved in the negotiations? How did they proceed? What were the results? What are some "guides to effective negotiation" which might be suggested?

14. Trace the steps taken in the *organization* or reorganization of some specific agency or service. What problems were encountered? How were these problems dealt with?

15. Study the organization chart of a community welfare council or a chest-council. What does it tell about the organization of the agency? What does it not tell? What are some of the values and limitations of organization charts in community organization?

SUGGESTIONS FOR READING

References in this and the succeeding chapter are listed under specific methods or topics, arranged alphabetically.

ANALYSIS AND EVALUATION

Flesch, Rudolph, *The Art of Clear Thinking* (New York, Harper, 1951, 212 pp.).

Keyes, Kenneth S., Jr., *How to Develop Your Thinking Ability* (New York, McGraw-Hill, 1950, 246 pp.). Has a bearing on the method of analysis.

Trecker, Harleigh B., *Guide for Agency Self-Appraisal* (New York, Federation of Protestant Welfare Agencies, 1953, 24 pp.).

CONFERENCE

(See also bibliography for ch. 22, Committees. Under Periodicals, see especially *Adult Leadership.*)

Bergevin, Paul and Morris, Dwight, *A Manual for Discussion Leaders and Participants* (Greenwich, Connecticut, Seabury Press, 1954, 73 pp.).

Brinton, Howard H., *Reaching Decisions: The Quaker Way* (Wallingford, Penna., Pendle Hill, 1952, 30 pp.). A discussion of practice in Friends' business meetings. The text of this pamphlet appears also as ch. 6 of Brinton, *Friends for 300 Years* (New York, Harper, 1952, 239 pp.).

Cartwright, Dorwin and Zander, Alvin, *Group Dynamics: Research and Theory* (Evanston, Illinois, Row, Peterson and Company, 1953, 642 pp.).

Chase, Stuart and Chase, Marian Tyler, *Roads to Agreement: Successful Methods in the Science of Human Relations* (New York, Harper, 1951, 250 pp.). Contains valuable material regarding communication, conference, conflict and integration, negotiation, etc.

Follett, M. P., *The New State* (New York, Longmans, Green, 1920, 373 pp.). Contains a classic description of "group thinking," pp. 3–59.

Lasker, Bruno, *Democracy through Discussion* (New York, Wilson, 1949, 376 pp.). Conference method as an aspect of democracy.

Lippitt, Gordon L. and Schmidt, Warren H., *My Group and I* (New London, Connecticut, Educator's Washington Dispatch, 1952, 31 pp.). Group process and conference, with the approach of modern research in "group dynamics."

Lippitt, Ronald, *Training in Community Relations: A Research Exploration Toward New Group Skills* (New York, Harper, 1949, 286 pp.). An account of an application of the group dynamics approach in a specific situation.

Thelen, Herbert A., *Dynamics of Groups at Work* (Chicago, University of Chicago Press, 1954, 379 pp.).

CONSULTATION

Marx, Fritz Morstein (ed.), *Elements of Public Administration* (New York, Prentice-Hall, 1946, 637 pp.), ch. 12.

National Social Welfare Assembly. *Resource Book on Field Service Administration* (New York, 1952, 24 pp.).

Siegel, Doris, "Consultation: Some Guiding Principles." In: *Administration, Supervision, and Consultation,* Papers from the 1954 Social Welfare Forum, National Conference of Social Work (New York, Family Service Association of America, 1955, 114 pp.), pp. 98–114.

Springer, Gertrude, "It's the Way You Do It," *Survey Midmonthly,* Vol. LXXVI, April 1940, pp. 131–132. Field service and consultation.

FACTFINDING

(See also articles on "Research in Social Work" in *Social Work Year Book.*)

Carter, Genevieve W., "Action Research in Community Planning," *Social Work Journal,* Vol. XXXIII, January 1952, pp. 23–28.

Council of Jewish Federations and Welfare Funds. *Social Surveys: A Guide for Use in Social Planning* (New York, 1949, 29 pp.).

French, David G., *An Approach to Measuring Results in Social Work.* A Report on the Michigan Reconnaissance Study of Evaluative Research in Social Work, sponsored by the Michigan Welfare League (New York, Columbia University Press, 1952, 178 pp.).

National Social Welfare Assembly. *Shall We Make a Survey?* (New York, 1949, 23 pp.).

Webb, Sidney and Webb, Beatrice, *Methods of Social Study* (New York, Longmans Green, 1932, 263 pp.). Includes chapters on studying social institutions, documents, interviews, note-taking, etc.

Young, Pauline V., *Scientific Social Surveys and Research* (Englewood Cliffs, N.J., Prentice-Hall, 3rd ed., 1956, 540 pp.).

NEGOTIATION

Chase and Chase, *Roads to Agreement.* (See above, under Conference.)

Peiser, Kurt, "The Place of Mergers in Community Planning." In: Wayne McMillen, *Community Organization for Social Welfare,* pp. 143–152.

ORGANIZATION

Dimock, Marshal Edward, *The Executive in Action* (New York, Harper, 1945, 276 pp.). Especially chs. II, III, IV, VI, VIII, and XIV.

Lepawsky, Albert, *Administration: The Art and Science of Organization and Management* (New York, Knopf, 1952, 669 pp.). Readings on administration. Especially Part II.

Metcalf, Henry C. and Urwick, L., (eds.), *Dynamic Administration: The Collected Papers of Mary Parker Follett* (New York, Harper, 1940?, 320 pp.).

Mooney, James D., *The Principles of Organization* (New York, Harper, rev. ed., 1947, 223 pp.).

White, Leonard D., *Introduction to the Study of Public Administration* (New York, Macmillan, 4th ed., 1955, 531 pp.).

PLANNING

Deardorff, Neva R., "Areas of Responsibility of Voluntary Social Work during Period of Changing Local and National Governmental Programs" (NCSW, 1936, pp. 312–323). A basic analysis of the nature of social welfare planning.

Himes, Joseph S., *Social Planning in America: A Dynamic Interpretation* (Garden City, N.Y., Doubleday, 1954, 59 pp.). A sociological discussion of social planning.

Marx, (ed.), *Elements of Public Administration.* (See under Consultation above.) ch. 6.

Trecker, Harleigh B., *Group Process in Administration.* (New York, Woman's Press, 2nd. ed., 1950, 330 pp.) ch. 12.

21.

EDUCATION, PROMOTION, AND FINANCING

EDUCATION AND PROMOTION

THREE METHODS: education, legislative promotion, and non-legislative social action are grouped under this heading.

EDUCATION

Education as a method of community organization includes: informing; interpreting; seeking to promote understanding of facts, problems, issues or alternatives; seeking to produce conviction and to enlist and retain goodwill and support; developing and maintaining sound public relations for an agency.

Public relations includes the whole area of relations with the public and with groups and individuals outside the agency.

As a function of a social agency public relations is concerned . . . broadly with whatever makes the agency known, understood, liked, used and supported. Its content includes analysis of public opinion; identification of groups and individuals whose use of services or support should be cultivated; appraisal of available factual and illustrative material for use in nontechnical presentations; selection and skilled use of media of communication; timing of public relations efforts in relation to current interests; development of teamwork among staff and board interpreters; and participation in joint efforts with other agencies in campaigns to win public response.[1]

[1] Mary Swain Routzahn, "Public Relations in Social Work," SWYB, 1949, p. 400.

Education is one of the most important and frequently used methods of community organization. Every social worker uses it at one time or another; therefore, every social worker needs some understanding of it and some facility in its use.

The fundamental reason for education by social welfare agencies is to make it possible for these agencies to serve, as effectively as possible, the community as a whole or those who need particular services.

There are at least four different motivations that may enter into educational efforts by health and welfare agencies:

The enlistment of support — moral and financial — is the motivation that comes first to mind. Probably most social welfare interpretation is designed primarily for this end. Unless the agency is completely endowed (a state fortunately rare), it must get its funds from the public, in one way or another. The agency, then, depends upon public understanding and support for the continuance of its program of service.

Defense is sometimes necessary against opposition to specific social welfare programs. Such opposition may be based upon program deficiencies or mistakes on the part of individual workers. In this case prompt correction of the deficiencies or errors is required. Sometimes, however, opposition is based upon misunderstanding, prejudice, or adverse economic or political interests.

A direct attack upon a program or a budget which involves the welfare of several thousand people may call for the mobilizing of educational and public relations methods for the defense of the threatened services and the values they represent.

Promoting understanding of the aims, services and methods of social welfare agencies, so that these services may be used as adequately and effectively as possible is another use of education. Such interpretation may be directed to the actual and potential consumers of the service, to probable sources of referrals, to cooperating organizations and to the general public.

The educational activities of health and welfare agencies may be directed also to *"education for better living,"* that is, developing understanding, acceptance, and practice of sound standards and ways of living by the public or special portions of the public — parents, children, teachers, workers, young people, etc. Health and mental health education, safety education, and parent education are examples of this type of interpretation.

Two outstanding authors on social work interpretation have diagrammed the social agency and its publics, with the agency in the center of a series of eight concentric circles, representing, respectively, the agency family — board, committees, staff; volunteers; consumers; cooperating organizations and individuals; supporters — contributors, members, special friends; key persons; special publics — professions, industries, veterans, students, racial and cultural groups; and the general public.[2] Education, then, may be directed to any one or more of these "publics" — it may vary all the way from self-education of the board or membership to the furnishing of factual information to ministers or members of labor unions, or the sending out of a news release intended to reach the general public through the newspapers.

The principal media of interpretation have been concisely summed up as follows:

> Here, not listed in order of importance, are the major methods available to you:
>
> Newspapers . Radio . Television . Motion Pictures . Displays and Exhibits . Meetings and conferences sponsored by your own organization . Participation in meetings and conferences sponsored by others . Interviews, including telephone interviews . Informal contacts by board, staff and volunteers . Letters, both form and individual . Bulletins and house organs of other groups . Booklets, pamphlets, folders, leaflets . Magazines.[3]

The key to the selection among all the media of interpretation, the writer points out, is the question: *"What method is best suited to my particular purpose and my resources?"*

The best method of education is participation. Membership on boards and committees, volunteer service, participation in discussion groups, meetings, campaigns — all these are valuable not only because these citizen contributions enrich social welfare programs and services, but also because these activities bring the citizen on the inside of the social welfare fence and give him a new understanding of the enterprise in which he has become a partner and an active participant.

There is a substantial literature on the subject of interpretation and publicity for social welfare, and a much larger literature on interpretation and public relations, in general, beyond the bounds of social welfare. No attempt is made here to discuss the various aspects of the

[2] Helen Cody Baker and Mary Swain Routzahn, *How to Interpret Social Welfare* (N.Y., Russell Sage Foundation, 1947), p. 10.
[3] Sallie E. Bright, *Public Relations Programs: How to Plan Them* (New York, National Publicity Council for Health and Welfare Services, 1950), p. 27.

subject in detail. Some brief comments seem desirable, however, on certain general factors that relate to education as a method of community organization.

First, we may consider what are some of the *qualities that make for effective interpretation.*

Effective interpretation:

1. Must be based on sound service. "Selling" must start with a product worth selling. Poor standards of service cannot be overcome by "good publicity."

2. Is founded on facts.

3. Is honest. Social work should not "oversell" its claims. The caution of the medical profession in assessing the value of new medical discoveries provides a salutary example for social work.

4. *Is easy to understand.* There are no more important rules for good interpretation than, "Tell your story simply and directly" and *"Don't use technical language to a lay audience. Say it in English."* [4]

5. Is vivid. It must attract attention and capture and hold interest at least long enough to get over its message. It was a skilled social work interpreter, Karl de Schweinitz, who once remarked that, "An appeal leaflet must be short enough so that the man will get the message while he's throwing it into the waste basket!" What interests most people? Human beings, most of all — especially children; also action, the interplay of human emotions, drama, conflict, puzzles — not abstract discussions, statistics nor most conventional charts. A picture, a story, or a vivid illustration will often make a point better than many pages or minutes of exposition.

6. Starts from scratch. It begins with the hypothesis of the cub reporter, writing his story: "Assume that nobody knows anything about anything."

7. Is aimed at a particular audience. It begins where that audience is, and adapts itself to their interests.

8. Repeats the message. A backwoods minister, with little formal education but with unusual power as a preacher, explained his procedure: "I divides my discourses into three parts: first, I tells 'em what I'se gonna tell 'em; then I tells 'em; then I tells 'em what I done told 'em!"

9. Is education — not mere propaganda. The object is to create

[4] In this connection, see: Sidney Hollander, "Confessions of a Board Member," NCSW, 1939, pp. 552–553. Zilpha C. Franklin, "Publicity and Research. I. As the Publicity Worker Sees It," *Channels,* Vol. XVII, September 1939, p. 3. Stuart Chase and Marian Tyler Chase, *Power of Words* (New York, Harcourt Brace, 1954), ch. 23, "Gobbledygook."

understanding, not merely passive acceptance of what the interpreter says.

Every social welfare agency should have a year-round planned *program of public relations* rather than depend upon sporadic efforts or unrelated episodes. Such a program would involve defining the objectives, formulating the message, identifying the audience to be reached, selecting the media to be used, working out a time schedule and budget, and providing for evaluation of the efforts and results.[5]

Public relations efforts should be tied in with the attempt to *build and maintain a constituency*. Every agency — governmental or voluntary — needs a constituency, including key people and leaders of community groups, who will have enough basic understanding about the agency and about social welfare problems and objectives, methods and resources so that they — the constituents — will "know what it is all about" and will be able to make sound and intelligent decisions about ultimate questions of policy. This kind of education is in harmony with democracy and the democratic ideal.

Public relations is basically a state of mind — not a bag of tricks nor a bundle of clever techniques. Fundamentally, it is a philosophy, a way of looking at and feeling about the job and the community for whom the job is being done. Public education is an expression of the recognition of a partnership between the professional social worker and the citizens whom he serves.

Public relations is the business of everybody connected with the agency. Everybody — executive, social workers, professional and non-professional staff, board members, volunteers — has a responsibility for representing and interpreting the agency and its program. And the receptionist, the telephone clerk and the janitor are frequently in key positions for building good public relations!

PROMOTING LEGISLATIVE OBJECTIVES

Promoting legislative objectives means attempting to bring about the passage or defeat of proposed measures of legislation.

Services in respect to legislation may include a great variety of activities. Legislative service is likely to be most important in the case of statewide agencies, such as statewide citizens associations or state conferences on social welfare; although both national and local agencies may participate in legislative service.

[5] E. G. Routzahn, *Elements of a Social Publicity Program* (New York, Russell Sage Foundation, 1920).

The first few types of legislative activities, as listed below, do not directly or necessarily involve *promotion* of legislation, but they are part of a comprehensive legislative service, and they form a foundation upon which legislative promotion is often built.

Reviewing bills and legislative documents. Legislative documents may include: copies of bills and resolutions; legislative agenda or lists of bills on order for reading or final passage on a given date; legislative "histories" or "status lists" indicating the status of each bill introduced; legislative journals; reports of legislative committees; and records of hearings by legislative committees.

The reviewing and keeping abreast of current legislative proposals in its field is a normal function of any statewide or national agency concerned with community organization. As a matter of fact, no state is well-equipped or even properly safeguarded in the area of social welfare if it does not have some machinery by which *all* legislative proposals relating to social welfare are promptly and automatically reviewed by a competent social welfare agency.

Preparing briefs, abstracts and analyses of bills. The first step in dealing with any legislative proposal is to *read the text of the bill*. The next logical step, in dealing with any bill is to analyze the provisions of the bill, objectively. The analysis should strip the bill down to essentials — penetrate the maze of legal language and get at the substance of the proposal. One simple way of approaching such an analysis is to go through the bill, underlining the essential substantive words and sentences in each section.

In the case of bills which are of major importance from the standpoint of the agency, it is frequently desirable to prepare a "legislative brief." [6] This brief may contain any or all of the following features: (1) A statement regarding the background or setting of the bill — other existing or proposed legislation in regard to the subject, etc. (2) The analysis of the provisions of the bill. These may be annotated or supplemented with: (3) Queries in regard to the meaning, effect, or probable legal interpretation of provisions, where these do not seem entirely clear. (4) The arguments for and against the bill. Both sides should be stated, as fairly and strongly as possible. A brief of this sort is an extremely valuable tool in subsequent promotional activities concerning the bill.

Following the progress of bills. From the standpoint of reporting and of promotion, it is important to know, week by week, and often day by day, the exact status of a bill: whether it has been introduced,

[6] Cf. Sidney Maslen, "Social Action and Housing," NCSW, 1944, pp. 274-275.

referred to a committee, been reported out of committee, and so on.

Reporting the progress of social legislation, through a bulletin, such as those issued by statewide citizens associations.

Sending letters or issuing statements regarding bills. Such letters or statements may be purely informative, but they are more likely to be primarily promotional.

Consultation service to legislators and leaders concerned with legislation. The more the agency and its staff members know about the field of social welfare, governmental departments and legislative procedure, the more valuable they may become as consultants to whom legislators may turn.

Formulating the substance of a proposed bill. Much time can usually be saved in the preliminary stages of the discussion of a potential legislative proposal by preparing a memorandum outlining the *substance* of the proposals, stripped to their essentials, and unencumbered by the legal verbiage which will probably adorn the final bill.

Drafting a bill. This involves the preparation of the bill in proper form for introduction by a legislator. Bill-drafting is a specialized technical job; it is usually a task for a lawyer with special experience and skill in bill-drafting. The work of the drafter will be immensely simplified if he has a clear and rather detailed statement of what the bill is intended to accomplish and of the substance of the provisions which it is desired shall be included.

Arranging for the introduction of a bill. This involves questions such as the following: (1) Shall the bill be introduced in the Senate or House or concurrently in both houses? (2) Shall there be one sponsor or several, assuming that the bill is to be introduced in one house only? If so, should sponsors be sought from both major parties? (3) What are the "specifications" for the sponsor? For example: commitment to the objectives of the bill, position, strength, reputation, and following in the legislature; political position or leadership; geographic location; identification with acute political controversies (will he automatically alienate certain groups?); relation to the Governor and administration; interest in the subject; knowledge of the subject; integrity; intelligence; skill in parliamentary and legislative strategy; skill as a speaker and debater; willingness to give time and leadership to the bill; willingness to cooperate with the agency. (4) When should the bill be introduced? Early in the session? Later, when certain trends and developments may be observed and appraised?

Supporting and promoting bills. There are various degrees of activity in respect to legislative support and promotion, from mild expressions of approval to the assumption of major responsibility for an all-out legislative campaign. An agency which is interested in many different legislative proposals, or which can devote only a fraction of its time and energy to legislation, must make realistic decisions as to the degree of responsibility which it can assume, the investment of time which it can afford in reference to specific bills, and how many different bills it wishes to endorse, support or promote.

The agency's relationship to various legislative proposals might include any or all of the following: (1) Endorsing or opposing a bill. This need not be anything more than a public statement of the agency's position on the bill. (2) Giving incidental support. This implies some activity in behalf of the bill in addition to mere sponsorship, but without the assumption of the major responsibility by the agency for "carrying the ball" in the effort to have the legislation passed. Usually this degree of activity implies cooperation with some other agency which has assumed the major promotional responsibility. (3) Carrying major responsibility for promoting a specific bill. This means assuming primary responsibility for promotion: carrying on educational propaganda and pressure activities on behalf of the bill. (4) Planning, organizing and carrying out an all-out legislative campaign for a major piece of legislation.

THE LEGISLATIVE CAMPAIGN

A campaign involves an organized series of operations designed to bring about the passage or defeat of a particular legislative proposal. It usually implies widespread educational and promotional efforts, as contrasted, for example, with placing the sole emphasis on quiet negotiations with a few political leaders. While the campaign is directed toward securing favorable action by the legislators, often much effort is directed toward influencing the constituents of the legislators — "the folks back home" — so that they, in turn, may make their wishes known to their representatives.

Legislative campaigns vary tremendously, but a well-organized state-wide campaign is likely to include most of the following steps or some approximation of them.

1. Recognition of the problem.
2. Genesis of the idea for legislation.
3. Formulation of the *substance* of the proposal. This may in-

clude: analysis, factfinding, discussion by interested groups, and formulation of a statement of the substance of the proposal.

4. Planning of the campaign, appointing a Statewide Campaign Committee, and building the campaign organization.

5. Drafting the bill.

6. Securing the sponsor(s) and arranging for the introduction of the bill.

7. Carrying out the campaign, while the bill passes through the various prescribed steps of the legislative procedure. The campaign may include:

(a) A statewide educational campaign, which may involve: statewide news releases; production and distribution of campaign literature and supplies; efforts to secure support and endorsement by statewide organizations and leaders; perhaps a speakers bureau; and so on.

(b) "Legislative strategy," including: determination and execution of strategic moves; liaison with the sponsor; following through on legislative procedure; "nursing the bill along"; seeking to win the support of legislative and political leaders, the state administration, etc.; participation in legislative hearings; meeting of emergencies and crises.

(c) County or district campaign committees may be organized in some campaigns. Under the leadership of the Statewide Committee, these county committees concentrate on educational campaigns in their respective counties, directed primarily toward seeing that the legislators from the county hear from their constituents, frequently and urgently, in behalf of the bill. These county committees should receive suggestions, supplies, support, consultation, and some field service from the Statewide Committee, if they are to operate with maximum effectiveness.

In one Pennsylvania campaign for an increase in the appropriation for mothers' assistance (predecessor of aid to dependent children), the statewide Public Charities Association (now Pennsylvania Citizens Association) supplied the county "mothers' assistance trustees" and county committees with a "fact manual" and a handbook of methods for conducting county campaigns. Many of the county groups carried on vigorous and effective campaigns, and it was felt that their efforts played a large part in securing the increased appropriation.

8. After the bill is passed and signed (assuming that the campaign is successful), comes the wind-up of the campaign, sending letters

of thanks to those who cooperated, and analyzing, evaluating and making a permanent record of the campaign, as a basis for future legislative efforts.

It is sometimes suggested that, even in the case of an important bill, all that may be necessary is to "win over the right political leaders — the legislators will take their orders from them." Generally speaking, this advice is unsound both on principle and from the standpoint of expediency. From the standpoint of principle, it is a distortion of democracy to let the enactment of social legislation depend upon back-of-the-scenes political "wangling" rather than popular education and demand. Even from the standpoint of expediency, the method of mere political manipulation is unsound. If a bill is passed this year at the nod of a political boss, it may with equal ease be repealed a year from now, at the behest of the same boss or of his successor. The only safe basis for important social legislation is, not only a real attempt to convince the legislators, but also the slow but sure building of a constituency of informed and concerned citizens who will communicate their wishes to the legislators.

Generally speaking, legislative campaigns should combine (1) education and political strategy, and (2) statewide leadership and local operation.

Sometimes a social welfare agency must plan, organize and carry out a campaign in reference to a matter to be submitted to the voters for their decision. Such matters may include constitutional amendments, bond issues, and questions submitted to the voters under the initiative and referendum. A "voters' campaign" of this sort is of even wider scope than the legislative campaign, mentioned above, because of the necessity in the voters' campaign of attempting, so far as possible, to reach all the voters in the state. Such a campaign depends, to a large degree, on the organization of local groups and the effectiveness of their efforts.

NON-LEGISLATIVE SOCIAL ACTION

Social action may, of course, be directed to non-legislative ends.[7] The method here discussed is the attempt to prevail upon a group or official to take some desired action, other than the passage or approval of legislation, for a social welfare objective sought by the social actionist.

[7] See ch. 6.

Some examples of non-legislative objectives and action are: efforts to induce the mayor to appoint a qualified director of welfare; bringing pressure on the state welfare commission to forestall a reduction in assistance grants; urging the board of a hospital to admit qualified Negro physicians to practice in the hospital.

Tactics may include: persuasion; appeals to both reason and emotions; emphasizing the favorable and unfavorable results of the alternative courses of action: attempting to make a particular position or course of action untenable or unpleasant. Other possible devices such as "high-pressure salesmanship," flattery, and threats would probably be rejected by most social workers as being both socially undesirable and inappropriate to professional practitioners.

Most methods of social action [8] may be used interchangeably for either legislative or non-legislative objectives. A few specific methods which have not been discussed in connection with legislation are mentioned below.

One of these methods might be called *personal promotion.* The essence of the method is the attempt to influence an official, legislator, or other leader through a personal contact by a person who is close to the leader (or close to someone who is close to the leader!) or who has an outstanding position of leadership in business, politics or some other field. The essential points are the utilizing of more or less personal contacts or relationships and the bringing of personal influence to bear upon the leader.

Marshalling expressions of public opinion is another method. Petitions and public mass meetings to promote or protest are examples.

"Direct action" methods, such as mass resignations, parades, picketing, strikes, work stoppages, boycotts, non-cooperation and passive resistance are more characteristic of labor organizations and of militant organizations for "social reform" than of most conventional social welfare agencies; however, these methods may be and on occasion have been used in situations involving social welfare problems and issues. Opinions will differ as to which of these methods may be appropriately used, by what organizations, and under what circumstances.

Withdrawing or threatened withdrawal of funds or other threats of punitive action are not unknown in the field of social welfare, however much some of them may be deplored.

[8] If non-legislative social action is the general method, the activities discussed below are technically "secondary methods." For simplicity, however, they are referred to in this discussion merely as "methods."

INVOKING AUTHORITATIVE ACTION

Invoking authoritative action is one of the most drastic forms of non-legislative social action. Authority may be derived from several different sources: the law; authoritative organizational relationships (the authority of a national over a chartered local agency, for example); and authority established on the basis of contract or agreement. This last would include the authority of a chest budget committee to make decisions regarding agency budgets, and the authority of a national agency to exclude from membership a local affiliate that did not observe the membership standards of the national.

One aspect of the use of this method is enforcing compliance or prohibiting action under the terms of a contract or agreement entered into voluntarily. This is probably the mildest type of authoritative action, since it would, in most cases, be possible, at least theoretically, for the agency which is being subjected to the authority to withdraw from the agreement. Usually, however, the withdrawal would mean either loss of funds, status, or prestige, or all of these. An example would be:

> The Social Security Administration demands that a state remedy certain abuses in its civil service procedure concerning public assistance workers or risk the withdrawal of federal funds for these services.

A variation of this method would be an agency's *enlisting the administrative authority of some other agency or official* for a purpose related to community organization. For example:

> A local branch of a highly centralized national agency is a member of the local chest-council, but the agency has a long record of low standards and failure to cooperate with the chest-council. A community welfare survey has made some far-reaching recommendations regarding modifications in the agency's program and standards. For a year following the survey, the agency has ignored or evaded the issues raised by the report. The chest-council at length appeals to the national for authoritative administrative action to bring about necessary changes in the local agency and its program.

A third variation would be *an appeal to a governmental administrative agency or to the courts.* For example:

A family agency initiates action to bring about the condemnation of certain sub-standard dwellings by the health department.

Some students of community organization may reject the idea that community organization should ever have anything to do with authority or compulsion. The issue would seem to be one of fact and not of theory. Are any of the methods illustrated above ever actually used to bring about an adjustment between needs and resources? The answer is that on occasion they are.

An entirely different question, and one which presents a vital issue in community organization practice, is this: *Is it ever sound professional practice to use or invoke authority in community organization, and if so, when?* [9]

FINANCING

Under the heading of Financing are listed three methods: fund-raising (other than federated financing); federated financial campaigning; and joint budgeting. The two latter methods have been discussed in Chapter 11, so only non-federated fund-raising is considered here.

FUND-RAISING

Fund-raising, as the term is here used, means obtaining the requisite funds for the operation of a voluntary agency. Obtaining the budget for a governmental agency involves primarily administrative operations; although the agency's presentation of its budget to a budget director or a legislative committee has much in common with the submission of a chest-agency's budget to the chest budget committee.

The basic significance of fund-raising for voluntary agencies has been thus described:

Fund-raising is a great deal more than mere solicitation of money. It is a barometer of membership and community interest. It is like a vote of confidence in the objectives and program of an organization. It is democracy at work, involving a test of the organization among a wide variety of people. . . . The fundraisers must conceive of their efforts as part and parcel of the growth and maturation of the organization itself. In this context, their tasks

[9] See discussion of this in ch. 23.

become really those of community organization, in which fund-raising, as a process, is integrated with program, membership retention and expansion and public relations.[10]

Some of the major aspects of fund-raising may be briefly noted.

Raising operating funds through voluntary contributions. It is assumed that the organization here referred to is a voluntary agency, not a member of a community chest and not included in a national campaign such as the Christmas Seal Sale or March of Dimes. A variety of methods of money-raising may be used, including mail appeals; solicitation of individuals — by volunteers or by regular members of the paid staff; special types of appeals including tag days, benefits, canisters in stores, Christmas kettles campaign, etc.; a fund-raising campaign with an organization of volunteer solicitors. A full-scale fund-raising campaign for an individual agency is unusual unless the agency is a large one (a large hospital, for example) or unless the campaign is for a building fund or other capital objective.

Raising capital funds. Funds for erection or purchase of buildings, and sometimes for other types of major equipment are "capital funds." Usually these funds must be raised separately from the annual operating funds. If an agency is a member of a community chest, the agency may undertake a capital fund campaign only with the approval of the chest.

A large proportion of capital funds must usually be obtained primarily from wealthy persons rather than from the general public. Plans for a new building should also provide plans for maintenance by endowment or self-support.[11] New buildings normally mean increased operating expenditures, and sound capital fund-raising involves also planning for meeting these increased annual expenditures.

Soliciting bequests. This means encouraging testators to include in their wills bequests for social welfare purposes. This is usually done by an individual agency or a community trust; but it may be done also by community welfare councils or community chests, in behalf of their member agencies.

Soliciting grants from foundations and similar bodies. A great deal is known about this subject by foundation heads and by experienced leaders of national agencies and other bodies, but little is available in published form.[12] One of the chief tools which has been developed in

[10] Edwin S. Newman and Leo J. Margolin, *Fund-raising Made Easy* (N.Y., Oceana Publications, 1954), pp. 13–14.
[11] William J. Norton, *The Cooperative Movement in Social Work*, pp. 310–311.
[12] See, however, two articles by William H. Whyte, Jr., in *Fortune*, Vol. LII, "What

connection with this method is the "brief" or letter of request, setting forth and describing the proposed project and stating the case for a grant in support of it.

A fund-raising campaign is essentially an organized solicitation of the public, or a portion of the public, for voluntary contributions of funds in behalf of a cause or of certain programs and services as represented by one or more agencies. The public campaign is usually confined to a specified and rather brief period of time, such as a week or two weeks. The campaign is usually based primarily upon solicitation through personal interviews. A campaign implies an organization and usually a considerable number of volunteer solicitors or other workers.

There are two major types of cooperative campaigns: the local joint fund-raising campaign carried on by the community chest or united fund; and the national or state fund-raising campaign in a specialized field, such as the Christmas Seal Sale, Easter Seal Sale or March of Dimes.

The community chest campaign has been described in Chapter 11, and a specialized technical literature on financial campaigns is available. The various types of campaigns differ in emphases, in procedures, and in many details.

The campaign executive has one of the most trying jobs in the field of social welfare. He must work through a large-scale organization involved in a high-pressure undertaking. Most of the things that are done are not and cannot be done by the director, but *he must see that all of them are done;* he must spark-plug the whole undertaking; "facilitate" and "energize" at many different points; supervise some jobs personally — or supervise the supervisors; be sensitive and alert at all times to the general movement and progress of the undertaking; build and maintain morale; exert quiet, consistent, indirect leadership; and be ready to leap into the breach at any point when a crisis develops.

INTERVIEWS

The interview is a "tool" that may be used in connection with most of the methods of community organization. (See ch. 19.)

An interview is a conversation with a purpose, as distinguished

---

are the Foundations Up To?", October 1955, pp. 110–113+, and "Where the Foundations Fall Down," November 1955, pp. 140–141+; also F. Emerson Andrews, *Philanthropic Foundations* (New York, Russell Sage Foundation, 1956), ch. 7.

from mere casual talk. The interview may be purposeful from the standpoint of only one participant (as in many research interviews) or from the standpoint of both (as in consultation interviews). An interview is usually confined to two persons, and it is ordinarily held in private. The language is usually extemporaneous, although a research interview may include certain set questions or phrases.

Interviews are used in all sorts of vocations — psychiatry, social work, journalism, law enforcement, etc. Interviews are constantly used in community organization. Some of the major purposes for which they are employed are: factfinding; analysis of a problem or diagnosis of a situation; planning; integration (an attempt to arrive at a meeting of minds); consultation; negotiation (bargaining); liaison; education, information-giving, interpretation; promotion (an attempt to convince, persuade, or sell an idea); recruiting (enlisting volunteers for the chest campaign, for example); and financial solicitation. The supervisory interview, essentially an administrative procedure, is of course used in community organization agencies. The parties to the interview may be two professional workers, a professional and a volunteer, or two volunteers (in a chest campaign, for example).

No attempt is made here to discuss the techniques of interviewing. Much that has been written in the general literature of interviewing and in the literature of casework interviews can be applied or adapted to the uses of community organization. There is real need, however, of research focused on the interview in community organization and on the ways of using it most effectively.

MEETINGS

The meeting is another "tool of communication" frequently used in community organization. Meetings are expensive in time and in the money which time represents. A two-hour meeting of 100 people in a large city probably means at least 300 man-hours in attendance and travel, to say nothing of preparation or follow-up. At the rate of $2 per man-hour, the meeting represents a cost of $600 in the time spent on it by the attendants. Every proposal for a meeting should be subjected to the queries: Is this meeting really necessary or important? Why?

In planning a program meeting, the following decisions are basic and should be made at the outset: (1) What is the purpose of the meeting? (2) What is the topic, theme or "message" of the meeting?

(3) What is the general type of program to be planned: formal address, open forum, etc.? [13] (4) Who will comprise the audience? Will it be a ready-made audience, a federation of settlements, women's club, etc.? If not, what types of persons are to be invited — board members, residents of a local community, etc.?

After these basic matters are decided, the planners are ready to proceed to such matters as: the date, hour, length of meeting; whether or not it is to be a meal meeting; the place of the meeting; and the persons to be invited to serve as participants — chairman, speakers, panel members, etc. Much of the success of the meeting will depend not only upon the quality of the participants but also upon communicating to each participant just what it is that he is being asked to do, and how this fits into the general plan for the meeting.

QUESTIONS AND PROBLEMS

1. What are some of the most effective methods of social work *education?*

2. Obtain a sample of interpretative or publicity material from a social welfare agency. Criticize and evaluate it from the standpoint of its aim, content, form, appeal or interpretative-value, etc. What are its strong and weak points? — Someone with specialized knowledge of public relations may hold a "publicity clinic;" evaluate several pieces of publicity material and encourage questions and comments from the audience. Each member of the audience should have a copy of each piece of publicity under discussion.

3. Select an important current *legislative bill* in the area of social legislation. (a) Prepare an objective, factual digest of the major provisions of the bill. (b) Prepare a "legislative brief" in regard to the bill.

4. What would be involved in planning a statewide legislative campaign for a major public welfare reorganization in your state? Assume that the lead is taken by some specific statewide organization, that this organization wants to promote statewide discussion of the issues involved, and wants to bring about widespread agreement as to what provisions should be embodied in the bill. Assume also that there will probably be considerable opposition to the bill, particularly from certain local officials and political leaders.

5. If possible, talk with someone (either a professional or layman) who has had substantial experience in promoting social legislation. What methods and principles seem to him important to effectiveness in legislative promotion?

[13] For an analysis of various types of program meetings, see Paul Bergevin and Dwight Morris, *Group Processes for Adult Education* (Bloomington, Ind., Community Services in Adult Education, 1951).

6. Analyze an instance of *non-legislative social action*. What were the issues involved? Who were concerned? What methods were used? What happened?

7. Give an example of the *invocation of authoritative action* for purposes of community organization. What organizations were involved? What happened?

8. What methods of *financing* social welfare agencies are used in your community? List as many as you can. Try to analyze what is involved in the use of these methods, and their probable effectiveness.

9. Analyze the organization and operation of a financial campaign for a social welfare objective, outside of the community chest, in your community. What are some of the special campaign methods and procedures that have been developed?

10. A role-playing situation may be staged, in which one person solicits a contribution from another for the community chest or for some other designated social welfare purpose.

11. What are the chief similarities and differences between casework *interviews* and community organization interviews?

12. To what extent can experience and skills in casework interviewing be utilized in interviewing in connection with community organization?

13. Attend, observe, and report on a formal program *meeting* with some relation to social welfare. What were its strong and weak points?

SUGGESTIONS FOR READING

EDUCATION, INTERPRETATION, AND PUBLIC RELATIONS

Baker, Helen Cody and Routzahn, Mary Swain, *How to Interpret Social Welfare* (New York, Russell Sage Foundation, 1947, 141 pp.). A textbook on public relations in social welfare.

Bright, Sallie E., *Public Relations Programs — How to Plan Them* (New York, National Publicity Council for Health and Welfare Services, 1950, 44 pp.).

Chase, Stuart and Chase, Marian Tyler, *Power of Words* (New York, Harcourt, Brace, 1954, 308 pp.). A study of "communication."

Freeman, Lucy, *Better Human Relations: The Challenge of Social Work*. Public Affairs Pamphlet 97A (New York, Public Affairs Committee, 1956, 28 pp.). A popular interpretation of social work, prepared primarily for recruiting purposes.

Granger, Lester B., "Educational and Promotional Process in Community Organization," NCSW, 1947, pp. 218–226.

Levy, Harold P., *Public Relations for Social Agencies: A Guide for Health, Welfare, and Other Community Organizations* (New York, Harper, 1956, 208 pp.).

National Publicity Council for Health and Welfare Services, 257 Fourth

Ave., New York. Publications, including periodical, *Channels*, and a "how-to-do-it" series of pamphlets.

FUND-RAISING

(See also the three books by Andrews, listed in bibliography, ch. 11.)

Gamble, Charles W. and Gamble, Winona W. *How to Raise Money: Fund Raising Programs for Social and Religious Organizations* (New York, Association Press, 1942, 265 pp.).

Newman, Edwin S., and Margolin, Leo J. *Fund Raising Made Easy* (New York, Oceana Publications, 1954, 158 pp.).

INTERVIEWS

Bingham, Walter Van Dyke and Moore, Bruce Walter, *How to Interview* (New York, Harper, third revised edition, 1941, 263 pp.).

Fenlason, Anne Ferguson, *Essentials in Interviewing* (New York, Harper, 1952, 352 pp.).

Young, Pauline V., *Interviewing in Social Work* (New York, McGraw-Hill, 1935, 416 pp.).

LEGISLATIVE PROMOTION AND NON-LEGISLATIVE SOCIAL ACTION

(See also bibliography for ch. 6, Social Action.)

Bond, Elsie M., *Methods of Securing Social Welfare Legislation* (New York, State Charities Aid Association, 1941, 14 pp.)

Improving Your Community and State. Proceedings: Institute on Methods of Social Action, New Orleans, November 1953. Institute sponsored by National Conference of Social Work (Columbus, National Conference of Social Work, 1954, dittoed, variously paged). Includes papers on community organization and social action.

Wickenden, Elizabeth, *How to Influence Public Policy: A Short Manual on Social Action* (New York, American Association of Social Workers, 1954, 39 pp.). A handbook on methods of legislative promotion.

MEETINGS

(See also references under Conference, bibliography, ch. 20; note especially Thelen, *Dynamics of Groups at Work*, ch. 6.)

Bergevin, Paul and Morris, Dwight. *Group Processes for Adult Education* (Bloomington, Indiana, Community Services in Adult Education, 1951, 86 pp.). Types of and devices for meetings.

Strauss, Bert and Strauss, Frances. *New Ways to Better Meetings* (New York, Viking Press, 1951, 177 pp.). Suggested methods for conferences and meetings.

22.

COMMITTEES

A VAST AMOUNT OF COMMUNITY organization activity is carried on through committees. Arlien Johnson once observed that, "The committee is to community organization as the interview is to casework"; and someone else has remarked that while casework and group work might conceivably be carried on without committees, community organization could not be carried on without them.

A committee may be defined as a group of persons, limited in membership by selective appointment, usually appointed by some superior authority, and having joint responsibility for inquiry, deliberation, decision, action, sponsorship, or related activities in regard to matters assigned to them.[1] The word "committee" is here used generically to cover many groups which may be designated as boards, commissions, cabinets, councils (e.g., an interclub house council in a settlement), etc. as well as those which are called committees. A committee may be either a group or an "inter-group" body.

Let us examine the elements of the definition given above.

A committee is a *group.* A committee, as here conceived, must consist of two or more persons; a "committee of one" is a figure of speech.[2]

A committee is almost always *limited in membership* by definite, selective appointment. One normally becomes a member of a com-

---

[1] For some other definitions, see: Audrey R. Trecker and Harleigh B. Trecker, *Committee Common Sense* (New York, Whiteside and Morrow, 1954), pp. 18–19; Herrymon Maurer, "Management by Committee," *Fortune,* Vol. 47, April 1953, p. 146; Henry M. Robert, *Robert's Rules of Order, Revised* (Chicago, Scott, Foresman & Co., 1943), p. 206.
[2] For a different view, see *Robert's Rules of Order,* p. 206.

mittee by invitation, rather than by taking the initiative and joining it. In this respect the committee differs from most associations or membership organizations.

In the case of the committee, appointment is generally *selective*: a selection is made of a number of persons who it is thought can best contribute to carrying on the work of the committee.

A committee is usually *appointed by some superior authority*. Etymologically, "committee" is derived from the Latin verb *committere,* meaning to entrust. Thus, a committee is usually a secondary rather than a primary body; it is normally subsidiary to some other authority or "parent body." The superior authority may be either a group or an individual; for example, it may be an association, a community welfare council, a board, another committee, or an executive. In some cases there may be two or more superior authorities: as, for example, in the case of a joint committee representing two or more organizations.

Not all committees, however, are appointed by superior bodies. The self-appointed committee is a matter of fairly common observation. A group of interested citizens may band together as a committee to bring about the organization of a family service society; another group organizes as a "Committee of One Hundred" to investigate moral conditions within a community or to sponsor the passage of proposed legislation. Even with the self-appointed committee, appointment is usually selective: the original members "select" themselves from a larger potential number of persons; and often the original nucleus co-opts additional members.

Occasionally, a whole organization is called a committee: for example, the National Child Labor Committee and the American Friends Service Committee. In such cases the name of the originating body or the governing body has usually been extended to the whole organization; that is, there is usually a committee at the head of the organization, but the total organization is obviously an association.

The committee members have *joint responsibility* for discharging the committee's assignment. Urwick stresses this factor in his definition of a committee as "a group of persons to whom certain functions have been assigned on condition that they discharge those functions conjointly in a corporate capacity. The necessary authority adheres to the group as such, not to any individual member of the group." [3]

This is an important qualification. It distinguishes the committee

[3] L. Urwick, *Committees in Organisation* (reprint from *British Management Review,* London, date ?), p. 5.

from a squad of soldiers, a gang of men working on the railroad, a class studying under a teacher, or a group of caseworkers working under the supervision of a case supervisor. Each of these instances presents a "hierarchical" form of organization, where the leader is vested with certain administrative authority to direct or supervise or teach. But in the case of the committee, the assignment and the requisite authority to carry out the assignment is committed not to the chairman or to any other individual but *to the group*. The individual committee members are not "responsible" to the chairman; they are individually responsible to the committee, and the committee, *collectively*, is responsible to the appointing authority. The chairman is a leader, but he does not possess executive authority; as Urwick points out, he is merely *primus inter pares*, the first among equals.

The committee usually illustrates two characteristics of democracy: first, there is essential equality of power and control by its members; and, second, the committee, within the limits of its assignment, usually operates with a high degree of autonomy and freedom as to its procedure and actions.

The committee may have *responsibility for inquiry, deliberation, decision, action, or sponsorship,* or for any combination of these activities. Inquiry relates to the ascertainment of facts. Deliberation is probably the most typical committee activity; it includes the exploration of a subject, analysis of a problem, consideration of possible alternatives, and other discussion related to the committee's assignment. Decision implies, of course, agreement or determination upon some specific plan, recommendation, policy, or action. Action and sponsorship are discussed below, in connection with the functions of committees.

Finally, the committee receives, or formulates for itself, *terms of reference* — an assignment and definition of its nature and task. Its duties may be defined by a constitution or a set of by-laws, by the minutes of the appointing body, by an executive order, or by agreement on the part of the committee itself. The assignment may be broad or narrow, precise or vague; but in any case the committee is limited to this assignment.

A committee is usually a relatively small body, but this is not always true. A board may sometimes have 30, 50, or even a larger number of members; and a sponsoring committee may include a hundred or more members.

The committee is an instrument of community organization, or, even more commonly, of administration. It is a type of organization unit; it usually employs group discussion or conference as its chief method, but it also uses other methods of community organization, such as factfinding, planning, and so on.

TYPES OF COMMITTEES

COMMITTEES MAY BE CLASSIFIED in at least the following ways: by length of life; organizational status; method of creation; method of appointment; authority to which they are accountable; and major functions.

From the standpoint of length of life, there are permanent or standing committees and temporary, special, or *ad hoc* committees.

Organizational status includes such variations as the public commission, directive or policy determining board, advisory board, administrative (plural executive) board, "cabinet" of department heads, "committee of the whole," sub-committee, etc.

Committees may be created in at least four ways: (1) by the provision of some administrative document, such as a statute, legislative resolution, constitution, or by-laws; (2) by action of a group, such as a membership body, a board, or another committee; (3) by action of an executive or other individual; or (4) by action of the persons forming the committee.

The members of the committee may be appointed in various ways: the whole committee may be appointed by some superior body, such as a board of directors, or by the chairman of the board; the chairman of the committee may be appointed by the superior body and may be given power to appoint the other members; the committtee may be self-appointed; or the committee may have and exercise the right to "co-opt" additional members, that is, to add to its membership.

The committee (unless it is self-appointed) is responsible either to a group (a board, another committee, etc.) or to an individual, such as the Governor, the president of an agency, the agency executive, a district supervisor, etc. A committee created by action of a group or individual is usually responsible to the creating authority; a committee established by a constitution, or other document, is ordinarily responsible to the governing board of the organization or to the appointing authority.

MAJOR FUNCTIONS OF COMMITTEES

IT HAS ALREADY BEEN SUGGESTED that committees have joint responsibility for inquiry, deliberation, decision, action, sponsorship, or related activities. A more detailed analysis of committee activities suggests that committees may exercise at least the following functions. These are not completely hard-and-fast separate categories. In many cases it is impossible to classify a committee completely by any one function, as the same committee may perform several functions; thus, an executive committee may have power to decide certain matters, to recommend in other cases, to nominate a new executive to the board, and so on.

The major functions are:

1. *To make decisions* on matters of policy, program, or action. This is the familiar "determination of policy" or the "power to act." It is also the function of planning when the committee has power to make actual decisions regarding proposed action.

2. *To make recommendations* regarding policy, program, or action. In this case the committee usually submits its recommendations to the parent body, which reserves the right to make decisions. A special committee is frequently appointed to study and make recommendations regarding some proposed course of action.

3. *To give advice* to an executive or perhaps to some policy-determining body. An advisory committee often submits definite recommendations, but the giving of advice is broader in scope than mere formal recommendations. It may include an informal type of discussion where the executive or other advisee may be more anxious to explore, or "talk through" a problem, or to "get the thinking" of the advisory body than to obtain a specific and formal recommendation.

4. *To direct or supervise* an executive, sub-executive, or staff member. This represents the familiar board-executive relationship, in which an executive or department sub-executive is responsible to a governing board or committee. This function is usually united with the function of making decisions regarding policies and program.

5. *To effect coordination* among the members and the departments, groups, or other units which they represent. A "cabinet" of department heads, an interclub council in a settlement, or an inter-agency committee on referrals might be primarily concerned with this coordinative function.

6. *To study, make inquiries, or carry on factfinding.* A survey or study committee and a Congressional or legislative investigating com-

mittee are two very different types of committees having factfinding as a primary function. In both cases the committee may carry on its activities largely through direction or supervision of a technical staff.

7. *To visit or inspect.* This function is closely related to inquiry and factfinding. The visiting committees of the New York State Charities Aid Association in their visitation of state and local institutions are examples of this function. A budget committee of a community chest which visits the offices and institutions of the chest member-agencies illustrates another use of this function.

8. *To educate the committee members.* This is likely to be a secondary rather than a primary function of a committee. A committee of a state conference, appointed to make recommendations regarding revisions in the state's adoption law, may hold several meetings devoted to the study of adoption laws in its own and other states. It is assumed, however, since a committee is ordinarily not merely a study group for the education of its own members, that eventually its study will result in some decision, recommendation, or action.

9. *To promote sound public relations.* This may include statements, conferences with other bodies or officials, informal conversations, and so on. Governing boards, public relations or publicity committees, and advisory boards are among committees which exercise this function.

10. *To carry on administrative or service activities.* This is the committee function which is concerned not merely with deciding or recommending but with executing. The outmoded state "board of control" where the members actually serve as a plural executive, and the traditional "poor board," where the members actually disburse public relief, are examples — and warnings — of one application of this function. There are other instances, however, where it is necessary and desirable that a committee should take direct action: for example, a Special Gifts Committee of a community chest may be appointed primarily to solicit prospective large givers; an agency and a union may appoint a committee to negotiate with each other; and an Arrangements Committee for an agency's annual meeting may be expected to reserve a meeting room, arrange decorations and place cards, provide refreshments, receive guests, usher, etc.

11. *To select, appoint, or approve personnel.* Nominating committees and personnel committees may be charged primarily with this function, but a directive board also exercises one of its most important prerogatives in the appointment of the agency's executive. A membership committee, which passes on applications for individual or or-

ganization membership exercises this function in a somewhat different way.

12. *To render judgment or to arbitrate* in cases of conflicting claims or interests. Illustrations may be found in an agency committee on grievances or personnel adjustments; a committee on "fair hearings" (appeals) under the public assistance provisions of the Social Security Act; or a committee of a professional association chapter requested to adjudicate a conflict between an agency board and executive.

13. *To sponsor or endorse* an agency, program, or undertaking. Sometimes, in the case of a drive for funds or a legislative campaign, a large committee may be formed with no other purpose than formal endorsement and sponsorship of the undertaking. Some such national or statewide committees may never meet; they may function entirely as lists of names on letterheads and campaign literature. Such bodies have sometimes been referred to as "scenery committees" rather than working committees. This method has been subject to much abuse; well-intentioned and prominent persons have sometimes lent their names to causes about which they knew very little. A committee that has no real function except sponsorship should be given a title such as Sponsoring Committee, which clearly indicates this fact. To call such a committee a "board of directors" or even an advisory committee is patently dishonest. It is of course true that any directive board, and usually an advisory board, exercises this function of sponsorship as a minor aspect of its responsibilities.

14. *To assist in a ceremonial function.* The legislative "committee to escort the Governor to the rostrum," a reception committee at a social function, or a committee of a Council board to attend the dedication of a new building of a member agency all illustrate this function.

These fourteen functions may be applied to all varieties of subject matter in all types and sizes of organizations. There may be a committee to study the boundaries of geographical units for the community chest campaign and a committee of the United Nations to study education for social work throughout the world. The important thing is to understand the particular functions and the specific assignment of any given committee.

THREE TYPES OF BOARDS

Three types of boards or committees may be briefly noted here since they occur so often in social work. The *directive board* is usually the governing body for an agency, organization, or a department of an organization. The agency board usually makes decisions regarding program, policies, and allocation of funds within the approved budget. It ordinarily adopts and recommends the budget to some outside budgetary authority such as the community chest budget committee, a budget director, or a legislative committee. The board may make recommendations, from time to time, to the national agency in its field, the community welfare council, the community chest, or public bodies and officials. The board ordinarily appoints the executive, who is accountable to the board. The board serves as a sponsoring body for the agency, and individual members may participate incidentally in interpretation or other "action" in connection with administrative or service activities. The board may at times exercise various other functions among those listed.

The advisory board's primary function is giving advice and making recommendations, usually to the agency executive. The executive is not appointed by and is not responsible to an advisory board, and he is not obliged to follow its advice. When a public board or a departmental committee is created, it is a matter of major importance to make clear whether the body is directive or advisory.

An advisory board may be a citizen group of non-professionals, a technical advisory committee of professionals, or a mixture of the two. Sometimes the executive who is being advised presides over the advisory committee; usually, however, the committee has more status, strength, independence, and objectivity if one of its members serves as its chairman.

Observation and experience suggest these comments in regard to advisory boards and committees. First, the functions of giving advice and making decisions should not be combined in one committee. To create a board to *advise* a public official and then to give it also the right to promulgate rules and regulations for the department is a confusion of functions and is inviting friction. Second, an advisory committee should not be created unless the advisee really wants advice. It is unfair to inveigle busy and responsible persons into serving on an advisory committee and then to use the committee merely as "window-dressing." Third, if the committee is to retain self-respect and vitality, it must be actually asked to advise; the matters submitted to it must include questions of substance and importance; and the advisee must accept or use the advice in a reasonable proportion of cases.

The administrative board, as the term is here used, is a full-time working board, the members of which receive salaries for full-time service. It is usually a small board of three or five members. The administrative board not only makes decisions regarding program and policies, but it also acts as the plural chief executive of the agency and its members participate directly in administrative activities. Illustrations of this type of board include the old full-time state boards of control (some of which still survive), the traditional "poor boards" for the administration of public poor relief, and the Social Security Board (1935–1946). (Quasi-judicial bodies, such as public utility commissions are in a different category.) While some of these boards have honorable records of achievement, they have probably achieved these records in spite of, rather than because of, their form of organization. The administrative board is a flagrant violation of the principle that the final executive authority and responsibility for the management of an agency should rest in a single executive. The plural executive is a clear invitation to friction and administrative inefficiency; it is essentially a cumbersome, wasteful, and ineffective form of organization.

As has already been pointed out, there are many instances in which committees may and do properly participate in direct administrative action (as in the case of the Special Gifts Committee, mentioned above), but the administrative board as the plural executive of an agency has no place in modern social welfare organization.

ORGANIZATION AND PROCEDURE

Usually a committee has at least a chairman and secretary, and sometimes also a vice-chairman. Often a committee of a social agency has a staff member who is attached to the committee to give what may be called executive service. The term "committee aide" will be used in this discussion to designate such a staff member. The committee aide is often designated as the secretary of the committee. The functions of the chairman, secretary, and committee aide will be discussed below, in connection with the topic of leadership.

SOME BASIC PRINCIPLES IN RESPECT TO COMMITTEES

Since a committee is a *group of persons*, the most important factor is always the human element — the personalities of the individuals involved and the ways in which they relate to each other and to the group process.

John Galsworthy once dealt with the subject of committees and conference process, succinctly, in a passage which all students of the subject should know:

> In an age governed almost exclusively by Committees, Michael knew fairly well what Committees were governed by. A Committee must not meet too soon after food, for then the Committeemen would sleep; nor too soon before food, because then the Committee-men would be excitable. The Committeemen should be allowed to say what they liked, without direction, until each was tired of hearing the others say it. But there must be someone present, preferably the Chairman, who said little, thought more, and could be relied upon to be awake when that moment was reached, whereupon a middle policy voiced by him to exhausted receivers, would probably be adopted.[4]

The following principles are suggested as a basis for the achievement of maximum effectiveness by committees.[5]

1. **The objectives and functions of the committee should be clear.** Why is a committee needed? What is it trying to do? What is its purpose? Is the committee really necessary or desirable? Defining the objective of the committee is the starting point; it is a basis for decision as to whether or how important it is that there should be a committee. The specific functions of the committee should also be defined. The list of committee functions suggested above may be used as a checklist for this purpose.

To make sure that the committee's objective and functions are clearly formulated and understood, *there should be a written assignment or "charge" for the committee.* In the formal language of public administration, this statement may be called the "terms of reference" of the committee.[6] If the committee receives no such written assignment from the parent body, the committee should draft its own assignment and check it back with the appointing authority.

The assignment to the committee should cover such points as the following: (a) the name of the committee; (b) the authority for the

---

[4] John Galsworthy, *Swan Song* (New York, Scribner, 1928), p. 201. This chapter is a delightful narrative of an English committee meeting to further housing reform. See also an earlier chapter, "Forming a Committee."

[5] For other formulations of the factors making for effective committee work, see Trecker and Trecker, *Committee Common Sense,* pp. 145–153 and Edward F. Sheffield, *Making Committees Effective* (Toronto, Ryerson Press, 1950), p. 1.

[6] See: Sheffield, *Making Committees Effective,* pp. 5–6, E. H. Simpson, *The Mechanics of Committee Work* (Brussels, International Institute of Administrative Sciences, 1952), pp. 3–4.

appointment of the committee (by-laws, action of board, action by executive, etc.); (c) the designation of the appointing authority; (d) the members of the committee; (e) the officers of the committee, or an indication that the committee is to elect its own officers; (f) the date of appointment, the period for which the committee is to function, and the terms for which the officers and members are appointed: (g) any time schedule or deadlines that are binding upon the committee or are suggested for its guidance, and (h) above all, a clear statement of the committee's objective and functions — why it has been created and what it is to do.

A community welfare council, national agency, or any other agency that has a considerable number of committees needs an up-to-date looseleaf book or card index giving, for each of the agency's committees, at least the information indicated above.

2. There should be appropriate selection of members. No problem is ever solved merely by appointing "a committee" — the results depend on the persons who are appointed to the committee and what they do. The effectiveness of committees would be vastly increased if appointing authorities would utilize the administrative device of "job specifications" and would start out, not by a random reviewing of names, but by formulating a statement of what the committee members are to do and what, therefore, should be their qualifications.

The selection of committee members should be appropriate from the standpoint of the following:

(a) Number. How many persons should serve on the committee depends upon the nature of the task and extent to which various groups, interests or points of view must be represented. For adjudication or for the drafting of a constitution a committee of three may be better than a larger group; for a representative body, 25, 50, or even more may be required. For the average committee, where freedom, informality, and full participation in group discussion are desired, probably the most desirable size is between five and ten. In general, the committee should be small enough for informal group discussion and free participation, and large enough to represent the types of experience, interests, or groups which should be represented.

(b) The members should be reasonably well equipped for the work of the committee in terms of education, experience, knowledge, skill, and other qualifications, *or* should be willing to work toward bringing themselves up to the necessary level of competence through reading, study, observation, faithful attendance, and service on the committee itself. Most committees in social welfare need not be made up mainly of experts or specialists. In fact, committee service is one of the best means of education and participation, in most organizations; and on many committees it is highly desirable to train some younger and less experienced persons. The new member of a chest budget committee, a public welfare board, or a council divisional committee may not at the outset measure up to the level of ideal competence; but if not, he ought at least to be educable and willing to work up gradually to the requirements of the job.

(c) The members of the committee should be interested and willing to serve and should have sufficient time, health, and strength.

(d) The committee membership should adequately represent the constituency or the parent body and also any special groups or interests that need to be represented.

(e) *The members should be able to work together as a group.* Committee work means teamwork. Five brilliant, exceptionally able, but highly individualistic persons may be infinitely less useful for committee purposes than five less brilliant individuals who are better "group persons," who believe in and are more skillful in the give and take of the group process.

3. **The committee should have competent leadership and adequate executive and clerical service.** One of the truths that must be learned by all who work with committees is that *a committee must have leadership.* A committee is a cooperative venture, and its leadership should be appropriate to a cooperative undertaking. In practice, "intellectual leadership" or "working leadership" is sometimes given informally by a member of the committee, or by various members at various times. The chairman and committee aide exercise two types of formal leadership.

THE CHAIRMAN

The job of the chairman of the committee involves: serving as the official head of the committee, for purposes of both internal and external relationships; deciding when meetings shall be held (unless the committee decides this); presiding at meetings of the committee; and officially presenting reports to superior authorities or outside bodies.

Presiding at meetings may mean ability to lead an informal group discussion, to conduct a parliamentary meeting, or sometimes to conduct a combination of the two. Whatever the form of meeting, the chairman must always try to keep the committee on the track and moving forward, but at the same time preserve an atmosphere of freedom and vitality of participation. Even in a parliamentary setting, the chairman is concerned primarily with helping the group to come to a decision or to arrive at an integration of its thinking.

THE COMMITTEE AIDE

Staff service to committees in social welfare is an administrative device of immense importance in community organization and in social welfare administration.[7] Frequently a staff aide may have responsibility in three different areas. These are:

(a) Program service. This implies assistance in developing the committee's program of work and requires an understanding of the aims and task of the committee. It calls for ideas, imagination, initiative, and resourcefulness.

(b) Organizational service. This involves a continuing responsibility for working with the appointing authority and the committee chairman to assure that the committee has the requisite manpower and organization for its task. When the committee is first authorized, its personnel must be appointed by the proper authority; and the committee must be organized, with at least a chairman and secretary. Thereafter, the personnel must be kept at full strength.

(c) Administrative service. This may include the following activities: (1) Planning when meetings shall be held and planning the agendas, both in conference with the chairman. (2) Making the physical arrangements and other necessary preparations for meetings. (3) Sending out the notices for meetings. (4) Keeping the minutes or seeing that the minutes are kept; and seeing that they are distributed to the members of the committee. (5) Handling correspondence for the committee and seeing that members are notified or reminded of assignments given them by the committee.

The committee aide may have also a deeper and more delicate type of administrative responsibility: seeing that the committee meets regularly and functions actively, that actions taken at meetings are followed up, and as far as possible insuring that it "gets somewhere."

The committee aide gives indirect rather than direct leadership. His job involves working with and strengthening the position of the chairman, the official head, rather than usurping or infringing upon his prerogatives. Fundamentally, the committee aide must be an "enabler" and not a director or a manipulator. His basic task is to

[7] See: Simpson, *The Mechanics of Committee Work.*

facilitate the work of the committee, to help or enable it to perform its task effectively, but never to dictate or determine its course of action nor to usurp or infringe upon the functions of the chairman.

4. **There should be appropriate arrangements for the meetings of the committee.** A committee's life has three recurring phases: preparation for meetings; meetings; and follow-up action after meetings.

Meetings should be held at appropriate intervals, considering the nature, functions, and membership of the committee. The time of the meeting should be convenient, adequate to the business to be performed, but not too prolonged. An hour or an hour and a half is often better than two hours; two hours should usually be the limit, unless the meeting is broken by an intermission.

The question of a "meal meeting" versus a non-meal meeting must often be determined. Generally speaking, the meal meeting tends to promote informality, sociability, and fellowship, and thus, solidarity; but the serving of the meal uses up valuable time, and the non-meal meeting is usually better adapted to concentrated group thinking and discussion.

There should be an appropriate physical setting for the meeting. This means a separate room of appropriate size; quiet; satisfactory conditions of heat, light, and ventilation; comfortable chairs; and an informal arrangement of the seating, where all the members may see each other. Meeting around a table — round, oval, square, or oblong — is usually the best arrangement if it can be managed. If a table is not available, the next best arrangement is probably the circle or semi-circle. In any event, the seating should be such that the members of the committee can see each other, so that they will find it easy and natural to talk back and forth.

It was Francis Bacon who observed that

A long table and a square table, or seats about the walls, seem things of form, but are things of substance; for at a long table, a few at the upper end, in effect, sway all the business; but in the other form there is more use of the counsellors' opinions that sit lower. A king, when he presides in council, let him beware how he opens his own inclination too much in that which he propoundeth. For else counsellors will but take the wind of him, and instead of giving free counsel, will sing him a song of *placebo*.[8]

5. **There should be appropriate procedure at meetings.** Most activities of committee meetings fall under the following heads: (a)

[8] Francis (Lord) Bacon, *Essays.* "Of Counsel."

The committee carries on certain procedural activities. This includes the adoption of the agenda and the formal approval of the minutes. (b) The committee usually spends a good deal of time listening to the presentation of material — reports, formal and informal, testimony (in the case of formal committee hearings), proposals, and other presentations. (c) The committee engages in discussion, including "debate" on motions, if the committee observes the formalities of parliamentary law. (d) The committee may make decisions or recommendations. It may act on resolutions; it may formulate matters of substance to be later embodied in a more complete formal statement or report; or it may act in detail on the various parts of a constitution, report, or other document. Ordinarily a committee should direct its discussion and action to matters of substance, leaving detailed or technical drafting of documents to be done between meetings. It is usually futile for a committee to try in a group meeting to compose or edit a lengthy document. It is frequently difficult enough to get a fifty-word motion stated to the satisfaction of the committee!

Lucile Lippitt, writing of YWCA committees, suggests that a committee meeting may be thought of "as falling quite naturally into three parts: (1) *study and information,* which give the necessary background for (2) *discussion and decision or action,* which must not end with the committee meeting but which require (3) *definite assignment of responsibilities to individual committee members* with specific time limits for carrying them out." [9]

Obviously all committees do not proceed on the strict basis of parliamentary law. Actually any given committee may carry on its meetings on the basis of parliamentary law, informal conference or group discussion, or semi-formal conference, where the committee reaches its agreements mainly through group discussion but confirms them by parliamentary motions or other action. The committee should be completely pragmatic in deciding which procedure will best fit the requirements and circumstances for that particular committee.

The device of the "open committee meeting" is one that may often prove useful in social welfare organizations. This is a meeting of a committee to which interested members of the parent organization, or others who are interested, may be invited. The visitors may be invited to participate in the discussion, to listen and observe, or they may be asked to abstain from participation until near the end, when the meeting may be thrown open to questions and discussion from the floor.

[9] Lucile Lippitt, *Committee Cues* (New York, Woman's Press, 3rd ed., rev., 1944), p. 19.

For example:

A committee of a family and child welfare division of a large-city community welfare council is attempting to formulate a statement of suggested policies to govern intake and referral of cases by the agencies. All members of the division should not be expected to attend these committee meetings; nevertheless the committee knows that a good many representatives of the agencies feel a keen interest in this project. The committee arranges to hold a series of open committee meetings on this subject, which any interested representatives of agencies in the division or the council may attend.

The board of a state or local public welfare agency regularly holds its meetings in public, open to representatives of the press and interested citizens.

A committee "hearing" is somewhat allied to the "open meeting." In the hearing, however, the committee usually addresses itself primarily to hearing statements and addressing questions to persons who appear before it, either voluntarily or at the request or summons (if it is a governmental body) of the committee. The hearing does not imply that the normal business of the committee will be transacted before an audience; the open committee meeting does carry more or less this implication.

6. There should be adequate preparation for and follow-up after meetings. The effectiveness of a committee meeting frequently bears a direct relationship to the amount and quality of the preparation for the meeting. Preparation involves: (a) Deciding when and where the meeting shall be held. (b) Preparing the agenda. (c) Preparing and sending out the notices of the meeting. (d) Gathering and compiling material. (e) Preparing material, such as draft reports, memoranda, and statements; statements of issues, alternatives, arguments pro and con, etc.; lists of nominees, and so on. (f) Studying material. This is frequently a function of all the committee members, whereas most of the foregoing activities are usually performed by the chairman, secretary, committee aide, or by members who have received special assignments.

The follow-up after meetings may involve: (a) Writing up and distributing the minutes. (b) Seeing that sub-committees or members are informed of assignments. (c) The carrying out of assignments by sub-committees or members. (d) Sometimes the chairman, committee aide, or secretary must follow up to make sure that special assignments are being carried out.

Tead makes the point that "if some overt actions are to be taken (such as submitting a budget, hiring a housekeeper, directing the alterations or repairs of a plant) some *member* of the committee as an individual should be specifically charged with the task." The committee "is fitted to take counsel, reach agreements, adopt policies . . ." but it "is *not* qualified for activity which requires individualized, clear-cut active performance of specific duties. . . . The work gets done only as the whole task on its operating side is broken down into a group of correlated but individualized duties and *each member is directed to specific tasks* so that his labors comprise a needed part of the whole assignment." [10]

7. **The committee should have adequate records.** The chief records of the committee are usually: a personnel list of the members of the committee; notices of meetings; agendas; minutes; and reports. The last three items are especially important.

THE AGENDA

Almost without exception, any committee meeting requires a written *agenda* or list of things to be done. The chairman and the committee aide (or secretary) should usually prepare the agenda, jointly; certainly both of them should be thoroughly familiar with the agenda before the meeting begins.

Items for the agenda may be drawn from: unfinished business from the last meeting; items previously scheduled by the committee for consideration on this date; matters suggested by a member of the committee; communications from outside the committee, which require consideration by the committee; and matters which the chairman, committee aide, or secretary believes ought to be listed for discussion or action. If possible, copies of the agenda should be distributed to all members present at the meeting.

Items on the agenda may be stated in various forms; the following are some of the possible variations:

FIGURE 14

VARIETIES OF AGENDA ITEMS

FORM OF AGENDA ITEM	ILLUSTRATION
a. *As a subject.*	Consideration of application for membership in the Council by the Pleasant View Day Nursery.

[10] Ordway Tead, *Democratic Administration* (New York, Association Press, 1945), p. 30.

| FORM OF AGENDA ITEM | ILLUSTRATION |

b. *As a question.*

Shall the Child Welfare Division of the Council recommend that the Council endorse House Bill 236, amendments to the Adoption Act?

c. *As a question, followed by a summary of arguments pro and con.*

Shall the Budget Committee recommend a study of the youth-serving and recreational agencies in the community?

IN FAVOR OF SUCH A STUDY:

1. Findings and recommendations needed for more intelligent budgeting.
2. Five or six of the agencies definitely want such a study.
3. Study is needed to clarify certain problems and areas of confusion.
4. Study would probably strengthen the hand of the Recreation Commission in its plans for further development of the city recreation program.
5. Study may shake the complacency of and get some dynamic action from certain large, expensive, but static agencies.

AGAINST SUCH A STUDY:

1. The cost — estimated at $15,000. Chest funds are "tight."
2. A substantial minority of the agencies are probably opposed to the idea of a study.
3. Opposition of certain community leaders to "having outside experts tell us what to do."
4. Do we need more facts — or do we need the courage to act on the facts that we have?
5. Will the report of the study be *used,* or will it be just "one more survey?"

d. *As two or more alternatives.*

In the case of the Child Health Society, shall the committee recommend:
1. a self-study
2. a study by an outside specialist
3. a self-study with some consultation by an outside specialist
4. a consultative field visit from the national agency

e. *As a recommendation (This form may be appropriate particularly for routine items. In writing up the minutes, later, it may be necessary only to change "recommended" to "voted.")*

Recommended, that the Board of Directors of the Community Chest approve the recommendations of the Budget Committee, as listed below, and that the executive director be authorized to communicate the amounts of the approved budgets to the member agencies.

The faculty of a school of social work developed an administrative device which might be utilized by boards or committees having many items which require at least review and routine approval. At the end of the agenda for the faculty meeting appeared a section designated, "For the Record." This contained draft minutes of items of report and proposed action, in more or less routine matters. Each member of the faculty looked over these items during the meeting; at the end of the meeting they were approved as a whole unless someone wished to call up a particular item for separate consideration and action.

One of the helpful contributions which students of group dynamics have made to the study of committees is the concept of the "hidden agenda." This hidden agenda is the sum of the personal attitudes, interests, and needs which the members of the committee bring to the committee meeting. In many meetings the hidden agenda may be much more potent than the formal written agenda which everyone can read! The committee leader or aide who recognizes the reality and importance of the hidden agenda will avoid oversimplifying the task of the committee and will be more understanding of the factors that are operative in the committee meeting.[11]

MINUTES

The minutes, or the official account of what was done at a meeting, are an important record and a major administrative tool in community organization. They should be carefully recorded so as to give an adequate account of the meeting; they should be signed and certified by the secretary of the meeting, and officially approved by the committee.

The minutes, plus any documents appended to them, should stand as a complete and self-contained record of the meeting. They should begin by identifying the body that is meeting; the date, hour, and place; and the presiding officer, members present, and members absent.

The minutes should ordinarily be chronological; they should follow the actual order of events. The minutes should contain a clear statement of all actions taken or decisions made — votes, agreements, appointments. In addition, the minutes should ordinarily give a summary of the discussions, which will make it clear *why* certain action

[11] For illustrations see Mildred C. Barry, "Community Organization Process: An Approach to Better Understanding," *Social Work Journal*, Vol. XXXI, October 1950, pp. 157–163; and Phyllis Bentley's novel, *Quorum* (New York, Macmillan, 1951).

was taken and which will cover certain matters that may have resulted in no specific action and yet may have been more important than any action which was taken at the meeting. Much of the art of good minute-taking lies in the selection of material to be recorded. In style, minutes should be clear, direct, factual, objective, and reasonably concise. When a long report or other document is submitted or discussed, this may be referred to briefly in the body of the minutes and the full document may be appended.

The secretary usually takes notes during the meeting — some of them perhaps on his copy of the agenda — and dictates or writes up the minutes in corrected form as soon as possible after the meeting. If the minute-taker is not participating actively in the discussion, he may sometimes find it possible, with a little practice, to record full sentences as he goes along, rather than fragmentary notes. Where the committee proceeds informally it may be helpful for the secretary to read to the group his draft minutes of important agreements, to be sure that he is correctly recording the sense of the meeting.[12]

In the typed or mimeographed minutes it is desirable to indicate by side headings the topics which have been considered. If possible, copies of the minutes should be distributed to all members of the committee. The official copy of the minutes should be signed by the secretary and kept in a permanent binder, together with appended materials.

REPORTS

Committee *reports* vary from brief oral reports of progress to formal, comprehensive, and carefully prepared documents. Sometimes a committee reports only when it has concluded its assignment; other committees may report monthly, annually, or at irregular intervals. If the committee has anything of importance to say, its report should be in writing. Committee reports should conform to the general rules and practices governing other reports.[13]

The report should be self-identifying; it should indicate the name of the reporting committee, its membership, to whom the report is addressed, the subject of the report, and the date. The material should

[12] Compare the method used in the Society of Friends (Quakers), where the minutes are written up, read, and approved as the business meeting proceeds. Howard H. Brinton, *Guide to Quaker Practice* (Wallingford, Penna., Pendle Hill, revised edition, 1950), pp. 30–34. Also Brinton, *Reaching Decisions: The Quaker Method.*

[13] Cf. John M. Pfiffner, *Research Methods in Public Administration* (New York: Ronald Press, 1940), Chapter XVI, "Preparing the Report," pp. 367–386.

be well organized and broken up by appropriate headings and sub-headings; if the document is lengthy, it should have a title page and table of contents. Detailed tables, documents, or other materials may often be appended rather than included in the body of the report. The style should be clear, untechnical, and readable. Findings, conclusions, and recommendations should be made particularly clear; if there are many of these, it may be desirable to summarize them at the beginning or end of the report.

A draft report should be prepared by an individual — the chairman, committee aide, secretary, or a committee member — usually on the basis of previous committee discussion regarding the substance of the items to be included. The draft should be sent to the committee members in advance of the committee meeting, so that they may study it beforehand and come prepared with suggestions as to revisions.

8. **The committee should develop into a cohesive group, with a sense of solidarity and group loyalty.** There is no formula and no magic for accomplishing this; it must be achieved through sustained and patient effort, and must come as a result of a gradual growth. A basic test of a good committee is expressed in this question: Is the committee a mere list of names, is it an aggregation of individuals, or is it a *group?* Regular attendance, free participation by all the members of the committee, good leadership, responsible execution of specific assignments, mutual acceptance and creative relationships among the members, an understanding of group process and group discussion — all these are elements in helping the committee to grow into an effective group. The community organization worker who is to work successfully with committees must learn that a good committee does not happen; it is the result of effort, growth, participation, and the delicate and complex interweaving of thinking, feeling, and action that makes up the group process.

9. **The performance of the committee should be periodically evaluated.** Sometimes such an evaluation is accomplished by the committee's report to the parent body. If not, the committee itself should probably undertake a self-evaluation periodically. If for any reason it seems impracticable to draw the whole committee into this process, an administrative evaluation may be made by the chairman and the committee aide, or by either of them.[14]

---

[14] The Outline for a Report on a Committee, Appendix C, suggests questions as a basis for both a descriptive and evaluative report on a committee. The principles suggested in this chapter also may be used as criteria in evaluation. For

10. When the committee has served its purpose, it should be discharged or disbanded. Every community organization agency should seek to keep its committees limited to an active working number performing necessary functions. An annual "committee inventory" or review and evaluation of all the agency's committees will be an additional safeguard in eliminating committees which have served their purpose or which are performing no useful function.

THE WORKER'S COMMITTEE RESPONSIBILITIES

Because the committee is so important an instrument of community organization, the community organization worker, like the agency executive, tends to become involved in a large and growing number of committee relationships, commitments, and responsibilities. The more effective he is as a committee member, the more these demands will tend to increase.

Any such worker will find, sooner or later, that he must limit his work-load of committee responsibilities. Two practical suggestions may be helpful in this connection. First, the worker will do well to maintain an index or list of the committees on which he serves or for which he acts as committee aide. For each committee, the salient facts should be given regarding its organization and functions, and the worker's relations to it. This index gives the worker a realistic summary of the nature and extent of his committee responsibilities. It will be useful in reviewing past and planning future activities, and in deciding whether or not to accept additional committee responsibilities and other assignments. Second, the worker, upon being asked to assume an additional committee responsibility may apply such tests as the following as an aid to arriving at a decision: How important is this committee? What is its relation to my job? Do I have some obligation to accept this assignment? What contribution am I qualified to make? *How much time will this committee assignment take?* If I take this on, what will have to give way? Am I interested in undertaking this assignment?

Committees are invaluable instruments of community organization. As Sheffield has said: "When committees are at their best they are valuable aids to administration, they contribute to the active kind of

---

other suggestions regarding the evaluation of committees, see: Trecker, *Group Process in Administration,* pp. 224–226; Trecker and Trecker, *Committee Common Sense,* ch. 15.

democracy which is our goal, and they enrich the lives of the people who belong to them." [15]

QUESTIONS AND PROBLEMS

1. Write a descriptive report on a social welfare committee. See Appendix C, Outline II, Part A.

2. If an agency or department is interested, one or more students may make a "committee inventory" for the organization, using or adapting the outline referred to above. Such an inventory may, of course, be undertaken also as a staff activity.

3. What are some of the advantages and disadvantages of committees?

4. Select some committee on which you have served or about which you can get fairly full information. Analyze this committee in terms of the principles suggested in this chapter. Try to evaluate it, using the outline in Appendix C, Outline II, Part B.

5. Attend a committee meeting and prepare an analysis of the strong and weak points of the meeting, from the standpoint of sound committee procedure.

6. What are some of the most common problems or difficulties encountered in respect to committees? How can these problems best be dealt with?

7. Interview a social worker who is a committee aide for some committee. What are his functions in reference to the committee?

8. Prepare an agenda for a committee meeting.

9. Criticize a set of minutes for some social welfare committee.

10. Write the minutes for a committee meeting. How well do they conform to the suggestions given in the chapter and in other readings on minutes?

SUGGESTIONS FOR READING

The most valuable single reference on committees for social workers or laymen interested in social welfare is the Treckers' *Committee Common Sense.* Sheffield's briefer handbook is excellent, also.

Case materials on committees will be found in the items by Barry, Bentley, King, Pfeiffer, and Van Valen.

For other related materials, see bibliography for ch. 20, under "Conference."

Barry, Mildred C., "Community Organization Process: An Approach to Better Understanding," *Social Work Journal,* Vol. XXXI, October 1950, pp. 157–163.

Bentley, Phyllis, *Quorum* (New York, Macmillan, 1951, 309 pp.). A

[15] Sheffield, *Making Committees Effective,* p. 2.

novel focused on the operation of a committee and reaching its climax in a committee meeting.

Blumenthal, Louis H., *How to Work with Your Board and Committees* (New York, Association Press, 1954, 64 pp.). "A guide to productive board-staff relations."

King, Clarence, *Your Committee in Community Action* (New York, Harper, 1952, 114 pp.). Case materials with brief comments.

Pfeiffer, C. Whit, "The Community Organization Worker in Action." In *The Job of the Community Organization Worker* (New York, Community Chests and Councils of America, and Association for the Study of Community Organization, 1948), pp. 15–24. Primarily a discussion of the community organization worker and committee process.

Routzahn, Mary Swain, *Better Board Meetings* (New York, National Publicity Council for Health and Welfare Services, 1952, 112 pp.).

Sheffield, Edward E., *Making Committees Effective* (Toronto, Ryerson Press, 1951, 46 pp.). An excellent handbook on committees.

Simpson, E. R., *The Mechanics of Committee Work: An Essay on the Tasks of a Committee Secretary* (Brussels, International Institute of Administrative Sciences, 1952, processed, 31 pp.). Number XI in a series of administrative monographs, undertaken by the Institute for the United Nations. (May be purchased through the Public Administration Service, Chicago.)

Sorenson, Roy, *The Art of Board Membership* (New York, Association Press, 1950, 160 pp.).

Street, *A Handbook for Social Agency Administration.* (See bibliography, ch. 16.) chs. 4, 5, 6.

Trecker, Audrey R. and Trecker, Harleigh B., *Committee Common Sense* (New York, Whiteside and Morrow, 1954, 158 pp.). An excellent non-technical guide to the effective use of committees.

Van Valen, Donald, "Community Organization, Manipulation or Group Process?" (NCSW, *Social Work in the Current Scene,* 1949, pp. 325–342).

23.

SOME GUIDING PRINCIPLES

———

PRINCIPLES OF COMMUNITY ORGANIZATION, in the sense in which the term is here used, are essentially generalized expressions of *rules of sound practice* in employing the process of community organization for social welfare. Principles are expressions of value judgments. Such formulations of values obviously have a large subjective element. Values differ between groups and between individuals within the same group. Moreover, there has been no explicit, comprehensive, or generally accepted formulation of basic ethical and social values by any representative group of community organization practitioners.

However, this does not mean that a formulation of principles of community organization must be merely the unsupported subjective opinions of one individual. There is a general test which may be applied to any such suggested principle. It is this: Is this principle in harmony with the spirit and purpose of social work in a democratic society?

Community welfare organization has been defined as the process of bringing about or maintaining adjustment between social welfare resources and social welfare needs. Now the adjustment of these needs and resources is not an end in itself; it is only one aspect of social work. The purpose of social work may be stated, broadly, as helping families and individuals to lead normal lives, in terms of health, education, work, recreation and spiritual development [1] or "helping human beings to find the opportunity and the incentive to make the most of themselves and so make the largest possible contribution to the progress and well-being of the whole society." [2]

[1] Porter R. Lee, *Treatment* (New York, Russell Sage Foundation, 1918), p. 3.
[2] Kenneth L. M. Pray, *Social Work in a Revolutionary Age*, pp. 229–30. Also in NCSW, 1946, p. 6.

These conceptions of social work are oriented to a *democratic* society; they would not be expressive of the aims or philosophy of a totalitarian or aristocratic state, for example. We are concerned with the dignity and worth, the freedom, the security, the participation, and the wholesome and abundant life of *every* individual; and this implies democracy.

We thus assume that democracy is the most desirable type of society and form of government. Most of us regard this assumption not merely as an act of faith but as deduction, from our own experience, from the recorded thoughts and experiences of others, and from the study of history.

The following pages contain a statement of 28 suggested principles of community organization.[3] They are grouped under seven headings:

Democracy and social welfare.

Community roots for community programs.

Citizen understanding, support, and participation, and professional service.

Cooperation.

Social welfare programs.

Adequacy, distribution, and organization of social welfare services.

Prevention.

DEMOCRACY AND SOCIAL WELFARE

1. **Social welfare agencies and services should be democratic in spirit, organization, and operation.** In particular, social welfare programs should lie within the ultimate control of the people. The field of social welfare should bring itself into closer harmony with democratic concepts, by divesting itself increasingly of the psychology of charity or philanthropy extended by one favored group to other persons in need; it should move toward the goal of social welfare programs maintained, for the most part, by the great body of citizens, as necessary functions of a democratic society.

This does not mean that all social welfare programs should operate under governmental auspices. There is an important place for the voluntary group, especially in the stages of pioneering, experimentation, or demonstration. This principle does mean that most basic,

[3] These owe much to Florence G. Cassidy's pioneer statement of "Principles of Community Organization," appended to the *Second Report of the Michigan Committee on the Study of Community Organization, for the Year 1939–1940*, Detroit, 1940, mimeographed.

accepted social welfare services should operate either under governmental auspices or under other forms of organization and support which will represent the large body of citizens. It means also that voluntary social welfare agencies should operate under some degree of governmental supervision, such as may be expressed in control of incorporation, licensing, visitation, inspection, power to require reports, and, under certain conditions, power to dissolve.

2. **In general, the support and control of social welfare programs should be representative of the whole population of the geogaphic areas within which these programs operate.** This principle has several corollaries.

First, it suggests that, generally speaking, social welfare agencies should be widely supported and that their boards should be representative of the entire community rather than being drawn primarily from limited higher-income groups, for example.

Second, this principle suggests that, as a general rule, *social welfare agencies should be community-wide in auspices and service.* This does not mean that there is no place for a "sectarian" agency under specialized auspices. However, this principle suggests that the burden of proof is on those who propose a sectarian agency, in the sense of an agency controlled by a specialized interest group or serving a specialized clientèle such as members of a racial or religious group, organized labor, veterans, etc.

Third, social welfare agencies should not be controlled by special economic or political interest-groups. Specifically, social welfare agencies should not support or be affiliated with political parties. Also, partisan politics should have no place in the administration of public welfare programs.

Fourth, we must recognize the right of a membership organization to extend certain social welfare services to its own membership. We must recognize also the right of a concerned group — even a small group — to attempt to initiate a social welfare program or service which they believe is needed in the community. Such a program is of concern to the community as a whole, if the welfare of dependent clients is involved or if community support is sought for the program.

Fifth, self-perpetuating boards are not in harmony with democratic principles, and are usually undesirable.

3. **There should be participation in the direction and operation of social welfare programs by all groups affected by them.** Such groups include those who support the service; those who serve on boards, committees, or as working volunteers; those who serve as paid em-

ployees, professional and non-professional; and those who are consumers of the service.

The fact that there is as yet relatively little consumer representation in social welfare agencies — outside of certain group work agencies — does not affect the validity of this principle or its soundness as a goal to be striven for.

A corollary of this principle is that in working out inter-group problems, the effort should be made to assure the opportunity of participation by every group that has a stake in the situation.

4. Social welfare agencies and programs should exemplify and promote community solidarity and the practice of democracy, and should seek to overcome divisive influences which threaten the well-being of the community and the vitality of democratic institutions. In the social welfare services in a democracy, discrimination and segregation should be avoided; integration and mutual acceptance should be promoted.

COMMUNITY ROOTS FOR COMMUNITY PROGRAMS

5. A continuing local community welfare program should have its roots in the community. It is generally desirable for local community services to be indigenous, grass-roots developments rather than to be imposed from without. Whenever possible, then, a community welfare program should have its origin in a need felt by the community or by some substantial number of persons in the community; and there should be vital community participation, and usually essential community control, in its development.

Federal and state programs will, of course, operate in the community; but the people of the community have representation in the control of such programs.

The nation has also the right — and many people believe, the duty — to establish a national minimum standard of living as a right of all families and individuals. Such a national minimum would, of course, apply to every community within the nation.

Sometimes the recognition of a need and the concern for providing a service arises outside the community. An outside group may be concerned for a neglected group within the community (children, the aged, a minority group, the unemployed, etc.), and may initiate a program for them in the face of indifference or even hostility on the part of the dominant group in the community. But, in the long run, unless a resident constituency can be developed — from supporting groups or from the consumers or both — the program will probably not have a satisfactory long-time foundation.

CITIZEN UNDERSTANDING, SUPPORT, AND PARTICIPATION, AND PROFESSIONAL SERVICE

6. **Every continuing social welfare program should be based upon the understanding and the moral or financial support of a substantial body of citizens.** In the long run, every social welfare program, governmental or voluntary, needs to be understood if it is to be supported; and it needs, moreover, a constituency of interested citizens, even if this must begin as nothing more than a carefully selected mailing list.

7. **So far as possible, every social welfare program should enlist active and vital citizen participation and leadership. "Self-help" by citizen or consumer groups should be encouraged and fostered.** Such media as directive boards, advisory and cooperating committees, volunteers, and membership or other constituency groups may be utilized in enlisting citizen participation. Generally, such participation should be as widespread and representative as possible.

The concept of self-help, which has been so much stressed in relation to community development, is broadly applicable to community welfare organization. In general, resident-participation and consumer-participation in social welfare programs should be encouraged, from the standpoint both of democratic principle and of expediency — that is, the direct involvement in the program of those who have the primary stake in its results.

Certain corollaries to this principle are:

First, a completely hierarchical organization should generally be avoided in social welfare, even in governmental programs. Directive or advisory boards are of basic value and importance.

Second, active lay participation is vitally important to sound community organization. Ordinarily, the professional worker should perform no functions that can be performed equally well by lay participants.

Third, it is usually desirable to spread active participation to as large a proportion as possible of the membership, constituency, or consumer group.

8. **Fundamentally, the role of the professional community organization worker is to provide professional skill, assistance, and creative leadership in enabling citizen groups and organizations to**

achieve social welfare objectives. Basic decisions regarding program and policy should be made by lay groups — by the community, or the constituency or their representatives — not by the professional. This is the accepted pattern of democratic organization. While the community organization worker plays a variety of roles in different situations, he is basically concerned with enabling citizen expression and leadership to achieve community organization goals, and not with control, domination, or manipulation.

COOPERATION

9. Voluntary cooperation is the key to effective community organization. Fundamentally, and with rare exceptions, sound community organization must be based upon mutual understanding, voluntary acceptance, and mutual agreement. Community organization, if it is to be in harmony with democratic principles, cannot be regimentation; it should not be imposed from without, but must be derived from the inner freedom and will-to-unite of those who practice it.

10. The spirit of cooperation rather than competition, and the practice of coordination of effort should characterize the operation of social welfare agencies within a geographical area or a functional field. Cecil C. North points out that, if a community program is to be achieved, "In the attitude of the agencies toward one another, the spirit of mutual assistance must predominate over that of competition." [4]

11. Community organization at its best is characterized by coordinated and sustained programs attacking major problems rather than by a series of separate and unrelated efforts. The history of community organization demonstrates that the most effective advances are made through cooperative effort, directed toward objectives of major importance, rather than through sporadic efforts by various groups.

12. Invoking the application of authority or compulsion may sometimes be necessary in community organization; but it should be used as little as possible, for as short a time as possible, and only as a last resort. When compulsion must be applied, it should be followed as soon as possible by resumption of the cooperative process. Sometimes — though rarely — it is sound community organization to invoke the application of authority and the use of compulsion to attain a social welfare objective.

However, the qualifications stated in the principle are important.

[4] Cecil Clare North, *The Community and Social Welfare*, p. 20.

Compulsion always represents a less desirable method. It is justifiable chiefly where action must be taken to protect the health or welfare of the general public or of some group of helpless or dependent persons, where the situation is emergent, and where no other method will serve.

For example: A state welfare department, after two years of unsuccessful efforts at education, initiates legal procedure for the dissolution by court order of a babies' home which has maintained children under extremely bad conditions and which has refused to follow requests, demands, or orders from the department.

The state department is working for the improvement of standards in the babies' home; it is performing a community organization function. But these standards are not a mere written document; they have to do with the lives and health of helpless infants.

It would be more satisfactory if the state department could succeed in "educating" the institution, and enlisting the voluntary cooperation of the superintendent and board in making the necessary improvements. But there comes a point where the department may have to abandon education and cooperation and invoke authority for the sake of protecting the babies. So after the proper series of requests, demands, orders, and warnings, the department seeks a court order which will close the institution and remove the babies from this dangerous and unwholesome environment.

On the basis of the facts as stated, this is a sound use of the process of community organization.

One further point may be suggested. Let us suppose that the members of the board of the institution are shocked into action by the drastic step taken by the department. At the time of the court hearing the attorney for the board produces testimony that the board has investigated the situation, that they have dismissed the former superintendent and are prepared to employ a well-qualified person as his successor, and that they are ready and willing to cooperate with the state department in giving proper care to their charges. If the department is convinced of the good faith of the board, it will probably be willing to withdraw from its attempt to close the home, and to resume cooperative relationships. This illustrates the statement in the principle that when compulsion must be applied it should be followed as soon as possible by the resumption of a cooperative process.

SOCIAL WELFARE PROGRAMS

13. **Social welfare programs should be based upon and responsive to needs. Such programs should be initiated, developed, modified, and terminated on the basis of the needs of the recipients or potential recipients of the service and on the basis of the availability of other comparable services. When the need for a service is past, the program should be modified or terminated. There is no place for "vested interests" in the field of social welfare.** As has been mentioned in chapter 3 there is no completely objective means of measuring the needs of a community or other area. Porter Lee's "elements of normal life" (referred to earlier in this chapter) and the "community yardsticks" suggested in chapter 2 should be helpful in appraising such needs. But value judgments, and therefore subjective judgments, will necessarily enter in.

14. **So far as possible, social welfare programs should be the product of careful planning, on the basis of ascertained facts, rather than an expression of guesswork, "hunches," or mere trial and error.** The importance of factfinding and planning in social welfare has already been discussed. However, in the present state of social research, it is frequently impossible to obtain in advance a complete or precise answer to the question, how valuable will this particular program be to a specific community or group of potential consumers. Pioneering, the sense of social adventure, and well-thought-out experimentation are to be encouraged in the field of social welfare.

15. **The fullest possible use should be made of existing social welfare resources, before creating new resources. It is often necessary to establish a new service, a new program, or a new agency; but the burden of proof is upon such a proposal.** Along with the utilizing of present resources must go recognition of the fact that these resources may sometimes need extensive overhauling before they will meet certain needs.

16. **A social welfare agency, institution, or program should be such a size as to be an efficient and economical unit of organization and operation. So far as possible, an agency should be limited to an area in which it can give effective service.** Little research seems to have been done on the subject of the optimum size of various types of social welfare agencies. An agency may be either too small or too large. A one-man or two-man community center or casework agency in a large city may be too small to justify all that is involved in operat-

ing a separate agency. Where this is true, combinations of agencies should be effected.

An agency may also be too large — whether in terms of number and variety of services it offers, the number of consumers it serves, or the territory which it seeks to cover.

A public casework agency is usually charged by statute with serving a county or city. If the city or county is large, the agency must manage as well as it can with a mass load, and must cope with the familiar problems of large organizations, using such devices as departmentalization and district organization to overcome the handicap of its size.

A voluntary agency with aggressive leadership may have a tendency to expand continually; but there is a point of diminishing returns in such expansion. It was J. Prentice Murphy who once spoke of the "invisible walls" that bounded the case load which could be served effectively by a foster family placement agency.

17. The programs, functions, and services of social welfare agencies should be conceived of as dynamic, flexible, and subject to change — not as static, crystallized, or unchangeable. This principle is basic to sound community organization. Social welfare agencies and programs *must* be responsive to the changing conditions, problems, and needs of community life. "Flow is king," as Walter Lippmann once paraphrased the teachings of an ancient Greek philosopher.

Teachings regarding the inviolability of the "function of the agency" are sound only if they are united with the recognition that *agency functions may be changed* and often should be changed, through proper community organization procedures, to meet changed needs.

Some of the foes of agency flexibility may be: tradition; large investments in buildings; self-perpetuating boards; conservative, timid, complacent, and unimaginative management; and general "institutional hardening of the arteries." Fresh, vital, far-visioned, creative leadership, on boards and in executive positions, is likely to be the strongest single factor making for flexibility in programs and agencies.

18. Any social welfare program should be constantly viewed, by its sponsors as well as by others, in the light of the total situation of the geographic area or functional field. No social welfare program can be isolated from the social welfare needs and resources of the community as a whole. The welfare of the whole community is always more important than the interest or the well-being of any one agency in the community.

ADEQUACY, DISTRIBUTION, AND ORGANIZATION OF SOCIAL WELFARE SERVICES

19. **The total social welfare services available in a community or other area should be adequate in quantity and quality to meet the social welfare needs of the area.** If it asked, who shall decide upon the adequacy of the services, the answer would seem to be, the people of the community, partly through the instrumentalities of government and partly through a democratically organized voluntary body such as a community welfare council.

20. **There should be an overall social welfare program for a community, and not merely a number of unrelated agencies, services, and programs. Such a program should avoid both "overlapping and overlooking." It should seek to achieve effective, efficient, and economical disposition of social welfare resources, meeting social needs as fully and effectively as possible, and eliminating duplication of programs or services.** The functions and services of individual agencies should be clearly defined, and should bear some logical relationship to the overall community welfare program.

Some of the basic questions that arise in reference to a community welfare program are these: What unmet needs are there? What duplications of service exist? How effective are existing services? How effectively are they coordinated? How well are they understood by the community? How adequately are they supported?

21. **The social welfare services of an area should be distributed among the whole population of the area in proportion to their needs. Special care should be taken to see that facilities and services are made available to members of minority racial, nationality, or other groups, and to neighborhoods and communities with special problems, in proportion to their needs.** Services should be extended to those who need them, in proportion to the incidence of need and not merely on the basis of size of population. A section of the city, inhabited largely by low-income families, or a minority group composed largely of such families, may need much more in the way of health, casework, and recreational facilities, per 10,000 population, than is needed for the community as a whole.

22. **Both governmental and voluntary agencies are needed in the field of social welfare. Governmental agencies should normally provide social welfare services which are accepted by the public as a whole: those which involve permanent or long-time care, extensive**

programs, or large financial outlay; and those which involve the use of authority or compulsion. Voluntary agencies should normally provide social welfare services which seek to "bridge the gap between need and statutory provision for need"; which are accepted or understood by only limited groups within the community; which serve special sectarian, racial, nationality or other similar groups; which are experimental or demonstrational in nature; or which involve a substantial measure of social action or character education. The inclusion of "character education" as a desirable function of voluntary agencies reflects what appears to be the prevailing opinion in this country: that we do not wish government to go much beyond the law or the citizenship education of the public schools in engaging in systematic ethical or "character" education. We prefer to have youth organizations such as the Boy Scouts and Girl Scouts, for example, operate under voluntary auspices rather than run the risk of a governmentally directed or politically dominated "youth movement."

23. In general, there should be voluntary citizens organizations paralleling major public welfare services, and concerned with the development and maintenance of sound public welfare programs and standards. The experience of the statewide citizens' associations and of statewide and national agencies in specialized fields points rather clearly to this principle as applicable under the American system of government, at least. Governmental agencies are necessarily concerned primarily with the administration of their respective programs. The electorate is not well acquainted with specific governmental programs; legislative assemblies are concerned with many different subjects, legislators are involved in political activities, and few of them have the time or inclination to become really well informed regarding specific public welfare programs. Independent, non-political citizens' organizations are needed, concerned with the integrity and development of the public welfare services and ready to study, educate, criticize, promote, defend, attack, or fight for legislative and other objectives, as the need may be.

24. The organization and administration of social welfare services should be as simple as practicable.[5] Simplicity in the organization and administration of social welfare services is not easily attained. Some of the factors that militate against simplicity are: the size of many communities and population groups which are served; the complexity of modern community life; the large degree of autonomy ex-

[5] *Health, Welfare, and Leisure Time Activities: Post-War Planning Report of the Syracuse Council of Social Agencies*, Syracuse, mimeographed.

ercised by the several states; our tradition of freedom for voluntary groups; and tradition and vested interests.

Some of the practical ways of attaining greater simplicity of social welfare organization and administration are these: (a) In many cases, one agency instead of several may perform a particular function. Most counties would probably benefit immeasurably from a single, well-administered, integrated county welfare department administering public assistance, various services to children, and a number of related services. Among voluntary agencies, many mergers could be effected with advantage to consumers and communities, and without surrender to any policy of ruthless or wholesale consolidation. (b) The functions of each agency should be clearly defined. (c) An overall community welfare program and long-time planning for rational community welfare patterns will be a major constructive force. (d) Through community information and referral bureaus and other cooperative devices it should be made as easy as possible for an individual who needs social service to find out what social welfare services are available and which agency is the appropriate one to help him with his particular problem. (e) A conscious effort should be made by all social welfare agencies and leaders to keep organization structure simple and rational. (f) "Study to keep things simple" would be a sound rule for all social welfare administrators. Unremitting efforts are needed, to avoid useless administrative formalities; to reduce the appalling numbers of documents; to keep techniques, machinery and "standard operating procedure" in their place; to talk and write clear and simple English; and to eliminate the clutter of needless red tape. (g) Perhaps the most effective contribution of all would be for executives and workers to maintain a basic, uncluttered *simplicity of spirit*, and sense of human values even amidst the noise and whirl of the machinery of large organizations.

25. If a social welfare service can be equally well administered by an agency on a lower or higher geographical level, local administration, or administration on the lower level, is to be preferred because it is closer to the people who receive the service. In the case of most locally administered public welfare services, there should be statewide leadership and supervision united with local administration. Lord Bryce has said that this idea of administration on lower rather than higher levels is an "American dogma." It rests, however, upon common sense and experience. Programs of social welfare must be taken to the local communities, where people live. Services should be readily accessible. Moreover, it seems desirable that most of these services should "belong to" the local community and should not be mere hierarchical extensions of state or national agencies.

In the case of most public welfare services, however, the county, or a group of counties, is likely to be the smallest desirable territorial unit of organization, except that a city of considerable size should usually constitute a separate unit.

26. The federative principle is widely applicable in community organization. Federation means united effort for doing those things that can best be done together. Federation implies a large degree of individual autonomy, with voluntary joint efforts in relation to common concern. Federation in social welfare offers a middle ground between amalgamation on the one hand and separation or independent and un-related units on the other. Federation has peculiar pertinence to the American scene, where there are many autonomous voluntary agencies and where joint effort is needed also by both governmental and volun-tary agencies. Federation may exemplify the principle of unity through diversity. Many of the most impressive results that have thus far been seen in community welfare organization have been attained through federated forms of organization — community chests, community wel-fare councils, national agencies, and so on.

One aspect of federation must always be remembered: *Federation and complete autonomy are incompatible.* Some limitation upon free-dom is the price of the benefits of united effort. This is true all the way from the United Nations down to a community chest in a city of 25,000.

Where groups are represented in an inter-group body, the rep-resentatives should carry on a "two-way, from-and-to process," of reporting, interpretation, and expression, between the respective mem-ber groups and the inter-group body. The representative should be-come the chief means by which his group plays an active and vital part in the life and activities of the inter-group body.[6] The more careful observance and application of this principle would bring greater vitality to many federated efforts.

27. Leadership in community organization in a geographical area or functional field implies a conscious and persistent effort to bring about such a development, alignment, and mobilization of social welfare resources as will meet most effectively and efficiently the social welfare needs of that unit. This is likely to involve the necessity of bringing about the creation of new agencies and programs,

---

[6] Wilbur I. Newstetter, "The Social Intergroup Work Process," NCSW, 1947, pp. 205–217.

and the realignment and modification and in some cases the termination of existing programs. These are tasks which sound community organization leadership cannot shirk. These tasks should be carried out in a democratic and cooperative spirit. A majority is not identical with the whole community; and the rights of minorities should be zealously safeguarded. Due regard should be paid to the autonomy and freedom of decision of individual agencies and groups and to the importance of the time element in bringing about far-reaching changes. At the same time there should be a clear recognition that the welfare and interests of the community as a whole must not be subordinated to the interests of any special group.

PREVENTION

28. **Social welfare programs should become increasingly concerned with prevention. Cure and rehabilitation are socially more valuable than mere continued care; prevention, in turn, is more valuable than cure. "Much for care, more for cure, most for prevention" is a sound slogan and a sound principle of community organization.** Within certain limits, social prevention, like public health, is purchasable. We have enough funded knowledge and understanding today, if we will only use it, to prevent a great volume of need and distress which now claims the attention of social welfare agencies. Social welfare agencies and their leaders should be concerned with the building and maintenance of a more perfect democratic social-economic order, as well as with the provision of specific social services for those who are now in need of such services.

QUESTIONS AND PROBLEMS

1. Compare one of the formulations of principles listed in the bibliography and the formulation in this chapter. Consider: scope, general point of view, ideas expressed, content, conflicts of ideas, issues raised, etc.

2. Consider critically the formulation of principles in this chapter. What additions, deletions, and modifications would you propose?

3. Is it a sound principle that "there should be participation in the direction and operation of social welfare programs by all groups affected by them?" If so, what are the implications for (a) staff representation on boards, (b) consumer representation on boards, (c) other forms of staff and consumer participation in control, policy-determination, and direction of programs? (See Ordway Tead, *Democratic Administration*.)

4. Are lay boards, generally speaking, an essential and valuable factor or

a necessary evil in social welfare? What should be the functions of boards? What should be the place of directive or advisory boards in public welfare agencies?

5. Do we have volunteers chiefly because we haven't enough money to pay sufficient professional workers, or would we use volunteers even if financial pressure did not make it necessary? What are the unique contributions of volunteers, if any? What, if anything, can they do that professionals could not do?

6. How would you apply principles of community organization in the following cases:

a. In a small company mining town bad conditions exist in housing, health, recreation, etc. A committee of a state conference on social welfare discusses attempting to obtain a foundation grant to initiate a demonstration program of community improvement in this community. A member of the committee asks what would be the probable attitude of the company toward such a program. "Indifference — or at most, bored acquiescence," another committee member replies. "It's not even certain that the people of the community would vote for the program unless a lot of educational work were done." "Should we force such a program on the community if the community doesn't want it?" the first member asks.

b. A large voluntary casework agency has chiefly untrained personnel, poor standards of work, and highly regimented administrative practices. The secretary of the Family and Children's Division of the Community Welfare Council has worked with the agency, for some years, without success, in an effort to enlist their interest in improving their standards. A committee of the Division considers: Should the Council recommend pressure from the Chest through the Budget Committee? Or would this be a violation of the agency's freedom and autonomy?

c. With the rise of community chests, the former "members" of (that is, contributors to) individual agencies have largely passed out of the picture. As a result, many agency boards are now self-perpetuating. This is not usually considered a democratic pattern. What can be done to develop more democratic patterns of organization?

d. A social welfare leader urges drastic reduction in the number of separate social welfare agencies. He advocates: (1) consolidation of most local governmental public welfare agencies in a county department of welfare; (2) amalgamation of practically all voluntary agency casework services under one large casework agency, with adequate staff, districts, specialized medical, psychological, and psychiatric service, etc.; (3) amalgamation of most voluntary institutional recreational agencies (YMCA, YWCA, settlements, community centers) under one large agency which would then attempt to supplement the public recreational program, and locate or develop facilities in special geographical areas of need.

e. The late Robert P. Lane once said: "If the slate were wiped clean of all social and health agencies, for any large community, no sane person would ever conceivably lay out the pattern of agencies and services that we have today." Most persons who are well-informed about social welfare would probably agree. — Suppose a community of a given population could "start from scratch" in developing its social welfare agencies and services. What are some of the major improvements it might make in its social welfare patterns?

SUGGESTIONS FOR READING

Among the Basic References, explicit statements of principles will be found particularly in the texts of Johns and De Marche and Ross; and (in relation to community welfare planning) in the volume by Buell and associates.

Three of the references below (those listed under Dunham, Tead, and Trecker) are statements of principles for other aspects of social work, but with implications also for the practice of community organization.

Community Chests and Councils of America, *Community Planning for Social Welfare: A Policy Statement* (New York, 1950, 15 pp.).

Dunham, Arthur, "Administration of Social Agencies," SWYB, 1949, pp. 20–21.

Greater Boston Community Survey, Conducted by the Committee of Citizens to Survey the Social and Health Needs and Services of Greater Boston (Boston, 1949, 148 pp.). See especially pt. II, Principles of Action, and section VII, Planning and Financial Services.

Howard, Donald S., "The Common Core of Social Work in Different Countries," (NCSW, *Social Welfare Forum*, 1951, pp. 19–36).

McNeil, C. F., "Community Organization for Social Welfare," (SWYB, 1954, p. 123).

Miles, Arthur P., *American Social Work Theory: A Critique and a Proposal* (New York, Harper, 1954, 246 pp.), pp. 200–203.

North, Cecil Clare, *The Community and Social Welfare* (New York, McGraw-Hill, 1931, 359 pp., OP), pp. 20–24.

Pray, "When Is Community Organization Social Work?" (See bibliography, ch. 3.)

Tead, Ordway, *The Art of Administration* (New York, McGraw-Hill, 1951, 223 pp.), ch. 12.

Trecker, Harleigh B. *Social Group Work: Principles and Practices* (New York, Whiteside, rev. ed., 1955, 442 pp.). Includes chapter on principles of group work.

United Nations, *Social Progress Through Community Development*. (See bibliography, ch. 15.) See Basic Elements of Community Development, pp. 8–13.

24.

FRONTIERS OF COMMUNITY ORGANIZATION

————

THE ESSENCE OF COMMUNITY ORGANIZATION

THE DISCUSSION OF COMMUNITY organization in this book may be thus summarized:

1. Community welfare organization is the process of bringing about and maintaining a balance between social welfare needs and social welfare resources in a community or other geographical area.

2. Community organization expresses itself through the channels of: factfinding; program development; establishment and development of standards; development of coordination; education; and enlistment of support and participation.

3. Community organization operates on and between all geographic levels.

4. Community welfare organization is a pervasive process: all social welfare organizations and many other groups make use of it.

5. The practice of community organization involves certain methods and skills. Among these methods are factfinding, analysis, planning, conference, consultation, organization, education, and legislative promotion. The committee is a tool frequently used in community organization.

6. Community organization involves cooperation of groups and individuals, and the participation of both laymen and professionals.

7. Professional service in community organization is based upon the possession of certain knowledge, skills, and attitudes. The equipment of the professional involves personal qualities, education, experience, and a personal and professional philosophy. The role of the

professional includes the functions of the "enabler," the specialized consultant and practitioner, and the creative participant.

8. There are principles of community organization oriented to a democratic ideology and expressing value-judgments as to what is sound community organization. Some of the basic ideas that underlie such principles are: community organization should be democratic in spirit and practice; community social welfare programs and agencies should be rooted in the community; social welfare undertakings require citizen understanding, support, participation, and leadership; voluntary cooperation is the key to effective community organization; the federative principle is widely applicable; welfare programs and services should be developed, modified, distributed, and operated on the basis of needs; programs and services should be dynamic, flexible, and subject to change in the light of changing needs; governmental and voluntary social welfare agencies are both essential and are complementary; community organization should lay increasing stress on prevention.

THE IMPORTANCE OF COMMUNITY ORGANIZATION

COMMUNITY ORGANIZATION FOR SOCIAL welfare is important because it deals with:

The lives and welfare of human beings.

Human relationships.

In particular, group and intergroup relationships.

The community and community life.

The achievement of the "good life."

The effecting and influencing of social change.

Democracy, not only as a form of political and social organization, but as a way of life.

The participation of the individual in group activities, in community living, in a democratic order.

Acting together, cooperation, integration of thinking and action, the spirit of community, and translation into practice of the ideal of human brotherhood.

Community organization, then, has a place in the achievement of democratic living, a world order based upon cooperation rather than war, and the good life for the people of the world.

American democracy is based upon the willing cooperation of free individuals and groups. Its basic problem is to work out the concepts of democracy, in practice, equitably and effectively, in terms of co-operative living. To this undertaking community organization has a considerable contribution to make.

THE FRONTIERS OF COMMUNITY ORGANIZATION

WHAT ARE THE FRONTIERS OF COMMUNITY organization, as we enter the second half of the twentieth century? At what points and in what directions should we move? The following seem to be some of these frontiers:

1. There appear to be several *new emphases in community organization*. There is a growing acceptance of *community organization as a generic process* of social work, rather than something that is a specialized property or function of chests and councils or any other types of specialized agencies. There appears to be an *increased interest today in community organization* on the part of both social workers and laymen, a somewhat better understanding of it, and more acceptance of its validity as a professional process. There is an emphasis on *citizen participation and citizen leadership* in social welfare. At the same time, there is more emphasis on *professionalization* among community organization practitioners.

2. There is a new interest in working out the *theoretical bases of community organization* and in identifying and defining more precisely its concepts, its principles, and its relationships to the social sciences.

3. There are new *implications of community welfare organization for special settings and for various geographical levels*. There are new problems, new insights, new learnings as community organization is consciously and thoughtfully applied to any "new" field — or field of increased importance — in social welfare. For example, we are learning a good deal today about community organization for the aging, for the prevention and control of juvenile delinquency, and for vocational rehabilitation.

Beyond these areas that are clearly recognized as social welfare, there are marginal or related areas of social activity. What are the implications of community welfare organization for such areas as: city, town, and regional planning; housing; neighborhood redevelopment; community councils; "block" and neighborhood organization; rural improvement programs; community development; cooperative communities, under religious auspices or otherwise; resettlement programs; programs of organized labor; education, and especially adult education and "mass education;" informal education for youth ("work camps" and other summer programs, for example); economic development; consumers cooperatives; improvement of intercultural relations; religious and interfaith organization; health and medical care; civic organization and citizens' movements?

What are the directions which community welfare organization should take in respect to geographic levels other than local? How can more effective statewide community organization and planning be developed? How many and what kinds of national agencies do we need? What further cooperative patterns and what realignments should be worked out on the national level, and how can national agencies, governmental and voluntary, make their greatest contribution to our national life? What are the greatest opportunities for the application of community organization in international social welfare, and what contribution can be made to international social welfare by American social work and American community organization?

4. *Community development*, particularly in its application to newly developing societies, is one of the most exciting and rewarding frontiers on which community organization is active today. The focus on improvement of total community life, the inter-professional team, self-help, the multi-purpose community worker, and experimentation with new or modified techniques and forms of organization — all these are aspects of community development. Practitioners and teachers of community organization face these questions: What contribution can social work — and, in particular, community welfare organization — make to community development? Basically, what have we to offer? How can we best equip and train social workers to make their most effective contributions in this area? Is it possible that we may see the rise of a new type of professional worker, a generalist in community development?

5. Closely allied to both of the preceding topics is the challenge to social workers to produce some "*social generalists*" and "*social statesmen*."

Hertha Kraus has suggested:

. . . that we stand ready to claim and assume *our rightful role as social generalists* — among many specialists — willing and able to help transform a competitive into a social economy. We should rebalance our traditional knowledge and skill, and perfect it so as to become wiser generalists, more imaginative social designers, more

convincing interpreters of valid design, more effective renewers of
outdated service policies and patterns.[1]

Donald S. Howard speaks of two "new horizons for social work":

The first of these is the gradual enlargement of our technical
fields of competence and the growing realization that there are still
further fields in which we — or if not we then some other profession
— must develop a competence. The second is the movement of
social work away from a patching up operation to more constructive
kinds of activity . . .

The important new role for social work which I envisage involves the ability to analyze broad economic, social, physical, educational, and cultural aspects of world, national, and community
life; to appraise their effect upon the welfare of the men and women
and children concerned; to ascertain ways in which these broad areas
of life may better promote the well-being of individuals and communities; and to bring together the professions and resources needed
to improve them. The whole, which would add up to a sort of social
statesmanship, might be termed "social organization" in that it
would bring to the solution of broad social questions a combination
of skills, much as "community organization" brings a defined group
of skills to the solution of community problems.[2]

6. Community organization shares with other areas of social work
the need for *a better factual foundation,* and therefore for more *adequate research.* At too many points today we depend upon opinions
and guesswork rather than established facts. Research is needed in
respect to the whole area of social welfare. We need, among other
things, an intensification of the study of group and community behavior as well as of individual behavior.

The principles of "action research" ("research which underlies
social action") have been ably formulated by Genevieve W. Carter.
The final principle suggested is that "An action research project
should result in recommendations for social change." [3]

[1] Hertha Kraus, "The Future of Social Work: Some Comments on Social Work
Function," *Compass,* Vol. XXIX, January 1948, p. 7. The italics are not in the
original.
[2] Donald S. Howard, "New Horizons for Social Work," *Compass,* Vol. XXVIII,
November 1947, p. 9. (Published by American Association of Social Workers.)
The point of view developed in this volume does not, of course, limit community
organization to "community problems," but sees it as a process which may operate
on or between any geographic levels.
[3] Genevieve W. Carter, "Action Research in Social Planning," *Social Work Journal,*
Vol. XXXIII, January 1952, pp. 23–28.

The importance of basic and evaluative research has been stressed. In this whole area of research, we need to draw more largely upon the experience, the points of view, and the research skills of the social sciences. The practice of social work is rooted in the social and psychological sciences, and social work research and social-science and psychological research should form a closer working partnership than has sometimes been true in the past.[4]

7. Community welfare organization must become more concerned with *the broad strategy of health and welfare planning,* as distinguished from the details of coordination and inter-agency adjustments. There is a need for some basic re-designing of social welfare patterns, for some major overhauling of agency structure and programs, and for much greater emphasis on social prevention rather than fair success in rehabilitation, cure, or care.

A good deal of community organization has been, in effect, "playing around the edges" of basic problems instead of driving boldly to the center. Community organization agencies have frequently devoted a disproportionate amount of attention to factfinding, education, fundraising, and a mild degree of coordination, and have failed to grapple with the basic problems of program development, standards, and real integration of effort.

8. There are *major problems of social welfare policy* that have a bearing on community organization, and other *problems of community organization policy* as such. Some examples of such problems are these: What social welfare services do we want? How much social welfare can we afford? What should be the major emphases and priorities? What should be the functions and relationships of governmental and voluntary agencies? What shall we do about the financing of voluntary agencies? To what extent do we want cooperative or federated financing? To what extent do we prefer that major health and welfare agencies should finance themselves through separate and individual efforts? How can we develop the most effective machinery for health and welfare planning? What should be the relationships between organizations and programs for health and welfare planning and for joint financing? How can we develop greater precision and better tools for measuring financial ability and the needs and results of health and welfare planning?

9. As is the case with any developing professional specialization, community welfare organization has a host of *technical problems* that

---

[4] See David G. French, *An Approach to Measuring Results in Social Work.* (New York, Columbia University Press, 1952.)

need solution. Methods, skills, and techniques, organization structure, committee operation, administration, and records all need improvement. Along with this must go more work in hammering out working principles and standards of community organization.

Personnel is the key to the practice of community organization. Professional education, in turn, is the key to the provision of competent professional personnel. How can we develop enough well-trained workers for this type of service? More adequate recruitment and better professional education and training in community organization are two of the basic needs. This is part of the broader problem of education for social work, in general. But there are also special problems connected with the training of those who are to practice community organization — problems of advanced courses, field work, research, and so on.

Great strides have been made during the past ten years in the development of a technical and professional *literature;* but even so, scarcely more than a good beginning has been made. There is a special need for a variety of usable community organization case records, case problems, and documents for teaching purposes; for materials interpreting community organization to lay citizens; and for materials concerning community organization on state, national, and international levels.

10. Among the greatest problems that face social work and community organization are the problems of *communication and interpretation.* As Robert MacRae has written:

> We have learned to design good campaign posters. We have learned to stir some people's emotions either of sympathy or fear. What we have largely failed to do is to interpret to the mass of citizens their personal stake in strong social welfare programs. Understanding continues to rest all too widely on a base of patronizing charity. It is imperative that we deepen that understanding. Social welfare will gain status when we discipline its sentimentalism and communicate its significance to a good society.[5]

Closely related to this need for better communication is the need for *more adequate citizen leadership and participation* in community welfare organization. Only as this is achieved does community welfare organization become really integrated into the democratic process.

11. Finally, there seems to be a trend in the direction of the

[5] Robert MacRae, "New Wine and Old Bottles," *Community,* Vol. 30, May 1955, p. 175.

broadening and democratizing of community organization for social welfare. Evidences of this are found in the increased interest in neighborhood and other forms of local community organization in urban communities; the emphasis upon citizen participation and leadership; the examples of self-help in social welfare; the more active participation of organized labor; the increased emphasis upon improving inter-racial and inter-cultural relations and attaining a greater degree of unity in American life; the widespread interest in community councils and community development, transcending the field of social welfare. While it is clear that community welfare organization is a specialized area of professional service, it is becoming increasingly evident that neither individual, group, nor community life can be successfully compartmentalized. It seems likely that social welfare will be more and more broadly construed, and that community organization for social welfare will become more and more an integral part of broad movements to improve community life and well-being.

There should be a *deepening* as well as a broadening of community organization. Robert MacRae has well stressed the need of community organization leaders who have "spiritual identification with the social work movement." [6] This is profoundly true. If community organization is to make a really creative contribution to the world of today, its leaders and practitioners must have conviction as well as objectivity, passion as well as skill, commitment as well as competence. Community organization can become sterile, brittle, mechanistic, unless it is rooted in the deep soil of religion, humanitarianism, democracy, and man's long collective struggle for the good life and the good society.

Philosophies and religious interpretations differ, but Josiah Royce has captured the essence of our quest in words that go deeper than a commitment to any one religious or philosophical approach:

> *I believe in the beloved community and in the spirit which makes it beloved, and in the communion of all who are, in will and in deed, its members. I see no such community as yet; but none the less my rule of life is: Act so as to hasten its coming.[7]*

SUGGESTIONS FOR READING

Carter, Genevieve W., "Action Research in Community Planning," *Social Work Journal,* Vol. XXXIII, January 1952, pp. 23–28.

[6] *Ibid.*
[7] Josiah Royce, *The Problem of Christianity* (New York, Macmillan, 1913), p. 360. By permission of the Macmillan Company.

French, *An Approach to Measuring Results in Social Work.* (See bibliography, ch. 20.)

Hendry, "The Contribution of Community Organization to the Raising of Standards of Living in Under-Developed Areas of the World." (See bibliography, ch. 15.)

Howard, "Fifty Years of Social Work in the World." (See bibliography, ch. 14.)

Howard, Donald S., "New Horizons for Social Work," *Compass,* Vol. XXVIII, November 1947, pp. 9–13, 28.

Kraus, Hertha, *Common Service Resources in a Free Society: Attempt at a Frame of Reference* (Community Organization Materials, No. 5; New York, Association for the Study of Community Organization, 1954, mimeographed, 26 pp.).

——— "The Future of Social Work: Some Comments on Social Work Function," *Compass,* Vol. XXIX, January 1948, pp. 3–9.

MacRae, Robert. "New Wine and Old Bottles," *Community,* Vol. 30, May 1955, pp. 163–164, 175. An outlook on community organization in 1955.

Basic References on Community Welfare

Organization

The following list of Basic References includes 13 books and other items which contain material relating to many or most of the aspects of community organization. For the most part, these references are not cited in the chapter bibliographies, but it should be recognized that the *Basic References are an additional resource for all chapters.*

To avoid burdensome repetition of the titles of two major series of reference volumes, the following abbreviations are used, with the years of the volumes, in both footnotes and bibliographies:

National Conference of Social Work, Proceedings   NCSW
(Where there is more than one volume of Proceedings for
a particular year, the title of the specific volume is added,
thus: NCSW, *Social Welfare Forum,* 1956.)
Social Work Year Book   SWYB
The abbreviation OP is used where an item is known to be out of print.

Following the Basic References, below, is a brief selected list of Periodicals which are likely to contain a substantial amount of material on community welfare organization. Where a periodical is concerned with one specific topic, such as community development, it is listed in the appropriate chapter bibliography rather than in the general list below.

BASIC REFERENCES

Buell, Bradley and associates, *Community Planning for Human Services* (New York, Columbia University Press, 1952, 464 pp.). Against the background of an intensive study in St. Paul, Minnesota, this volume discusses the historical developments, current situation, and needs in the areas of dependency, ill-health, maladjustment, and recreational need; and it poses basic problems for community welfare planning. A number of "follow-up" reports on experiments in particular communities have been issued by Community Research Associates, New York, which conducted the St. Paul study.

Green, Helen D., *Social Work Practice in Community Organization* (New York, Whiteside and Morrow, 1954, 253 pp.). Emphasizes "social intergroup work" and expresses the point of view of the School of Social Work of the University of Pittsburgh in respect to community organization. Part II contains several case records.

Hillman, Arthur, *Community Organization and Planning* (New York, Macmillan, 1950, 378 pp.). Stresses the interlocking of the concepts and activities of community organization and planning for various aspects of community life.

International Conference of Social Work, Proceedings. Each volume has a descriptive title. The last three volumes are: *Social Service and Standards of Living,* Madras, 1952; *Self-Help in Social Welfare,* Toronto, 1954; *Industrialization and Social Work,* Munich, 1956. Information regarding the Conference and its publications may be obtained from the United States Committee of the Conference, 345 East 46th St., New York 17, N.Y.

Johns, Ray and De Marche, David F., *Community Organization and Agency Responsibility* (New York, Association Press, 1951, 274 pp.). A simplified general introduction to community welfare organization, plus a detailed discussion of the role of direct-service agencies in community organization.

King, Clarence, *Organizing for Community Action* (New York, Harper, 1948, 202 pp.). Vivid collection of case materials, with some discussion of general principles, under the broad headings of promotion and coordination.

Lane, Robert P., "The Field of Community Organization," NCSW, 1939, pp. 495–511. A committee report — the "First Lane Report" — based on the discussions of local community organization discussion groups. A landmark in contemporary thinking about community welfare organization. For the "sequel" to this report, see bibliography, ch. 3.

McMillen, Wayne, *Community Organization for Social Welfare* (Chicago, University of Chicago Press, 1945, 658 pp.). The first textbook with an orientation to contemporary thinking about community welfare organization. Comprehensive, scholarly, and authoritative. Contains also "documents" relating to various aspects of community organization.

Murphy, Campbell G., *Community Organization Practice* (Boston, Houghton Mifflin, 1954, 444 pp.). Seeks to orient community welfare organization to the broader aspects of social work, and to assess current trends, controversies, problems, and developments.

National Conference of Social Work, Proceedings (NCSW). Annually, 1874 to date. (Published by Columbia University Press, New York, since 1939; by the University of Chicago Press, 1920–1938; earlier, by the Conference itself.) The best single stream-record of social welfare experience and ideas in the United States. Beginning with 1950 the main volume of the Proceedings has had the title, *The Social Welfare Forum,* and there have been various subsidiary volumes. In 1956 the name of the Conference was changed to National Conference on Social Welfare.

Ross, Murray G., *Community Organization: Theory and Principles* (New York, Harper, 1955, 239 pp.). A theoretical approach to community organization, from the standpoint of the social sciences. Presents a distinctive definition of community organization, interprets it as being applicable to many areas of human needs, and seeks to construct underlying theory and principles on the basis of sound philosophical and social science foundations.

Social Work Year Book (SWYB), 1929–1957 — 13 volumes. (Published by the Russell Sage Foundation, 1929–1949, by the American Association of Social Workers, 1951–1954, and by the National Association of Social Workers beginning with 1957. Recent volumes have been published at three-year intervals.) Essentially an encyclopedia regarding social work and social welfare in the United States and Canada. Among the materials in the 1957 *Year Book* which have some relation to community welfare organization are: (1) The "history and context" articles on the development of social welfare programs and economic and cultural contexts of social work, in the United States. (2) Topical articles on: administration, Canadian social welfare, Catholic social services, community chests and united funds, community organization for social welfare, community welfare councils, conferences, education for social work, federal agencies, financing, foundations, housing, intergroup relations, international social welfare, Jewish social services, national defense and social welfare, national organizations, Protestant social services, public relations, research, social action, social service exchanges, social work as a profession, state and regional welfare organization, and volunteers in social welfare. (3) Directories of national and international agencies.

Stroup, Herbert Hewitt, *Community Welfare Organization* (New York, Harper, 1952, 612 pp.). Systematic descriptive text, from a social science background. Indicates wide acquaintance with and scholarly use of literature and materials on the subject.

PERIODICALS

Adult Leadership   Published monthly, except July and August. Chicago, Adult Education Association of the United States of America. Contains much material regarding conference, group dynamics, group leadership, meetings, committees, evaluation, consultation, social action, and related topics.

Community   Bulletin of United Community Funds and Councils of America. Monthly except July, August, and October. Contains articles on topics of interest to chests and councils; includes a department, "The Council Hopper."

Social Service Review   Quarterly. "Devoted to the scientific and professional interests of social work." Edited by the faculty of the University of Chicago, School of Social Service Administration.

Social Work   Journal of the National Association of Social Workers. Quarterly. Established January 1956. Succeeded *Social Work Journal* (earlier, *The Compass*), published by the American Association of Social Workers.

Major Chronological Developments in Community

Welfare Organization in the United States, 1870-1957

(Where a specific agency is listed, this is usually the first agency of its kind to be established in the United States. Some international events are included in this list.)

1872   State Charities Aid Association, New York

1873   National Conference of Charities and Correction (now, National Conference on Social Welfare)

1876   Boston Registration Bureau — precursor of the social service exchange

1877   Buffalo Charity Organization Society

1881   Wisconsin Conference of Social Work

1886   Neighborhood Guild, New York — first settlement in the United States. Later named University Settlement.

1905– Survey of the city of Washington, D.C. by staff of magazine, *Charities*
1906   *and Commons* (later, *The Survey*). Beginning of the "social survey movement."

c 1906   Beginnings of modern type of social service exchange (central index)

1908   Pittsburgh "central council" of Associated Charities (first council of social agencies)

1909   First White House Conference on child welfare called by President Theodore Roosevelt (later conferences, 1919, 1930, 1940, 1950)

1911   Margaret F. Byington — *What Social Workers Should Know About Their Own Communities*. First important monograph on community welfare organization.

1912   United States Children's Bureau

1913   Cleveland Federation of Charities and Philanthropies — first modern community chest

1917   Illinois Department of Public Welfare — first modern state welfare department

1917– Rise of the war chests
1918

1917– Cincinnati Social Unit experiment
1919

1918   American Association for Community Organization (now United Community Funds and Councils of America)

1920– Widespread organization of community chests and councils of social
1930   agencies. Many social service exchanges organized under or transferred to auspices of councils and chests.

1920– League of Nations
1946

1921   National Health Council
        American Association of Social Workers

1922   National Social Work Council (1922–1945)

1925   Jesse F. Steiner — *Community Organization* — pioneer textbook

1926   International Conference of Social Work organized (First Conference held at Paris, 1928)

1929– Depression — widespread unemployment
1939

1930   *Social Work Year Book* founded. (First volume designated *Social Work Year Book, 1929*. Articles on various aspects of community organization included in this and subsequent volumes.)

1933   Federal Emergency Relief Administration (1933–1936)

1935   Social Security Act

1939   Federal Security Agency

1939   "The Field of Community Organization." Report of committee under chairmanship of Robert P. Lane, *National Conference of Social Work, Proceedings, 1939*. Followed activities of a number of local committees for study of community organization, 1939.

1942   National War Fund (1942–1947)
        State war chests

1943   United Nations Relief and Rehabilitation Administration (UNRRA; 1943–1948)

1945   United Nations
        UN Economic and Social Council (ECOSOC)
        National Social Welfare Assembly (succeeded National Social Work Council, 1922–1945)
        Wayne McMillen — *Community Organization for Social Welfare* — first contemporary textbook on community welfare organization

1946   Association for the Study of Community Organization (1946–1955)
        UN Secretariat — Department of Social Affairs

1948   Universal Declaration of Human Rights adopted by United Nations
       Assembly
1949   United Foundation, Detroit (united fund) organized as a response to
       the problem of multiple appeals
1950   United Community Defense Services (1950–1956)
       United Defense Fund (1950–1955)
1952   UN unit on Community Organization and Development established
       in Secretariat, Bureau of Social Affairs (Unit now designated as
       Community Development Group)
1953   U.S. Department of Health, Education, and Welfare (Cabinet depart-
       ment, succeeding Federal Security Agency, 1939–1953)
1955   National Association of Social Workers organized as the result of a
       merger of the American Association of Social Workers and six other
       professional associations, including Association for the Study of
       Community Organization
1956   Committee on Community Organization, NASW
1956– Curriculum study of schools of social work initiated by Council on
 1957 Social Work Education; includes place of community organization in
       the curriculum.
       National Conference papers on various aspects of theory underlying
       community welfare organization

APPENDIX **B**

Definitions—References

This appendix contains five series of references to definitions or closely related statements on the subjects of (1) social work, (2) the community, (3) community organization in general, (4) community welfare organization, and (5) social action. The items on each list are arranged chronologically, except for the definitions of the community, where the relative dates appear to be of less importance. Where a book has two or more editions, the first is usually cited here.

Where only the author's last name and the title of the volume are given in these lists, the full bibliographical citation to the book will be found in the Basic References (BR) or in a chapter bibliography, which is indicated in parenthesis.

In general, only published material which is fairly accessible is included. Statements which are merely repetitive of earlier definitions have been omitted.

A few of the definitions use variant terms as synonyms for those listed above: for example, "social welfare planning" for "community organization", "social reform" for "social action", etc.

SOCIAL WORK

1. Cabot, Richard C. *Social Service and the Art of Healing.* (New York, Dodd Mead, 1909), pp. 55–56.

2. Devine. *Social Work* (1922), pp. 19, 21–22 (ch. 7).

3. Halbert, L. A. *What Is Professional Social Work?* (New York, *Survey*, 1923), p. 25.

4. Ritter, Halsted. "A Message to Take Home with You," NCSW, 1925, p. 79.

5. Cheyney, Alice S. *The Nature and Scope of Social Work* (New York, American Association of Social Workers, 1926), p. 24. Contains additional definitions, besides the one proposed by the author.

6. Warner, Queen, and Harper. *American Charities and Social Work* (1930), pp. 5, 556 (ch. 7).

7. Whipple, Leon. "The Philosophical Basis of Educational Publicity in Social Work," NCSW, 1930, p. 569.

8. Kelso, Robert W. "Tomorrow's Social Work Training," *Survey,* Vol. LXXII, September 1936, p. 260.

9. Klein, Philip and others. *A Social Study of Pittsburgh* (New York, Columbia University Press, 1938), pp. 4–8. (Objectives of social work.)

10. Hamilton, Gordon. *Theory and Practice of Social Case Work* (New York, Columbia University Press, 1940), pp. 4–6.

11. Brown, Esther Lucile. *Social Work as a Profession* (New York, Russell Sage Foundation, 1942), pp. 15–16.

12. Witmer, Helen L. *Social Work: An Analysis of a Social Institution* (New York, Farrar and Rinehart, 1942), pp. 39, 43, 121, and *passim*.

13. Fink, Arthur E. *The Field of Social Work* (New York, Holt, 1942). pp. 2–3.

14. *Education for the Public Social Services: A Report of the Study Committee, American Association of Schools of Social Work* (Chapel Hill, University of North Carolina Press, 1942), pp. 9–10.

15. Johnson, Arlien. "Social Work as a Profession," SWYB, 1943, p. 511. (Definition repeated in several later issues of SWYB and elsewhere.)

16. Clarke, Helen I. *Principles and Practice of Social Work* (New York, Appleton-Century, 1947), p. 16.

17. Stroup, Herbert Hewitt. *Social Work: An Introduction to the Field* (New York, American Book Co., 1948), p. 1.

18. Altmeyer, Arthur J. "Social Work and Broad Social and Economic Measures," NCSW, 1948, pp. 101–102.

19. Pray. *Social Work in a Revolutionary Age* (1949): see items in various papers included in this volume: pp. 18–19 (1942), 236–238 (1946), 276–278 (1947). (ch. 1.)

20. United Nations. *Training for Social Work: An International Survey* (Lake Success, New York, 1950), pp. 8–17.

21. Youngdahl, Benjamin E. "Social Work as a Profession," SWYB, 1951, p. 491. See also SWYB, 1954, p. 506.

22. Howard. "The Common Core of Social Work in Different Countries," NCSW, 1951, *Social Welfare Forum*, p. 26. (ch. 1.)

23. U.S. Department of Labor. *The Outlook for Women in Social Work: General Summary* (Women's Bureau Bulletin 235–8, Washington, Government Printing Office, 1952), pp. 1–2.

24. *Social Work as a Profession* (1953), pp. 3, 6–8 (ch. 1).

25. Friedlander. *Introduction to Social Welfare* (1955), p. 4 (ch. 1).

26. Wilensky and Lebeaux. *Industrial Society and Social Welfare* (1958). (ch. 1).

COMMUNITY

1. Bernard. *American Community Behavior,* pp. 34–35 (ch. 2).

2. Biddle. *Cultivation of Community Leaders,* pp. 29–30 (ch. 2).

3. Brownell, Baker. *The Human Community* (New York, Harper, 1950), pp. 195–210.

4. Lindeman, E. C. "Community," *Encyclopedia of the Social Sciences* (New York, Macmillan, 1931), pp. 102–105.

5. Hawley, Amos H. *Human Ecology* (New York, Ronald Press, 1950), pp. 180, 257–258.

6. Hillman. *Community Organization and Planning,* pp. 3–13, 17 (BR).

7. Johns and DeMarche. *Community Organization and Agency Responsibility,* pp. 9–12 (BR).

8. Lindeman. *The Community,* pp. 8–14 (ch. 2).

9. MacIver. *Community,* pp. 22–23, 109–110 (ch. 2).

10. McMillen. *Community Organization for Social Welfare,* pp. 28–31 (BR).

11. Morgan. *Small Community,* pp. 20–30 (ch. 2).

12. Murphy. *Community Organization Practice,* pp. 9–11 (BR) (ch. 23).

13. North, Cecil Clare. *The Community and Social Welfare,* p. 3.

14. Orton, William A. *The Liberal Tradition.* Quoted by Leonard W. Mayo, NCSW, 1946, p. 138.

15. Poston. *Democracy Is You,* pp. 15–16 (ch. 2).

16. Ross. *Community Organization: Theory and Principles,* pp. 40–42 (BR).

17. Sanderson, Dwight. *The Rural Community* (Boston, Ginn, 1932), pp. 1–13.

18. Sanderson and Polson. *Rural Community Organization,* pp. 49–54 (ch. 2).

19. Steiner. *Community Organization* (1930), pp. 18–21 (ch. 7).

20. Stroup. *Community Welfare Organization,* pp. 6–9 (BR).

21. Warner, W. Lloyd and Lunt, Paul S. *The Social Life of a Modern Community* (Yankee City Series, Vol. 1, New Haven, Yale University Press, 1941), pp. 16–17.

22. Zimmerman, Carle C. *The Changing Community* (New York, Harper, 1938), pp. 12–16.

COMMUNITY ORGANIZATION

General Community Organization (not restricted specifically to social welfare)

1. Daniels, John. *America Via the Neighborhood* (New York, Harper, 1920), pp. 462–463.

2. Lindeman. *The Community* (1921), p. 173 (ch. 2).

3. Wood, Arthur E. "The Philosophy of Community Organization."

American Sociological Society, Papers and Proceedings, Seventeenth Annual Meeting (Chicago, 1922), Vol. XVII, pp. 178–184.

4. Burr, Walter. "The Philosophy of Community Organization: The Rural Community Ideal," NCSW, 1925, p. 399.

5. Eldridge, Seba. "Community Organization and Citizenship," *Social Forces*, Vol. 7, September 1928, pp. 132–140.

6. Steiner. Community Organization (1930), pp. 160–174 (ch. 7).

7. Steiner, Jesse F. "Community Organization," *Encyclopedia of the Social Sciences*, Vol. IV (1931), pp. 106–108.

8. Gist, Noel P. and Halbert, L. A. *Urban Society* (New York, Crowell, 1933), pp. 641–642.

9. Sanderson and Polson. *Rural Community Organization* (1939), p. 76 (ch. 2).

10. Barnes, Harry Elmer and Ruedi, Oreen M. *The American Way of Life* (New York, Prentice-Hall, 1945), p. 473.

11. American Association for Adult Education. *Community Education in Action: A Report on Community Organization and Adult Education*, p. 8 (ch. 8).

12. Hendry. "The Contribution of Community Organization to the Raising of Standards of Living in Under-Developed Areas of the World," in *Social Service and the Standards of Living: Proceedings, Sixth International Conference of Social Work*, pp. 117–118 (ch. 15).

13. Ross. *Community Organization: Theory and Principles* (1955), p. 39 (BR).

14. United Nations. *Social Progress Through Community Development* (1955), p. 6 (ch. 15).

COMMUNITY WELFARE ORGANIZATION

1. Devine, *Social Work* (1922), pp. 66–68 (ch. 7).

2. McClenahan, Bessie A. *Organizing the Community* (New York, Century, 1922), pp. 36–41.

3. Halbert, L. A. *What Is Professional Social Work?* (1923), pp. 64–74. (See under Social Work, item 3, in this Appendix.)

4. Pettit, Walter W. "Some Prognostications in the Field of Community Work," NCSW, 1925, pp. 681–682.

5. Warner, Queen, and Harper. *American Charities and Social Work* (1931), pp. 31, 554–556 (ch. 7).

6. Pettit, Walter W. "Is Community Organization Social Work?", *Social Forces*, Vol. X, October 1931, pp. 62–66.

7. Dunham, Arthur. "Social Welfare Planning," SWYB, 1937, p. 482 (see also SWYB, 1933 and 1935).

8. Lane. "The Field of Community Organization," NCSW, 1939, pp. 497–498. The three definitions included in this report were those formulated by the New York, Chicago, and Michigan Study Committees, in the order mentioned. (BR)

9. Hamilton. *Theory and Practice of Social Case Work,* p. 8. (See under Social Work, item 10, in this Appendix.)

10. Kurtz, Russell H., "The Range of Community Organization," NCSW, 1940, pp. 401, 412.

11. Bondy, Robert E. "Community Organization in Times of Crisis," NCSW, 1941, p. 547.

12. Newstetter, Wilber I. "Teaching Community Organization in Schools of Social Work," in McMillen, *Community Organization for Social Welfare,* pp. 61–62 (BR). For a later statement by Newstetter, see item 22, below.

13. King, Clarence. "Community Organization for Social Work," SWYB, 1941, pp. 128–129.

14. Mayo, Leonard W. "Community Organization at the National Level," NCSW, 1942, pp. 229–230.

15. Fink. *The Field of Social Work* (1942), p. 443. (See under Social Work, item 13, in this Appendix.)

16. Community Chests and Councils. *Organizing a Community and War Chest* (New York, 1943), p. 1. See also later editions of this pamphlet.

17. Devine, Thomas. "Community Organization under Public Auspices. I. From the Federal Viewpoint," NCSW, 1944, p. 402.

18. McMillen. *Community Organization for Social Welfare* (1945), pp. 22–23 (BR).

19. Community Chests and Councils. *Health and Welfare Planning in the Smaller Community* (New York, 1945), p. 6.

20. Mayo, Leonard W. "Community Organization in 1946," NCSW, 1946, p. 129.

21. McMillen, Wayne. "Community Organization in Social Work," SWYB, 1947, p. 110.

22. Newstetter, Wilber I. "The Social Inter-Group Work Process. How Does It Differ from Social Group Work Process?," NCSW, 1947, pp. 205–206.

23. King. *Organizing for Community Action* (1948), pp. 17–18 (BR).

24. Community Chests and Councils of America. *Getting Things Done in Community Organization* (Proceedings, Blue Ridge Institute for Social Work Executives, New York, 1948), p. 8.

25. Kurtz, Russell H. "Community Organization for Social Welfare," SWYB, 1949, p. 129.

26. Stone, Walter L. *Community Welfare Planning and Organization* (Hanover, Ind., Informal Education Service, 1949), p. 7.

27. Hillman. *Community Organization and Planning* (1950), pp. 13–14, 355 (BR).

28. Barry, Mildred C. "Community Organization Process: An Approach to Better Understanding," *Social Work Journal,* Vol. XXXI, October 1950, p. 157. (ch. 22).

29. Community Chests and Councils of America. *Community Planning for Social Welfare: A Policy Statement* (1950), p. 5 (ch. 10).

30. Johns and DeMarche. *Community Organization and Agency Responsibility* (1951), pp. 2, 77–79 (BR). Discusses several definitions.

31. McNeil, C. F. "Community Organization for Social Welfare," SWYB, 1951, p. 123.

32. Stroup. *Community Welfare Organization* (1952), pp. 138–144 (BR). Discusses several definitions.

33. Dillick. *Community Organization for Neighborhood Development — Past and Present* (1953), pp. 89, 135.

34. Murphy. *Community Organization Practice* (1954), pp. 7–9 (BR).

35. Friedlander. *Introduction to Social Welfare* (1955), pp. 187, 589 (ch. 1).

36. Murphy, Campbell G. "Community Organization for Social Welfare," SWYB, 1957, p. 179.

37. Sieder. "The Tasks of the Community Organization Worker" (1957) (ch. 17).

SOCIAL ACTION

1. Richmond, Mary E. *What Is Social Case Work?* (New York, Russell Sage Foundation, 1922), pp. 223–224.

2. NCSW, 1934, Minutes, p. 597.

3. Lee. "The Social Worker and Social Action" (1935), in *Social Work as Cause and Function*, p. 259 (ch. 1).

4. Coyle, Grace. "Social Workers and Social Action," *Survey Midmonthly*, Vol. LXXIII, May 1937, pp. 138–139.

5. Fitch, John A. "Social Action," SWYB, 1939, p. 398.

6. ———— "The Nature of Social Action," NCSW, 1940, p. 488.

7. Hamilton. *Theory and Practice of Social Case Work* (1940), pp. 7–8. (See under Social Work, item 10, in this Appendix.)

8. Lurie, Harry L. "Social Action: A Motive Force in Democracy," NCSW, 1941, p. 631.

9. Pray, Kenneth L. M. "Social Work and Social Action," NCSW, 1945, p. 348.

10. Maslen, Sydney. "Social Action," SWYB, 1949, p. 473.

11. Hill, John G. "Social Action," SWYB, 1951, p. 455.

12. Stroup. *Community Welfare Organization* (1952), pp. 529–534 (BR).

13. Friedlander. *Introduction to Social Welfare* (1955), pp. 189, 613 (ch. 1).

14. Solender, Sanford. "Social Action," SWYB, 1957, pp. 517–518.

APPENDIX C

Working Outlines

This appendix contains the following working outlines for use by practitioners and students of community organization.

(I) Outline for a descriptive report on a social welfare agency.

(II) Outline for a report on a committee.

(III) Outline for analysis of a community organization project.

(IV) Outline for work progress report.

I. OUTLINE FOR A DESCRIPTIVE REPORT ON A SOCIAL WELFARE AGENCY

1. Name of agency

2. Address

3. Under what auspices does the agency operate? Governmental? Voluntary? Special auspices: religious denomination, fraternal order, labor organization, etc.?

4. In what functional field(s) does the agency operate?

5. What are the agency's specific functions or services?

6. What territory does the agency serve?

7. On what geographic level does the agency operate? Local? State? National? International?

8. Is this a consumer-service agency — does it serve consumers or clients directly?

9. Is this agency: institutional, semi-institutional (nursery school, day camp, etc.), non-institutional?

10. In what year did the agency originate?

11. How was it established — by law, voluntary association, etc.?

12. Does the agency have a board? How designated? If there is no board, what official is the policy-determining and directing head of the agency?

13. Who appoints the executive?

14. Is the agency a member or branch of any of the following? If so, note the name in each case: community welfare council or council of social agencies; social service exchange; community chest; state agency; national agency; other coordinating or planning body.

15. Is the agency licensed or supervised by any governmental agency? If so, give name of such governmental agency.

16. From what sources does the agency obtain most of its funds?

17. Give the following figures, if they are available: (a) total operating expenses for last ended fiscal year; (b) total approved budget for current fiscal year.

18. Give key service statistics for last completed year; for example, members, active groups (group work agency); cases active at beginning and end of year, cases active at some time during year (casework agencies), etc.

19. What is the total number of persons on the professional staff of the agency? What are the major types of professional workers?

20. How many service volunteers are active during a year? (Do not include administrative volunteers, members of boards, and committees.)

II. OUTLINE FOR A REPORT ON A COMMITTEE

Part A. Descriptive Material

1. Name of committee

2. Parent body

3. Standing (permanent) or special (temporary, *ad hoc*)

4. Functions — Are there written terms of reference or a written charge or assignment to the committee? If so, quote or summarize and indicate source of the official statement.

5. By what authority was the committee created?

6. By whom was the committee appointed? To whom is it responsible?

7. When was it appointed?

8. Number of members on committee? Give names and positions if this seems important for purposes of this particular report.

9. Chairman; secretary; staff aide, if any. (Name and position of each.)

10. How many times did the committee meet during the past year? Give dates or indicate frequency of meetings. What was the average attendance?

11. What other activities did the committee carry on during the past year?

12. Identify the documents available in regard to the committee: minutes, reports, etc.

Part B. Evaluative Material

13. How important is the committee's assignment?

14. Is the task well suited to a committee?

15. How active is the committee?

16. What has the committee accomplished during the past year?

17. What is the current program and what are the current activities of the committee?

18. What are the plans of the committee for the future? What does it see as its next steps?

19. How does the committee rate according to principles underlying effective committee operation? (See ch. 22.)

20. What are the committee's strengths and weaknesses? Consider such matters as: membership, leadership, productivity, effectiveness of group process.

21. Should the committee be continued? If so, why?

22. If it should be continued, what should it seek to accomplish during the coming year?

III. OUTLINE FOR ANALYSIS OF A COMMUNITY ORGANIZATION PROJECT

(Note: This outline is written primarily in terms of a current project, but it can also be adapted to a completed project.)

1. Designation of project

2. Background and origin

3. Sponsoring agency or organization chiefly concerned

4. Nature and purpose of project

5. Organization of project (agencies, committees, staff, etc.)

6. Worker having executive responsibility for project: name, position, agency

7. Time of project (Current? Specified period of past time?)

8. Territory to which project relates

9. What is involved in budgeting or financial expenditure?

10. Approximately how many professional staff hours per month are being spent on this project?

11. What have been the major chronological steps in the development of the project?

12. What is the present status of the project?

13. What seem to be the next steps that should be taken?

14. What major methods have been used in connection with the project?

15. What major problems have been encountered?

16. What is your estimate of the actual or potential value of the project?

17. If the project has been completed — (a) What was accomplished?

(b) Evaluate the project and the performance in respect to it.

(c) Why was it successful, partially successful, or unsuccessful?

IV. OUTLINE FOR A WORK PROGRESS REPORT

The following general outline is suggested for the periodical Work Progress Report for a community organization agency. (See ch. 18.) Adaptations may be desirable for a specific agency.

A. Heading: "Work Progress Report" — agency, department, and worker preparing report; period covered; date on which report is submitted.

B. Summary (optional). If the report is long, a summary will be useful. This summary should highlight the most important developments of the period, and should refer to the pages of the report where further details are given. The summary should be written after the rest of the report is completed, but it should appear at the beginning of the report.

C. Projects. For each project, list these items:

1. Project number

2. Designation of project

3. Organization unit and worker in charge of project

4. Date of initiation of project

5. Developments during period covered by report (referred to hereafter as "report period")

6. Present status, recommended next steps, and remarks

D. Recurrent services (joint budgeting, joint fund-raising campaign; annual city-wide welfare conferences, etc.)

1. Service (designate or describe briefly)

2. Organization unit and worker in charge

3. Developments during report period

4. Present status, recommended next steps, and remarks

E. Major contacts with other agencies or organizations (other than those included under Sections C, D, F, or I)

1. Organization with which contact was made

2. Date of contact

3. Form of contact: personal, telephone, correspondence

4. Worker making contact

5. Subject of contact

6. Suggested next steps: remarks

F. Meetings under the auspices of the agency (Record such meetings as seem important for the purposes of the particular agency.)

1. Public and semi-public meetings

a. Group holding meeting

b. Date; hour of beginning and ending

c. Place

d. Attendance (Mark "e" if estimated)

e. Program and/or major actions

f. Next steps; remarks

2. Administrative meetings. (Same sub-heads as under 1, above. Omit "major actions" under e if covered elsewhere.)

G. Collateral activities (Record only important collateral activities.)

1. Date

2. Nature of activity (speech, consultation, outside meetings, etc.)

3. Worker carrying on activity

4. Person or group involved

5. Subject; action; etc.

6. Next steps, if any; remarks

H. Publications

1. Number (serial number used in agency's Scrapbook, if any)

2. Title

3. Author

4. Organization unit issuing; or outside publisher

5. Date of issue

6. Form (printed, mimeographed, etc.)

7. Number of pages

8. Number of copies issued

9. Remarks

10. General nature or purpose of publication

I. Continuous services. Enter whatever type of monthly statistical summary is maintained for each kind of continuous service, such as social service exchange, community information or referral service, volunteer bureau, etc.

J. Administrative developments. Note such matters as:

1. Administrative projects listed in Work Plan

2. Changes in organization units, such as departments, divisions, districts, etc. (Include a revised organization chart if extensive organizational changes have occurred.)

3. Creation or discharge of any committee

4. Change of location of agency, department or district office

5. Changes in personnel of board, staff, or committees. If there are many changes in personnel, attach a revised personnel list as of the last day of the month.

K. Extra-agency developments

1. Objectives or projects listed in Work Plan

2. Other extra-agency developments

L. Other developments

M. Current problems

1. Note any current major problems which confront the agency but which are not covered elsewhere in the report.

2. Note pending requests for service, not covered elsewhere.

This report may be presented either in chart or textual form. If the chart form of report is used, the information regarding projects, for example, might be presented in a chart with columns headed: project number; designation of project; organization unit and worker in charge; date of initiation; developments during past month; present status, recommended next steps, and remarks. Similar charts could be designed for other sections of the Report.

The textual type of report has a less formal appearance, is more flexible, and reads more smoothly. On the other hand, the columns provide a kind of automatic checklist on entries, so that items are less likely to be overlooked; and where there are many projects it is possible to compare projects more easily as to their organization units, length of operation, developments, status, etc.

SOURCES OF THE PROGRESS REPORT

The sources from which the Progress Report is compiled may include:

1. The agency's Work Plan

2. The Work Progress Report for the preceding report period. This serves as a checklist of items to be considered, and a point of departure for noting changes and developments.

3. Workers' day sheets

4. Minutes of meetings

5. Copies of publications

6. Workers' appointment books or appointment calendars

7. It is desirable that every worker charged with making up a report of this sort should have a folder, "Work Progress Report — Current," into which he may put, as the ideas occur to him, memoranda of matters that ought to go into the report. Extra carbons (not file copies) of important outgoing letters; newspaper clippings, and other appropriate material may be included.

8. The workers' memories are obviously the final unsatisfactory and uncertain resource. If the basic records are adequate, dependence upon memory alone will be reduced to a minimum.

In a small agency, with perhaps one to four workers, a single report may be compiled by the executive on the basis of conferences with the other workers. In larger agencies, each organization unit (department, division, etc.) should compile a separate report. The report for the agency as a whole should then be compiled by the chief executive or an assistant, from the various departmental and divisional reports, plus material cutting across divisional lines or relating to the whole agency.

If the Report is to be of practical value for program direction, it should be completed promptly after the end of the report-period.

Types of Community Organization Jobs

The following chart presents, in tabular form, certain data regarding major types of community organization jobs and the functional specializations which seem to apply to them. (See chapter 17.) Except as it relates to the CCC job descriptions, this chart is based upon empirical observation and study of available material rather than comprehensive job studies. It includes judgments on the part of the author as to the nature of certain jobs, the functional specializations related to them, and so on. The chart as a whole is offered primarily as a basis for further research and discussion.

The chart lists, in alphabetical order, the 23 jobs listed in chapter 17.

Column 1 gives each job a serial number. It contains also initials designating any of the following characteristics of the job.

B   Borderline job between social work and some other profession or vocation, which is listed in parenthesis.

C   Chest-council job, included in CCC job descriptions.

C+ Job found in chest-councils *and* other agencies. Included in CCC job descriptions.

L   ⎫
S   ⎪ These initials designate the geographic levels on which the job is
N   ⎬ likely to be found: Local, State, National, International.
I   ⎭

Column 2, Type and Nature of Job, gives the job title used in this list, with a brief description of the nature of the job.

Column 3 lists Illustrative Jobs for this type of position.

Column 4 of the chart, headed Major Functional Specializations, refers to the 15 functional specializations, described in chapter 17. In this column are entered what appear to be the primary and secondary functional specializations for this type of job. The primary specialization is printed in ALL

CAPITALS: the secondary specializations in Capitals and Small Letters. The titles of some specializations are abbreviated, as follows:

Fund-raising other than in financial federation — Fund-raising other than federated

Health and welfare planning — Planning

Legislative analysis and promotion — Legislative service

Planning and promotion of program in specialized field — Planning specialized program

Public relations and interpretation — Public relations

Column 5, the last column, includes any remarks.

TYPES OF COMMUNITY ORGANIZATION JOBS

1. NUMBER / CLASSIFICATION / GEOGRAPHIC LEVEL	2. TYPE AND NATURE OF JOB	3. ILLUSTRATIVE JOBS	4. MAJOR FUNCTIONAL SPECIALIZATIONS	5. REMARKS
1. B (Accounting) C L-S-N	*Budget Secretary.* Secures, analyzes and prepares information regarding budgets in a community chest; furnishes executive service to Budget Committee.	Budget secretary or budget analyst in a community chest or in a council acting as agent of the chest for budgeting; budget secretary for a state united fund or for National Budget Committee.	BUDGETING Community chest operation	One of the jobs that verges on another professional or technical field, aside from social work — in this case, accounting. In practice, the incumbent may have social work training or experience and may add the accounting skills required; or he may have accounting training and experience and add the knowledge of social work content. This knowledge of social work content would seem to be essential in all cases to a sound job of community organization.

2. C+ L	*Bureau (or Department) of Community Councils Secretary.* Directs an organization unit concerned with the coordination and program development of two or more local community councils.	Secretary of a federation or department of local urban community councils, which is likely to be a part of or affiliated with a community welfare council.	PLANNING Public relations Research	
3. B (Fund-raising) C+ L-S-N	*Campaign Director.* Plans and directs fund-raising activities.	Campaign director in a joint fund-raising agency or in a local, national, or state agency conducting a highly organized financial campaign.	CAMPAIGNING Community chest operation Public relations	Skill and experience in fund-raising are primary requirements. The worker should have also an adequate understanding of the field of social welfare and of community organization.
4. B (Fund-raising) C+ L, usually	*Campaign Division Secretary.* Plans and directs a major division of a financial campaign.	Campaign division secretary for a division of a joint fund-raising campaign (firms, employee groups, individual contributors, etc.); or for other type of agency with highly organized financial campaign.	CAMPAIGNING Community chest operation Public relations	Skill and experience in fund-raising are primary requirements. The worker should have also an adequate understanding of the field of social welfare and of community organization.

1. NUMBER CLASSIFI-CATION GEOGRAPHIC LEVEL	2. TYPE AND NATURE OF JOB	3. ILLUSTRATIVE JOBS	4. MAJOR FUNCTIONAL SPECIALIZATIONS	5. REMARKS
5. C L-S	*Chest Executive Secretary.* Directs the year-round administration of the chest, including management of the annual campaign, collection and distribution of funds, budgeting, publicity, development of community leadership, and serving as secretary to the board of directors and policy-making committees.	Executive of a community chest, local united fund, state united fund, or sectarian financial federation.	COMMUNITY CHEST OPERATION Budgeting Campaigning Planning Public relations	This is the basic specialized community chest type of job. Jobs 1, 3, and 4 are specializations derived from it. In a small community, this is largely a practitioner job; in a larger community it is more administrative in nature.
6. C L	*Chest and Council Executive Secretary.* Gives leadership in health and welfare planning and joint fund-raising: directs the year-round administration of the community chest and community welfare council.	Executive of a combined chest-council; common executive of a separate chest and council; executive of Jewish or Catholic welfare federation.	COMMUNITY CHEST OPERATION PLANNING Budgeting Campaigning Public relations Research	In the smaller community this is more of a practitioner job; in a larger community it is more administrative in nature. This kind of position, in the smaller community, is one of the most nearly "generic" community

	Community Development Worker. Works for the improvement of total community life in a village or rural area.	Village worker in certain newly developing areas in foreign countries. Frequently a "multi-purpose worker." There are some more or less similar jobs under various auspices in this country.	PROMOTION OF GENERAL COMMUNITY IMPROVEMENT Planning Public relations Research	welfare organization jobs to be found anywhere. It is likely to involve 6 of the 16 functional specializations. In a large chest and council the executive may give primary attention to one unit and have an assistant who carries major responsibility for the other. The basic training of the worker may be in social work, agriculture, education, public health, health education, etc., or other specializations. In the area of social work, the worker may do individual counseling, group work, and community organization. The job appears, however, to require substantial understanding of and skill in community organization, if the service of the worker is to be effective.
7. B (See remarks) L				

1. NUMBER / CLASSIFICATION / GEOGRAPHIC LEVEL	2. TYPE AND NATURE OF JOB	3. ILLUSTRATIVE JOBS	4. MAJOR FUNCTIONAL SPECIALIZATIONS	5. REMARKS
8. S-N-I- possibly L	*Conference executive.* Carries on the direction of a national, state, or possibly local welfare conference whose primary function is the holding of an annual conference or convention and closely related activities.	There are few such jobs. Executive of the National Conference on Social Welfare and of certain state conferences would be examples. (Conferences with "action programs" are included under job 14.)	CONFERENCE ADMINISTRATION Planning Public Relations	A highly specialized and rare type of job.
9. C+ L-some S and N	*Council Division Secretary.* Gives professional leadership in health and welfare planning in a functional field of health, welfare or recreation.	Secretary of a functional division of a community welfare council. There are also a few somewhat similar jobs in statewide citizens associations and in certain national agencies.	PLANNING Planning specialized program Research	This job obviously requires specialized knowledge of the content of the particular field or fields with which the division is concerned: family welfare, child welfare, health, recreation, etc.

			This is a basic "health and welfare planning" type of job, because it is carried out on the community level, where people live.
		PLANNING Budgeting Public relations Research Social service exchange administration Volunteer bureau administration	
10. C L	*Council Executive Secretary.* Gives professional leadership in health and welfare planning; directs the administration of a community welfare council.	Executive of a community welfare council or other local organization concerned with overall health and welfare planning such as a health and welfare division of Office of Civilian Defense during World War II. The job of the executive of a broad "community council" or "community association" in a small community might be quite similar, except that the content of these jobs would probably be broader and would be concerned only in part with matters of health and welfare planning.	

1. NUMBER — CLASSIFICATION — GEOGRAPHIC LEVEL	2. TYPE AND NATURE OF JOB	3. ILLUSTRATIVE JOBS	4. MAJOR FUNCTIONAL SPECIALIZATIONS	5. REMARKS
11. C+ L	District Community Council Secretary (or Neighborhood Worker). Gives executive service to one or more neighborhood, district, or community councils in an urban community; participates in development of community leadership and health and welfare planning in neighborhoods and other local areas.	Secretary of a department of community councils in a community welfare council; secretary to one or more such councils; "area worker;" community organization worker for a settlement or community center; community organization or block worker for an Urban League. Some of the jobs mentioned tend to shade into group work and direct consumer-service at certain points.	PLANNING Public relations Research	
12. N, I	Executive of a national or international agency for co-ordination and broad health and welfare planning. Car-	Executive or staff member of agencies such as National Social Welfare Assembly or former United Community	PLANNING Legislative service Public Relations Research	These jobs relate to overall health and welfare planning on the national or international levels. They normally

	Job description	Where employed	Field	Comments
	...ries on health and welfare planning and coordination on the national level or international level, for the field of social welfare as a whole or in some broad area as health, youth service, casework, etc.	Defense Services; also certain positions in Department of Health, Education and Welfare, certain other federal agencies, and United Nations.		involve an unusual degree of responsibility and leadership. They vary in their relation to legislation; they may require understanding and analysis of legislation rather than legislative promotion.
13. L-S-N-I	*Executive of program promotional agency in a specialized field.* Promotes program development, and improvement of standards, and carries on related activities in a specialized field.	Executive of: a local housing association, tuberculosis association, committee on unity (or inter-cultural or race relations agency); a state society for mental health, crippled children and adults, social hygiene, the blind; and most national agencies, such as those concerned with family service, child welfare, health, recreation, corrections, etc. Also certain positions in the federal Department of Health, Education and Welfare, state public welfare agencies, state commissions on children and youth, etc.	PLANNING SPECIALIZED PROGRAM Fund-raising other than federated Planning Legislative service Public relations Research	These jobs usually combine promotion and health and welfare planning with knowledge of a specialized field of content. In some cases fund raising campaigns require a large amount of attention.

1. NUMBER CLASSIFICATION GEOGRAPHIC LEVEL	2. TYPE AND NATURE OF JOB	3. ILLUSTRATIVE JOBS	4. MAJOR FUNCTIONAL SPECIALIZATIONS	5. REMARKS
14. S	*Executive of statewide agency for health and welfare planning.* Directs year-round statewide program of health and welfare planning, which may include factfinding, education, promotion of legislation, cooperation with governmental and voluntary agencies, and development of citizen leadership.	Executive of a statewide citizens welfare association or similar organization; executive of a state welfare conference with a year-round "action program."	PLANNING Legislative service Public relations Research	These are basic health and welfare planning jobs on the state level. There are relatively few such jobs. Sometimes statewide citizens agencies have functional departments on family and child welfare, public health, mental health, the aging, corrections, etc.
15. S-N-I	*Field representative* (concerned primarily with community organization rather than administration). Carries on field service for a state or national agency	Field representative jobs for many national and state agencies, including certain field service jobs in governmental agencies.	FIELD SERVICE Planning Planning specialized program Public relations Research	The essence of this job is carrying on program promotion and/or health and welfare planning in the field, away from "home base." Requires knowledge of the

	where the contacts are primarily consultative, co-operative, and liaison in nature rather than authoritative, administrative, or procedural.			specialized content of the field in which the agency operates.
16. B (Fund-raising) L-S-N-I	*Financial secretary.* Carries on year-round fund-raising activities in behalf of a local, state, or national agency, other than a community chest. This job sometimes involves direction of a highly organized national or state financial campaign.	Financial secretary, membership secretary, extension secretary, etc. for a national or state agency or a local agency outside a chest. Staff member in the campaign department of a national or state agency.	FUND RAISING OTHER THAN FEDERATED Public relations	Skill and experience in fund-raising are primary requirements. The worker should have also an adequate understanding of the field of his agency.
17. C+ L-S-N	*Labor representative.* Develops understanding and co-operation between labor groups and the community or other health and welfare services.	Labor relations secretary in a council, chest-council, local or state united fund, or in certain national agencies, particularly those concerned with joint fund-raising.	LIAISON WITH ORGANIZED LABOR Planning Public relations Research	This type of job requires an intimate understanding of organized labor as well as of health and welfare planning.

1. NUMBER ——— CLASSIFICATION ——— GEOGRAPHIC LEVEL	2. TYPE AND NATURE OF JOB	3. ILLUSTRATIVE JOBS	4. MAJOR FUNCTIONAL SPECIALIZATIONS	5. REMARKS
18. S-N	*Legislative representative.* Analyzes, interprets, and promotes legislation for a statewide or national voluntary agency.	Legislative representative for a state or national agency. Except in large agencies this position is likely to be combined with some other job.	LEGISLATIVE SERVICE Planning Public relations Research	A highly specialized job, requiring specialized knowledge of legislation and legislative procedure, and skill in legislative promotion. Rare as a separate job.
19. B (Public relations) C+ L-S-N-I	*Public relations director (or publicity director).* Develops a program of public relations and/or interpretation for an agency.	Public relations director or publicity director or worker for a chest, chest-council, or other agency — governmental or voluntary, consumer-service or otherwise. Sometimes called Educational Secretary. Sometimes combined with Financial Secretary.	PUBLIC RELATIONS	A border-line job, combining need for public relations skills and understanding of social work and social welfare.

20. B (Research) C+ L-S-N-I	*Research director.* Plans and conducts social research and factfinding for an agency. In larger agencies, directs a staff of professional workers.	Research director or research worker for a council, chest-council, or for any other social welfare agency —governmental, voluntary; consumer-service or non-consumer service; local, state, or national.	RESEARCH Planning	A border-line job, relating to both social work and social science research. A combination of knowledge and skills from both areas is desirable.
21. C+ L	*Social service exchange secretary.* Plans and directs the work of a social service exchange.	Secretary of a social service exchange operating as a department of a council, public welfare agency, or other agency; or operating as an independent agency.	SOCIAL SERVICE EXCHANGE ADMINISTRATION Planning	This is a highly specialized position; it is not infrequently combined with some other job on a council staff.
22. C+ L	*Volunteer bureau director.* Plans and carries out a program of citizen participation involving promotion of the use of, recruiting, training, and placing volunteer workers in health and welfare agencies in the community.	Secretary of a volunteer bureau operating as a department of a council or under other auspices.	VOLUNTEER BUREAU ADMINISTRATION Planning Public relations	

1. NUMBER CLASSIFI-CATION GEOGRAPHIC LEVEL	2. TYPE AND NATURE OF JOB	3. ILLUSTRATIVE JOBS	4. MAJOR FUNCTIONAL SPECIALIZATIONS	5. REMARKS
23. B (See re-marks) C+ L	*Volunteer bureau referral secretary.* Carries out refer-ral of volunteers in social welfare and related organi-zations in the community.	Referral secretary of a vol-unteer bureau operating un-der a council or other aus-pices.	VOLUNTEER BUREAU ADMINISTRATION	This job involves some of the skills of employment service and vocational guid-ance. It may be regarded as a border-line job between social work and these two fields. The incumbent needs substantial understanding of social work and social welfare.

INDEX

Refugees, 243
Report, 304, 316, 317, 409, 410
Report. *See also* Work progress report
Research. *See* Factfinding
Robert, Henry M., 390
Robinson, Dorothy, 89
Role-playing, 358
Roles in groups, 357
Roman, Gloria, 310, 330
Ross, Murray G., 27, 295, 429, 441
Routzahn, E. G., 375
Routzahn, Mary Swain, 371, 373, 388, 413
Royce, Josiah, 437
Rural service, 108
Rusk, Dean, 244
Russell Sage Foundation, 75, 77

Saint Louis Social Planning Council, 133, 134
Salvation Army, 11
Sanders, Irwin T., 214
Sanderson, Dwight, 20, 108, 279
Schaffer, Ruth Connor, 20
Schmidt, Warren H., 368
Schuyler, Louisa Lee, 205
Seeley, John R., 192
Seifert, Harvey, 109
Self-help, 88, 89, 253
Settlement, 73, 74, 100-104
Seymour, Harold J., 163, 192
Sheffield, Edward F., 399, 411-413
Shenefield, Virginia S., 317
Sheps, Cecil G., 20
Sieder, Violet M., 28, 29, 59, 66, 158, 159, 183, 302, 337
Siegel, Doris, 368
Silver, Harold, 104
Simcox, Beatrice R., 123
Simplicity, 424, 425
Simpson, E. H., 399, 402, 413
Skill, 335
"Snowball technique," 365
Social action, 52-64
  definition, 52, 451
  nature, 52-57
  non-legislative, 380, 381
Social action. *See also* Legislative promotion
Social casework. *See* Casework
Social generalist, 433, 434
Social group work. *See* Group work
Social intergroup work. *See* Intergroup work
Social sciences, 435
Social Security Act, 79
Social service exchange, 72, 111-122
  casework, in relation to, 120-122

defense of, 121, 122
equipment, 115
history, 112
operation, 115-120
opposition, 120-122
principles, 113, 114
research, 122
Social Service Review, 442
Social statesmanship, 434
Social welfare administration. *See* Administration
Social welfare
  agencies, analysis, 452, 453
  agencies, classification, 7-9
  agencies, functional fields, 8
  agencies, functions, 422
  agencies, income, 48-49
  agencies, organization, 424, 425
  agencies, origins, 9-11, 72
  agencies, personnel, 6
  agencies, size, 421, 422
  agencies, social action, relation to, 57-60
  agencies, unification, 140
  agencies. *See also* Governmental and voluntary agencies
  characteristics, 6
  cost, 7, 183, 184
  definition, 5
  methods, 7
  needs, 24, 25, 421
  policy, 435
  resources, 25, 421
Social welfare attachés, 242, 243
Social welfare services—adequacy, distribution, arrangement, 423-427
Social work
  community development, relation to, 255-257
  definition, 5, 446, 447
  function, 11, 414
  nature, 38
  processes, 7
  profession, 5, 6
  sources, 3, 4
  values, 39
Social Work (periodical), 442
Social Work Journal, 90
Social Work Publicity Council. *See* National Publicity Council for Health and Welfare Services
Social Work Year Book, 29, 439, 441
Social workers
  social action, participation in, 60-64
Social workers club, 95, 96
Society for Superseding the Work of Climbing Boys, 69, 70
Solender, Sanford, 57
Sorenson, Roy, 140, 413